(Un)veiling Bodies
A Trajectory of Chilean
Post-Dictatorship Documentary

LEGENDA

LEGENDA is the Modern Humanities Research Association's book imprint for new research in the Humanities. Founded in 1995 by Malcolm Bowie and others within the University of Oxford, Legenda has always been a collaborative publishing enterprise, directly governed by scholars. The Modern Humanities Research Association (MHRA) joined this collaboration in 1998, became half-owner in 2004, in partnership with Maney Publishing and then Routledge, and has since 2016 been sole owner. Titles range from medieval texts to contemporary cinema and form a widely comparative view of the modern humanities, including works on Arabic, Catalan, English, French, German, Greek, Italian, Portuguese, Russian, Spanish, and Yiddish literature. Editorial boards and committees of more than 60 leading academic specialists work in collaboration with bodies such as the Society for French Studies, the British Comparative Literature Association and the Association of Hispanists of Great Britain & Ireland.

The MHRA encourages and promotes advanced study and research in the field of the modern humanities, especially modern European languages and literature, including English, and also cinema. It aims to break down the barriers between scholars working in different disciplines and to maintain the unity of humanistic scholarship. The Association fulfils this purpose through the publication of journals, bibliographies, monographs, critical editions, and the MHRA Style Guide, and by making grants in support of research. Membership is open to all who work in the Humanities, whether independent or in a University post, and the participation of younger colleagues entering the field is especially welcomed.

ALSO PUBLISHED BY THE ASSOCIATION

Critical Texts
Tudor and Stuart Translations • *New Translations* • *European Translations*
MHRA Library of Medieval Welsh Literature

MHRA Bibliographies
Publications of the Modern Humanities Research Association

The Annual Bibliography of English Language & Literature
Austrian Studies
Modern Language Review
Portuguese Studies
The Slavonic and East European Review
Working Papers in the Humanities
The Yearbook of English Studies

www.mhra.org.uk
www.legendabooks.com

STUDIES IN HISPANIC AND LUSOPHONE CULTURES

Studies in Hispanic and Lusophone Cultures are selected and edited by the Association of Hispanists of Great Britain & Ireland. The series seeks to publish the best new research in all areas of the literature, thought, history, culture, film, and languages of Spain, Spanish America, and the Portuguese-speaking world.

The Association of Hispanists of Great Britain & Ireland is a professional association which represents a very diverse discipline, in terms of both geographical coverage and objects of study. Its website showcases new work by members, and publicises jobs, conferences and grants in the field.

Editorial Committee
Chair: Professor Trevor Dadson (Queen Mary, University of London)
Professor Catherine Davies (University of Nottingham)
Professor Sally Faulkner (University of Exeter)
Professor Andrew Ginger (University of Bristol)
Professor James Mandrell (Brandeis University, USA)
Professor Hilary Owen (University of Manchester)
Professor Christopher Perriam (University of Manchester)
Professor Philip Swanson (University of Sheffield)

Managing Editor
Dr Graham Nelson
41 Wellington Square, Oxford OX1 2JF, UK

www.legendabooks.com/series/shlc

STUDIES IN HISPANIC AND LUSOPHONE CULTURES

1. *Unamuno's Theory of the Novel*, by C. A. Longhurst
2. *Pessoa's Geometry of the Abyss: Modernity and the* Book of Disquiet, by Paulo de Medeiros
3. *Artifice and Invention in the Spanish Golden Age*, edited by Stephen Boyd and Terence O'Reilly
4. *The Latin American Short Story at its Limits: Fragmentation, Hybridity and Intermediality*, by Lucy Bell
5. *Spanish New York Narratives 1898–1936: Modernisation, Otherness and Nation*, by David Miranda-Barreiro
6. *The Art of Ana Clavel: Ghosts, Urinals, Dolls, Shadows and Outlaw Desires*, by Jane Elizabeth Lavery
7. *Alejo Carpentier and the Musical Text*, by Katia Chornik
8. *Britain, Spain and the Treaty of Utrecht 1713-2013*, edited by Trevor J. Dadson and J. H. Elliott
9. *Books and Periodicals in Brazil 1768-1930: A Transatlantic Perspective*, edited by Ana Cláudia Suriani da Silva and Sandra Guardini Vasconcelos
10. *Lisbon Revisited: Urban Masculinities in Twentieth-Century Portuguese Fiction*, by Rhian Atkin
11. *Urban Space, Identity and Postmodernity in 1980s Spain: Rethinking the Movida*, by Maite Usoz de la Fuente
12. *Santería, Vodou and Resistance in Caribbean Literature: Daughters of the Spirits*, by Paul Humphrey
13. *Reprojecting the City: Urban Space and Dissident Sexualities in Recent Latin American Cinema*, by Benedict Hoff
14. *Rethinking Juan Rulfo's Creative World: Prose, Photography, Film*, edited by Dylan Brennan and Nuala Finnegan
15. *The Last Days of Humanism: A Reappraisal of Quevedo's Thought*, by Alfonso Rey
16. *Catalan Narrative 1875-2015*, edited by Jordi Larios and Montserrat Lunati
17. *Islamic Culture in Spain to 1614: Essays and Studies*, by L. P. Harvey
18. *Film Festivals: Cinema and Cultural Exchange*, by Mar Diestro-Dópido
19. *St Teresa of Avila: Her Writings and Life*, edited by Terence O'Reilly, Colin Thompson and Lesley Twomey
20. *(Un)veiling Bodies: A Trajectory of Chilean Post-Dictatorship Documentary*, by Elizabeth Ramírez-Soto

(Un)veiling Bodies

A Trajectory of Chilean Post-Dictatorship Documentary

ELIZABETH RAMÍREZ-SOTO

LEGENDA

Studies in Hispanic and Lusophone Cultures 20
Modern Humanities Research Association
2019

Published by Legenda
an imprint of the Modern Humanities Research Association
Salisbury House, Station Road, Cambridge CB1 2LA

ISBN 978-1-78188-701-1 (HB)
ISBN 978-1-78188-429-4 (PB)

First published 2019
Paperback edition with minor corrections 2021

All rights reserved. No part of this publication may be reproduced or disseminated or transmitted in any form or by any means, electronic, mechanical, photocopying, recording or otherwise, or stored in any retrieval system, or otherwise used in any manner whatsoever without written permission of the copyright owner, except in accordance with the provisions of the Copyright, Designs and Patents Act 1988, or under the terms of a licence permitting restricted copying issued in the UK by the Copyright Licensing Agency Ltd, Saffron House, 6–10 Kirby Street, London EC1N 8TS, *England, or in the USA by the Copyright Clearance Center, 222 Rosewood Drive, Danvers MA 01923. Application for the written permission of the copyright owner to reproduce any part of this publication must be made by email to legenda@mhra.org.uk.*

Disclaimer: Statements of fact and opinion contained in this book are those of the author and not of the editors or the Modern Humanities Research Association. The publisher makes no representation, express or implied, in respect of the accuracy of the material in this book and cannot accept any legal responsibility or liability for any errors or omissions that may be made.

Trademark notice: Product or corporate names may be trademarks or registered trademarks, and are used only for identification and explanation without intent to infringe.

© *Modern Humanities Research Association 2019*

Copy-Editor: Dr Ellen Jones

CONTENTS

	Acknowledgements	ix
	Explanatory Notes	xii
	Abbreviations	xiii
	Introduction	1
1	Contextualizing Chilean Documentary and the Memory Struggles	33
2	(Un)veiling Bodies: From Human Remains to Torture Survivors	62
3	Chilean Documentary Wanderings: Journeys of *Desexilio*	96
4	On Glimpses of Childhood and Other People's Memories	125
5	Extending the Circle: Nostalgia for the 1980s and Unsettling Accounts	150
	Conclusion	178
	Bibliography	183
	Filmography	202
	Index	206

Para mi tata

ACKNOWLEDGEMENTS

Like many of the documentaries it examines, this is a travelling book. It has been written in various places and owes its existence to the contributions of many people and institutions around the world.

I am grateful to the Association of Hispanists of Great Britain and Ireland and to Legenda for supporting this project, and to Laura Rascaroli and Alison Ribeiro for recommending my work to these institutions. My editor, Graham Nelson, has been very supportive from the beginning.

The bulk of this investigation was undertaken while I was a Ph.D. candidate in the Department of Film and Television Studies at the University of Warwick, where I had the good fortune to have Stella Bruzzi and John King as my supervisors. I could not have dreamt of two better sets of eyes to guide my research. I am grateful for their unrelenting support and encouragement; it is an enormous honour to have them both as my mentors. Stephen Gundle, Alastair Phillips, Charlotte Brunsdon, and the late Victor Perkins also left an indelible mark on me during these formative years.

This research would have been impossible to carry out without the support of numerous filmmakers, in particular: Ignacio Agüero, Macarena Aguiló, Gastón Ancelovici, René Ballesteros, Claudia Barril, Pablo Basulto, Germán Berger-Hertz, Andrés Brignardello, Pachi Bustos, Alejandra Carmona, Francisco Casas, Carmen Castillo, Hernán Castro, Cristóbal Cohen, Gerardo Cáceres, Silvio Caiozzi, Pedro Chaskel, Cecilia Cornejo, Andrés Daie, Carla Dávila, Mario Díaz, Sergio Gándara, Lorena Giachino, Leopoldo Gutiérrez, Patricio Henríquez, Marcelo Hermosilla, Marianne Houghen-Moraga, Pablo Insunza, Yura Labarca, Sebastián Larraín, Pablo Lavín, Orlando Lübbert, Marilú Mallet, Hermann Mondaca, Sebastián Moreno, Iván Osnovikoff, Emilio Pacull, Tiziana Panizza, Carmen Luz Parot, Bettina Perut, Andrés Racz, Paula Rodríguez, Antonia Rossi, Pablo Salas, Marcela Said, Lucía Salinas, Claudio Sapiaín, Juan Diego Spoerer, Paco Toledo, Andrés Vargas, Angelina Vázquez, and Juan Pablo Zurita. A special thanks to Patricio Guzmán for authorizing the reproduction of a still from *Nostalgia de la luz* (2010) for the book cover.

In Chile, I am indebted to María Luisa Ortíz, María Teresa Viera-Gallo and José Manuel Rodríguez from the Museo de la Memoria y los Derechos Humanos, who were instrumental in bringing this project to fruition. For their invaluable help accessing archives, finding films or locating festival catalogues, I am grateful to Pamela Pequeño, Isabel Mardones, Claudia Posadas, Babi Salas, Paola Castillo, Raúl Camargo, Rocío Ramos, and Hernán Venegas. My work has also benefitted from the conversations I have had with many colleagues in Santiago and elsewhere:

Constanza Vergara, Iván Pinto, María Paz Peirano, Jorge Iturriaga, Carolina Ramírez, Sarah Barrow, and Rosa Olmos. I am hugely indebted to Claudia Bossay, for her camaraderie and contagious passion for Chilean film history.

While working on my Ph.D. I had the chance to become a visiting student researcher in the Department of Spanish and Portuguese at UC Berkeley. Little did I know how important this research trip would be in shaping my investigation, and to some extent, my career, as I find myself now writing these lines back in this city. I would like to thank Francine Masiello, Linda Williams, Jorge Ruffinelli, and Jason Sanders for such a stimulating stay in the Bay Area.

In addition to Becas Chile-CONICYT, which allowed me to pursue my doctoral program, the following grants funded research and conference travels, and helped me organize academic events: ASSECC, SLAS, HRC Doctoral Fellowship Competition, and the Warwick-Santander Universities Agreement.

For many challenging and fun conversations I would like to thank my friends in Warwick: Santiago Oyarzabal, Filippo Trentin, Katharina Karcher, and Rosario Undurraga. Also, thanks to my friends in London and Paris: Carmen Richards, Denisse Glavic, Jez Stewart, Mónica Henríquez, Nigel Fountain, and Katya Peña. All of them made the long European winters feel less cold; I am so grateful for their warmth.

The support of my wonderful colleagues Britta Sjogren, Jenny Lau, Celine Shimizu, Aaron Kerner, Steve Kovacs, and Steve Choe in the School of Cinema at San Francisco State University has made my insertion into US academia so much smoother. My friend Marissa Rosemblat has always been ready to introduce me to the area's best kept secrets.

I would like to thank Carl Fischer for providing thoughtful feedback on the introduction for this book. Legenda's anonymous reader also provided useful comments on the manuscript. Mark Wyers helped proofread earlier versions of these drafts.

I owe so much to José Miguel Palacios. Throughout these years we have exchanged countless ideas and conversations which have enriched the pages of this book. He also had the patience to read the entire manuscript, providing invaluable comments on how to improve it.

A very special thanks to my fellow traveller Beatriz Tadeo for always being here, disregarding the oceans between us. Her integrity and commitment as a scholar have been truly inspiring and have pushed me to keep going.

In Japan, I would like to express my sincere appreciation to the Fujisaki family; I always carry them in heart. My deepest gratitude goes to Taiji Fujisaki, who accompanied me during such a long part of this journey and was my home for so many years. Finally, I would like to say a huge thanks to my parents, who have always respected and encouraged my intellectual and nomadic urges.

Some sections of the Introduction and the Conclusion appeared in Spanish in my 'De restos a imágenes hápticas: un intinerario del documental chileno de la post-dictadura', in *Memorias y representaciones en el cine chileno y latinoamericano* (LOM, 2016), reprinted in *Cine chileno y latinoamericano: Antología de un encuentro* (LOM, 2019). A much earlier version of Chapter 4 was also published in Spanish in my 'Estrategias para (no) olvidar: notas sobre dos documentales chilenos de la postdictadura', *Aisthesis* 47 (2010), 45–63. Parts of Chapters 3 and 4 appeared in 'Journeys of Desexilio: The Bridge Between the Past and the Present', *Rethinking History: Journal of Theory and Practice*, 18: 3 (2014) 438–51, and in 'Travelling Memories: Women's Reminiscences of Displaced Childhood in Chilean Post-dictatorship Documentary', published in *Doing Women's Film History: Reframing Cinemas Past & Future* (Urbana: University of Illinois Press, 2015), 139–50. I thank Louise Spence, and Christine Gledhill and Julia Knight, respectively, for their generous advice when writing those articles.

July 2019

EXPLANATORY NOTES

1. The titles of films in Spanish are given first in the original language, followed by their best-known English titles in square brackets, e.g. *Chacabuco, memoria del silencio* [*Chacabuco: Memory of Silence*]. When this information is not available I have provided my own translation in round brackets, also in italics, e.g. *La venda* (*The Blindfold*). After the first reference, which includes other information (i.e. the director's name and production year), only the Spanish titles are given, except when extra information has been deemed helpful. The same applies for titles in other languages.

2. All English translations of original sources in Spanish are mine, unless otherwise indicated.

ABBREVIATIONS

ADOC	Asociación de Documentalistas de Chile (Association of Chilean Documentarians)
AFDD	Agrupación de Familiares de Detenidos Desaparecidos (Association of Relatives of the Detained and Disappeared)
APCTV	Asociación de Productores de Cine y TV (Association of Film and TV Producers)
CAIA	Consejo del Arte y la Industria Audiovisual (Council of the Arts and the Audiovisual Industry)
CE	Cine Experimental (Experimental Cinema)
CLP	Chilean Peso
CNCA	Consejo Nacional de la Cultura y de las Artes (National Council for the Culture and the Arts)
CNI	Central Nacional de Informaciones (National Information Centre)
CNTV	Consejo Nacional de Televisión (National Council for Television)
CNVR	Comisión Nacional de Verdad y Reconciliación (National Commission on Truth and Reconciliation)
CORFO	Corporación de Fomento de la Producción (Chilean Economic Development Agency)
DINA	Dirección Nacional de Inteligencia (National Intelligence Agency)
DIRAC	Dirección de Asuntos Culturales (Direction of Cultural Affairs)
EE.UU.	Estados Unidos de América (United States of America)
FICValdivia	Festival Internacional de Cine de Valdivia (Valdivia International Film Festival)
FIDOCS	Festival Internacional de Documentales de Santiago (Santiago International Documentary Film Festival)
FONDART	Fondo Nacional de Desarrollo Cultural y las Artes (National Fund for the Development of Culture and the Arts)
FPMR	Frente Patriótico Manuel Rodríguez (Manuel Rodríguez Patriotic Front)
H&S	Walter Heynowski and Gerhard Scheumann
MIR	Movimiento de Izquierda Revolucionaria (Revolutionary Left Movement)
n.d.	No data
NGOs	Non-governmental Organizations
ONR	Oficina Nacional de Retorno (National Office for Return)
P+O	Perut and Osnovikoff

UP	Unidad Popular (Popular Unity)
SML	Servicio Médico Legal (Medical Legal Service)
TVN	Televisión Nacional de Chile (National Television Channel)
UK	United Kingdom
US	United States
USD	United States Dollars

INTRODUCTION

At the long-awaited local premiere of Ignacio Agüero's *Como me da la gana II* [*This is the Way I Like it II*] (2016) at the Cineteca Nacional de Chile, among the film community, family and friends who attended, there was Elena Maureira, wearing the black and white photographs of her five lost loved ones on her chest. Her husband and four of her sons were murdered during Augusto Pinochet's military rule (1973–90), and their bodies were found inside the limestone furnaces of Lonquén, outside Santiago, in 1978. Her tiny, wrinkled figure testified not only to the persistence of the violence, but also to the intimate bond between Chilean documentary filmmakers and human rights struggles. The Lonquén case, as it came to be known, was the focus of Agüero's first documentary, *No olvidar* [*Not to Forget*] (1982), released under a pseudonym in the midst of the dictatorship. Agüero returns to this production in *Como me da la gana II*, a peculiar retake of his *Como me da la gana* [*This is the Way I Like it*] (1986), in which he registered the work being carried out by national filmmakers under military rule. The sequel, a sophisticated essay about the expressive possibilities of the documentary form, inevitably draws attention to the commitment of local filmmakers to keeping the memories of this past alive as well as to an incessant aesthetic quest for an appropriate language to address it.

Focusing on the cinematic treatment of memories of the dictatorship and its legacies, this book analyses the rich territory of Chilean documentary during the first two decades that followed the restoration of civilian rule in 1990. My main argument is that in addressing this contested past, post-dictatorship documentary performs *a revelation of bodies* — in a trajectory that shifts from revealing the bodies of direct victims to unveiling the body of the film itself. This transition is closely intertwined with the historical, political, and cultural developments of the country.

(Un)veiling Bodies: A Trajectory of Chilean Post-Dictatorship Documentary contributes to the study of contemporary non-fiction cinema in Chile, in particular during the post-dictatorship period, which, despite some recent and discreet efforts, remains largely under-researched and unknown to the general public outside specialized circles. The book brings visibility to the work of many directors who remain overshadowed by a handful of emblematic names. Whilst doing so, it establishes connections and disjunctions between productions of different generations. Additionally, my study goes beyond Chilean post-dictatorship documentaries' self-evident testimonial value as well as beyond restricted readings of them as works

about trauma. Although undoubtedly bound to a catastrophic event — the *coup d'état* and its aftermath — the relevance of these documentaries is not limited to the witness they bear to a particular period or to the content they transmit, as urgent as it may be. My overall project arises from the conviction that favouring subject matter over form (this is, to the detriment of their specific cinematic strategies) accomplishes little in building understanding of the complexities and richness of Chilean documentary.

Ever since the bombing of the country's presidential palace La Moneda on the 11 September 1973, contested versions of the meaning of the military coup and its aftermath have emerged and continue to be subject to interpretation. Significantly, this event has been described as a 'coup against representation'.[1] Its fortieth anniversary in 2013 displayed an apparent common agreement across different political sectors: there is a shared 'wound' that needs to be 'healed'. Yet in moments like these, the most polarized divisions in the country resurface, featuring the voices of those who (albeit perhaps less loudly than before) still think of the coup as a triumph, and those who see it as an utterly incurable wound. Certain words and their meanings permanently call attention to these ingrained discordances: depending on their political loyalties, people say either 'military coup' or *pronunciamiento*; they either call Pinochet a tyrant or a saviour; and the names given by intellectuals to the country's political system range from an 'incomplete democracy' to an 'imperfect dictatorship'.[2] After an atrocity of this dimension, language — and hence representation — turns into a battlefield.[3]

Documentary plays an essential role in the struggles over the meanings of the nation's recent past by challenging official discourses and constantly reshaping individual and cultural memories. Chilean documentary filmmakers have closely, passionately, and incessantly documented, created, and reenacted memories of the coup and its aftermath both inside the country and abroad. In the period covered by this research, they have constantly challenged the official dictum of 'turning the page' to start anew. As this study demonstrates, post-dictatorship documentary adopts a wide range of strategies and topics to refer to the recent past. Whether these accounts are narrated by directors who experienced repression directly or by younger generations who did so less straightforwardly, and whether the testimonies gathered come from survivors, activists, or even agents of the dictatorship, I am interested in exploring the aesthetic features these documentaries present, while also paying close attention to the historical juncture in which they emerge. These documentarians generate narratives of the past, actively engaging and participating in the continuous struggle to influence how Chilean cultural memory is conceived and how national identity is constructed or reconstructed after years of repression and violence. In this sense, documentary filmmakers' active intervention in the country's memory battles ought to be seen as a political struggle, as scholars have forcefully argued with regard to the disputes over the meanings of Chile's recent past as a whole.[4]

Rather than being motivated by the study of single cases, my point of departure was the urge to reflect in broader terms about the transformations experienced by documentary during the two decades that followed the restoration of civilian rule. After reviewing nearly one hundred productions released between 1990 and 2011, one of the main conclusions that emerged was this: the trajectory of Chilean post-dictatorship documentary is characterized by a revelation of bodies. Before explaining what I mean by this particular itinerary, I would like to briefly clarify why the book spans this particular period.

On 11 March 1990, President Patricio Aylwin took office after seventeen years of a terrorizing dictatorship that subjected Chilean society to profound cultural transformations under the shadow of the implementation of a radical free-market economy. Since the mid-1950s, the revolutionary aspirations that had begun to shake the pillars of Chilean society, characterized by severe inequalities, deepened under the moderate social reforms proposed by the 'revolution in liberty' of Christian Democrat Eduardo Frei, reaching its peak with the election of Marxist president Salvador Allende in 1970 in his fourth bid for office. Allende's distinctive 'Chilean road to revolution' — a pacifist and democratic way to socialism — and his radicalized agenda, which included a strong nationalisation programme, was met with a spiralling economic crisis, social polarization, and political violence, while confronting a series of internal obstructions and the external intervention of the United States (US) which feared the advances of the 'red tide' of communism. Many expected an abrupt end to the experiment of the Unidad Popular (Popular Unity, UP) but few could imagine the violence in which it came to a halt, with a military *junta* overthrowing Allende's government and bombing La Moneda. The images of this display of unprecedented violence were broadcast around the world, furthering the international interest in Chilean politics that had developed since Allende's ascension to the presidency.[5] The *junta* immediately made its goal explicit: to 'extirpate the Marxist cancer' from the political body. Death, exile, and fear paralyzed the country until a major social outburst in 1983 eventually led Pinochet to negotiate a political solution with the opposition. The 1988 national plebiscite, in which Chilean citizens voted 'No' (54.71%) or 'Yes' (43.01%) for Pinochet to remain in power, demonstrated that the dictator had constructed a profoundly divided country. He stepped down from office in 1990 but remained as commander in chief of the Army, even assuming in 1998 the position of senator-for-life, sheltered by the 1980 Constitution that is still in effect (albeit with some modifications). The Concertación de Partidos por la Democracia (the Coalition of Parties for Democracy, the centre-left alliance constituted to defeat Pinochet, hereinafter *Concertación*) remained in power for the next two decades, inaugurating a seemingly endless post-dictatorial order. This order was significantly challenged, however, by an external factor: Pinochet's arrest and detention in London in 1998. The dictator eventually returned to Chile in early 2000 and notoriously managed to escape local justice after his defence argued he was unable to face trial due to senile dementia. Pinochet died in 2006 without ever being tried. The dictatorship's legacy includes an official estimation of three thousand *detenidos desaparecidos* (hereinafter disappeared); over twenty-seven thousand cases of torture, a number which, while official, is difficult to evaluate with precision not least due to the fact that the terror imposed upon civilians proved to have a multiplying and long-lasting effect on Chilean society; and nearly two hundred thousand exiles.[6]

My research begins with the first civilian administration in 1990 and covers a period of over twenty years. Whether to name this period 'transition to democracy' or post-dictatorship has long been debated among sociologists, historians, and cultural critics alike.[7] In referring to films from this era as 'post-dictatorship' documentaries, I am not suggesting a radical break between the dictatorship and the democratic rule that followed. Rather, I am recognizing the continuities and deep intimacy between the two, as asserted by numerous authors from Tomás Moulian to Armando Uribe and Miguel Vicuña.[8] The years 2010–11, the cut-off point of my study, are defined by a series of significant factors, including the inauguration of the Museo de la Memoria y los Derechos Humanos (Museum of Memory and Human Rights, hereinafter Museo de la Memoria) founded by the outgoing government of Michelle Bachelet; the presidential election of the right-wing billionaire Sebastián Piñera, who put an end to twenty years of continuous *Concertación* rule; the celebrations of the country's bicentennial, accompanied by a series of historical and cultural revisions; the unprecedented post-dictatorial awakening of Chilean society, led by the 2011 student movement; and a striking 'redefinition of victimhood'[9] which would transform public discourse about the past and the landscape of post-dictatorship documentary in the ensuing years.

Twenty years of filmic production offer abundant material for an evaluation of the transformations experienced by documentary, in close interconnection with the country's historical, political, and cultural trajectory towards democracy. Having said this, it must also be acknowledged that setting the year 1990 as a starting point for this research early on proved insufficient for dealing with the richness and complexities of the Chilean documentary landscape. Therefore, although the main focus of my research is post-dictatorship production, I found myself necessarily and continuously returning to the previous decades, not only to images of the coup or the UP, but notably, to the 1980s, a period marked by the return of exiled directors to the country and by a burgeoning video scene that laid the groundwork for the creation of the corpus under examination. It is my contention that the development of post-dictatorship documentary cannot be understood without considering these preceding works.

Specifically, my main argument is that between 1990 and 2011, Chilean documentary oscillates — intersecting at times — between the unveiling of two types of bodies: those of the direct victims and those of the films. Therefore, I propose a documentary trajectory that shifts from an emphasis on the revelation of the literal body to the foregrounding of the cinematic one, more precisely, of the *film's skin*, as described by Laura U. Marks in her book *The Skin of the Film*.[10] I claim that while post-dictatorship documentary stresses the revelation of the actual bodies of the victims during the first period (1990–2003), the emphasis shifts towards the materiality of the images during the last decade (2003–11). As I see it, documentaries undertake a trajectory from what I call a 'cinema of the affected' towards a 'cinema of affect', at times overlapping and even conflating the two, while at other times departing from one other.

More precisely, by a 'cinema of the affected' I refer to documentaries that, for the most part, i) seek to reveal the 'truth' about what happened; ii) focus on the 'directly affected', by which I mean that they adopt a limited view of direct victims of state political violence, particularly on the disappeared, their female relatives, and later on, torture survivors; iii) rely heavily on onscreen testimony and other realist or representational strategies; iv) avoid using a first-person narrator in order to emphasize a sense of objectivity; and v) circulate images of past atrocities that may shock the spectator. By a 'cinema of affect', in turn, I refer to documentaries that, i) seek to reveal the materiality of the image rather than a certain 'truth'; ii) feature other voices aside from those of the direct victims, including those of younger generations that did not experience the coup or the UP first hand, as well as more unsettling voices, such as Pinochet's supporters or collaborators; iii) favour creative and non-representational strategies other than onscreen testimony or direct address; iv) endorse the use of a first-person narrator, embracing a subjective point of view; and v) occlude images of past atrocities in order to elicit more sensorial, affective responses from the audience. The differences between these two modes of approaching the past are by no means straightforward and are largely a matter of degree. Furthermore, encountering the affective force of a number of exilic works from the 1980s, most of which are still unknown even to scholars, compelled me to bring them into the discussion, further challenging any attempt to perform a teleological reading of the fertile and heterogeneous corpus under analysis.

The itinerary I am proposing here does not seek to suggest a lineal reading of Chilean documentary. Nor could it, because first and foremost the question of the destiny of the disappeared remains unsolved. Bodies are still missing, and in some cases, relatives' quests have been subjected to an outrageous saga of recognitions and misrecognitions of the remains of their loved ones. Indeed, occasionally these disappeared bodies haphazardly resurface to haunt Chile's post-dictatorial order. Therefore, I hope that when I say that Chilean post-dictatorship documentary performs a trajectory from a revelation of literal bodies towards a revelation of the film's skin, the use of the words 'from' and 'towards' are not misleading. I do not suggest that revelations of atrocious and unsettling facts have come to an end, or that there is a chronological development experienced by non-fiction production. Rather, I am suggesting *a shift of emphasis* within documentary, the development of which is closely intertwined with Chile's own trajectory towards democracy.

Certainly, the pursuit of 'truth' that dominated the first period has not come to a conclusion, but some cumulative, if extremely difficult, advances have been made in the arena of human rights. For that reason, in spite of the continuities between the dictatorial period and the civilian administrations that followed, historian Steve Stern has made efforts to nuance debates on this matter in his painstaking trilogy devoted to the topic. Stern has described the country's process of reckoning with its past as an 'unravelling of the memory impasse', a paradoxical process characterized by a constant tension between 'blockage and movement' of the memory struggles, with some social actors pushing forward while others refuse to advance in human rights issues.[11] In addition to Stern's conceptualization of memory as an 'unravelling impasse', his notion of an expanding 'symbolic circle' of those affected by the regime — a circle that widened throughout time from a limited focus on the direct victims to a less restrictive view, including the rest of civil society — is fundamental to understanding the trajectory of documentary that I am proposing.[12] Throughout the chapters of this book, it will be clear that documentary responses to the dictatorship's aftermath followed a similar path: from a constrained idea of the victim as embodied in the figure of the disappeared and their relatives, to a gradual opening towards other voices such as the tortured subject and later on younger generations, including but not limited to children of direct victims. Around the years 2010–11, however, other actors begin to appear in the scene, an emergence that would indicate not a mere expansion of the symbolic circle of victimhood but a complex redefinition of the notion of victim as Michael J. Lazzara asserts.[13] Military conscripts, civilians who were supporters of the dictatorship, and collaborators of the secret police, figures that were 'previously excluded' from 'the country's collective memory narrative', gain visibility in public discourse and pose new challenges to the memory struggles.[14] The emergence of these disruptive voices is most clearly embodied in the figure of Jorgelino Vergara, the main subject of El mocito [The Young Butler] (Marcela Said and Jean de Certau, 2011), the documentary that closes this study. The path opened by this film, centring on a former functionary of the secret police, signals a further shift in current Chilean post-dictatorial documentary landscape, which will widen in recent years to include the voices of perpetrators, as in the case of El pacto de Adriana [Adriana's Pact] (Lissette Orozco, 2017). The ethical challenges posed by the eruption of these discourses and the strategies mobilized by younger directors to address them (such as first-person narratives) remain to be examined and are outside the scope of this study.

It is in light of this 'unravelling impasse' that I see a shift from a 'cinema of the affected' to a 'cinema of affect'. This book therefore offers a historical narrative of twenty years of Chilean documentary production, which, I argue, needs to be understood in close connection with the larger cultural and political struggles shaping the nation's recent past. This historical interpretation emerged from my study of the documentary films themselves. In this sense, the book also performs a critical appraisal of Chilean post-dictatorship documentary, by unpacking some of the most relevant aesthetic features as they unfold throughout the period under study. I believe that the undeniable historical importance of these documentaries has often occluded their style and creativity. Since the number of productions is large and elusive, I have chosen to focus on their cinematic aspects, such as reenactment, the use of the travelling shot, the treatment of archival material, and the mobilisation of the close-up, performing close textual analysis of some sequences. I foreground a few works that I consider to be more illustrative of the different arguments that I am making throughout the chapters of this book, but these are taken in the context of how they serve to trace a broader picture of my proposed trajectory.

My reasons for stating that the works under analysis are elusive are quite practical in nature: when I started this research the material was incredibly difficult to access, and to some extent, this is still the case. The vast amount of documentary production engaged in the anti-dictatorial struggle has only recently begun to be compiled, in some cases transferred from 16mm or U-matic to digital formats, 'returned' or donated from foreign archives, and even unearthed from directors' garages. Nor are contemporary productions easily accessible; seldom (though increasingly) commercially available, these films can often only be obtained through direct contact with the documentary filmmaker. In fact, my investigation started in tandem with that of the Museo de la Memoria, which began collecting an audiovisual archive of memories of the past, including documentary. Although I have tried to access as much material as I could from the period under analysis and the decades that preceded it, in order to be able to understand the transformations that have impacted documentary, I have not been able to trace or access the entire documentary production. Unfortunately, John King is right when he asserts that 'film historians in Latin America are faced with the painstaking task of reconstructing data from many imperfect sources'.[15] In this case, accessing the entirety of works is virtually impossible, as many of the exilic films have proven unobtainable, scattered as they are in different public and private archives all over the world. In addition, the number of documentaries produced in the last decades has grown explosively, largely allowed by the use of digital cameras and the proliferation of new platforms. The lack of channels of distribution only aggravates this situation. Cultural institutions have been gradually redressing this state of affairs through websites such as the very recent Ondamedia, run by the Ministry of Cultures, along with earlier initiatives such as Cineteca Nacional Online run by Cineteca Nacional de Chile (National Film Archive), and Cineteca Virtual run by Cineteca Universidad de Chile (Film Archive of the University of Chile).[16] Directors themselves have also contributed to making these works more accessible online. Nonetheless, despite this rapid emergence of online platforms and digital archives, access to Chilean documentaries remains a difficult task and an important number of productions are yet to be known.

The corpus analysed in this book consists of a wide range of documentaries produced under varying conditions and different formats (from U-matic to high definition video, from Super-8 to 35mm) and are of diverse lengths (short, medium, and feature). When I use the word 'film', I generally refer to documentary in any of these formats and will indicate the production format when it seems necessary. Some of these works have received public funding, while others came to fruition through international funding or, in some cases, received no funding at all. What they primarily share, however, is restricted circulation and distribution; most were constrained to national and international film festival circuits, and were seldom aired on Chilean network television. In the absence of a complete catalogue I have constructed my corpus by reviewing film festival catalogues, bibliographical references, and online sources.[17]

Expanding the Study of Chilean Documentary

Despite the fact that Chilean documentary has a long-standing and rich tradition of engaging actively and creatively with historical processes, it has been little studied both inside and outside Chile. The heyday of foreign academic attention on Chilean cinema was triggered by the so-called 'Nuevo Cine Latinoamericano' (New Latin American Cinema, hereinafter NLAC) of the 1960s and 1970s, and by the solidarity that followed the devastating violence that put an end to those culturally and politically vibrant years in the region. Soon after the coup, Michael Chanan provided an early and urgent focus in *Chilean Cinema*.[18] Chile's national cinema was also discussed in general historical accounts of cinemas in the region, as well as in two early anthologies on 'committed' and 'social' documentary, edited by Thomas Waugh and Julianne Burton, respectively.[19] Zuzana M. Pick developed the most nuanced and sustained interest in Chilean cinema in exile, compiled the most complete catalogue of exilic production, and elaborated sophisticated readings of some of these works.[20] Her project is particularly relevant for this book and I will return continuously to it.

What these publications demonstrate overall is the fascination of Anglophone academia with politically engaged filmmakers. In terms of Chilean documentary in particular, these writings reveal a special interest in the extraordinary allure exercised by the figure of Patricio Guzmán and his pivotal trilogy *La batalla de Chile* [*The Battle of Chile*] (1975–79).[21] In fact, the title of Guzmán's first documentary directed in the country after the democratic restoration, *Chile, la memoria obstinada* [*Chile: Obstinate Memory*] (1997) — the obstinate memory — has become a catchphrase in Latin American memory studies. It would be wrong to underestimate the fundamental place of Guzmán in the contemporary documentary landscape. Not only is he the director of *La batalla de Chile*, one of the most complete accounts of Salvador Allende's government and a key piece of the 1960s and 1970s political documentary, but he also founded the Festival Internacional de Documentales de Santiago (Santiago International Documentary Film Festival, hereinafter FIDOCS), the most important documentary film festival in Chile. Furthermore, he has promoted the work of younger Chilean documentary filmmakers abroad through the organization of film programmes, and he has also taught numerous seminars about documentary in Chile and elsewhere. Unfortunately, the overwhelming scholarly attention on Guzmán's work has occluded most of the other Chilean documentarians. Paulo Antonio Paranaguá already cautioned a decade ago: 'Como suele ocurrir con las piedras conmemorativas, lo malo es que a veces obstruyen las perspectivas o el paisaje. *La hora de los hornos* y *La batalla de Chile* son los monumentos del documental latinoamericano' [As it often occurs with commemorative stones, the bad thing is that they obstruct perspectives or the landscape. *La hora de los hornos* and *La batalla de Chile* are the monuments of Latin American documentary].[22] The academic and critical enthusiasm generated by Guzmán's oeuvre has resulted in scant attention to other documentary filmmakers, obscuring the broader picture and the interconnectedness, or disjunctions, of the post-dictatorship documentary scene. *(Un)veiling Bodies* seeks precisely to redress this limited knowledge of Chilean documentary. I do take the work of this fundamental director into consideration; in fact, readers will notice that the cover of the book is a still from his *Nostalgia de la luz* [*Nostalgia for the Light*] (2010), an important film for the trajectory proposed here. Nonetheless, it should not come as a surprise that this book presents Guzmán's production in a rather elliptical fashion. It is time to grant scholarly attention to other documentary filmmakers as well.

Chilean academia, in turn, has seen a point of inflection with the emergence of film studies as a scholarly discipline.[23] Within this incipient field, research on post-dictatorship cinema has been largely devoted to fiction films. The tendency to overlook or even exclude documentary from accounts of contemporary Chilean cinema drew in 2002 a somewhat enraged reaction from a reputed local documentary filmmaker, Cristián Leighton, who complained in an article about what he called the 'ellipsis' of documentary film — its historical absence — in critical discourse.[24] Only very recently has this situation started to be redressed, with a handful of books and articles published in Chile from 2005 onwards.

One of the most prominent trends of this recent upsurge in film historiography is the revision of the period between the 1950s and the 1973 military coup, when documentary was the dominant mode of production.[25] These publications provide important insights into a time that remained largely obscure, enhancing an understanding of Chilean documentary as both authorial and political. The reappraisal of these fertile decades has also been accompanied by the recuperation of foundational figures such as those of Sergio Bravo, Raúl Ruiz, Pedro Chaskel, and Patricio Guzmán, and the valorisation of the work of Ignacio Agüero and Carlos Flores, who can be seen as a sort of linkage between this generation and that of younger filmmakers (as a matter of fact, both Agüero and Flores have been actively involved in the formation of students in filmmaking schools).[26] The more recent visibility of key women directors, notably Valeria Sarmiento, Marilú Mallet, and Angelina Vázquez, who began their careers during the UP and continued it in exile, has challenged this masculine canon.[27] Emphasis has also been put on examining the extensive video production in the 1980s, most significantly in Germán Liñero's *Apuntes para una historia del video en Chile* and its complementary online project called *U-matic*.[28]

Within this landscape, Chilean scholars have provided useful succinct overviews of documentary production since the 2000 onwards, either highlighting their material operations, such as Iván Pinto, or examining the way they represent the dictatorial past in an overt way, valuing them in their role of 'guardians of popular memory', as Claudia Bossay does following Teshome Gabriel.[29] Authors analysing documentary tend to focus on the rise of first-person narratives, normally on those directed by the sons and daughters of direct victims or militants.[30] These different stances significantly extend scholarly attention to lesser-known directors, notably women and younger documentary makers. My book expands on some of the issues examined by these authors while offering new perspectives. These previous works bring into discussion a number of titles that I also examine here; however, numerous productions required further exploration and closer readings. Indeed, documentaries from the first democratic decade are often overlooked and I hope to shed light on their particularities. Furthermore, my study deals exclusively with documentaries concerned with memories of the dictatorship and its legacies in order to offer a broad picture of its development over two decades. To my knowledge, this is the first research with such an aim and scope: offering a narrative of Chilean post-dictatorship documentary in terms of a *trajectory* performed over twenty years, drawing particular attention to the transformation of its aesthetic features in specific historical junctures.

If this section of the introduction has distinguished academic studies written in English and published in North America and Europe from those written in Spanish and published in Chile, it is because their differences cannot be overlooked. While authors writing in English tend to produce specific case studies about a handful of titles directed by established directors and/or to highlight the testimonial value of these documentaries, Chilean authors present a more inclusive and broader stance in their studies. In this regard, it is worth clarifying that my own position cuts across these two academic worlds. As a Chilean scholar trained in the UK and currently working in the US, one of my tangential goals with this book is to build connections and to establish a dialogue between scholarly traditions which do not always converse. Although contemporary attention to Chilean documentary can be explained in the context of the current interest in non-fiction practices both world-wide and within the Latin American region as a whole,[31] it is important to highlight that consideration from abroad can be most clearly understood in the context of the memory struggles in the Southern Cone, in which non-fiction film has played a fundamental role. Scholars based in Latin American Studies or Literature departments, especially in the US, often approach documentary as just one more artefact along with other artistic and cultural practices such as memorial sites, literature, and the visual arts, to illustrate how these myriad responses have contributed to questions of memory.[32] Unlike these approaches, documentaries constitute the main object of study in this book, and it is through the analysis of their specific aesthetic and narrative strategies that I engage in discussions about memory struggles in post-dictatorship Chile.

The notion of trauma has dominated a great part of these debates, as evidenced in the work of Antonio Traverso, a Chilean scholar based in Australia.[33] His approach is concerned with underlining strategies of what psychoanalysis calls 'working through', that is, exploring how these documentaries contribute to overcoming the cultural trauma of dictatorship. Similarly, my first impulse was to approach this complex corpus through trauma studies. After all, as Idelber Avelar influentially asserted, 'The imperative to mourn is the postdictatorial imperative par excellence'.[34] Nonetheless, I soon became wary of wholeheartedly embracing such a perspective, which has largely been shaped by discussions developed in the context of the Holocaust. Not only did it seem that looking through the lens of trauma studies would further overload these works with the burden of negativity, but the stress of this approach on the impossibility of representing cataclysmic events also seemed increasingly baffling to me as I gathered and reviewed documentary after documentary produced as a response to the coup. In addition, as its main focus is on victims and survivors of trauma, such an approach was not enough to tackle the wide range of responses that the dictatorship has prompted, which certainly goes well beyond primary victims and their children. The way in which these directors refer to their own productions further challenge therapeutic readings — even when dealing with loss and death. Germán Berger-Hertz, for instance, who made a documentary on the disappearance of his father, forcefully states: 'My purpose was always to make a film, not family therapy.'[35] Assertions like this reinforce claims by authors such as Jill Bennett who, in her eloquent examination of the relation between the visual arts and affect in contexts of trauma, writes: 'To identify any art as "about" trauma and conflict potentially opens up new readings, but it also reduces work to a singular defining subject matter in a fashion that is often anathema to the artists, who construe the operations of their work as exceeding any single signifying function'.[36]

This is not to say that I completely eschew this influential approach. Indeed, I draw upon a number of film scholars who have been mobilizing psychoanalytical concepts to explore the limits and possibilities of the representation of traumatic events, a paradigm commonly traced back to the authors who expanded the notion of trauma into the cultural field in the early 1990s, notably Shoshana Felman, Dori Laub, and Cathy Caruth.[37] As E. Ann Kaplan, one of the leading critics seeking to depart from this model that sees trauma 'as a debilitating kind of memory'[38] explains, one of the main criticisms is the stress these authors place on the 'unrepresentability' and 'unspeakability' of the traumatic event.[39]

In turn, I found productive solace in scholarship developed in the wake of the 'affective turn' in the arts and the humanities — a shift that foregrounds the realm of the senses and emotions and conceives of perception as embodied — an emphasis that partially emerged as a response to the overwhelming presence of psychoanalysis in the cultural field.[40] Although film scholars have played a leading role in such a theoretical shift, this approach has seldom been adopted with regard to the cinema of the region. A notable exception is Laura Podalsky's *The Politics of Affect and Emotion in Contemporary Latin American Cinema*.[41] In her exploration of the complex interconnections between affect and politics, Podalsky criticises dominant accounts of the New Latin American Cinema, which have read its 'consciousness-raising impulse' as an outcome of Brechtian techniques of distanciation while disregarding, in turn, these films' 'sensorial dynamics'.[42] Although her focus is primarily on popular fiction films from Argentina, Cuba, Mexico, and Brazil, interestingly, she arrives at such an argument by analysing Guzmán's *La batalla de Chile* and *Chile, La memoria obstinada*, of which she offers a brief, yet nuanced, reading as profoundly emotional films.[43] It is not by chance that Podalsky compares both documentaries as she aims to develop a genealogy between the militant cinema of the 1960s and 1970s and post-1990 production by highlighting their 'visceral aesthetics'.[44] *(Un)veiling Bodies* can be seen as a contribution in the same direction. Although revisiting the so-called New Chilean cinema is beyond the scope of the book, I do build larger genealogies through the most sensorial films developed in the 1980s by exilic directors. Above all, by moving away from the prevailing notion of trauma, I explore Chilean documentary in its affective features, including, though not limited to, its traumatic aspects.

Beyond trauma studies: the crafting of a 'cinema of the affected'

I approach post-dictatorship documentaries as eclectic responses to the cultural trauma of the military coup and the almost two decades of terror and repression endured by Chilean society. Like the 9/11 attack on the Twin Towers in the US, Chile's coup, which occurred on another 11 September, was a highly visual event. La Moneda in flames, after being bombed by the Hawker Hunter jets, quickly and enduringly became the most iconic of the images of this 'event at the limits'.[45] It is difficult not to see the relentless repetition of the bombing — in the media in general, but particularly in post-dictatorship documentary — as a 'symptom' of this traumatic event for Chilean society, particularly if one follows Cathy Caruth's influential assertion that 'to be traumatized is precisely to be possessed by an image or event'.[46]

The theoretical framework of trauma, however, was not enough to account for the ways in which these documentaries are able to *move* and affect spectators so intensely. In answering this question, it has been very useful to approach these works through film scholarship that has been drawing from phenomenology and Gilles Deleuze's philosophical writings; what has been called the 'turn to the tactile'[47] or the 'haptic turn'.[48] By refusing to impose pre-established interpretative models that would constrain appreciation of this rich artistic production, I have chosen to draw upon varying theoretical frameworks to develop an interdisciplinary approach informed by the so-called affective turn, trauma and memory studies, cultural studies, film studies, history, and gender. In a way, the overall trajectory that I am visualising for Chilean documentary, which shifts from a 'cinema of the affected' towards a 'cinema of affect', demands a similar move from an approach based on trauma studies to one grounded in affect theories.

On the one hand, the notion of 'cinema of the affected' I am proposing here arises most evidently from the notion of the 'directly affected', which is used in the Southern Cone to refer to individuals who have suffered in their own 'flesh and blood' the horrors of repression.[49] It is also partially inspired by the notions of a 'cinema of duty' set forth by Sarita Malik and a 'cinema of the affected' as described by Rob Burns, who deal with Black British cinema and Turkish-German cinema respectively.[50] Both authors see these diasporic cinemas as having developed a strong sense of responsibility that seeks to create alternative views or to redress those offered by hegemonic discourses by aligning themselves with individuals perceived as being oppressed or victims of a system at a particular historical juncture. I am only partly influenced by these terms, because a 'committed' or 'social' cinema guided by the urgencies of the region has its own strong tradition in Latin America. On the other hand, my understanding of a 'cinema of affect' draws upon film scholarship that has underlined the affective dimension of cinema through the notion of touch. This notion is key to the affective turn in film studies, as it helps scholars foreground how the cinematic experience is embodied and not merely visual. As Thomas Elsaesser and Malte Hagener explain, leading authors within this theoretical shift such as Vivian Sobchack, Steven Shaviro, and Laura U. Marks (I would add Martine Beugnet to that list as well), have foregrounded the tactile-like qualities of images not as a 'negation of the visual' but rather to try 'to understand the senses in their interplay and perception as embodied'.[51] Before expanding upon this theoretical framework, I will first refer to some of the key features that I draw from trauma studies developed within the film studies field.

The enormous critical attention on how societies remember and forget in the last thirty years has led some authors to talk about a 'memory boom'[52] and even of a 'memory industry'.[53] While in Europe and in the US this contemporary interest emerged mainly through discussions centred on the Holocaust, in Latin America this attention has reflected on the social and cultural legacies of dictatorships during their transitions to democracy. It therefore cannot be understood outside the pursuit of justice and redress, particularly for the direct victims of state terrorism. As a consequence, the concepts of trauma, mourning, and melancholia have been central to the literature and the artistic practices dealing with the aftermath of these authoritarian regimes.[54] Because of the prominence of these Freudian categories, whose significance seem self-evidently useful to address the memories prompted by the most devastating event of the twentieth century for Chilean society, I initially approached the documentaries from a trauma studies perspective. Although trauma does not have a precise definition, scholars within the humanities commonly turned to what Caruth glosses as a 'response, sometimes delayed, to an overwhelming event or events, which takes the form of repeated, intrusive hallucinations, dreams, thoughts or behaviors stemming from the event'.[55] In fact, trauma's allure for film scholars emerges primarily from the fact that there can be found a 'match between the visuality common to traumatic symptoms (flashbacks, hallucinations, dreams) and the ways in which visual media like cinema become the mechanism through which a culture can unconsciously address its traumatic hauntings'.[56]

Numerous authors have argued that cultures or communities present similar reactions to individuals when faced with natural disasters or catastrophes brought about by humans such as wars, genocide, or mass displacements.[57] In her important work *Trauma Culture*, inspired by her own experience of 9/11, Kaplan argues that the 'complex interconnections between individual and cultural trauma' are such 'that, indeed where the "self" begins and cultural reactions end may seem impossible to determine'.[58] She draws particularly on the later writings of Freud to argue that 'cultures too may be traumatized, and that they too may "forget" horrendous actions performed in the past'.[59] Despite the recognition that 'cultural traumas are not "remembered" in the usual sense because of the specificity of trauma', Kaplan claims that 'the impact on past crimes in a nation-state may evidence itself in the form of cultural "symptoms" in a similar way to traumatised individuals'.[60] In the same vein, Kai Erikson claims that the tissues of a community can be damaged by a traumatic experience just as a body can. Aware of the scepticism such an analogy may arouse, he asserts that although 'communities do not have hearts or sinews or ganglia',[61] to speak of trauma in the context of a natural or human-caused catastrophe is useful for understanding the social dimensions of such an event, which indeed goes beyond 'the sum of the private wounds that make it up'.[62] A cultural trauma, in this sense, damages the 'fabric' that binds the individuals together while at the same time ends up bonding wounded people in such a way that 'estrangement becomes the basis for commonality'.[63]

Pinochet's military coup has been extensively understood as such a shattering event, both at an individual and cultural level. Alberto Moreiras has described the post-dictatorial climate as being 'more suffering than celebratory'.[64] For cultural critic Nelly Richard, the coup was a violent 'break in signification', which radically disturbed every aspect of social life from language and identity to history and politics, no longer considered safe categories of understanding.[65] Melancholy has characterized post-dictatorship Chile, she argues, which seems to be caught in narratives that lie between 'muteness' (reproducing the subject's stupor) and 'overstimulation' (ongoing reenactments that ineffectively seek to overcome depression).[66] Due to the particularities of the aftermath of the dictatorship, Chileans have insufficiently addressed their recent past. As a result, the country has been sporadically disturbed by social convulsions. People who went out into the streets either to celebrate or mourn Pinochet's death in 2006 illustrate precisely such convulsions. In an influential article, Alexander Wilde refers to these sudden social outbursts as 'irruptions of memory' which he defines as 'events that break in upon Chile's national consciousness, unbidden and often suddenly, to evoke associations with symbols, figures, causes, ways of life' that are still significantly linked to a past political experience.[67] These events disrupt the socio-political order of the transition to democracy by triggering, in the present, the extremely contested versions of the recent past. These public disruptions, Wilde explains, might be activated by unanticipated events, such as the discovery of bodies of the disappeared or by external factors that occur independently of the government in power, such as Pinochet's detention. In Wilde's account, these irruptions can be interpreted as a civic response to the inability of political institutions and leaders to cope with unresolved issues, related mostly to human rights.

Trauma studies, then, particularly as theorized by film scholars, proved productive when it came to analysing the first decade of the post-dictatorial era, which was marked by a quest for truth and a revelation of the human remains of the victims, as well as by the circulation of the testimonies of their relatives and those of torture survivors. As mentioned above, the notion of trauma has provided fertile ground for film studies because of its particular visual traits and the mechanisms articulated by filmmakers to convey it on the screen. As a result, scholars have coined terms such as 'shell shock cinema', 'trauma cinema' or 'posttraumatic cinema' to deal with responses to catastrophic events on screen.[68] It must be recalled, however, that the dominant model in trauma studies has been largely criticized for its focus on the impossibility of representing traumatic experience.[69] As Francis Guerin and Roger Hallas remark in their collected volume *The Image and the Witness*, trauma studies is indeed built upon this paradox, as it persists in returning to an 'iconoclastic notion of the traumatic event as that which simultaneously demands urgent representation but shatters all potential frames of comprehension and reference'.[70] These authors stress that it is necessary to move beyond such 'aporia'.[71] Yet, two concerns have constrained these possibilities, as summarized by Kaplan and Wang: a fear of an aestheticization of politics and history in general and, as a consequence, their trivialisation by media representations.[72] Hayden White, in his influential 'The modernist event', argues that it is precisely the previously inconceivable characteristics of the twentieth century catastrophic events — such as wars, massive poverty, and systematic genocide, with the Shoah being a paradigmatic case — that demand alternatives modes of representation.[73] The challenges posed to traditional frameworks of knowledge by such 'holocaustal events', in White's conceptualization, are most appropriately dealt with by the stylistic features of modernism.[74]

This is why scholars dealing with the depiction of traumatic events on the screen often favour the use of experimental or self-reflexive techniques, which they see as more suited for addressing conflictive and contested pasts. This is the case with authors like Linda Williams, Janet Walker, and Joshua Hirsch, all of whom foreground the potentialities of non-fiction in staging memory, stressing documentary's importance as alternative historiographies, or, in Walker's words, as 'imperfect historiography'.[75] For Walker, it is precisely the contested memories, multiple vantage points, and fictional strategies that mark these documentaries as 'effectively political' texts, more powerful than realist representations 'to redress real abuses of the past'.[76] Walker's foregrounding of the 'less realist' strategies has persuaded me to look carefully for such devices in the texts under analysis, particularly reenactment (due to its creative possibilities), which I have found deployed in these productions in varied forms.

Yet, even when documentary productions engage less eagerly with fictional strategies, this does not make them any less powerful. Significantly, I would argue, these documentaries' shifting strategies in addressing the past reveal the historical moment of their emergence. As Jo Labanyi states via Raymond Williams' concept of 'structure of feeling': 'it is clear how attention to textures of emotion can tell us much about the cultural specificity of a historical period.'[77] The celebration of experimental aesthetics is common in scholarship dealing with the representation of the dictatorial trauma in the Chilean artistic practices as well, as perhaps more clearly illustrated by the writings of Nelly Richard.[78] Nonetheless, I would advocate for a less prescriptive view such as that fostered by authors as distinct as Kaplan and Wang, Podalsky, or Huyssen.[79] In Kaplan and Wang's view, although 'the obsession with the meaning-defying dimensions of trauma and *mise-en-abîme* may offer stark or provocative aesthetics, such an obsession risks becoming a closure in its own turn, a fetishized taboo sealing off a domain of non-meaning and nonsense' (emphasis in the original).[80] Such obsessions, the authors argue, may occlude the importance of why we need to remember in a broader historical context and what we can do to change the social structures that have produced such cultural traumas.[81]

I take these cautionary words seriously. Many of the documentaries discussed here engage fully or partly in sophisticated formal quests. Indeed, many could be seen as belonging to the 'essayistic cinema' as described by Laura Rascaroli: variations of first-person works that are 'irreducibly plural' and characterized by 'doubt and self-scrutiny [...] still authorial, still experimental, still radical'.[82] However, I have been careful not to overlook productions on the grounds that they are not 'sufficiently' experimental. Local commentators have dismissed many Chilean documentaries, usually on the grounds that they are not aesthetically sophisticated or formally challenging, significantly eroding the knowledge that can be derived from them. For instance, Jacqueline Mouesca claims, with regard to the phenomenon of Chilean cinema in exile, that 'Decenas de documentales quedaron en el olvido y sus méritos, si es que hoy pudieran ser recogidos y visionados, son probablemente puramente testimoniales' [Dozens of documentaries have been forgotten. If one could recover them and watch them now, it is likely their value will be solely testimonial].[83] Not only do recently rediscovered films prove such generalizations mistaken, but I would also argue that even when documentaries do not fully engage with self-reflexive strategies, they nonetheless draw upon cinematic resources that are worth looking at closely. As will emerge from my study, the deployment of different aesthetic mechanisms often responds to particular historical junctures. Understanding why and how these formal and aesthetic elements change throughout time is an essential part of this book.

Indeed, my project is guided by an interest in tracing how history has shaped documentary responses to a devastating event with particular attention on which cinematic strategies have been mobilized in different periods. In doing so, the work of Joshua Hirsch has been particularly helpful, as it enables the visualization of the trajectory performed by Chilean post-dictatorship documentary.[84] In *Afterimage* he carefully traces the historical development of the representation of the Holocaust from the newsreel and compilation film to that which he calls 'posttraumatic' postmodern cinema. In his account, what defines the traumatic aspect of cinema is not the presence or the absence of a particular image of horror but the formal exploration of the visual depiction of trauma.[85] He suggests that there are two phases that can be distinguished in a society that has experienced a traumatic event. Hirsch claims that there is a period

> after the initial encounter with a traumatizing historical event but before its ultimate assimilation — in which there arises a discourse of trauma. [...] One may be traumatized by an encounter with the Holocaust, one may be unable to assimilate a memory or an image of atrocity, but the discourse of trauma as one encounters it in conversation, in reading, in film — gives one a language with which to begin to represent the failure of representation that one has experienced.[86]

The initial stage of this process is characterized by the revelation of images of atrocities, which 'may need relatively little narrative support in order to cause vicarious trauma'.[87] Hirsch argues that it is sufficient for the image to be introduced by a reliable source (a newspaper, for example), historically contextualized (by explaining that they belong to a former concentration camp, for instance), and validated (via the truthfulness of its source). Soon, however, public interest in these images diminishes, and gets limited to the field of specialists, in a process commonly termed 'collective numbing'. It is in the following stage, he argues, when these images are no longer able to shock viewers, that films develop other strategies to overcome this numbness. At this point, films appear to be less defined by the specific content of an image of atrocity (whether this be fictional, non-fictional or even absent), and more by an 'attempt to formally reproduce for the spectator an experience of suddenly seeing the unthinkable'.[88] Thus, films engage in a formal exploration that aims to cinematically mimic traumatic features.

My perception of documentary as shifting to a 'cinema of affect' that tends to move away from images of horror in favour of more affective ones, is inspired but also departs from Hirsch's ideas. First of all, I would like to insist on the fact that my proposed itinerary does not follow a close chronological development; not least because of the fundamental role exiled directors have played in creating alternative ways to refer to the coup. Distancing themselves from overt militant discourses characteristic of the 1960s and 1970s, a number of such directors produced deeply affective works. I see their films as crucial precedents to first-person documentaries that emerged most clearly at the turn of the century, many of which I see as being part of a 'cinema of affect'. In addition, rather than reading the form exhibited by documentaries in the second stage proposed by Hirsch as one that seeks to formally convey aspects of trauma only, documentaries seem to be seeking to defeat Chilean society's so-called 'collective numbness' by moving beyond images of atrocity. These works are clearly not confined to memories of pain or loss, but rather expand to include a wide range of affective images of the past. Many of these images refer to everyday life under the dictatorship, drawing on childhood memories, experiences of solidarity and friendship in detention centres, and collective action and political resistance.

The Texture of the Past: Towards a 'Cinema of Affect'

There was something in these documentaries that did not seem contained by the notion of trauma, an intensity that is still not easy to describe. Part of this visceral, affective appeal seems to emanate from an aspect usually overlooked in political documentary, as Jane M. Gaines argued in 'Political Mimesis'; these are the 'aesthetic supplements' that can be found in the most realist of these productions.[89] I am interested in exploring precisely such creative devices: the audiovisual strategies they mobilize and the textual operations they deploy in order to address the dictatorial past and its legacies. In this sense, although I conceive of these productions as responses to a specific cultural trauma, I would like to assert that this does not mean that readings of them should be confined to trauma theory or that the memories included by these responses are solely of a traumatic nature. Such an approach, I believe, not only limits their understanding as artistic practices, but has political implications as well.

Antonio Traverso and Mick Broderick contend that trauma studies and memory studies have developed in such close interconnection that it is, 'in fact, virtually impossible to separate them out; their underlying difference being more of *emphasis* than any intrinsic specificity to be delineated from a historical, thematic or methodological perspective'[90] (my emphasis). Nonetheless, it seems that much accent has been placed on trauma. Criticising such a stress, Andreas Huyssen writes:

> It has been all too tempting to think of trauma as the hidden core of all memory. After all, both memory and trauma are predicated on the absence of that which is negotiated in memory or in the traumatic symptom. Both are marked by instability, transitoriness, and structures of repetition. But the collapse of memory into trauma, I think, would unduly confine our understanding of memory, marking it too exclusively in terms of pain, suffering and loss. It would deny human agency and lock us into compulsive repetition. Memory, whether individual or generational, political or public, is always more than only the prison house of the past.[91]

In line with Huyssen's remarks, I believe that it makes a difference — and a significant one for that matter — if one chooses to frame one's research as 'archives of suffering',[92] as Bhaskar Sarkar and Janet Walker do, or if one chooses instead, like Ann Cvetkovich does, to refer to it as 'archives of feelings'.[93] While Sarkar and Walker explicitly align their collection on documentary and catastrophic events with the current shift away from victimhood towards one of survivors and agency, their emphasis remains attached to 'social suffering'.[94] Cvetkovich, building on the notion of trauma as experienced in everyday life in her examination of lesbian culture, fosters an understanding of 'trauma as a category that embraces a range of affects, including not just loss and mourning but also anger, shame, humor, sentimentality and more'.[95] Seeking to move beyond what she considers pathologising approaches to this concept, Cvetkovich argues that 'traumatic events refract outward to produce all kinds of affective responses and not just clinical symptoms'.[96] Like Cvetkovich, several authors have tried to engage in more productive ways with concepts burdened by a dark veil. This is the case of Svetlana Boym with her work on nostalgia or David L. Eng and David Kazanjian's engagement with the notion of loss, which fosters an understanding of it as a creative force, shifting the focus from that which is absent to that which remains.[97]

Within the Chilean context, Stern forcefully argues that an important yet often overlooked aspect of the dictatorship is that memory is a battle 'for hearts and minds'.[98] Chilean post-dictatorship documentaries make this struggle clear. They present a vast 'archive of feelings' even when dealing with losses of political projects and loved ones, or take up topics such as exile, displacement, and torture. In many cases, these memories acquire a sensorial, even synaesthetic, presence.[99]

Therefore, my overall understanding of documentary is in line with the work of several authors who have questioned documentary's affiliation to 'discourses of sobriety', in Bill Nichols' influential formulation.[100] According to Nichols, documentaries are aligned with 'nonfictional systems' such as science, politics, economics, education, or religion, which 'assume they have instrumental power [...]. Discourses of sobriety are sobering because they regard their relation to the real as direct, immediate, transparent.'[101] Consequently, he argues, documentary distances itself from erotics, being determined instead by 'a pleasure in knowing' which he defines as 'epistephilia'.[102] Authors writing on documentary, such as Stella Bruzzi, Michael Renov, and Belinda Smaill, have variously criticized this approach to non-fiction, on the grounds that by privileging the realm of reason and knowledge, it dismisses affect, emotions, and desire too rapidly.[103] Renov offers a substantial critique to such an understanding of documentary. Defending the role of desire, he challenges the conception of sobriety in non-fiction film, judging it as 'unduly separatist and deeply rationalist' in its favouring of consciousness over the unconscious, knowledge over pleasure and 'sobriety at the expense of the evocative and delirious'.[104] According to Renov, documentary's appeal not only derives from its subject matter, but also from the spectator's 'historiographic curiosity'.[105] There is something else, he argues, 'along the lines of Barthes' notion of punctum, the explosive prick of contact with one's own image repertoire evoked by the documentary image'.[106] Renov champions an understanding of non-fiction 'in relation to both knowledge and desire, evidence and lure, with neither term exerting exclusive control'.[107]

Such an approach has significantly influenced this book, since Chilean documentaries have been committed to informing and educating viewers about the dictatorial period, delivering historical facts and gruesome details in order to explain the scope and legacies of state terrorism to foreign and local audiences. At the same time, however, these productions have engaged in imbuing such knowledge and memories with particular textures, feelings, and affects. In this respect, because the notion of affect refers to the mind and the body alike, as much to the passions as to reason, as Michael Hardt stresses,[108] I have drawn on it as well. Affects, Hardt argues, building on the ideas of Baruch Spinoza, shed light on 'both our power to affect the world around us and our power to be affected by it'.[109] This point is crucial as it allows thinking of these documentaries as 'things' that may move us not only to reflect on the past but also, significantly, to affect the future. Thus authors such as Jo Labanyi invite us to think about cultural texts in their dimension as cultural practices, as '"things that do things": that is, things that have the capacity to affect us'.[110] It is worth recalling that Brian Massumi has influentially equated the notion of affect with intensity.[111] He distinguishes affect from emotion, in that while the latter is of a 'qualified' nature, lending itself to be narrativized, the former is 'unqualified', defined by its irreducibility.[112] Albeit acknowledging this difference — emotion and affect as distinctive yet intertwined[113] — I will deal with both affect and emotion, as the works under analysis here mobilize at times clearly distinguishable emotions (such as terror, fear, or anger) but also less graspable affective responses, often prompted by what Marks defines as 'haptic' images.[114]

Relying on the notion of touch, haptic images foreground how the cinematic experience is embodied and is not simply visual.[115] When I argue that the trajectory of Chilean documentary manifests a shift from a revelation of literal bodies to a revelation of the film's skin, I am thinking precisely in Marks' formulation. She develops the notion of the film's skin as

> a metaphor to emphasize the way film signifies through its materiality, through a contact between perceiver and object represented. It also suggests the way vision itself can be tactile, as though one were touching a film with one's eyes: I term this *haptic visuality*. (emphasis in the original)[116]

Marks turns to art historian Alois Riegl to describe haptic vision as a way of looking in which 'the eyes themselves function like organs of touch'.[117] Haptic visuality 'tends to move over the surface of its object rather than plunge into illusionistic depth, not to distinguish form so much as to discern texture. It is more inclined to move than focus, more inclined to graze than gaze'.[118] Although she argues that the difference between optical and haptic vision 'is a matter of degree' (as both are usually involved), she contends that the former 'privileges the representation power of the image' while the latter 'privileges the material presence of the image'.[119] A haptic image, therefore, invites the spectator to linger on the screen's surface before she realizes, if ever, what she is looking at.[120] Marks claims that despite their medium-specific differences, tactile features are shared both by video and film, such as their distinct graininess, the effects of over- and underexposure, as well as changes in focus.[121] As she argues, these characteristics foster a relationship between the spectator and the screen as a whole, while discouraging the discernment of the objects in it.[122] Her understanding is not so much concerned with the differences between video (usually conceived as an optical medium) and film (considered a tactile one), but rather on how the eye is invited to 'touch' that which is on the screen.[123] I find her work very useful, since the directors under analysis here utilize different gauges of film, from Super-8 to 16mm, as well as low and high definition video. Regardless of the medium they choose, they seek to invest their images with particular textures that endow their works with a tactile quality alike to that described by Marks.

Building significantly on Marks' project, Martine Beugnet develops a clarifying description of a 'cinema of sensation' in her study of contemporary French film, similar to the 'cinema of affect' I am envisaging. This 'cinema of sensation' is characterized by the following:

> Changes in focus, unusual angles and framing, long shots alternating with close-ups and extreme close-ups, graphic editing and the combination of different media (8mm, 16mm, 35mm, high- and low-definition digital footage) with their variations in ratio and graininess and so on: the choice of techniques operates a constant passage from optical to haptic perception, where the material presence of the image competes with, and often supersedes, its representational power.[124]

Such a cinema, Beugnet argues, is particularly important to history, as it 'specifically re-endorses film's often undervalued yet most essential of privileges: the ability to reach a spectator's mind through the intelligence of the affective'.[125]

Like Marks, Hamid Naficy focuses on exilic and diasporic filmmakers, foregrounding the fact that these directors' experiences of dislocation present a strong consideration on the senses and on memories of the quotidian in their works.[126] As Naficy puts it, 'since some of the most poignant reminders of exile are non-visual and deeply rooted in everyday experiences, they tend to emphasize tactile sensibilities'.[127] In the same line, Marks develops the notion of 'sense memories', understood as 'a nontransparent and differentially available body of information' which though certainly available to any individual, acquires a key role in that it helps minority groups protect '*cultural* knowledge' (emphasis in the original).[128] She argues that 'the sensorium is [often] the only place where cultural memories are preserved. For intercultural cinema, therefore, sense experience is at the heart of cultural memory'.[129] Naficy and Marks' scholarly works are particularly productive for developing an understanding of Chilean documentary as profoundly affective; as already mentioned, exiled filmmakers have played a pivotal role in its development. Also, younger directors from a wider diaspora have studied or pursued careers abroad, rising as some of the leading actors in Chile's contemporary documentary landscape. It is not by chance that I first encountered an important number of recent Chilean productions or coproductions at their premiere at international film festivals held in Europe (such as in France and the United Kingdom), while many others were generously sent to me via airmail by directors based in countries such as Canada, France, and the US This distinctive nomadic feature of Chilean cinema led me to think about these documentaries as 'travelling memories'.

By referring to the notion of travelling, I consider the material experience of displacement endured by many of these filmmakers, but I also align myself with a more transcultural approach to memory studies which seeks to go beyond the nation-state model, accounting for the fundamental role that media plays in the construction and circulation of cultural memory. In this sense, my understanding of memory is influenced by the work developed by scholars such as Marita Sturken, Alison Landsberg, Astrid Erll, and Marianne Hirsch, who tackle from various perspectives the means by which media and other artistic practices help in the circulation and construction of cultural memories in the contemporary world.[130] I draw on these various theoretical approaches that stress mobility, as they help me highlight the fact that the directors I am dealing with both incorporate and elaborate memories that circulate and are in permanent motion. 'Memories do not hold still', Erll argues, 'on the contrary, they seem to be constituted first of all through movement'.[131] Travelling through time and space, these cinematic memories are incorporated through other people's narrations, images, and sounds, and are not exclusively acquired by an experience lived directly. Thus these memories are transmitted and transformed from generation to generation and from one documentary to another, and they circulate from one country to another, *touching* different audiences.[132] At the same time, however, while these documentaries are inserted into a global world, and this is fundamental, they remain historically and politically grounded. They have emerged as artistic responses to the shattering individual and collective experiences of the military coup, the ensuing seventeen years of dictatorial rule, and the constrained democracy that followed.

As I have argued throughout this introduction, my project goes beyond an understanding of Chilean post-dictatorship documentaries as being merely about trauma. Instead, I approach these productions more broadly as 'memory works', as suggested by Annette Kuhn. Not all of these documentaries question the authenticity of the memories they convey as proposed by Kuhn's elaboration (this is done most notably by productions I conceive of under the broad notion of 'cinema of affect').[133] Yet, despite their differing political and aesthetic approaches, what these documentaries share is the fact that they consciously engage in 'an active practice of remembering which takes an inquiring attitude towards the past and the activity of its (re)construction through memory'.[134]

I have mentioned above that emphasizing a model based on trauma carries political implications. Lessie Jo Frazier provides culturally specific reasons to not embrace too eagerly such a perspective in the Chilean context.[135] She argues that 'psychologistic models have come to pervade contemporary political discourse, and mourning as a path to social reconciliation has proven inadequate for the politics of memory'.[136] The issue at stake is that the official posture has co-opted such a discourse in the model of 'mourning-as-reconciliation'[137], which claims 'that the nation can reconstitute itself as a whole through a common experience of mourning'.[138] This 'culturally specific model of mourning', similar to the Freudian one, has benefited some political parties and sections of the military as it has helped both 'smooth over the national tragedy of the Chilean coup and military dictatorship as a "problem"'.[139] In opposition to this state-led model, Frazier underscores the role of human rights activists and organizations, which have on the contrary 'linked intimate processes of mourning with political action'.[140] In her view, these actors' 'passionate refusals' to leave the past behind opposes this model that seeks to constrain 'affective states (such as sorrow, anger, passionate love for the lost one — seen as dangerously chaotic in and of themselves)' in order to achieve 'an emotionally neutral point of functional stability'.[141] Despite Frazier's analysis overall remaining attached to a narrow focus on human rights activists and those directly affected, and thereby understating the role of a wider spectrum of society, her remarks are refreshing as they point to the risks of lingering on the concepts of trauma and mourning in this particular setting. I see Chilean post-dictatorship documentary as another, and key, 'passionate refusal' to let go of the past.

If the post-dictatorship period has been characterized by a generalized *desencanto* (disenchantment) in Chilean society, or in Richard's words, by 'disaffection'[142] or a 'dismantling of drama',[143] I argue that these documentaries seek to return *intensity* to it. In Richard's account:

> The will to remember and commemorate the loss that the victims' relatives try to keep alive collides with the passive universe of sedimented indifference that today conjures up machinations and spontaneities, calculations and automatisms, impositions and inclinations, all enmeshed at the moment where they jointly produce an exhaustion of the meaning of acts and words that were previously charged with rigor and emotion. The question 'Where are they?' has no place in which to lodge itself in this current Chilean landscape without intense narrative or dramatic voice.[144]

Within this context of cultural indifference, post-dictatorship documentaries have offered a space for a wide spectrum of voices, significantly but not exclusively victims, so that they can inscribe their counter-narratives. In this sense, I would like to think, figuratively, of my proposed trajectory of post-dictatorship documentary as one that seeks to restore the senses to a social body that is numb, *anaesthetized* after the shock of the coup. Here, I follow the work of Susan Buck-Morss, who has sophisticatedly argued that Walter Benjamin's closing remark in his famous essay 'The Work of Art in the Age of Mechanical Reproduction'[145] is a call for art to return to the sensorial realm.[146] In this argument, Buck-Morss returns to the etymological root of the word aesthetics:

> *Aisthitikos* is the ancient Greek word for that which is 'perceptive by feeling'. *Aisthisis* is the sensory experience of perception. The original field of aesthetics is not art but reality — corporeal, material nature. As Terry Eagleton writes: 'Aesthetics is born as a discourse of *the body*'. It is a form of cognition, achieved through taste, touch, hearing, seeing, smell — the whole corporeal sensorium (emphasis in the original).[147]

In her view, Benjamin's call for a 'politicization of art' in the wake of fascism is not a call to embrace propaganda but 'to *undo* the alienation of the corporeal sensorium, to *restore the instinctual power of the human bodily senses for the sake of humanity's self-preservation*, and to do this, not by avoiding the new technologies, but by *passing through them*' (emphasis in the original).[148] Film, Buck-Morss remarks citing Benjamin, 'reconstitutes experience'.[149] More recently, Judith Butler, in her reflections on how media 'frames' armed conflicts, claims that:

> in some sense, every war is a war upon the senses [...] There is no thinking and judgement without the senses, and there is no thinking and judgement about war without the senses assuming a social form that can be reliably reproduced over time.[150]

Although comparing the Chilean case to a war would be misleading — there was no 'state of internal war', even though the *junta* declared as much in order to justify the coup and the pervasive use of violence — aggression against the tissue of the social body could certainly be seen as an attack on the senses. Following such a line of thought, it does not seem an overestimation to argue that in the aftermath of the brutal military rule, Chilean post-dictatorship documentary fosters a restoration of the senses. If by returning incessantly to the iconic images of La Moneda being bombed, testimonies of pain and loss, and images of horror, these productions have initially mimicked society's shock, it is also true that they have moved beyond this repertoire of atrocity to seek out more affective and sensorial ways to refer to this past. Haptic images, argues Marks, are usually deployed as 'an explicit critique of visual mastery, in the search for ways to bring the image close to the body and other senses'.[151] In this way, 'cinema may reconfigure, rather than shatter, a subjectivity'.[152] By following a trajectory from a 'cinema of the affected' to a 'cinema of affect', post-dictatorship documentary contributes, metaphorically speaking, towards Chilean society's restoration of the senses.

The structure of the book is as follows. In Chapter 1, I offer a historical background of Chilean documentary from the mid-1950s until today and explore the country's politics of memory to stress how intimately entrenched non-fiction's development is with the country's own historical trajectory. In addition to providing key insights into the memory struggles, the chapter traces the phases of the dismantling and re-articulation of Chilean documentary, both during the era of dictatorship and during the post-dictatorial period, focusing on public and private initiatives that have contributed to its current revitalization. The chapter also briefly examines the vexing relationship between documentary and local television. In Chapter 2, I argue that between 1990 and 2003 documentary was dominated by a focus on the directly affected, characterized by a revelation of images of atrocities, particularly of the human remains of the disappeared, and by a focus on victims' female relatives, extending later to torture survivors. I compare two documentaries set in the Atacama Desert and constructed upon missing bodies in order to illustrate the changes and continuities in my proposed trajectory: *Huellas de sal* [*Salt Traces*] (Andrés Vargas, Grupo Proceso) produced in 1990, and Patricio Guzmán's *Nostalgia de la luz*, released twenty years afterwards, in 2010. I also argue that documentaries retreat from overt representations of torture, favouring instead the use of reenactments in which atrocity is evoked but not displayed. Chapter 3 establishes continuities between different generations of filmmakers via the enduring experience of exile, centring on deeply affective homecoming documentaries. The focus is on 'travelling memories': first-person accounts by exilic filmmakers and by the subsequent generation raised or born abroad, particularly women directors. In turn, Chapter 4 stresses the generational differences as present in the first-person documentaries of younger directors who turn to the family trope to grapple with the dictatorial past. I deal both with the work of the children of direct victims and their memories of childhood and loss, as well as with directors who, though not the children of the directly affected, also turn to the family trope to formally reflect about the possibilities of making other people's memories their own in their intrinsically haptic documentaries. Chapter 5 focuses on younger directors who nostalgically shift their lenses to the vibrant anti-dictatorial struggle of the 1980s, most clearly since 2004. These productions perform a revelation of archival material often relegated from the screen: photographs and video images of that same resistance in which rebellious youth played a crucial role. I also focus on two works from the end of the decade that further challenge the traditional debate over memory by revealing abject bodies that disturb and defy the dominant accounts about the past: *La muerte de Pinochet* [*The Death of Pinochet*] (Bettina Perut and Iván Osnovikoff, 2011) and *El mocito*. In the Conclusion, I highlight some of the main arguments of this book in relation to the itinerary traced by Chilean documentary from a 'cinema of the affected' to a 'cinema of affect'. In addition, I look into more recent developments of Chilean documentary and propose further trajectories for future studies.

Notes to the Introduction

1. Chilean philosopher Patricio Marchant in Nelly Richard, 'The Reconfigurations of Post-dictatorship Critical Thought', *Journal of Latin American Cultural Studies*, 9: 3 (2000), 273–82 (p. 273).
2. For further discussion on 'incomplete democracy', see Manuel Antonio Garretón, *Incomplete Democracy: Political Democratization in Chile and Latin America*, trans. by R. Kelly Washbourne and Gregory Horvath (Chapell Hill: University of North Carolina Press, 2003). For the qualification of a 'dictadura imperfecta' (imperfect dictatorship), see Armando Uribe and Miguel Vicuña, *El accidente Pinochet* (Santiago: Editorial Sudamericana, 1999), pp. 49–50.
3. See Richard, 'The Reconfigurations', p. 278; Idelber Avelar, 'Five Theses on Torture', *Journal of Latin American Cultural Studies*, 10:3 (2001), 253–71 (p. 262), and Tomás Moulian, *Chile actual: anatomía de un mito*, 3rd edn (Santiago: LOM, 2002), p. 37.
4. See, for example, Steve Stern's trilogy 'The Memory Box of Pinochet's Chile': *Remembering Pinochet's Chile: On the Eve of London 1998*. Book One (Durham: Duke University Press, 2004),

Battling for Hearts and Minds: Memory Struggles in Pinochet's Chile, 1973–1988. Book Two (Durham: Duke University Press, 2006); *Reckoning with Pinochet: The Memory Question in Democratic Chile, 1989–2006*. Book Three (Durham: Duke University Press, 2010); and *The Politics of Memory in Chile: From Pinochet to Bachelet*, ed. by Cath Collins, Katherine Hite, and Alfredo Joignant (Colorado: Firstforum Press, 2013).

5. Alan Angell, *Democracy After Pinochet: Politics, Parties, and Elections in Chile* (London: Institute for the Study of the Americas, 2007), pp. 1–2.
6. These figures have been discussed in detail by Stern in his 'Introduction to the Trilogy: Memory Box of Pinochet Chile', pp. xxi–xxxiv (reprinted in all three volumes; hereafter I will be quoting from the introduction to Book Three), pp. 390–93 n. 3. Stern, offering a conservative number of deaths and disappearances, suggests an estimate between 3,500 and 4,000. The state figures provided by the Truth and Reconciliation Commission (known as the Rettig Report) and its follow-up, the Corporation of Repair and Reconciliation, amount to 2,905 documented cases of death and disappearance and 139 deaths via political violence, most often civilians shot by state agents during curfew hours, as he explains. For figures regarding exile, see Stern, p. 395 n.3.
7. Manuel Antonio Garretón argues that — though incomplete and imperfect — Chile's transition to democracy was prompted by the democratic elections of 1988 and ended with the inauguration of the first democratic administration in 1990. See Garretón, *Incomplete Democracy*, pp. 146–47. Other authors, like Idelber Avelar argue that the real transitions in countries like Brazil and Chile were not the return to civilian rule, but the dictatorships themselves, in that they signal 'epochal transitions from State to Market'. See Idelver Avelar, *The Untimely Present: Postdictatorial Latin American Fiction and the Task of Mourning* (Durham: Duke University Press, 1999), pp. 58–59 and also 'Five Theses on Torture', p. 253.
8. See for example, Moulian; Uribe and Vicuña; Nelly Richard, *Cultural Residues: Chile in Transition*, trans. by Alan West-Durán and Theodore Quester (Minneapolis: University of Minnesota Press, 2004); and Avelar, *The Untimely Present*.
9. Michael J. Lazzara, *Civil Obedience: Complicity and Complacency in Chile since Pinochet* (Madison: University of Wisconsin Press, 2018), p. 123.
10. Laura U. Marks, *The Skin of the Film: Intercultural Cinema, Embodiment, and the Senses* (Durham: Duke University Press, 2000).
11. The concept of 'memory impasse' is key in Stern's account, and I shall return to it in Chapter 1. Stern, *Reckoning with Pinochet*, p. 4
12. On the 'symbolic circle' see Stern, *Reckoning with Pinochet*, esp. pp. 131–32; 194–95.
13. Lazzara, *Civil Obedience*, p. 123.
14. Ibid.
15. John King, *Magical Reels: A History of Cinema in Latin America*, 2nd edn (London: Verso, 2000), pp. 1–2.
16. See Onda Media, <http://ondamedia.cl>, launched in mid 2017 by the CNCA, as well as the digital archive of the Cineteca Nacional <http://cinetecadigital.ccplm.cl> and the online archive of the Cineteca Universidad de Chile <http://cinetecavirtual.cl>, which began functioning in 2013 and 2012, respectively. Other relevant initiatives where films can be accessed are: Cinemateca Virtual de Chile <www.cinechileno.org>, CineChile: Enciclopedia del cine chileno <http://www.cinechile.cl>, Chile desde fuera <http://vimeo.com/chiledesdefuera>, Archivo de Documentación Gráfica de la Universidad de Santiago <www.archivodga.usach.cl>, Proyecto U-matic (U-matic Project) <http://www.umatic.cl> (no longer available online), and Archivo Fílmico de la Universidad Católica de Chile <http://archivofilmico.uc.cl>.
17. These sources are: the catalogue of documentary production available on the website of the Asociación de Documentalistas de Chile (ADOC, Association of Chilean Documentarians) elaborated by Pamela Pequeño, *Catastro virtual de la producción documental chilena*, ADOC (2007) <http://www.adoc-chile.org/cat/?page_id=125> [accessed 23 December 2013] (no longer available online); every catalogue published by the Festival Internacional de Documentales de Santiago (Santiago International Documentary Film Festival, hereinafter referred as FIDOCS), since its creation in 1997 until 2011; a selection of catalogues from other relevant film festivals

such as the Festival Internacional de Cine de Viña del Mar (Viña del Mar International Film Festival), Festival Internacional de Cine de Valdivia (Valdivia International Film Festival, FICValdivia) and the Festival de Cine Recobrado de Valparaíso (Valparaíso Film Festival of Rediscovered Cinema); the online catalogue available on CineChile's website, which has been growing steadily since its creation in 2009. Foundational bibliographical sources consulted include Alicia Vega, *Itinerario del cine documental chileno, 1900–1990* (Santiago: Centro EAC, Universidad Alberto Hurtado, 2006), a major catalogue of production in celluloid. For Chilean cinema in exile, the most authoritative catalogue remains the one elaborated by Zuzana M. Pick (in collaboration with the Cinemateca Chilena), 'Cronología del cine chileno en el exilio 1973/1983', *Literatura chilena, creación y crítica*, 10:27 (January–March 1984), 15–21 and for video production, the catalogue elaborated by Yéssica Ulloa, *Video independiente en Chile* (Santiago: Ceneca, 1985). More recently, Pamela Pequeño compiled a catalogue for the Ictus video collection, *Productora Ictus TV, Videoteca: Memoria histórica 1978–1992* (Santiago: 2005) and Germán Liñero created Proyecto U-matic, which focuses on Chile's prolific U-matic production, cataloguing over 450 titles, some of which could be accessed online, although not available any more: <http://www.umatic.cl>.
18. *Chilean Cinema*, ed. by Michael Chanan (London: BFI, 1976).
19. See, for instance, *Les cinemas de l'Amérique latine*, ed. by Guy Henebelle and Alfonso Gumucio Dragón (Paris: L'Herminier, 1981); John King, *Magical Reels*, who provides some insights into the early post-dictatorial scene in its updated revision in 2000; and Peter B. Schumann, *Historia del cine latinoamericano*, trans. by Oscar Zambrano (Buenos Aires: Editorial Legasa, 1987). The articles on edited collections are Victor Wallis and John D. Barlow, 'Documentary as Participation: *The Battle of Chile*', in *'Show Us Life': Toward a History and Aesthetics of the Committed Documentary*, ed. by Thomas Waugh (London: Scarecrow Press, 1984), pp. 403–16. In Burton's anthology two articles deal exclusively with the Chilean case: Pick, 'Chilean Documentary: Continuity and Disjunction', and Ana M. López, '*The Battle of Chile*: Documentary, Political Process and Representation', both in *The Social Documentary in Latin America*, ed. by Julianne Burton (Pittsburgh: University of Pittsburgh Press, 1990), pp. 109–30 and pp. 267–87, respectively.
20. See amongst them 'Chilean Cinema: Ten Years of Exile (1973–83),' *Jump Cut*, 32 (1987), 66–70 <http://www.ejumpcut.org/archive/onlinessays/JC32folder/ChileanFilmExile.html> [accessed 23 July 2016] and 'Chilean Cinema in Exile (1973–1986). The Notion of Exile: A Field of Investigation and its Conceptual Framework', *Framework*, 34 (1987) 39–57, as well as her various essays in the special issue evaluating the state of Chilean cinema since the coup, *Literatura chilena, creación y crítica*, 10:27 (January–March 1984).
21. Among others, the list of publications includes: Patricio Guzmán and Pedro Sempere, *Chile: el cine contra el facismo* (Valencia: Fernando Torres, 1977); Thomas Miller Klubock, 'History and Memory in Neoliberal Chile: Patricio Guzmán's *Obstinate Memory* and *The Battle of Chile*', *Radical History Review*, 85 (Winter 2003), 271–81; Nelly Richard, 'Con motivo del 11 de septiembre: notas sobre *La memoria obstinada* (1996) de Patricio Guzmán', in *Escrituras, imágenes y escenarios ante la represión*, ed. by Elizabeth Jelin and Ana Longoni (Madrid: Siglo XXI, 2005) pp. 121–29 (first publ. in *Revista de Crítica Cultural*, 15 (1998)). See also the books by Jorge Ruffinelli, *El cine de Patricio Guzmán: En busca de las imágenes verdaderas* (Santiago: Uqbar, 2008) and Cecilia Ricciarelli, *El cine documental según Patricio Guzmán* (Santiago: FIDOCS, 2010).
22. Paulo Antonio Paranaguá, 'Orígenes, evolución y problemas', in *Cine documental en América latina*, ed. by Paulo Antonio Paranaguá (Madrid: Cátedra, 2003), pp. 13–78 (p. 58).
23. See Hans Stange and Claudio Salinas, 'La incipiente literatura sobre cine chileno', *La Fuga*, 7 (2008) <http://www.lafuga.cl/la-incipiente-literatura-sobre-cine-chileno/302> [accessed 27 August 2016] and also 'Hacia una elucidación del campo de estudios sobre cine en Chile', *Aisthesis*, 46 (December 2009), 270–83; Marcela Parada, 'El estado de los estudios sobre cine en Chile: una visión panorámica 1960–2009', *Razón y Palabra*, 77 (2011) <http://www.razonypalabra.org.mx/varia/77%205a%20parte/67_Parada_V77.pdf> [accessed 27 August 2016]; and Elizabeth Ramírez-Soto, 'Impertinent Interventions: On Raúl Ruiz and an Emerging Field', *Journal of Latin American Cultural Studies: Travesia*, 21:1 (2012), 49–59.

24. Cristián Leighton, 'La elipsis del documental', *EAC Magazine*, 2 [n.d] <http://jhcnewmedia.org/eacmagazine/> [accessed 28 August 2016] (first publ. in *Patrimonio Cultural*, Dibam, 25 (2002)).
25. Relevant titles include Pablo Corro and others, *Teorías del cine documental chileno, 1957–1973* (Santiago: Pontificia Universidad Católica de Chile, Facultad de Filosofía, Instituto de Estética, 2007); Mónica Villarroel and Isabel Mardones, *Señales contra el olvido: cine chileno recobrado* (Santiago: Cuarto Propio, 2012); and Claudio Salinas and Hans Stange (with the collaboration of Sergio Salinas), *Historia del Cine Experimental en la Universidad de Chile 1957–1973* (Santiago: Uqbar, 2008).
26. See, for example, Pablo Corro, 'Sergio Bravo y tendencias del montaje', *Aisthesis*, 47 (July 2010), 83–99; *El cine de Raúl Ruiz: fantasmas, simulacros y artificios*, ed. by Valeria de los Ríos e Iván Pinto (Santiago: Uqbar, 2010); Verónica Cortínez and Manfred Engelbert, *La tristeza de los tigres y los misterios de Raúl Ruiz* (Santiago: Cuarto Propio, 2011); Andrea Chignoli and Catalina Donoso, *(Des) montando fábulas: el documental político de Pedro Chaskel* (Santiago: Uqbar, 2013); Ruffinelli; Valeria de los Ríos and Catalina Donoso, *El cine de Ignacio Agüero: el documental como la lectura de un espacio* (Santiago: Cuarto Propio, 2015); and Jorge Morales and Gonzalo Maza, *Idénticamente desigual: el cine imperfecto de Carlos Flores*, 2nd edn. (Santiago: FIDOCS, 2014).
27. *Nomadías: el cine de Marilú Mallet, Valeria Sarmiento y Angelina Vázquez*, ed. by Elizabeth Ramírez-Soto and Catalina Donoso Pinto (Santiago: Metales Pesados, 2016).
28. Germán Liñero, *Apuntes para una historia del video en Chile* (Santiago: Ocho Libros, 2010).
29. Iván Pinto, 'Cine, política, memoria. Nuevos entramados en el documental chileno', *La Fuga*, 4 (2007) <http://2016.lafuga.cl/cine-politica-memoria/341> [accessed 4 June 2017] and 'Formas expandidas: Límites y entre-lugares del documental chileno 2004–2016', *Cine Documental*, 4 (2016) <http://revista.cinedocumental.com.ar/formas-expandidas-limites-y-entre-lugares-del-documental-chileno-2004–2016/> [accessed 4 June 2017]; and Claudia Bossay, 'Cineastas al rescate de la memoria reciente chilena', *Imagofagia*, 4 (2011) <http://www.asaeca.org/imagofagia/index.php/imagofagia/article/view/165/137 > [accessed 4 June 2017].
30. See Michelle Bossy and Constanza Vergara, *Documentales autobiográficos chilenos* (Santiago: Fondo de Fomento Audiovisual del Consejo Nacional de la Cultura y la Artes, 2010); María Teresa Johansson and Constanza Vergara, 'Filman los hijos. Nuevo testimonio en los documentales *En algún lugar del cielo* de Alejandra Carmona y *Mi vida con Carlos* de Germán Berger-Hertz', *Meridional*, 2 (2014), 89–105; and Catalina Donoso, 'Sobre algunas estrategias fílmicas para una propuesta de primera persona documental', *Comunicación y medios*, 26 (2012): 23–30, among others.
31. See Paranaguá; *Visual Synergies in Fiction and Documentary Film from Latin America*, ed. by Miriam Haddu and Joanna Page (New York: Palgrave Macmillan, 2009); *New Documentaries from Latin America*, ed. by Vinicius Navarro and Juan Carlos Rodríguez (New York: Palgrave Macmillan, 2014); and *Latin American Documentary Film in the New Millenium*, ed. by María Guadalupe Arenillas and Michael J. Lazzara (New York: Palgrave, 2016), among others.
32. See, for example, Macarena Gómez-Barris, *Where Memory Dwells: Culture and State Violence in Chile* (Berkeley: University of California Press, 2009); Michael J. Lazzara, *Chile in Transition: The Poetics and Politics of Memory* (Gainesville, FL: University Press of Florida, 2006) and *Civil Obedience*; and Ana Ros, *The Post-Dictatorship Generation in Argentina, Chile, and Uruguay: Collective Memory and Cultural Production* (New York: Palgrave MacMillan, 2012).
33. See, for instance, Antonio Traverso, 'Working through Trauma in Post-Dictatorial Chilean Documentary: Lorena Giachino's Reinalda del Carmen', in *People, Place and Power: Australia and the Asia Pacific*, ed. by Dawn Bennett, Jaya Earnest and Miyume Tanji (Perth, WA: Black Swan Press, 2009), pp. 208–29 and 'Dictatorship Memories: Working through Trauma in Chilean Post-Dictatorship Documentary', *Continuum*, 24:1 (2010), 179–91.
34. Avelar, *The Untimely Present*, p. 3.
35. Cinedirecto Producciones — Todo por las Niñas, '*My Life with Carlos*. A Film by Germán Berger-Hertz' (Press book) (n.d.). <http://www.gebrueder-beetz.de/produktionen/mein-leben-mit-carlos> [accessed 18 November 2017].
36. Jill Bennett, *Empathic Vision: Affect, Trauma, and Contemporary Art* (Stanford: Stanford University Press, 2005), p. 3.

37. Shoshana Felman and Dori Laub, *Testimony: Crisis of Witnessing in Literature, Psychoanalysis and History* (New York: Routledge, 1992); *Trauma: Explorations in Memory*, ed. by Cathy Caruth (Baltimore: Johns Hopkins University Press, 1995) and Cathy Caruth, *Unclaimed Experience: Trauma Narrative and History* (Baltimore: Johns Hopkins University Press, 1996).
38. E. Ann Kaplan and Ban Wang, 'Introduction: From Traumatic Paralysis to the Force of Modernity', in *Trauma and Cinema: Cross-Cultural Explorations*, ed. by E. Ann Kaplan and Ban Wang (Hong Kong: Hong Kong University Press, 2004), pp. 1–22 (p. 5).
39. E. Ann Kaplan, *Trauma Culture: The Politics of Terror and Loss in Media and Literature* (New Brunswick: Rutgers University Press, 2005), p. 37. See also Kaplan and Wang, pp. 3–15.
40. See particularly, Vivian Sobchack, *The Address of the Eye: A Phenomenology of Film Experience* (Princeton, NJ: Princeton University Press, 1992), pp. xiii–xvii and Steven Shaviro, *The Cinematic Body* (Minneapolis: University of Minnesota, 1993), pp. 67–81.
41. Laura Podalsky, *The Politics of Affect and Emotion in Contemporary Latin American Cinema: Argentina, Brazil, Cuba, and Mexico* (New York: Palgrave Macmillan, 2011). For more on the affective turn in the cinema of the region see Vinodh Venkatesh and María del Carmen Caña Jiménez, 'Affect, Bodies, and Circulations in Contemporary Latin American Film', *Arizona Journal of Hispanic Cultural Studies*, 20 (2016), 175–81.
42. Ibid., p. 30.
43. Ibid., p. 25–30.
44. Ibid., p. 56.
45. I allude to the notion used by Saul Friedländer; 'Introduction', in *Probing the Limits of Representation: Nazism and the 'Final Solution'*, ed. by Saul Friedländer (Cambridge, Mass.: Harvard University Press, 1992), pp.1–21 (p. 3).
46. Cathy Caruth, 'Introduction', in *Trauma: Explorations in Memory*, ed. by Cathy Caruth (Baltimore: Johns Hopkins University Press, 1995), pp. 3–12 (pp. 4–5).
47. Elizabeth Stephens, 'Sensation Machine: Film, Phenomenology and the Training of the Senses', *Continuum*, 26: 4 (2012), 529–39 (p. 530).
48. Thomas Elsaesser and Malte Hagener, *Film Theory: An Introduction Through the Senses* (New York: Routledge, 2010), p. 127.
49. Elizabeth Jelin, 'Victims, Relatives, and Citizens in Argentina: Whose Voice is Legitimate Enough?', in *Humanitarianism and Suffering: The Mobilization of Empathy*, ed. by Richard Ashby Wilson and Richard D. Brown (Cambridge: Cambridge University Press, 2009), pp. 177–201 (p. 177 n. 1).
50. Sarita Malik, 'Beyond "the Cinema of Duty"? The Pleasures of Hybridity: Black British Film of the 1980s and 1990s', in *Dissolving Views: Key Writings on British Cinema*, ed. by Andrew Higson (London: Cassell, 1996), pp. 202–15; and Rob Burns, 'Turkish-German Cinema: From Cultural Resistance to Transnational Cinema?', in *German Cinema: Since Unification*, ed. by David Clarke (London: Continuum, 2006), pp. 127–49 (p. 127–34).
51. Elsaesser and Hagener, p. 110.
52. Andreas Huyssen, *Present Pasts: Urban Palimpsests and the Politics of Memory* (Stanford: Stanford University Press, 2003), p. 18.
53. Kerwin Lee Klein, 'On the Emergence of Memory in Historical Discourse', *Representations*, 69 (Winter 2000), 127–50.
54. Richard, 'The Reconfigurations', p. 273 and Avelar, 'Five Theses on Torture', p. 253. Freud influentially discussed these concepts in Sigmund Freud, 'Mourning and Melancholia', in *The Standard Edition of the Complete Psychological Works of Sigmund Freud*, vol. 14, trans. and ed. by James Strachey (London: Hogarth Press, 1957), pp. 243–58.
55. Caruth, 'Introduction', p. 4.
56. Kaplan, *Trauma Culture*, p. 69.
57. See for example Kaplan, *Trauma Culture*; Elizabeth Jelin, *State Repression and the Struggles for Memory*, trans. by Judy Rein and Marcial Godoy-Anatavia (London: Latin American Bureau, 2003); Kai Erickson, 'Notes on Trauma and Community', in *Trauma: Explorations in Memory*, ed. by Cathy Caruth (Baltimore, London: Johns Hopkins University Press, 1995), pp. 183–99; and Hayden White, 'The Modernist Event', in *The Persistence of History: Cinema, Television and the Modern Event*, ed. by Vivian Sobchack (New York: Routledge, 1996), pp. 17–38 (p. 20).

58. E. Ann Kaplan, *Trauma Culture*, p. 2.
59. Ibid. p.68.
60. Ibid. p.68.
61. Kai Erikson, *Everything in its Path* (New York: Simon and Schuster, 1976), p. 194, quoted in Kai Erickson in 'Notes on Trauma and Community', p. 188.
62. Ibid., p.185.
63. Ibid., p.186.
64. Alberto Moreiras, 'Postdictadura y reforma del pensamiento', *Revista de Crítica Cultural*, 7 (1993), 26–35 (p. 27).
65. Richard, 'The Reconfigurations' p. 274.
66. Richard, *Cultural Residues*, p. 22.
67. Alexander Wilde, 'Irruptions of Memory: Expressive Politics in Chile's Transition to Democracy', *Journal of Latin American Studies*, 31: 2 (May 1999), 473–500 (p. 475). The author deliberately uses the term 'irruption' as this spelling matches more closely the Spanish word 'irrupción'. See p. 475, n. 5.
68. See Anton Kaes, *Shell Shock Cinema: Weimar Culture and the Wounds of War* (Princeton, NJ: Princeton University Press, 2009); Janet Walker, 'Trauma Cinema: False Memories and True Experience', *Screen*, 42:2 (2001), 211–16 and *Trauma Cinema: Documenting Incest and the Holocaust* (Berkeley: University of California Press, 2005); and Joshua Hirsch, *Afterimage: Film, Trauma, and the Holocaust* (Philadelphia: Temple University Press, 2004) and 'Post-Traumatic Cinema and the Holocaust Documentary', in *Trauma and Cinema: Cross-Cultural Explorations*, ed. by E. Ann Kaplan and Ban Wang (Hong Kong: Hong Kong University Press, 2004), pp. 93–122.
69. See Kaplan for an enlightening account of such critiques and the need to go beyond them: *Trauma Culture*, pp. 34–38 and Kaplan and Wang, p. 3–12.
70. Frances Guerin and Roger Hallas, 'Introduction', *The Image and the Witness: Trauma, Memory and Visual Culture*, ed. by Frances Guerin and Roger Hallas (London: Wallflower Press, 2007), pp. 1–20 (p. 3).
71. Ibid., p. 4.
72. Kaplan and Wang, pp. 10–11.
73. Ibid., p. 30–32.
74. Ibid., p. 32.
75. Walker, *Trauma Cinema*, p. 190, and Linda Williams, 'Mirrors without Memories: Truth, History, and the New Documentary', *Film Quarterly*, 46: 3 (Spring 1993), 9–21.
76. Janet Walker, 'The Traumatic Paradox: Documentary Films, Historical Fictions, and Cataclysmic Past Events', *Signs*, 22: 4 (1997), 803–25, p. 809.
77. Jo Labanyi, 'Doing Things: Emotion, Affect, and Materiality', *Journal of Spanish Cultural Studies*, 11: 3–4 (2010), 223–33 (p. 231).
78. See, for example, *Cultural Residues* and her collection of essays *Crítica de la memoria (1990–2000)* (Santiago: Ediciones Universidad Diego Portales, 2010). In *Cultural Residues*, for instance, she turns to the artistic and literary practices of the 1980s to argue that in their disarticulation of language, their 'poetics of the crisis' resonated better with 'the memory of disaster', p. 29.
79. See Kaplan and Wang, pp. 11–14, Podalsky, pp. 6–7 (she explicitly criticises Richard's elitist and nostalgic position in her favouring of such aesthetics) and Huyssen, pp.18–21.
80. Kaplan and Wang, p. 11.
81. Ibid., p. 12.
82. Laura Rascaroli, *The Personal Camera: Subjective Cinema and the Essay Film* (London: Wallflower Press, 2009), pp. 189–90.
83. Jacqueline Mouesca, 'Cine: un largo camino de ilusiones', in *100 años de cultura chilena 1905–2005*, ed. by Juan Andrés Piña (Santiago: Zig-Zag, 2006), pp. 331–80 (p. 357).
84. Joshua Hirsch, *Afterimage* and 'Post-Traumatic Cinema', pp. 93–22.
85. Hirsch, *Afterimage*, p.19; 'Post-Traumatic Cinema', pp. 101–02.
86. Hirsch, *Afterimage*, p. 19.
87. Hirsch, *Afterimage*, p. 18.
88. Ibid., p.19.

89. Jane M. Gaines, 'Political Mimesis', in *Collecting Visible Evidence*, ed. by Jane M. Gaines and Michael Renov (Minneapolis: University of Minnesota Press, 1999), pp. 84–102 (pp. 98–99).
90. Antonio Traverso and Mick Broderick, 'Interrogating Trauma: Towards a Critical Trauma Studies', *Continuum*, 24: 1 (2010), 3–15 (p. 5).
91. Huyssen, p. 8.
92. *Documentary Testimonies: Global Archives of Suffering*, ed. by Bhaskar Sarkar and Janet Walker (New York: Routledge, 2010).
93. Ann Cvetkovich, *An Archive of Feelings: Trauma, Sexuality, and Lesbian Public Cultures* (Durham: Duke University Press, 2003).
94. Bhaskar Sarkar and Janet Walker, 'Moving Testimonies', in *Documentary Testimonies: Global Archives of Suffering*, ed. by Bhaskar Sarkar and Janet Walker (New York: Routledge, 2010), pp. 1–34 (p. 4).
95. Cvetkovich, p. 48.
96. Ibid., p. 19.
97. Svetlana Boym, *The Future of Nostalgia* (New York: Basic Books, 2001) and David L. Eng and David Kazanjian, 'Introduction: Mourning Remains', in *Loss: The Politics of Mourning*, ed. by David L. Eng and David Kazanjian (Berkeley: University of California Press, 2003), pp. 1–25 (p. 2).
98. Stern, 'Introduction to the Trilogy', p. xxii–xxiii. Such, in fact, is the title of Book Two of his trilogy: *Battling for Hearts and Minds*.
99. The term synaesthesia is also central to the 'haptic turn' to stress that the film experience cannot be reduced to the optical realm and that the moving image can also appeal to other senses aside from vision. As Sobchack explains, 'in common usage synaesthesia refers not only to an *involuntary* transfer of feeling among the senses but also to the *volitional* use of metaphors in which terms relating to one kind of sense impression are used to describe a sense impression of other kinds' (emphasis in the original). Sobchack, 'What My Fingers Knew: The Cinesthetic Subject, or Vision in the Flesh', in *Carnal Thoughts: Embodiment and Moving Image Culture* (Berkeley: University of California Press, 2004), pp. 53–84 (p. 68). For more on the clinical term, see pp. 67–68.
100. Nichols, *Representing Reality* (Bloomington: Indiana University Press, 1991), pp. 3–4.
101. Ibid., p. 3–4.
102. Ibid., p. 178.
103. Stella Bruzzi, *New Documentary: A Critical Introduction*, 2nd edn (London: Routledge, 2006), p. 248; Michael Renov, 'Introduction: The Truth About Non-Fiction', in *Theorizing Documentary*, ed. by Michael Renov (New York: Routledge, 1993). pp. 1–11 (p. 3; 194 n. 5), and *The Subject of Documentary* (Minneapolis: University of Minnesota Press, 2004), pp. 93–103; and Belinda Smaill, *The Documentary: Politics, Emotion, Culture* (New York: Palgrave Macmillan, 2010), esp. pp. 3–20.
104. Renov, *The Subject of Documentary*, p. 98.
105. Ibid., p. 100.
106. Ibid., pp. 100–01.
107. Renov, *The Subject of Documentary*, p. 101.
108. Michael Hardt, 'Foreword: What Affects are Good for', in *The Affective Turn: Theorizing the Social*, ed. by Patricia Ticineto Clough and Jean Halley (Durham: Duke University Press, 2007), pp. ix–xiii.
109. Ibid., p. ix.
110. Labanyi, pp. 231–32.
111. Brian Massumi, 'The Autonomy of Affect', *Cultural Critique*, 31 (Autumn 1995), pp. 83–109 (p. 88).
112. Ibid. pp. 88–89.
113. In Labanyi's explanation: 'Affect, sensation, and emotion thus occupy different points on a continuum going from body to mind, each having a different temporality. All of them involve judgment in some way; sensation and emotion are felt consciously; and emotion forms a further continuum with reason in that both are forms of conscious moral thinking'; affect, in turn, is preconscious. Labanyi, pp. 224–25.

114. Marks, *The Skin of the Film*, esp. 162–82 and Marks, 'Video Haptics and Erotics', in *Touch: Sensuous Theory and Multisensory Media* (Minneapolis: University of Minnesota Press, 2002), pp. 1–20.
115. See, for example, Shaviro, pp. 50–55; Sobchack, *The Address of the Eye*, and in particular her eloquent essay 'What My Fingers Knew', in *Carnal Thoughts*, pp. 53–84; Marks, *Touch: Sensuous Theory and Multisensory Media* (Minneapolis: University of Minnesota Press, 2002); Martine Beugnet, *Cinema and Sensation: French Film and the Art of Transgression* (Edinburgh: Edinburgh University Press, 2007); and Jennifer M. Barker, *The Tactile Eye: Touch and the Cinematic Experience* (Berkeley: University of California Press, 2009).
116. Marks, p. xi.
117. Marks, *The Skin of the Film*, p. 162.
118. Ibid., p. 162.
119. Ibid., p. 163.
120. Ibid., pp. 162–63.
121. Ibid., p. 172.
122. Ibid., p. 172.
123. Ibid., p. 173.
124. Beugnet, *Cinema and Sensation*, pp. 67–68.
125. Ibid., p. 178.
126. Hamid Naficy, *An Accented Cinema: Exilic and Diasporic Filmmaking* (Princeton, NJ: Princeton University Press, 2001).
127. Ibid., p. 28.
128. Marks, *The Skin of the Film*, p. 199. On sense memory, see esp. pp.110–14; 194–242.
129. Ibid. p. 195.
130. Marita Sturken, *Tangled Memories: The Vietnam War, the Aids Epidemic, and the Politics of Remembering* (Berkeley: University of California Press, 1997); Astrid Erll, 'Travelling Memory', *Parallax*, 17: 4 (2011), 4–18; Alison Landsberg, *Prosthetic Memory: The Transformation of American Remembrance in the Age of Mass Culture* (New York: Columbia University Press, 2004); and Marianne Hirsch, *Family Frames: Photography, Narrative, and Postmemory* (Cambridge: Harvard University Press, 1997).
131. Erll, p. 11.
132. Marks emphasizes how intercultural cinema not only leaves its traces on other people, but also takes impressions of different audiences with it. 'The very circulation of a film among different viewers is like a series of skin contacts that leave mutual traces'. Marks, *The Skin of the Film*, pp. xi xii.
133. Annette Kuhn, *Family Secrets: Acts of Memory and Imagination*, new edn (London: Verso, 2002), pp. 157–58
134. Ibid., p. 157.
135. Lessie Jo Frazier, *Salt in the Sand: Memory, Violence, and the Nation-State in Chile, 1890 to the Present* (Durham: Duke University Press, 2007).
136. Ibid., p. 229. By a 'psychologistic' approach she means the mobilization of psychological concepts (as well as medical practices) by the state. p. 219.
137. Ibid., p. 195.
138. Ibid., p. 233.
139. Ibid., p. 232.
140. Ibid., p. 233.
141. Ibid., pp. 240–41.
142. Richard, *Cultural Residues*, p. 16.
143. Ibid., p. 26.
144. Ibid.
145. This is the most common translation into English, but the essay has also been published under the title 'The Work of Art in the Age of its Technological Reproducibility (Second Version)', in *Walter Benjamin: Selected Writings, vol.3, 1935–1938*, trans. by Edmund Jephcott and others, ed. by Howard Eiland and Michael W. Jennings (Cambridge, Mass: Harvard University Press, 2002), pp. 101–40. This is the version I will be citing in Chapter 3.

146. Susan Buck-Morss, 'Aesthetics and Anaesthetics: Walter Benjamin's Artwork Essay Reconsidered', *October*, 62 (Autumn 1992). Buck-Morss returns to Walter Benjamin's understanding of modernity as an experience centred on 'shock'. She writes, 'Bombarded with fragmentary impressions they see [the eyes] too much–and register nothing. Thus the simultaneity of overstimulation and numbness is characteristic of the new synaesthetic organization', pp. 16–18.
147. Ibid., p. 6.
148. Ibid., p. 5.
149. Ibid., p. 18 n. 62.
150. Judith Butler, 'Introduction to the Paperback Edition', in Judith Butler, *Frames of War: When is Life Grievable?* (London: Verso, 2010), pp. ix–xxx (p. xvi).
151. Marks, *The Skin of the Film*, pp. 151–52.
152. Ibid., p. 151.

CHAPTER 1

Contextualizing Chilean Documentary and the Memory Struggles

This chapter provides a general overview of the history of Chilean documentary and the complex memory struggles during the post-dictatorial period. Although the focus of this book is on documentary from 1990 onwards, it is necessary to look back to previous decades to understand its current development. In doing so, I stress the ways in which post-dictatorship documentary is deeply entangled with the works that preceded it and with Chilean society's transition to democracy. Addressing the complex history of advances and setbacks that have characterized the struggle for human rights, I focus on the most relevant turning points that have shaped documentary responses to the Chilean military coup since the democratic restoration. The chapter continues by tracing Chile's transformation from the virtually silent period of the early 1990s into a revitalized environment for cultural memory at the turn of the twenty-first century in order to understand the shifting production conditions faced by documentary films in that period. In the final section I discuss the paradoxical retreat of documentary that coincided with the arrival of civilian rule and the role that public policy, as well as private or semi-private initiatives, played in its renaissance. Lastly, I focus on the emblematic case of *El diario de Agustín* [*Agustin's Newspaper*] (Ignacio Agüero, 2008) which serves to examine the conflictive relation between public funding, documentary filmmakers, and television during the post-dictatorship period.

A Brief Overview of Chilean Documentary Before 1990

Chilean documentarians have a long-standing tradition of political commitment and engagement with formal exploration. This tradition can be traced at least to the mid-1950s when a new film culture began to emerge in the country. Previously, non-fiction films consisted largely of commissioned works by private companies or newsreels by state bodies. In the context of the Cold War and the Cuban revolution, Chilean filmmakers, as elsewhere in Latin America, began embracing 'documentary as an essential tool of political awareness and social transformation'.[1] A thriving film scene began taking shape mainly under the Instituto Fílmico de la Universidad Católica (Film Institute of the Catholic University) founded in 1955 and the Centro de Cine Experimental (Centre for Experimental Cinema, CE) created in 1957.[2]

Despite the extremely precarious conditions under which these filmmaking centres functioned, the young directors involved with them played a fundamental role in the development of Chilean cinema.[3] At least since then, Chilean documentary began developing what Zuzana M. Pick has aptly described as its 'political vocation', alongside formal experimentation.[4] Documentary dominated the cinematographic landscape, with filmmakers going into the streets and engaging eagerly in Salvador Allende's revolutionary process.[5] The transformations experienced by the country were so intense that led Pedro Chaskel to famously assert, 'No elegí el tema, fue la realidad que me lo impuso' [I did not choose the subject; it was reality that imposed it on me].[6]

Undoubtedly, the most well-known documentary of this period chronicling the rise and fall of Allende's government is *La batalla de Chile*, which was finished in exile in Cuba by Patricio Guzmán and edited by Chaskel. This film includes the iconic images of La Moneda being attacked by the Hawker Hunter jets, which came to symbolize both that which was lost and the violence that would fall over the nation after the collapse of the revolutionary project. Arguably, no other Chilean film has received the theoretical attention devoted to this trilogy, although it is closely followed by what is usually considered its sequel, *Chile, la memoria obstinada*, also directed by Guzmán. Because the interest dedicated to Guzmán's work is quite expansive, later in this chapter I will shift the discussion to the crucial role that the director has played in the reconfiguration of the Chilean contemporary documentary landscape, mostly through the foundation of the country's most important documentary film festival, FIDOCS.

After the military coup, most filmmakers who had trained between the mid-1950s and the early 1970s fled the country together with a vast contingent of people involved in the vibrant cultural scene, spreading all over the world. Chilean production resumed in exile, unexpectedly inaugurating the most prolific period of Chilean cinema. Although never a 'movement', as Pick has argued,[7] the massive exodus of film practitioners and their numerous works turned Chilean cinema in exile into an exceptional cultural phenomenon. Once again, documentary films dominated exilic production.[8]

Exiled directors, supported in most cases by European television channels, began their return to the country in the early 1980s, attracted by the awakening of civil society after a decade of terror and silence. Their numerous cinematic homecomings were motivated by the fact that between the years 1983 and 1986 the country was shaken by a series of protests. The harsh economic crisis that affected the country (from 1982 to 1983) had led, for the first time since 1973, Chilean people to take to the streets in massive riots on a national scale. The fear that had subjected Chilean society until then had been transformed into a strong civilian and partisan movement that would eventually lead to Pinochet's defeat in 1988 (after the first democratic elections that forced him to step down from the presidency). According to Paul W. Drake and Iván Jaksić:

> The resurrection of democratic forces in Chile began with the mass demonstrations of the early 1980s. Previously established social actors — like

labor unionists and students — overcame fear and recaptured a voice in national affairs. Less institutionalized groups — notably slum-dwellers and women — created novel forms of survival, organization, and expression.[9]

This process of redemocratization found a powerful ally in video. Between 1973 and 1978 Chilean cinema underwent a veritable process of dismantling, as María de la Luz Hurtado notes.[10] Most film schools were immediately closed while others survived only for a few more years; the state agency Chile Films underwent privatization and became dependent on official television; and the first Film law (1967) that protected Chilean cinema (which included tax reductions for local producers) was derogated. Hurtado argues, however, that around 1978, a gradual process of re-construction began. This new audiovisual sector was broadly characterized by an unparalleled growth of private activity through advertising agencies (in which many filmmakers were working), the production of spots for television instead of fiction films or documentaries, and, significantly, the arrival of video.

This new technology contributed enormously to the creation of so-called 'alternative' or 'independent' video production, mostly via U-matic, and its possible uses as a tool for redemocratization were documented and debated by practitioners themselves since its arrival on the scene.[11] Germán Liñero, an active member of the video landscape in the 1980s, recalls in his *Apuntes para una historia del video en Chile* that the first people to go into the streets to record the demonstrations were independent cameramen who had begun working for international television networks eager for news of Chile's political awakening.[12] Throughout the years, a number of audiovisual collectives blossomed, such as Ictus (1978), ECO (1980), Grupo Proceso (1982), and Teleanálisis (1982). These groups worked in close connection with grassroots movements and received funding mainly from international non-profit organizations.[13] Video became 'an example of oppositional media at a time when any form of opposition amounted to a defiant and risky gesture'.[14] Documentaries and alternative news reports circulated semi-clandestinely all around the country, featuring collective resistance and organization in shantytowns, mass demonstrations, and brutal state repression.[15] Thus these videos not only documented the period, 'but constituted a form of resistance in their own right'.[16]

Overall, the 1980s saw the emergence of a deeply heterogeneous audiovisual production, ranging from video-art to fiction, including the first-person documentaries of exiled filmmakers. Nonetheless, the period came to be largely identified with what is usually called *reportaje de trinchera* or cinema of *barricada*, terms that in fact place the emphasis on the street struggles.[17] The thousands of hours of footage and the enormous amount of videos unleashed in the context of the struggle for democracy constitute today a fundamental source of archival material which post-dictatorship documentaries draw upon when revisiting this past, as discussed in Chapter 6.[18]

This heterogeneous 'audiovisual resistance' came together as a fundamental force within the wider spectrum of the 'cultural resistance' mobilized by the 'No' campaign against Pinochet in the 1988 election.[19] Expectations placed by documentary filmmakers in the democratic restoration were, as in the rest of Chilean society, high, but in Liñero's view, silence came along with democracy.[20] I seek to develop a more nuanced stance in this study, and I will argue that though scarce and perhaps hesitant, Chilean documentary production continued throughout the early 1990s. Yet, to understand why documentary descended into this seeming silence it is necessary to look into the intricacies of the politics of memory in the country.

Chile and the Politics of Memory

The post-dictatorship period — in particular from 1990 to 1998, the year when Pinochet was detained in London — has been generally described as one in which oblivion defeated memory. This view is synthesized by the influential claim of Chilean sociologist Tomás Moulian, who stated in 1997 that 'El consenso es la etapa superior del olvido' [consensus is the higher stage of oblivion].[21] In his *Chile actual: anatomía de un mito*, Moulian goes beyond the general understanding of the transition to democracy as a system of bartering — the famous 'pacted transition' — in which political stability was sought through silence and impunity regarding the crimes committed during the regime.[22] He argues that a process of '*transformismo*' [transformism] took place that consisted merely of an apparent transformation of the institutional order imposed by the dictatorship to perpetuate the neoliberal system.[23] The first civil administrations, most of the political parties, and the military, in a concerted effort and with the aid of the mass media and a prevailing consumer culture, fostered what other authors have called a 'cultural model of promotion of oblivion'.[24]

Undoubtedly, numerous initiatives with regard to human rights have been initiated since the restoration of civilian rule. Two official truth commissions were created (1990 and 2003), policies of reparation have been established to redress direct victims and their families, leaders of Pinochet's notorious secret police and members of the armed forces have been condemned, numerous memorials and monuments have been inaugurated all around the country, and two important institutions were created: the Instituto Nacional de Derechos Humanos (National Institute of Human Rights), established in 2009, and the Museo de la Memoria, inaugurated in 2010. Yet, because the role of the state has been at best 'ambivalent' in its defence of human rights, as Cath Collins notes, the topic has been treated largely as a private matter with primarily non-state actors pushing forward the struggle towards memory.[25]

This is why Steve Stern proposes a more subtle understanding of the struggles over the past, challenging the dominant analysis of the 'pacted transition'.[26] The historian claims that it is precisely on the issue of memory that the 'notion of transition pacts must be cut down to more modest explanatory size'.[27] The agreements existed, he says, but they were only partial and restricted, focusing more on constitutional or economic aspects rather than the field of human rights. Additionally, in the beginning no one truly believed these agreements were going to be sustained. Lastly, he argues, even in an atmosphere of social demobilization, grassroots movements and other non-state actors have continuously maintained pressure to keep memories of the dictatorial past alive.[28]

Stern's analysis is in line with that of authors like sociologist Elizabeth Jelin, for whom the struggle over the meaning of a conflictive and painful past cannot be reduced to an opposition between remembering and forgetting, but one of 'memory against memory'.[29] Hence, rather than characterizing the Chilean post-dictatorial period as a 'culture of oblivion', Stern fosters an understanding of it as one of a 'memory impasse'.[30] He sees the country's memory struggles not as a static process but as a partially 'rolling' or 'unravelling impasse', notably since Pinochet's detention in 1998.[31] Stern talks about an impasse because, although a majority of Chilean society recognizes the crimes committed by the regime and comprehends the need for justice and redress, such understanding is accompanied by the belief that the minority defending the legacies of the military rule is too powerful.[32] There is a constant tension between social agents that seek to move forward the human rights issues against influential forces that strive to block those efforts. In his view, this is not a 'frozen' process, but one in which the balance does not stand still. Thus, he sees Chilean society as one that moves 'as if caught in moral schizophrenia — between prudence and convulsion'.[33] There have been advances with regard to truth, justice, and the memory struggles, although these have proved to be 'exceedingly slow and arduous'.[34] Significantly, Stern argues that this constant tension did not construct 'a society of amnesia but one of contradiction and ambivalence'.[35] These contradictions and ambivalences are echoed by the development of the documentary scene itself, as the following sections will demonstrate. If the 'memory question' has not remained frozen, the documentary field has not remained static either.

Chile During the 1990s: The 'Silent' Decade

The 1990s were characterized by a heavy silence that weighed upon the recent past, perceived as a 'conspiracy of consensus' forged by the political elites but which permeated Chilean society as a whole.[36]

In 1990, Pinochet stepped down from office and President Patricio Aylwin (1990–1994) inaugurated the first period of the *Concertación* that was to remain in power for the next two decades.[37] The characteristics of the early transition to democracy are usefully synthesized by Norbert Lechner and Pedro Güell. Firstly, it was framed by the legal and political framework put into place by the 1980 Constitution (which, though subjected to a series of reforms, still governs the country); secondly, it took place under an expansive capitalist market economy; thirdly, it was marked by Pinochet's continued influence in the political sphere; and fourthly, it occurred under a polarized division of the political actors (under a binominal electoral system).[38]

Overall, the early redemocratization process 'was constrained not only by the military regime but also by the memory of repression, the fear of provoking the political right and the military beyond their tolerance, and by the overwhelming consensus in Chile that this was to be avoided at all cost'.[39] Pinochet left everything 'tied, and well tied', thus creating a 'democracy on a tether' as Brian Loveman describes it.[40] These authoritarian remnants or 'enclaves' inherited from the regime created an 'incomplete' or 'low-quality democracy' as described by sociologist Manuel Antonio Garretón.[41] Pinochet remained in power as the commander-in-chief of the army until March 1998, when he was nominated senator-for-life (though not without the opposition of human right activists and a group of left-wing politicians). In October of the same year, however, the newly endowed Senator was detained in London, creating a major cultural and political watershed in the Chilean post-dictatorial order.

Aylwin's administration adopted a modest approach to redressing the violations of human rights, which came to be characterized by his phrase 'justicia en la medida de lo posible' [justice, within the limits of the possible].[42] The first official gesture towards direct victims was the creation of the Comisión Nacional de Verdad y Reconciliación (National Commission on Truth and Reconciliation, CNVR) in April 1990. The commission was appointed to investigate the truth of the crimes committed, considering the number of those who were executed and torture cases that resulted in death and disappearances, but it excluded torture survivors and the exiled, as well as other abuses such as exonerations. Released publicly in March 1991, it came to be known as the Rettig Report (after the name of its chairman, Raúl Rettig).[43]

Though the Rettig Report officially acknowledged that human rights violations were carried out by the military, it did not unveil the name of the perpetrators and it pursued no justice (as it had no subpoena power). Its narrow focus on direct victims, moreover, had an important negative outcome, as it eventually prevented a more complex understanding of the dictatorship as a multifaceted repression, as Stern forcefully argues.[44] In fact, if one follows historian Alfredo Jocelyn-Holt's interpretation, quite the reverse operation was at work. In his view, when Aylwin released the Report on his nationwide televised address, not only did he recognize the state as being responsible for the violation of human rights, but also, as perpetrators were not tried nor were they individualized, Chilean society as a whole was addressed as being responsible for the crimes. The guilt was so widespread, Jocelyn-Holt argues, that in the end no one could be proven accountable.[45] By the late 1990s, the official narrow focus on direct victims had already exacted 'a cost in social exclusion and social awareness', according to Stern.[46]

Only a few months after Aylwin took office, the country was *shocked* by the revelation of the discovery of bodies in a communal grave in Pisagua, the location of a former concentration camp in the Atacama Desert in the north of the country.[47] The bodies belonged to victims of 'La caravana de la muerte' (The caravan of death), an infamous murderous procession commanded by General Sergio Arellano Stark that travelled through the country on a *Puma* helicopter in October 1973 executing political prisoners.[48] 'The cultural impact of the find was huge', asserts Stern.[49] Other terrible findings had previously been made (as early as 1978 the discovery of the bodies of fifteen disappeared peasants in the depths of unused limestone furnaces in Lonquén emerged as the first proof of state terrorism), yet mass media coverage circulating images of mummified bodies in the Atacama Desert was unprecedented.[50] The wide circulation of these images together with those of other searches held in the following months in clandestine cemeteries all over the country — such as those of the other emblematic case known as 'Patio 29' (Graveyard 29) — complicated the political way out of the human rights issue.[51] I dwell upon these atrocious discoveries since these images entered forcefully into the post-dictatorship visual repertoire of the first decade and extended well beyond it, with numerous directors persistently turning their cameras to the northern desert and the remains of the disappeared, as will be discussed in the next chapter.

Towards the mid-to-late 1990s, the remnants of authoritarian rule and the failure to address human rights issues had produced widespread *desencanto* within Chilean society.[52] As Lechner and Güell explain, such a phenomenon is framed within one of the most radical transformations undergone by Chilean society during the dictatorship but which came to the forefront only after 1990; the absence of a collective political programme now meant a retreat to the domestic realm, accompanied by a concern for the private sphere and individual projects. A waning of a sense of future, they explain, debilitated readings of the past, and vice versa, the silencing of this past obstructed the construction of alternative horizons. In the authors' view, a certain frustration prevailed with regard to the democracy that could have been (but was not), as promised by the 1988 plebiscite through the rather deceitful motto from the *Concertación* — 'Chile, la alegría ya viene' ('Happiness is coming'), upon which the polemic film *No* (Pablo Larraín, 2011) draws. Democracy seemed unable, despite some economic success, to repair the deeply damaged bonds within Chilean society and mete out justice.[53]

Chile After 'The Pinochet Accident'

Glimpses of changes began occurring under Eduardo Frei's administration (1994–2000) before Pinochet's detention, most clearly in the judicial sphere.[54] 'The Pinochet Accident', however, as Armando Uribe and Miguel Vicuña termed it,[55] is seen as the major watershed in the Chilean post-dictatorial order and its impact went well beyond the judiciary and human rights arenas. This event, provoked by external forces (he was arrested while recovering in a London clinic from a routine operation upon a request from the Spanish courts which charged him with crimes of terrorism and genocide), contributed to the creation of a shifting awareness in Chilean society. As is known, however, despite the enormous symbolic and legal repercussions both at the national and international levels, Pinochet returned to the country and was never tried.[56]

What did happen was that Chile went from its distinctive 'muffled stasis' of the early post-dictatorial period into a new 'season of memory', as Wilde asserts.[57] A 'new consciousness' emerged with regard to the struggle for human rights that extended well beyond the relatives of the disappeared or the survivors.[58] 'It is they who bear the deepest wounds' Wilde asserts, 'but the victims of the harsh time are far more numerous than this tragic group'.[59] The 'symbolic circle' of victims, to return to Stern's notion already discussed in this book's introduction, was gradually opening up. Reverberations from the Pinochet case were wide-ranging and included young people outing torturers (known as Comisión Funa, the Funa Commission), the emergence of alternative media outside major conglomerates, and the creation of the polemic Mesa de Diálogo (Dialogue Table), active between August 1999 and June 2000.[60]

One of the most important cultural effects prompted by Pinochet's detention in London was that, having been one of the largest taboos in the country, the topic of torture was brought into open discussion.[61] Until 2001, torture remained 'un tema tácitamente vedado en Chile' [a topic tacitly banned in Chile].[62] This practice came to the forefront when the 'Agüero-Meneses case' was exposed in the media (former prisoner and academic Felipe Agüero had recognized a fellow colleague from the university, Emilio Meneses, as his torturer). As already stated, cases of torture were not included in the Rettig Report. According to journalist Patricia Verdugo, the fact that all early efforts of human rights organizations focused on finding the disappeared as well as on achieving justice and redress for those executed meant that the status of survivors became a 'suerte de privilegio' [sort of privilege] that required torture victims to remain silent.[63] Eventually, the 'Agüero-Meneses case' became one of the key events that prompted the establishment of the Comisión Ética contra la Tortura (Ethical Commission Against Torture) in 2001, a civil organization that sought the creation in 2003 of the Comisión Nacional sobre Prisión Política y Tortura (National Commission on Political Prison and Torture, known as the Valech Commission after its president, Monsignor Sergio Valech).[64] Inaugurated under Ricardo Lagos' administration (2000–06), this commission transformed Chile into the only country in Latin America to undertake a second official truth report.[65]

The Commission gathered nearly thirty-six thousands testimonies of individuals who claimed that they, or a deceased relative, had been tortured.[66] Released in 2004, the Valech Report verified almost twenty-eight thousand cases.[67] It also documented 1,132 sites used as detention and torture centres all over the country.[68] The Commission was not allowed to unveil the name of the perpetrators and victims' testimonies were to be kept in secrecy for fifty years.[69] Hence in Brian Loveman and Elizabeth Lira's critical evaluation, 'The struggle for truth certainly did not prove altogether successful, to say the least... [and] the commission report did not contribute directly to justice understood as criminal prosecution for crimes committed'.[70] Nonetheless, the Valech Report notably refuted the long-held claim made by the armed forces and their supporters that torture was not a systematic state practice but rather rare cases of 'excess' carried out by a few individuals.[71] Since then, the voices of these tortured bodies began belatedly, yet rapidly, to spread in post-dictatorship documentaries, as the next chapter will also discuss.

In the wake of the thirtieth anniversary of the coup, Lagos's administration began claiming 'a politics of commemoration'.[72] The Valech Commission was appointed two months before the anniversary of the fateful date, Allende's monument was erected in La Moneda, and Morandé 80, a door located on the side of the governmental palace that had been sealed since the coup, was ceremonially reopened.[73] The mass media joined the commemorations enthusiastically. Stern provides a vivid and celebratory description:

> Even before September, television and print media prepared for a big memory year. Television programmes injected a 'lost world' aspect — authenticity through attention to the human and the nostalgic, in addition to the standard focus on political crisis and violence on 1973. It was as if the trends of recent years — the retreat from earlier struggles to hegemonize memory, the emphasis on shared tragedy, still unfinished and festering, the breakdown of old taboos and silences, the cultural transformations that placed the foundational moment of "today" within a truly different yesterday world — readied many Chileans to return with fresh eyes to 1973. On the eleventh, television and radio competed to recapture the sights, sounds, and secrets of the historic days in documentaries, and in 'minute-by-minute' re-creations including radio-theatre.[74]

It is worth quoting Stern at length because both the audiovisual *excess* he is suggesting and the focus on the *tragedy* of 1973 he comments upon marked a major turning point in post-dictatorship documentary, which has circulated mostly outside television. Contrary to Stern's favourable reception of this eruption of the past, renowned local scholars such as Diamela Eltit did not embrace it so keenly. For Eltit, this assault of images, along with their compulsive repetition, seemed more like 'una carrera turística hacia el pasado' [a touristic race towards the past] that did not permit the distinguishing of any details.[75] This specific juncture demanded that documentary filmmakers respond to such images critically and its aftermath brought to the fore a proliferation of younger directors who were developing alternative ways to address the past.

The rehabilitation of Allende's figure in 2003 coincided with the decline of Pinochet's, according to Alfredo Joignant.[76] A combination of facts, notably the release of the Valech Report, a series of indictments in human right cases, and the revelation of economic corruption in the Riggs Bank case, contributed to Pinochet's demise. If the dictator's staunch support had remained rather stable in the most conservative sectors, it was the news of his involvement in the financial scandal that took a devastating toll on his public image.[77] This led to the assertion that even before his death, Pinochet was already a cadaver.[78] By 2011, few would deny that Pinochet had been a dictator.[79]

Pinochet's death, an 'irruption of memory' on a major scale that saw some Chileans burst into tears of sadness or joy, occurred under Michelle Bachelet's first administration (2006–10).[80] Bachelet was not only the first woman to become president of the country, but also the daughter of a general loyal to Allende who had died after being tortured. During her time as head of the government, she continued with what has been described as a shift towards a state-led 'mainstreaming of memorialization'[81] begun by Lagos. Bachelet inaugurated memorials and memory sites, and more significantly (though not without controversy), the creation of the Museo de la Memoria.

A year after Sebastián Piñera took office for the first time (2010–14), putting an end to twenty years of the centre-left coalition rule, the most significant social upheaval since the 1980s took hold of the country. First led by students who began demanding free quality public education for all in overt opposition to the discriminating educational system introduced by Pinochet, the rest of society soon joined the protests.[82] Chileans took to the streets once again in an enraged, albeit festive, manner. Describing this 'explosión de malestar' [outburst of malaise] as a reaction against the extreme neoliberal model of the nation, sociologist Alberto Mayol wrote: 'muchos miembros de esta sociedad se han sentido víctimas de un abuso enorme, de una injusticia feroz [...]. Si hay algo en el alma del Chile actual es la sensación de que finalmente se construyó un Chile sin victimarios y lleno de víctimas' [Many members of this society have felt that they are victims of an enormous abuse, a terrible injustice [...]. If there is something in Chile's contemporary soul, it is the feeling that the Chile that was eventually built lacked perpetrators but was full of victims].[83]

Similarly, Michael Lazzara has also remarked upon this widespread feeling of victimhood in his most recent work, albeit from a different stance.[84] In his view, both the rise of complicity and the radical expansion of the idea of victimhood in the public discourse mark this 2010–14 juncture. Civilians' responsibility in the dictatorship began to be acknowledged, as clearly encapsulated by Piñera's recognition of the role played by Pinochet supporters as 'cómplices pasivos' [passive accomplices] during his polemic speech for the fortieth anniversary of the military coup. As Lazzara explains, this shift was also accompanied by a complex redefinition of the idea of the victim, in which civilians who participated actively in the regime — such as conscripts and other functionaries — began to position themselves as victims of the dictatorial rule. The emergence of these civilians' disruptive voices will also unsettle the documentary scene, as most evidently indicated by the last case study of this book, *El mocito* (2011). This film follows Jorgelino Vergara, a functionary of the secret police whose testimony in 2007 contributed to make important advances in the human rights field. In the meantime, what was happening in Chilean documentary?

Documentary Production in the 1990s: Dismantling and Re-articulation

As noted by several scholars, democracy brought with it a radical transformation of the cinematographic scene.[85] Documentaries confronted economic instability but also, as Michael Chanan contends for the region as a whole, an identity crisis: 'Para un cine fundado en una concepción política de sí mismo, la transformación del espacio político en el que operaba como un resultado del cambio democrático en los ochenta, amenazó con dejarlo a la deriva' [For a cinema founded on the political understanding of itself, the transformation of the political space in which it operated, as a result of the democratic transformation of the eighties, threatened it to leave it adrift].[86] In Chile, only a few of the numerous alternative production companies managed to adapt to the new democratic scenario creating products for television channels, but the majority ended up disappearing.[87]

Chilean documentary faced an economic crisis due to the retraction of financial support from international cooperation agencies which had originally focused on the anti-dictatorial struggle.[88] In addition, early public initiatives that aimed to reconstruct the audiovisual sector favoured the production and distribution of fiction films produced in celluloid to the detriment of video.[89] In fact, according to Liñero's bleak account of the early post-dictatorial period, the vast amount of alternative video production suffered a veritable process of dismantling (once again, but now under democracy).[90]

For the first half of the 1990s, state efforts have been described as a period of 'mecenazgo' [patronage] in which available sources were restricted to well-known film directors so they could make feature films.[91] A selected group of organized directors and producers had access to a special bank loan provided by the Chilean State Bank with state endorsement (Banco del Estado). However, the initiative did not succeed after the films proved unable to generate the expected revenues in the box office.[92]

In 1992, the FONDART was created, and it eventually became one of the key public mechanisms to promote the development of the arts in general and the film sector in particular. After its conception, it financed productions through competitive grants for any format and genre (including fiction, non-fiction, and animation, in celluloid or video), yet only after 1998 did differentiation between these categories facilitate access to these funds for documentaries.[93] Public efforts to promote Chilean cinema abroad were also fiction oriented.[94] Only since 2001 has equal treatment for documentaries been achieved, thanks to the efforts of the Association of Chilean Documentarians (ADOC), created a year earlier.[95] For these reasons, Liñero described the 1990s in the following terms:

> Los noventa significaron un periodo de transición tanto temático como tecnológico para muchos documentalistas independientes. Las temáticas políticas fueron abandonadas y la mirada sobre los procesos sociales se restringió al mínimo, como parte quizás del acuerdo tácito de muchos sectores por no 'obstaculizar' la transición a la democracia. Los documentalistas de los ochenta estaban en su mayoría trabajando para la televisión y las pautas temáticas llegaron a ser manejadas por necesidades editoriales de los canales.
>
> [The nineties were both a technological and thematic transitional period for many independent documentary filmmakers. Political topics were abandoned and the critical view of social processes was restricted to a minimum, probably as a result of the tacit agreements amongst many sectors not to 'obstruct' the transition towards democracy. The majority of documentary filmmakers from the eighties were working for television, and the topics they covered were mandated by the editorial necessities of the television channels.][96]

Mouesca's interpretation is more nuanced, arguing that productions began diversifying in terms of topics (ranging from environmental issues to state repression against indigenous people), while interest in the dictatorship remained.[97] In her view, although undoubtedly the gaze of the documentarians changed, the topics inspired by the military rule and its on-going legacies were not eradicated.

It is true that documentaries concerned with the recent past were scarce and hard to trace, yet this issue was certainly not abandoned. It is also certain that the transformations brought about by democracy forced directors to take on difficult reckonings, or as Mouesca puts it, a change of gaze. Andrés Vargas, a member of the Grupo Proceso collective who directed *Huellas de sal* in 1990, one of the few documentaries explicitly addressing the topic of the disappeared during the early transition, points out the difficulties faced by some documentary filmmakers in this new setting:

> Nosotros pensamos que se abrían caminos de distribución y finalmente lo que nos encontrábamos era que teníamos mayores problemas que antes para distribuir. Que éramos más alternativos que antes, que lo que decíamos era más complicado que lo estábamos diciendo en época de dictadura. En época de dictadura las cosas estaban claras, o era blanco o era negro. Después nos encontramos con que la cuestión era sí, no, era todo súper abierto, pero en el fondo no había nada abierto, al contrario: los espacios se estaban cerrando. Yo creo que eso nos costó muchísimo entenderlo [...]. Nosotros teníamos mucha mejor distribución, llegábamos a mucha más gente en época de dictadura que después.[98]

> [We thought that new paths of distribution were opening up but what we found, in the end, was that we faced worse problems than before in the distribution of our work. Also, that we were now more alternative, and that what we were saying now was much more unsettling than what we were saying under the dictatorship. Under the dictatorship things were clear: either black or white. Afterwards, everything was super open, but truly, nothing was. On the contrary: the spaces were closing. I think that this was really hard for us to understand [...]. We had a much broader distribution network; we reached many more people during the era of the dictatorship than afterward.]

Indeed, accessing documentary production did not get any easier. According to Jorge Leiva, a young director who was to codirect the popular documentary *Actores secundarios* (*Supporting Actors*) in 2004 with Pachi Bustos, the circulation of nonfiction during the first democratic decade was very restricted and characterized by the same underground logic of the previous decade: 'el documental marcó durante los '90 la misma distribución que en los '80: de mano en mano, medio clandestino.' [During the 1990s documentary had the same distribution as in the 1980s: it circulated from hand to hand, semi-clandestinely].[99]

Considering this gloomy outlook, the pivotal role that FIDOCS — celebrated for the first time in May 1997 — played in the re-articulation of the national documentary landscape cannot be stressed enough.[100] It was during Patricio Guzmán's second return to the country from France, and in parallel to the shooting of his *Chile, la memoria obstinada* when he came to the idea of organizing a documentary film festival.[101] In Guzmán's words: 'Cuando llegué, me interesó filmar más que cualquier otra cosa, y lo que se me ocurrió enseguida no era quedarme, sino que ser un transmisor' [When I came back I was more interested in filming than anything else. But then I suddenly realized that I was not going to stay, but instead, I would act as a cultural mediator].[102] After sharing the idea of the festival with some fellow filmmakers, Guzmán secured funding from the Fondo Nacional de Desarrollo Cultural y las Artes (National Fund for the Development of Culture and the Arts, FONDART): 'ese proyecto no era más que contarle a mis colegas lo que yo había tenido oportunidad de ver aquí, ¿por qué no verlo allá?' [Originally this project was nothing more than telling my colleagues [in Chile] what I had been watching here [in Paris]'.[103] Yet it turned out to be so much more.

In order to grasp the significance of FIDOCS, its catalogues became invaluable primary sources. Since the festival does not have an institutional archive, these materials were incredibly difficult to trace, especially the early ones.[104] However, I managed to gather all of these precious documents and I shared them with María Paz Peirano, a colleague who used them to examine the history of FIDOCS and its role in the local documentary scene in a recently published article.[105] Here, I approach these materials through a different angle and propose to understand the emergence of the festival in close dialogue not only with the audiovisual sector but also with the development of Chilean society in relation to the memory struggles of the post-dictatorship.

Two retrospectives of Chilean documentary took place in the earliest editions of the documentary festival (the first showed sixteen films covering between 1967 and 1988; the second one programmed fourteen works, produced between 1970 and 1990). Significantly, Carlos Flores, Ignacio Agüero, and Pedro Chaskel, who were in charge of the first retrospective, introduced their selection with the following statement:

> Hemos elegido estos documentales, que no se filmaron para ser exhibidos en la televisión — es probable que nunca lo sean — para sacarlos del silencio en que circulan y reponerlos, por primera vez juntos [...] porque ellos representan un momento desconocido de la producción cinematográfica nacional y nos permiten apreciar las infinitas posibilidades creativas del género y su valor como documento. Si alguien, como en *Farenheit 451*, la premonitoria película de Truffaut, le preguntara a los autores de estos documentales: ¿qué han hecho?, ellos podrían contestar, **recordamos** (emphasis in the original).[106]

> [We have chosen these documentaries which were not filmed to be shown on television — it is likely they will never be — to rescue them from the silence in which they circulate and to rerun them together, for the first time [...] because they represent an unknown moment in the production of our national cinema that allows us to appreciate both the infinite creative possibilities of the genre and its value as a document. If someone, as in *Fahrenheit 451*, the admonitory film by Truffaut, were to ask the creators of these documentaries: What have you done? They could reply: we *remember(ed)*.]

The keyword, of course, is 'remember'. This first retrospective (as well as the one that followed) showed a wide selection of works by Chilean directors virtually unknown at the time, as the programmers remark. The *tour de force* led by Guzmán, who launched this initiative and pulled in the contributions of these three key figures in the Chilean documentary landscape, should not be seen in isolation. It is not accidental that historian Steve Stern distinguishes the festival as a prominent cultural initiative that signalled a wider shift in the country in which active members from civil society were seeking to bring the seemingly frozen issue of memory forward.[107] It is an early marker of the *new season of memory* about to begin.[108]

In addition to the retrospective, Guzmán's *La batalla de Chile* was shown in this first festival. As is widely known, the trilogy had *never* premiered in Chile, as the catalogue stressed.[109] It was also the premiere of *Chile, la memoria obstinada*, Guzmán's personal exploration of memory's vicissitudes in Chilean society. *La flaca*

Alejandra [*Skinny Alejandra*] (Carmen Castillo and Guy Girard, 1994), which deals with the topic of torture, was also screened in the international selection. Two lesser known films were shown in a parallel section: *Correcto... o el alma en los tiempos de guerra* (*Affirmative...or the Soul in Times of War*) (Orlando Lübbert, 1993) and *Hier, wo ich lebe/Aquí donde yo vivo* (*Here Where I Live*) (Carlos Puccio, 1994), which dealt with the issues of torture and the return of the children of Chilean exiles, respectively. Filmmakers who had lived under the UP and had fled into exile directed all of these works discussing problems seldom addressed in the public sphere before Pinochet's detention. Therefore, it would not be an exaggeration to say that the festival contributed significantly to an opening up of what has been called Chile's 'Pandora's box'[110] of memories to new generations.[111]

FIDOCS has been running yearly since its inception, sheltering, shaping, and promoting Chilean documentary. Its trademark is clear: a strong focus on the figure of the *auteur* and on 'creative' documentary, as well as an emphasis on the political, largely shaped by the strong figure of Guzmán.[112] The festival has been conceived not only as a space for diffusion but also of *resistance*:[113] Chilean documentary had finally found a home. Since FIDOCS' creation, students, filmmakers, and scholars began to be exposed not only to the work of local and Latin American directors, but also of international filmmakers such as Walter Heynowski and Gerhard Scheumann (hereinafter, H&S, who registered the most iconic images of the coup and its aftermath) and more contemporary ones such as Claude Lanzmann or Nicholas Philibert, both of whom attended the festival and introduced their works in its early editions.

Throughout the years, FIDOCS has established a series of activities to strengthen the production of documentary such as masterclasses, workshops for filmmaking students, documentary pitches, and 'school of spectators'. It was under the festival's wing too that ADOC was born in 2000 congregating documentary filmmakers and producers who have been forging better conditions for local production in several fronts including access to funding, distribution, and exhibition. Although in recent years the conduction of the festival has been somewhat inconsistent, suffering a series of modifications in terms of directorship, its position in the calendar year, and even programming, the festival has long been a veritable *fiesta* for the large documentary community in the country.[114] FIDOCS is now considered one of the most important documentary film festivals in the region, becoming a relevant hub for encounters between local producers and filmmakers, as well as with key figures of the international documentary scene, contributing to the professionalization of the field.[115]

Polyphonic Voices: Some Notes on Generations

Under the roof of FIDOCS as a space of encounter, a so-called 'new generation' of documentarians began to emerge in the late 1990s. These new voices acquired notable resonance outside the documentary circuit only after 2004, due to the unforeseen success of some of their creations.[116] It is not by chance that this happened in the aftermath of the thirtieth anniversary of the coup in 2003. This particular historical juncture made it evident that a focus on the directly affected or the powerful trope of La Moneda in flames and other images of atrocity seemed unable to address the complex issue of the recent past at that point in time (see Chapter 3 for a detailed discussion of this issue). The juncture helped bring to the forefront a number of younger directors who began exploring alternative ways to interrogate the country's violent past.

Because military rule lasted seventeen years, it has been argued that the notion of the 'post-dictatorship generation' is unable to 'fully capture' the experience of those who grew up in a country under siege.[117] In this sense, scholars talk about 'Pinochet's children' or the 'children of dictatorship' to describe the generation that came of age in the 1980s and in the constrained democracy of the first decade.[118] In my view, the notion of the 'post-dictatorship generation' is helpful to a certain extent in framing the work of directors who gradually began releasing their works in the late 1990s. Most were born from the mid-1960s to the mid-1970s and many consciously sought to break, or at least to create a distance with, the narratives that preceded them. A comment by Tiziana Panizza illustrates the position within which these directors locate themselves: 'Para una generación post-dictadura, post-apagón cultural, post-nada, los referentes eran escasos o más bien nos sentíamos huérfanos de una estirpe' [For a post-dictatorship generation, post-cultural or post-nothing, the referents were scarce; or rather, we felt ourselves to be orphans of a lineage].[119] Now, while useful to begin to approach the work of these younger directors (there is a certain sense of community, as this quotation suggests, and as I garnered from the conversations I sustained with a number of the directors), I think that such an umbrella term also risks occluding the differences between the directors themselves (as a matter of fact, differences that many of them stress). Their professional backgrounds are as varied as their works, and they hail from a wide range of disciplines such as journalism, anthropology, psychology, and audiovisual communications. A significant number of them attended filmmaking schools such as the renowned international filmmaking school Escuela International de Cine y Televisión de San Antonio de los Baños (The International Film and TV School, EICTV) in Cuba and other institutions in countries like the US, Germany, France, and the UK.

Bearing this in mind, and for lack of a better term, I refer here to the 'post-dictatorship generation(s)' to include both a 'broader' second generation and a 'narrower' or 'literal' second generation; hence the plural 's'. The former is used to refer to the work of directors who are not descendants of direct victims (or at least who do not inscribe this information explicitly in their works) and the latter points to the children of those who were directly affected. Even within this last group finer points of differentiation should be indicated, as methods of repression ranged from torture to disappearance and execution to exile, shaping these directors' personal stories in different ways.

The same is true, I believe, for the generations that preceded them. In this sense, I suggest three wide-ranging generational categories with the aim of emphasizing the polyphonic traits of the current landscape of documentary films, rather than proposing them as heuristic categories.[120] These generations are not only marked by a distinctive defining historical moment of 'origin' so to speak — proximity to or distance from the 1973 coup — but also, significantly, by the particular historical juncture of enunciation in which they coexist; in other words, the post-dictatorship period in which all these narratives converge. These coexisting generations of documentary filmmakers are comprised by i) directors who experienced the socialist revolution directly and went into exile, such as Raúl Ruiz, Patricio Guzmán, Marilú Mallet, Carmen Castillo, and Patricio Henríquez; ii) directors who were part of the so-called 'cultural resistance' in the 1980s who trained in film or audiovisual communication schools (in Chile or abroad), such as Ignacio Agüero, Andrés Vargas, Pablo Lavín, and Lucía Salinas, iii) directors who belong to the post-dictatorship generation(s), who, as discussed above, have diverse backgrounds but emerged in the late 1990s. This group includes both the literal and broader second generation. Amongst them are Esteban Larraín, Paco Toledo, Marcela Said, Tiziana Panizza, and Antonia Rossi.

Documentary Production Since 2000: Growth Despite Television

The rise of Chilean audiovisual production in the last decade has been explained by a series of factors including the increasingly widespread use of digital video, the proliferation of filmmaking schools and film festivals, and, above all, the creation of a new institutional framework.[121] Unfortunately, statistical information on documentary production is scarce, incomplete, and scattered. But approximate numbers can be found in the catalogue titled *Catastro virtual de la producción documental chilena*, which registers 181 documentaries from 1990–99, and a total of 244 from 2000–07.[122] Other figures can be found in CineChile's ever expanding database, which as of 2017 indicates ninety-six documentaries from 1990–2000, and a total of 496 for the years 2001–09.[123] A sorely needed report on this topic published by ChileDoc — a platform created in 2010 to develop an international network to commercialize and diffuse Chilean documentary — indicates that while in 2000 ten works were premiered at film festivals, cinemas, and other screenings, in 2010 this number grew to thirty, most of which where produced in the second half of the decade (its focus is mainly on feature length films).[124] Though disparate, all these figures indicate that there has been significant growth in documentary production in the last decade.

A new Film Law was finally approved in 2004, after a long campaign by the audiovisual sector. This law aims to develop, promote, disseminate, preserve, and protect local audiovisual productions and the audiovisual industry, as well as to encourage the development of new audiovisual languages and research.[125] It established the founding of the Consejo del Arte y la Industria Audiovisual (Council of the Arts and the Audiovisual Industry, CAIA) under the Consejo Nacional de la Cultura de las Artes (National Council for the Culture and the Arts, CNCA) established a year earlier. It also stipulated the creation of the Fondo de Fomento Audiovisual (Audiovisual Promotion Fund, FFA) which offers a wide range of areas to which documentary filmmakers may apply, from script development to distribution aids.

Since 1999, the Corporación de Fomento de la Producción (the Chilean Economic Development Agency, CORFO, under the Ministry of Economy) manages an important financial programme to support audiovisual projects (fiction, documentary, and animation). It co-finances audiovisual productions for television and cinema in the stages of development as well as marketing and distribution in Chile and abroad. Since 2010, CinemaChile has undertaken a strong campaign of internationalization for Chilean cinema. This private-public initiative created by the Asociación de Productores de Cine y TV (Association of Film and TV Producers, APCTV) seeks to promote Chilean audiovisual production in the international market. Tellingly, the opening image of its first catalogue is the famous black and white picture of Patricio Guzmán with Jorge Müller, the legendary young cameraman disappeared by the regime. The photograph also includes Guzmán's oft-quoted phrase: 'Un país sin cine documental es como una familia sin álbum de fotografías' [A country without documentary films is like a family without a photo album].[126]

Documentarians rely significantly on public funds made available by CAIA, FFA, and CORFO to finance and distribute their projects, in addition to their own self-funding.[127] Though less substantial according to ChileDoc's report, possibilities of coproduction have also expanded in the last years to include international funds. The international film festival circuit is considerable: over eighty documentaries considered by ChileDoc were premiered at festivals of different categories around the world.[128] According to Peirano, the international circuit — of which she highlights IDFA, DokLeipzig, and Visions du Réel — has provided significant input to local producers and directors in terms of networking, commercialization, and visibilization strategies, further contributing to the professionalization of the local landscape.[129]

In 2010, the film most viewed in Chile was a documentary: *Ojos Rojos* [*Red Eyes*] (Ismael Larraín, Juan Ignacio Sabatini, Juan Pablo Sallato, 2010), which was watched by nearly 120,000 spectators in cinemas. This is unanimously seen as an exceptional case; it was a commercial success because of the popularity of the subject, as it follows the tribulations endured by the national soccer team in their struggle to take part in the World Cup in 2010.[130] Previously, *Salvador Allende* (Patricio Guzmán, 2004) had reached over 40,000 spectators.[131] Despite exceptions like these, domestic audiences have tended to shun Chilean cinema and documentary is no exception.[132] In addition to FIDOCS, documentaries have found new venues in the proliferating local film festival circuit (a number of which are solely dedicated to non-fiction), as well as in a handful of art cinemas and other alternative spaces, to which MiraDoc, an initiative created in 2013 by ChileDoc to showcase Chilean documentaries throughout the country (supported by the FFA), has importantly contributed.[133] However, its circulation remains very limited with little to no airtime on national television.

The relationship between documentarians and the national television channel, Televisión Nacional de Chile (National Television Channel, TVN), has been riddled with political and economic tensions since the return to civilian rule, and public policies have been unable to secure the exhibition of such productions on television. This is partly due to the peculiar constitution of the channel as a state-owned yet autonomous institution that has to secure financing through advertisements. It is run by a director freely appointed by the President of the Republic and by a board of directors whose names are also proposed by the President and ratified by the Senate, designations that should guarantee pluralism.[134] However, it is the Senate that finally decides its degree of 'pluralism' by appointing representatives close to the political forces in parliament — and these are not necessarily representative of Chilean society.[135]

In 1990 TVN faced bankruptcy, low ratings, and an enormous crisis of credibility and legitimacy after seventeen years of dictatorship.[136] The channel began acquiring the programmes of independent production companies to modernize and diversify their offer.[137] These productions were, according to Liñero, an essential tool in constructing a pluralist corporate image, offering new ways of representing society and promoting the audiovisual sector.[138] Yet, in his view, this reactivation favoured only a few of these companies, and in the end, the process of externalization waned with the channel developing internal programmes, and focusing increasingly on entertainment.[139]

Few documentaries have made it onto local television. ChileDoc's findings are quite shocking: national television showed between 2000 and 2010 an average of five Chilean documentaries per year, less than ten hours annually.[140] To some extent, there are economic issues at stake. Valerio Fuenzalida et al. explain that television channels pay around USD 1,500–2,000 to local directors (which is the same amount they pay for foreign documentaries).[141] However, this amount is insufficient to recuperate the costs invested by local producers, to which the television sector responds by saying that it is unfeasible for them to absorb the costs of a production of this nature on their own.[142] To help to ease this situation, in 2005 the Consejo Nacional de Televisión (National Council for Television, CNTV) created a programme to support the distribution of already produced documentaries, an agreement via which CNTV co-finances the acquisition of these productions to be shown on free-view television channels.[143] The aid of this programme has been unsteady, however, funding very few documentaries since its inception.[144]

There are other reasons that explain the scarce presence of Chilean documentaries on national television. In 2009, Kristin Sorensen claimed that free-view national television was reluctant to address Chile's dictatorial past and human rights violations, the treatment of which remained 'partial and cryptic'.[145] The popular success in prime-time television of fiction and non-fiction series that revisited life under the dictatorship such as *Los 80* (*The 80s*) (Canal 13, 2008–2014) and *Chile, las imágenes prohibidas* (Chilevisión, 2013) [*Chile, the Forbidden Images*], respectively, pointed towards a potential transformation of this approach by the small screen.[146] However, none of these two aforementioned programmes were aired on TVN. Not only is the channel reticent to screen works that deal with the recent past (as mentioned earlier, most famously *La batalla de Chile* has never been shown), but also when broadcast such programmes are pushed into late night slots. Such was the case for instance, of the fiction series *Los archivos del cardenal* (*The Archives of the Cardinal*) (2012–2014, TVN), a polemic and critically acclaimed thriller that revisits the work of the Vicaría de la Solidaridad of the Catholic Church in the defence of human rights during the military rule, which lasted only for two seasons.[147] Moreover, even if TVN purchases documentaries, this does not necessarily guarantee that films will get aired. The state's erratic behaviour regarding both local productions and the human rights issue (it sustains these works via public funds but limits their circulation) was evidently exposed in the polemic provoked by the various obstacles placed in the way of Ignacio Agüero's *El diario de Agustín*. It is worth looking at this case closely.[148]

Agüero is, along with Guzmán, the leading and most respected figure in contemporary Chilean documentary, and virtually each of his productions can be considered a landmark of its time.[149] Nevertheless, it was only with *El diario de Agustín* that his work went beyond the limited documentary circuit and acquired the attention of the general public and media. *El diario de Agustín* follows an investigation carried out by a team of journalism students from the Universidad de Chile who set to uncover the complicity of the most influential and conservative newspaper *El Mercurio* with the military.[150] This is the country's longest-running newspaper and one of the largest press conglomerates. The documentary denounces the collaboration of the historical owner of the newspaper, the late Agustín Edwards Eastman (hence the title) with the dictatorship, including the gruesome covering up of some crimes.

El diario de Agustín is significantly distinct from the rest of Agüero's oeuvre. The director is himself a strong advocate of documentary, referring to it as 'el brazo experimental del cine' [the experimental branch of cinema].[151] Agüero's typically oblique approach to his topics, taken to the extreme in his recent *Como me da la gana II*, is replaced in this production by a more direct and conventional stance by means of 'talking heads', illustrative archival footage, images of atrocity (it seeks to reveal a truth that remains largely inconvenient), and written contextual information (Agüero refused to use a narrator as it would too easily convey his own views on the topic, as he explained to me). This anomaly in his cinematographic production occurred because he could not take any chances or allow himself any ambiguities with regard to the subject-matter. 'Tenía que ser finamente preciso' [I had to be skilfully precise].[152]

El diario de Agustín received state funding and its exhibition rights were bought in 2010 for a period of three years by TVN, yet the television channel continuously blocked its transmission. After years of a tug-of-war between the channel and the filmmakers, it broadcast it in July 2014 in *Zona D Realizadores*, a slot dedicated to Chilean cinema aired on Saturdays around midnight. The polemics began in December 2012, when after subsequent delays and uncertainties regarding its airing only months before the contract expiration, Fernando Villagrán, the coproducer and cowriter of the documentary declared to *The Clinic*, a popular newspaper: 'el directorio de TVN le tiene miedo a Agustín Edwards. Es tan simple como eso. Al final uno piensa que los tipos la compraron para no mostrarla' [the board of TVN is afraid of Agustín Edwards. It is as simple as that. In the end, it seems that they bought the documentary with the sole intent of not broadcasting it].[153] Following this interview, the executive director of the channel decided to put an early end to the contract, arguing that the network would not yield to public pressure, ultimately deciding not to broadcast the documentary at all.[154]

A similar situation occurred a few months later when a private channel cancelled the documentary's planned broadcast. The network argued that *El diario de Agustín* was going to be rescheduled, but following their experience with TVN, the team behind the film immediately decried the censorship at work.[155] The director of the private station tendered her resignation, rejecting the censorship.[156]

After six years of its premiere in FIDOCS in 2008, when it was screened as the opening film, the documentary was finally aired on TVN. Agüero said to the press that two things explained this change of scenery: the arrival of a new director to TVN, and the fact that the deadline for the channel to respond in the Supreme Court why they had bought the film and yet refused to air it, was approaching.[157] An agreement was reached then between the filmmakers and TVN, since in Agüero's words 'lo que nosotros queríamos era que la película se exhibiera. El canal accedió a darla por una vez, lo cual va a ocurrir este sábado, y nosotros desistimos de la demanda' [what we wanted was for the film to be aired. The channel agreed to broadcast it once, this coming Saturday, and we withdrew the lawsuit].[158] Nevertheless, before the several setbacks faced by *El diario de Agustín* (which included a controversy surrounding a panel to be held at the Museo de la Memoria on the topic),[159] the documentary had already circulated both in commercial and independent cinema circuits, and sold, according the director, six thousand copies in its DVD edition circulating with *The Clinic* until it went out of stock.[160] It had also received several awards locally and internationally, and was aired by television channels in other countries of the region.[161] After Edwards' decease in early 2017 the documentary was not aired by TVN, and in Agüero's view, it is unlikely that it will ever be broadcast again.[162]

Having said this, it would be an oversimplification to think that freedom of expression is at stake only when addressing issues related to the dictatorial past. As Agüero himself remarks in a recent interview, the 'anti-terrorist law' (another authoritarian remnant) has been used on different occasions by public prosecutors, enabling the confiscation of audiovisual materials from documentary filmmakers who aim to visibilize the violence perpetrated upon the Mapuche communities.[163] Focusing on the emblematic case of *El diario de Agustín,* however, serves to expose the sophisticated and intricate ways in which censorship and self-censorship still operates in national media and local institutions, as well as the difficulties national productions face in order to reach wider audiences in the small screen.

The lack of visibility of these productions is aggravated by the fact that most of the documentaries are at best self-distributed and at worst not even commercially available. This is why Guzmán stated in his 2012 editorial in FIDOCS that despite the growing presence of local production in festivals and cinemas abroad, it remained little known inside the country. Thus, in his view:

> the largest obstacle for the development of the audiovisual sector is the lack of distributors and exhibitors. It is not censorship or even the indiscriminate way in which state funds are allocated, but the lack of cultural agents with a vocation to distribute and promote good Chilean works that are never known well in their own country (slightly modified from the original text in English).[164]

Initiatives like ChileDoc, which has been recently mapping the state of the art and actively promoting the visualization of Chilean documentary domestically and abroad, seek to contribute to overcoming such obstacles.

This succinct overview of Chilean documentary film history has demonstrated that the nation's cinematic landscape has been characterized by the dominant presence of non-fiction rather than fiction films. Chilean documentary's *political vocation*, to borrow Zuzana Pick's expression, has persisted over time and endured the harsh production conditions to which it has been subjected in distinct historical periods. It has managed to survive contending with phases of dismantling and re-articulation (firstly, under the dictatorship, and later, under the recently restored democratic rule), adapting, not without difficulties, to the new conditions brought about in the post-dictatorship era. Today there is a thriving landscape in which various generations of directors coexist.

The detour undertaken in this chapter from a discussion of the struggles over memory in the last twenty years has sought to provide the background necessary to grasp the extent to which documentary production is intricately bound up with the country's cultural and historical trajectory. The apparent silence into which Chilean society was submerged in the early post-dictatorial period is mirrored, to some extent, by the fate of documentary production in the 1990s. The same could be said about Chile's revitalized relationship with the recent past (most notably triggered by the Pinochet case) and the re-articulation of the documentary scene on the threshold of the twenty-first century (brought about by a series of factors, including private and public initiatives).

Despite the fact that public support has increased for documentary production in the last decade, following the establishment of a new institutional framework along with developments in the field of human rights, the state's position has been at best erratic. This has been demonstrated most palpably by the continuous obstacles placed in the way of the broadcast of *El diario de Agustín*.

The programmers of the first retrospective of Chilean documentary in FIDOCS were right when they said that if anyone asked the filmmakers (including themselves) what they had been doing during these decisive decades, they would reply 'we remember[ed]'. The following pages seek to trace precisely how documentarians have recalled Chile's darkest periods and how these audiovisual approaches have changed throughout the years while remaining attentive to the intricacies of the country's politics of memory.

Notes to Chapter 1

1. Pick, 'Chilean Documentary', p. 109.
2. For a study of the documentaries produced in both universities see Corro and others, and for a history of the CE, see Salinas and Stange, *Historia del Cine Experimental*, pp. 35–42.
3. For early accounts, see Jacqueline Mouesca, *Plano secuencia de la memoria de Chile: veinticinco años de cine chileno (1960–1985)* (Santiago: Ediciones del Litoral, 1988), pp. 15–24 and Pick, 'Chilean Documentary'. For more recent studies see Mardones and Villaroel.
4. Pick, 'Chilean Documentary', p. 112.
5. See, for example, Ignacio del Valle, *Cámaras en trance: el Nuevo Cine Latinoamericano, un proyecto subcontinental* (Santiago, Cuarto Propio, 2014), p. 343.
6. Chaskel cited in Jacqueline Mouesca, *El documental chileno* (Santiago: LOM, 2005), p. 70.
7. Pick, 'Chilean Cinema in Exile', p. 42 and 'Chilean Cinema: Ten Years of Exile (1973–83)'.
8. Pick, 'Chilean Documentary', p. 118. According to Pick's catalogue, ninety-nine out of the total 176 are documentaries (sixty-five are fiction films and twelve are animations).
9. Paul W. Drake and Iván Jaksić, 'Introduction: Transformation and Transition in Chile, 1982–1990', in *The Struggle for Democracy in Chile*, ed. by Paul W. Drake and Iván Jaksić, revised edn (Lincoln: University of Nebraska Press, 1995), pp. 1–17 (p. 9).
10. María de la Luz Hurtado, *La industria cinematográfica: límites y posibilidades de su democratización*, 2nd edn (Santiago: Ceneca, 1986), pp. 12–20.
11. See, for example, Ulloa; Augusto Góngora, *Video alternativo y comunicación en democracia* (working paper) (Santiago, ILET: 1984); and Hernán Dinamarca, *El video en América latina: actor innovador del espacio audiovisual* (Santiago: ArteCien and Canelo de Nos, 1991). For a concise overview of the period in Chile in English, see Juan Carlos Altamirano, 'The Audiovisual Battle of Chile', in *Internal Exile: New Films and Videos from Chile*, ed. by Coco Fusco (New York: Third World Newsreel, 1990), pp. 18–22.
12. Liñero, pp. 45–47.
13. For more on these collectives, see Liñero, pp. 48–58 and Hermann Mondaca, *Las imágenes de un país invisible: historia del movimiento de video alternativo en Chile en el período 1980 a 1990 y su relación con los medios de comunicación* (unpublished bachelor thesis, Universidad Pedro de Valdivia, 2009), pp. 53–67. I am grateful to Hermann Mondaca for sharing this unpublished work with me.
14. Antonio Traverso and Germán Liñero, 'Chilean Political Documentary Video of the 1980s', in *New Documentaries in Latin America*, ed. by Vinicius Navarro and Juan Carlos Rodríguez (New York: Palgrave Macmillan, 2014), pp. 168–84.
15. The whole distribution and exhibition network that extended throughout the country was mostly sustained by Ictus through Babi Salas. Stern provides some details: Ictus established eleven agreements in the provinces with video-lending institutions — church and Christian-based community organizations, human rights groups and other non-governmental organizations (NGOs), and women's groups. In 1987 it added thirteen more agreements, and Ictus estimated it reached 150,000 people, more so in the provinces than in Santiago. Stern, *Battling for Hearts and Minds*, p. 309.
16. Traverso and Liñero, p.168
17. See, for example, Liñero, p. 217 or Mouesca, *El documental chileno*, p. 134.
18. Over 4,000 hours of video footage are in the hands of these independent cameramen and audiovisual collectives, according to Mondaca, p. 104. Documentary production in the country by 1983 had reached a total of eighty-three works, according to the catalogue provided by Ulloa, pp. 45–54. The online *U-matic* project, linked to Liñero's book on video registered over 450 audiovisual productions in general, produced between 1975 and 1995.
19. Liñero, pp. 156–60.
20. Ibid., pp. 161–97.
21. Moulian, p. 42.
22. Ibid., p. 38.
23. Ibid., pp. 141–43.
24. Arturo Arias and Alicia del Campo, 'Introduction: Memory and Popular Culture', *Latin American Perspectives*, 36: 5 (2009), 3–20 (p. 8).

25. Cath Collins, 'The Moral Economy of Memory', in *Accounting for Violence: Marketing Memory in Latin America*, ed. by Ksenija Bilbija and Leigh A. Payne (Durham: Duke University Press, 2011), pp. 235–63 (p. 236).
26. Stern, 'Introduction to the Trilogy', p. xxix–xxxi. For more on this rationale see *Reckoning with Pinochet*, pp. 364–68.
27. Stern, *Reckoning with Pinochet*, pp. 365–78.
28. Ibid., pp. 367–78.
29. Jelin, *State Repression*, p. xviii.
30. Stern, 'Introduction to the Trilogy', p. xxxi.
31. On the 'unravelling impasse' see esp. Reckoning with Pinochet, pp. xxxi–xxxiv, 2–4, 125–35, 145–48, 162–66, 193–99, 201, 210, 360–64.
32. Ibid., p. xxxi.
33. Ibid., p. xxxi.
34. Ibid., p xxxi.
35. Ibid., p. 361.
36. Wilde, 'Irruptions of Memory', p. 476. For the 'traumatic' silence of the political elite from the right and left, see Katherine Hite, 'La superación de los silencios oficiales en el Chile posautoritario', trans. by Horacio Pons, in *Historizar el pasado vivo en América latina*, ed. by Anne Pérotin-Dumon (Santiago: Universidad Alberto Hurtado, 2007), pp. 1–41 <http://www.historizarelpasadovivo.cl/downloads/hite.pdf> [accessed 24 October 2018].
37. For comprehensive analyses of this first democratic government, see Brian Loveman, 'The Transition to Civilian Government in Chile, 1990–1994', in *The Struggle for Democracy in Chile*, ed. by Paul W. Drake and Iván Jaksić, revised edn (Lincoln: University of Nebraska Press, 1995), pp. 305–37; Stern, *Reckoning with Pinochet*, Chapter 1 to Chapter 3; and Brian Loveman and Elizabeth Lira, *El espejismo de la reconciliación política: Chile 1990–2002* (Santiago: LOM, 2002), pp. 23–128.
38. Norbert Lechner and Pedro Güell, 'Construcción social de las memorias en la transición chilena', in *Subjetividad y figuras de la memoria*, ed. by Elizabeth Jelin and Susana Kaufman (Madrid: Siglo XXI, 2006), pp. 17–44 (p. 23).
39. Loveman, 'The Transition', p. 310.
40. The famous expression is 'todo atado y bien atado' (Loveman's translation). Ibid., p. 309. See also Loveman and Lira, *El espejismo de la reconciliación*, p. 33 and Wilde, 'Irruptions of Memory', p. 480.
41. Garretón, *Incomplete Democracy*, p. 146.
42. Instead, he adopted an 'expressive politics' in Wilde's appropriate description of the series of symbolic gestures he undertook. Wilde, 'Irruptions of Memory', pp. 483–84.
43. For a critically informed analysis on the role of this commission within the context of a broader historical perspective on the Chilean politics of memory and its emphasis on 'reconciliation', see Brian Loveman and Elizabeth Lira, 'Truth, Justice, Reconciliation, and Impunity as Historical Themes: Chile, 1984–2006', *Radical History Review*, 97 (Winter 2007), 43–76 (pp. 61–64).
44. Stern, *Reckoning with Pinochet*, pp. 131–32.
45. Alfredo Jocelyn-Holt, *El Chile perplejo*, 3rd edn (Santiago: Planeta-Ariel, 1999), p. 207. Aylwin's televised speech is analysed in depth by Stern, *Reckoning with Pinochet*, pp. 86–87.
46. Stern, *Reckoning with Pinochet*, pp. 131–32; 193–235.
47. Scholars have remarked on the *shocking* aspects of this atrocious discovery for the Chilean nation. See Loveman and Lira, *El espejismo de la reconciliación*, pp. 45–48; Stern, *Reckoning with Pinochet*, pp. 48–50; and Hite, 'La superación de los silencios', pp. 22–23.
48. On the denouements of this emblematic case, see Stern *Reckoning with Pinochet*, esp. Chapter 5 and Chapter 6.
49. Stern, *Reckoning with Pinochet Chile*, p. 48. The case was already widely known thanks to an exhaustive investigation carried out by Patricia Verdugo entitled *Los zarpazos del Puma* (The Puma's Claws) published in 1989, which rapidly became a bestseller. The death of seventy-two victims killed by this 'special commission', many of whom had given themselves up, are documented in this book, which sold over 125,000 copies (including pirate versions), according to Stern. Ibid., pp. 13–16.

50. Hite, 'La superación de los silencios', pp. 22–23.
51. Loveman and Lira, *El espejismo de la reconciliación*, pp. 45–49.
52. For an eloquent explanation of this phenomenon, see Lechner and Güell. See also Moulian, pp. 66–69; Wilde, 'Irruptions of Memory', pp. 476–77; and Stern, *Reckoning with Pinochet*, pp. 176–92.
53. Lechner and Güell, pp. 33–37.
54. These included a series of criminal accusations against Pinochet enabled by the reinterpretation of the Amnesty Law. Judge Juan Guzmán found a formula to surmount this by understanding disappearance as permanent kidnapping. Stern, *Reckoning with Pinochet*, pp. 212–22
55. Uribe and Vicuña, pp. 169–70.
56. For a detailed account of the case, see Naomi Roht-Arriaza, *The Pinochet Effect: Transnational Justice in the Age of Human Rights* (Philadelphia: University of Pennsylvania Press, 2005).
57. Wilde, 'A Season of Memory', p. 33.
58. Wilde, 'Irruptions of Memory', p. 495.
59. Ibid..
60. See Stern, *Reckoning with Pinochet*, Chapter 5. The Mesa de Diálogo was a special group created by president Eduardo Frei that aimed to discover the 'truth' of the destiny of the disappeared and to reflect on shared responsibilities leading to the coup and the ensuing violation of human rights. As it involved representatives of the military, some relatives of the victims and human rights lawyers opposed the initiative. The final report delivered by the armed forces soon fell apart; the information was not only vague, but also false, or at least, erroneous, as the discovery of new remains proved.
61. See the important collection of essays *De la tortura no se habla: Agüero versus Meneses*, ed. by Patricia Verdugo (Santiago: Catalonia, 2004).
62. Patricia Verdugo, 'Prólogo', in *De la tortura no se habla: Agüero versus Meneses*, ed. by Patricia Verdugo, (Santiago: Catalonia, 2004), pp. 11–16 (p. 15).
63. Patricia Verdugo, 'Los protagonistas', in *De la tortura no se habla: Agüero versus Meneses*, ed. by Patricia Verdugo (Santiago: Catalonia, 2004), pp. 19–44 (p. 28).
64. In reality, Verdugo explains, the creation of this commission was enabled by the fact that rather outrageously, the conservative right had announced in 2003 that they were preparing a project to deal with the pending human rights issues. Verdugo, 'Prólogo', p.11.
65. Collins, 'The Moral Economy of Memory', p. 236.
66. Comisión Nacional sobre Prisión Política y Tortura, *Informe de la Comisión Nacional sobre Prisión Política y Tortura* (Santiago: 2004). The Report can be accessed here <http://www.memoriaviva.com/Tortura/Informe_Valech.pdf> [accessed 30 October 2017].
67. Ibid., p. 8; p. 589.
68. Ibid., pp. 301–545.
69. On the practice of torture in Chile see Loveman and Lira, 'Truth, Justice, Reconciliation' and also their article 'Torture as Public Policy, 1810–2011', in *The Politics of Memory in Chile: From Pinochet to Bachelet*, ed. by Cath Collins, Katherine Hite, and Alfredo Joignant (Boulder: First Forum Press, 2013), pp. 91–132.
70. Loveman and Lira, 'Truth, Justice, Reconciliation', p. 67.
71. See Stern, *Reckoning with Pinochet*, pp. 286–97 and Loveman and Lira, 'Torture as Public Policy', p. 117
72. Katherine Hite, *Politics and the Art of Commemoration: Memorials to Struggle in Latin America and Spain* (London: Routledge, 2012), p. 82.
73. Stern, *Reckoning with Pinochet*, pp. 284–85 and Hite, *Politics and the Art of Commemoration*, p. 82.
74. Stern, *Reckoning with Pinochet*, p. 284.
75. Diamela Eltit, 'La memoria pantalla (acerca de las imágenes públicas como políticas de desmemoria)', *Revista de Crítica Cultural*, 32 (November 25) 30–33 (p. 31).
76. Joignant, *Un día distinto: memorias festivas y batallas conmemorativas en torno al 11 de septiembre en Chile, 1974–2006* (Santiago: Editorial Universitaria, 2007), p. 95.
77. Details of this transformation are given by Carlos Huneeus and Sebastián Ibarra, 'The Memory of the Pinochet Regime in Public Opinion', (trans. by Cath Collins), in *The Politics of Memory*

in *Chile: From Pinochet to Bachelet*, ed. by Cath Collins, Katherine Hite, and Alfredo Joignant, (Boulder: First Forum Press, 2013), pp. 197–238.
78. Joignant, *Un día distinto*, p. 143.
79. Huneeus and Ibarra, pp. 216–17; 220–34.
80. For vivid accounts on the political and cultural impact of Pinochet's death, see Joignant, *Un día distinto*, pp. 131–73 and 'Pinochet's Funeral: Memory, History, and Immortality', trans. by Cath Collins, in *The Politics of Memory in Chile: From Pinochet to Bachelet*, ed. by Cath Collins, Katherine Hite, and Alfredo Joignant, (Boulder: First Forum Press, 2013), pp. 165–95; Michael J. Lazzara, 'Pinochet's Cadaver as Ruin and Palimpsest', in *Telling Ruins in Latin America*, ed. by Michael J. Lazzara and Vicky Unruh (New York: Palgrave Macmillan, 2009), pp. 121–34; and Carmen Oquendo-Villar, 'Dress for Success', in *Accounting for Violence: Marketing Memory in Latin America*, ed. by Ksenija Bilbija and Leigh A. Payne (Durham: Duke University Press, 2011), pp. 265–85.
81. Collins, 'The Moral Economy of Memory', pp. 235–63 (p. 257).
82. For more on the student movement and widespread social mobilizations, see Carolina Segovia and Ricardo Gamboa, 'Chile: el año en que salimos a la calle', *Revista de Ciencia Política*, 32: 1 (2012), 65–85 [accessed 12 March 2019].
83. Alberto Mayol, *El derrumbe del modelo: la crisis de la economía de mercado en el Chile contemporáneo* (Santiago: LOM, 2012), p. 55.
84. Lazzara, *Civil Obedience*, pp. 120–47.
85. See Mouesca, *El documental chileno*, pp. 113–15; 118–36; Liñero, pp. 161–210; Michael Chanan, 'El documental y la esfera pública en América latina: notas sobre la situación del documental en América latina (comparada con cualquier otro sitio)', *Secuencias*, 18 (2003), 22–32 (p. 30).
86. Chanan, 'El documental,' p. 30.
87. Liñero, p. 172.
88. Ibid., pp. 171–72; also see Mouesca, *El documental chileno*, p. 114.
89. Liñero, pp. 180–83.
90. Ibid., p. 208.
91. Valerio Fuenzalida, Pablo Corro, and Constanza Mujica, *Melodrama, subjetividad e historia en el cine y televisión chilenos de los 90* (Santiago: Pontificia Universidad Católica de Chile — Fondo de Fomento Audiovisual del Consejo Nacional de la Cultura y las Artes, 2009), pp. 50–55.
92. According to Roberto Trejo the credit amounted to a total of one million dollars. Of the approximately ten productions expected to be released, only five achieved theatrical release and their commercial failure meant that directors had to pay the debts of the organizations as individuals. Roberto Trejo, *Cine, neoliberalismo y cultura: crítica de la economía política del cine chileno contemporáneo* (Santiago: Editorial ARCIS, 2009), p. 94 n. 42.
93. Mouesca, *El documental chileno*, p. 119.
94. Liñero, pp. 182–83. These initiatives were channelled by the Ministerio de Relaciones Exteriores (Ministry of Foreign Affairs) through the Dirección de Asuntos Culturales (Direction of Cultural Affairs, DIRAC) and ProChile (a department that promotes local exports).
95. Liñero, pp. 182–83.
96. Ibid., p. 219.
97. Mouesca, *El documental chileno*, pp.137–40; 133–34.
98. Interview with Andrés Vargas, 1 April 2013 (via Skype).
99. Leiva in Patricio Toledo, 'Entrevista a Patricia Bustos y Jorge Levia, *Actores Secundarios*', *Revista Chilena de Antropología Visual*, 6 (2005) <http://www.antropologiavisual.cl/actores_secundarios.htm> [accessed 23 October 2017].
100. The first version was called Primer Festival Internacional de Cine Documental (First International Festival of Documentary Cinema); since 2002, the festival's name changed to Festival Internacional de Documentales de Santiago, or FIDOCS. It has been funded by the state and supported by the French Embassy and the Goethe Institute since the outset. However, state funding has been unsteady, which in 2007 led Guzmán to resign as a director of the festival. See his resignation editorial in *11 Festival Internacional de Documentales de Santiago* [20–24 November 2007] (Santiago, 2007) pp. 10–11; 14.

101. Guzmán first return from exile was in 1986 when he filmed *En nombre de Dios* [In the Name of God].
102. Interview with Patricio Guzmán, Paris, 10 March 2012.
103. Ibid.
104. I am indebted to Claudia Posadas, Ignacio Agüero, and Isabel Mardones, who generously helped me to gather the FIDOCS catalogues.
105. María Paz Peirano, 'FIDOCS y la formación de un campo de cine documental en Chile en la década de 1990', *Cine Documental* 18 (2018), 62–89. <http://revista.cinedocumental.com.ar/indice-18/> [accessed 28 October 2018]
106. FIDOCS, *Catálogo Primer Festival Internacional de Cine Documental* (Santiago: FIDOCS, 1997), p. 5.
107. Stern, *Reckoning with Pinochet*, pp. 166–67. In the same year the Festival de Cine Recobrado was founded, with a clear focus on film heritage and archives.
108. I am borrowing this expression from Alexander Wilde's work, 'A Season of Memory: Human Rights in Chile's Long Transition', in *The Politics of Memory in Chile: From Pinochet to Bachelet*, ed. by Cath Collins, Katherine Hite, and Alfredo Joignant (Boulder: First Forum Press, 2013) pp. 31–60.
109. *Primer Festival Internacional de Cine Documental*, p. 14. Nonetheless, the film trilogy had circulated 'alternatively' in Chile since the dictatorship. Images of its screening to a young Chilean audience are included in *Les murs de Santiago* [*Chile: Ten Years of a Strong Man*] (1983), codirected by Fabienne Servan-Schreiber and Pierre Devert, and written by Carmen Castillo.
110. Lechner and Güell, p. 6.
111. According to the festival's organizers, more than 5,000 people attended over the twelve days that the festival lasted, the public being mostly young people between seventeen and twenty-seven years. Four times the doors of the Goethe Institute (which hosted the festival in its early stage) had to be closed, as the crowd could not fit in the screening room. See *Catálogo II Festival Internacional de Cine Documental en Santiago de Chile* (Santiago: FIDOCS, 1998), p. 3.
112. Since the first editorials of the festival, Guzmán called for an *authored* understanding of documentary. See, for example, the two first catalogues of the festivals, *Catálogo Primer Festival*, pp. 7–8 and *Catálogo II Festival Internacional de Cine Documental en Santiago de Chile* (Santiago: 1998), pp. 5–8. Ruffinelli has compiled many of Guzmán's writings in which he explains his conceptions of documentary in *El cine de Patricio Guzmán*, pp. 267–99.
113. Interview with Raúl Camargo (FIDOCS programmer until 2013 and current director of FICValdivia), Santiago de Chile, 12 January 2012.
114. Guzmán directed the festival from 1997 until 2007; his directorship was followed by Gonzalo Maza, from 2008 until 2012; and then by Ricardo Greene in 2013, who led it for one year. Since 2014, the festival has been directed by Carlos Flores. In 2008 the team behind the festival created CULDOC, a private non-profit corporation who oversees the organization of FIDOCS. See <https://corporacionculdoc.wordpress.com/quienes-somos/> [accessed 12 March 2019].
115. María Paz Peirano, 'Connecting and Sharing Experiences: Chilean Documentary Film Professionals at the Film Festival Circuit', in *Documentary Film Festivals*, ed. by Aida Vallejo and Ezra Winton (London: Palgrave MacMillan, 2019).
116. *Actores secundarios* lasted eight months in theatres, viewed by 8,000 spectators in just one screening room at the Cine Alameda. See Fernando Zavala, 'Actores Secundarios: el filme que consolidó a los nuevos documentalistas, *El Mercurio*, 22 August 2005, <http://diario.elmercurio.com/detalle/index.asp?id=%7B9ca462e5-8605-4099-96b4-1f7fbed9478f%7D> [accessed 8 July 2017].
117. Ros, *The Post-Dictatorship Generation*, p. 118.
118. See, for instance, Pamela Constable and Arturo Valenzuela, *A Nation of Enemies: Chile under Pinochet* (New York: W.W. Norton, 1991), pp. 247–70; Ros, p. 118; and Stern, *Reckoning with Pinochet*, p. 191.
119. Tiziana Panizza, 'Por mí y por todos mis compañeros', *Filmonauta*, 6 (April 2010) p. 7 <http://issuu.com/filmonauta/docs/filmonauta_06> [accessed 8 July 2017].
120. Chilean authors in their examinations of fiction film usually refer to at least five generations coexisting by the end of the 1990s. See Mónica Villarroel, *La voz de los cineastas: cine e identidad*

chilena en el umbral del milenio (Santiago: Cuarto Propio, 2005), p. 198 and Ascanio Cavallo, Pablo Douzet, and Cecilia Rodríguez, *Huérfanos y perdidos: relectura del cine chileno de la transición 1990–1999* (Santiago: Uqbar, 2007), pp. 32–33.

121. See, for example, Antonella Estévez, *Luz, cámara, transición: el rollo del cine chileno de 1993 al 2003* (Santiago: Radio Universidad de Chile, 2005), pp. 65–102 and Carolina Larraín, 'Nuevas tendencias del cine chileno tras la llegada del cine digital', *Aisthesis*, 47 (July 2010), 156–71. For critical accounts of the development of the Chilean audiovisual sector and its industrialization, see Bruno Bettati, *Why Not?: política industrial para el audiovisual chileno* (ebooks Patagonia, 2012), and Trejo.

122. The catalogue covers a period from 1902 until 2007 and it was born from a need to give an account of national production in its totality, or at least a close approximation of it, as indicates the researcher and filmmaker in charge of the catalogue. Pamela Pequeño, 'Catastro: nuestro universo documental' (January 2007) <http://www.adoc-chile.org/cat/?page_id=125> [accessed 20 October 2013] (no longer available online).

123. The database includes short to long features, in any format, either by students or professionals. See CineChile: Enciclopedia del cine chileno, *Documentales* <http://www.cinechile.cl/documentales.php> [accessed 5 June 2017].

124. ChileDoc, 'Comienzo del despegue: estado de la distribución y comercialización de documentales en Chile entre 2000 y 2010' (Santiago: Fondo de Fomento Audiovisual del Consejo del Arte y la Industria Audiovisual, 2014), p. 13 <http://www.chiledoc.cl/web/wp-content/uploads/2014/10/COMIENZO_DESPEGUE_25OCT_FINAL.pdf> [accessed 11 November 2018]. The focus of this study is a selection of 135 documentaries, mostly feature length (over fifty minutes). I am grateful to Paola Castillo from ChileDoc for sharing this publication with me when it was a work in progress. Further useful information can be found in Carolina Vergara's reports: 'La producción y exhibición del documental', in *Panorama del audiovisual chileno*, ed. by Valerio Fuenzalida and Pablo Julio (Santiago: Dirección de Artes y Cultura de la Pontificia Universidad Católica de Chile, 2011), pp. 80–91 (82–84); 'La producción y exhibición del documental', in *II Panorama del audiovisual chileno*, ed. by Valerio Fuenzalida and Pablo Julio (Santiago: Dirección de Artes y Cultura de la Pontificia Universidad Católica de Chile, 2012), pp. 107–23; 'Producción y exhibición del documental', in *III Panorama del audiovisual chileno*, ed. by Valerio Fuenzalida and Johanna Whittle (Santiago: Dirección de Artes y Cultura de la Pontificia Universidad Católica de Chile, 2013), pp. 55–62 (58–59), and 'La producción y exhibición del documental en 2013', *IV Panorama del audiovisual chileno*, ed. by Pablo Julio, Sebastián Alaniz y Francisco Fernández (Santiago: Dirección de Artes y Cultura de la Pontificia Universidad Católica de Chile, 2015), pp. 58–64 (61–62). All can be downloaded from <http://www.accionaudiovisual.uc.cl/prontus_accion/site/artic/20150120/pags/20150120182304.html> [accessed 30 October 2018]

125. Film Law 19.981 <http://www.leychile.cl/Navegar?idNorma=232277> [accessed 30 October 2018].

126. CinemaChile, *Chilean Films 2010/2011* (n.d.) <http://issuu.com/media.cinemachile/docs/cinemachile2010> [accessed 11 November 2018].

127. ChileDoc, pp. 19–20.

128. ChileDoc, p. 32.

129. Peirano, 'Connecting and Sharing Experiences'.

130. See for example, Vergara, 'La producción y exhibición del documental' (2010), p. 85 and ChileDoc, p. 30.

131. Detailed figures on these films can be found in Alejandro Caloguerea, 'El cine en Chile en el 2010' in *Panorama del audiovisual chileno*, ed. by Valerio Fuenzalida and Pablo Julio (Santiago: Dirección de Artes y Cultura de la Pontificia Universidad Católica de Chile, 2011), pp. 28–51 (pp. 49; 35). <http://www.accionaudiovisual.uc.cl/prontus_accion/site/artic/20111029/asocfile/20111029013029/panorama_corregido_22_noviembre___11.pdf> [accessed 30 October 2018].

132. For a detailed analysis of Chilean cinema and its audiences since 1990, see Trejo, pp. 100–17. For details on documentary consumption and exhibition, see Vergara's reports.

133. For a study on the local and international documentary film festival circuit see Peirano 'Connecting and sharing experiences'.
134. Law No 19.132 (1992) <http://www.tvn.cl/corporativo/documentos/Ley19132.pdf> [accessed 14 October 2013] (no longer available)
135. Bettati, (n.d).
136. Juan Carlos Altamirano, *¿TV or not TV?: una mirada interna de la televisión* (Santiago: Planeta, 2006), p. 340.
137. Ibid., p. 343.
138. Liñero, pp. 193–94.
139. Ibid., pp. 196–97.
140. ChileDoc, p.37.
141. Fuenzalida, Corro and Mujica, pp. 234–35. Unsurprisingly, this figure has not changed in the last years, according to the information provided by ChileDoc's director. Personal email communication with Paola Castillo, 17 July 2017.
142. Fuenzalida, Corro and Mujica, pp. 234–35.
143. The programme is called 'Apoyo a la difusión de documentales nacionales ya producidos'. Between 2009 and 2010, TVN succeeded in securing the fund, acquiring the rights to exhibit a number of Chilean documentaries for four years, and carrying out three 'airings' on their open and international channels. The producers in turn received approximately USD 8,500 from CNTV, plus a complementary sum of USD 1,000 from TVN. See Vergara's report from 2011, 'La producción y exhibición del documental', pp. 85– 86.
144. See Vergara, 'La producción y exhibición del documental en 2013' p. 63.
145. Kristin Sorensen, *Media, Memory, and Human Rights in Chile* (New York: Palgrave Macmillan, 2009), p. 32.
146. Both series circulated archival footage largely marginalized from television until then, as I shall refer to in Chapter 5.
147. The series was moved from a Thursday to a Sunday night slot. See Dusanka Obilinovic, 'Entre aplausos y bajo rating: Los archivos del cardenal llega a su final', *La Tercera*, 26 May 2014 <http://www.latercera.com/noticia/entre-aplausos-y-bajo-rating-los-archivos-del-cardenal-llega-a-su-final/> [accessed 22 October 2018].
148. Another case is Guzmán's *Nostalgia de la luz*. In July 2013 the documentary as aired on TVN suffered cuts, including the initial credits, and some fragments were even shown twice. Guzmán wrote a public letter to the executive director of TVN, Mauro Valdés, in which he accused the channel of sabotaging his film. Following the director's complaints, the channel apologized, arguing it was due to a technical error and promised to rerun it (which they did). Guzmán's letter can be accessed here: Patricio Guzmán, 'Carta abierta de Patricio Guzmán a Mauro Valdés, Director Ejecutivo de TVN', *CULDOC*, 31 July 2013 <http://corporacionculdoc.wordpress.com/2013/08/01/carta-abierta-de-patricio-guzman-dirigida-al-senor-mauro-valdes-director-ejecutivo-de-tvn/ > [accessed 22 October 2018].
149. For studies on Agüero's work see de los Ríos and Donoso, and *Ignacio Agüero: dos o tres cosas que sabemos de él*, ed. by Camila José Donoso and Eva Sangiorgi (Ciudad de México: Universidad Nacional Autónoma de México, 2017).
150. In addition to the documentary, the results of this investigation were published in a book. See Claudia Lagos, *El diario de Agustín* (Santiago: Lom, 2009).
151. Interview with Ignacio Agüero, Santiago de Chile, 21 January 2012. When this interview took place, the case had not yet exploded.
152. Ibid.
153. Macarena Gallo, 'El Directorio de TVN le tiene miedo a Agustín Edwards', *The Clinic*, 26 December 2012 <http://www.theclinic.cl/2012/12/26/el-directorio-de-tvn-le-tiene-miedo-a-agustin-edwards/> [22 October 2018].
154. Fernando Villagrán '¿Por qué "El diario de Agustín" no puede exhibirse en la TV chilena?, *The Clinic*, 19 March 2013 <http://www.theclinic.cl/2013/03/19/por-que-el-diario-de-agustin-no-puede-exhibirse-en-la-tv-chilena/> [accessed 22 October 2018]; Felipe Saleh, 'Las esquirlas de "El diario de Agustín" salpican ahora al Museo de la Memoria', *El Mostrador*, 12 December 2013

<http://www.elmostrador.cl/noticias/pais/2013/03/12/las-esquirlas-de-el-diario-de-agustin-salpican-ahora-al-museo-de-la-memoria/> [accessed 22 October 2018].
155. 'Realizador de "El diario de Agustín" sobre "censura" en ARTV: "Es extraño que esa mano negra sea tan larga"', *The Clinic-Online*, 24 April 2013 <http://www.theclinic.cl/2013/04/24/realizador-de-el-diario-de-agustin-sobre-censura-en-artv-es-extrano-que-esa-mano-negra-sea-tan-larga/> [accessed 22 November 2018] and 'ARTV saca de su programación "El diario de Agustín" y realizadores acusan nueva censura', *El Mostrador*, 24 April 2013 <http://www.elmostrador.cl/noticias/pais/2013/04/24/artv-saca-de-su-programacion-el-diario-de-agustin/> [accessed 22 October 2018].
156. 'Renuncia la directora de ARTV por censura a documental "El diario de Agustín"', *El Mostrador*, 1 May 2013 <http://www.elmostrador.cl/noticias/pais/2013/05/01/renuncia-la-directora-de-artv-por-censura-a-documental-el-diario-de-agustin/> [accessed 22 October 2018].
157. Cooperativa, 'Finalmente TVN estrenará "El diario de Agustín" este sábado', *cooperativa.cl*, 4 July 2014, <https://www.cooperativa.cl/noticias/entretencion/television/television-nacional/finalmente-tvn-estrenara-a-el-diario-de-agustina-este-sabado/2014-07-04/194235.html> [accessed 22 October 2018]. In January 2014, after two failed attempts, the Court of Appeals of Santiago accepted the petition for redress of constitutional violations (recurso de protección) against the national network for refusing to air the film despite owning the rights to do so. Ibid.
158. Ibid.
159. A panel organized to discuss precisely why the documentary was not broadcast on national television, which included former board members of TVN critical of the channel's management, was cancelled in the midst of the polemics. See the denunciation of this censorship made by one of them, journalist Faride Zerán, 'Premio Nacional de Periodismo denuncia grave censura del Museo de la Memoria', *DiarioUChile*, 7 March 2013 <http://radio.uchile.cl/2013/03/07/grave-censura-del-museo-de-la-memoria/> [accessed 22 October 2018] and Saleh, 'Las esquirlas de "El diario de Agustín"'. Somehow redressing this situation, a few days after the death of Agustín Edwards, the Museum organized an event called 'El diario de Agustín: Con derecho a réplica', attended by Agüero, Villagrán, and the President of the Journalists Association, Javiera Olivares.
160. Interview with Ignacio Agüero, Santiago de Chile, 21 January 2012.
161. The documentary was sold to channels like TeleSUR Venezuela, Ibermedia TV, and Iberoamérica TV. See Roberto Rubio 'Chilean documentaries and their multiplication within the industry', in *Documentary Pathways*, ed. by ChileDoc (Santiago: ChileDoc, 2014) <http://www.chiledoc.cl/web/wp-content/uploads/2015/08/Documentary-pathways1.pdf> [accessed 22 October 2018].
162. Personal email communication with Ignacio Agüero, 7 June 2017.
163. Patricio Olavarría, 'Ignacio Agüero, documentalista: "La ley antiterrorista es una provocación a la dignidad de los cineastas, aunque la mayoría de ellos ni lo sepan"', *El Mostrador*, 4 June 2017 <http://www.elmostrador.cl/cultura/2017/06/04/ignacio-aguero-documentalista-la-ley-antiterrorista-es-una-provocacion-a-la-dignidad-de-los-cineastas-aunque-la-mayoria-de-ellos-ni-lo-sepan/> [accessed 22 October 2018].
164. FIDOCS, *Catálogo 16° Festival Internacional Documentales Santiago Chile* (Santiago: FIDOCS, 2012), p. 9.

CHAPTER 2

(Un)veiling Bodies: From Human Remains to Torture Survivors

This chapter examines the documentaries dominating the early post-dictatorial landscape, and which featured the voices of those directly affected by state violence. It argues that from the 1990s until the early 2000s documentary traced a revelation of actual bodies — from human remains to torture survivors — a trajectory that is closely intertwined with the historical and political development of the recently restored democracy.

Initially, the revelations undertaken by this 'cinema of the affected' consist of the remains of the disappeared and the testimonies of those close to them, namely their female relatives. At the turn of the twenty-first century, the focus shifts to the revelation of tortured bodies, survivors who had been marginalized until then from the public sphere.

After providing a general overview of documentary representations of victims of state violence in the early post-dictatorial period and some key precedents, I analyse two productions set against the background of the Chilean desert: *Huellas de sal* (Andrés Vargas, Grupo Proceso, 1990) and *Nostalgia de la luz* (Patricio Guzmán, 2010), both of which are constructed upon a complex dynamic of veiling and unveiling of the disappeared. In the last section, I focus on works dealing with torture and argue that overt depictions of torments are often absent in post-dictatorship documentaries, which tend to evoke but not show these atrocities.

Early Post-dictatorship Revelations: The Urgency of a 'Cinema of the Affected'

As seen in the previous chapter, documentary not only faced economic instability and a period of adaptation during the early 1990s, but it also retreated significantly from discussions about human rights issues and the country's political development. Somehow mimicking Chilean society, documentary seemed perplexed.[1] Works concerned with memories of the dictatorship were minimal and intermittent until the turn of the century, although they traced an initial *revelation of bodies*, from the unearthing of actual human remains to the disclosure of the testimonies of torture survivors.

Fear is unlikely to simply fade away after years of state violence.[2] According to Manuel Antonio Garretón, although the recovery of democracy might make it possible for people to exorcize their fear, it is also true 'that many people do not undergo any such exorcism and that the survivors retain indelible scars'.[3] This violence marks people's lives as individuals and as members of society, undermining their trust in others and in institutions, and prompts a refusal to participate in politics.[4] Exploring the devastating effects of state repression in Chilean society, psychologists have explained that violence was employed not only to eliminate active opposition but also increasingly to dominate society as a whole by means of uncertainty.[5] Since for many citizens fear 'became the organizing structure of life' during those dark years, large swathes of the population emerged from it in a state of 'social amnesia' and 'numbness', with incalculable consequences at the political and social level.[6] In addition, those times were undercut in the political sphere by the haunting presence of General Augusto Pinochet who served as commander-in-chief of the Army, a fact that stressed both his untouchability and the fragility of democracy.

It is important to recall here Joshua Hirsch's illuminating reflection on the filmic representation of cataclysmic events, in which he suggests that there are two phases that can be distinguished within a society that has undergone such an experience.[7] He argues that there is an initial stage after the traumatic event and before its assimilation by society in which narratives and images of the atrocities committed begin circulating as a 'discourse of trauma' in various ways, in conversations and in the media. This stage is characterized by the revelation of images of horror, which need not be framed by very sophisticated narratives to shock the audience. It is precisely in this first phase where Chilean documentary responses to the early transition can be located. The public interest prompted by such images soon diminishes, however. It is in the second phase, Hirsch argues, when these images are no longer able to shock viewers and hence films are impelled to develop alternative strategies to overcome this process which is often referred to as 'collective numbing'. At this point, films are less defined by the specific content of an image of atrocity and more by an attempt to cinematically reproduce the experience of trauma, an effort to convey 'an experience of suddenly seeing the unthinkable'.[8]

Hirsch's proposed stages are particularly useful when visualizing in broad terms the trajectory of Chilean post-dictatorship documentary. In the early 1990s, television and other media widely circulated images of the atrocities committed.[9] These images provided undeniable proof of the crimes to those who were removed from state violence, but by the mid-1990s, general interest in the subject had already declined.[10] Documentary, then, was forced to develop new strategies to address the country's recent past. Yet, rather than stating that these productions shifted their focus to explore the formal depiction of trauma (as in Hirsch's account), I argue that Chilean post-dictatorship documentary's trajectory took a different direction.

In my conceptualization, the emphasis shifted from a 'cinema of the affected' — characterized by the deployment of images of atrocities and of the bodies attached to them — to a 'cinema of affect' — that tends to elaborate wider discourses about memory rather than focus solely on trauma, while at the same time opening up the debate about the past to a wider spectrum of Chilean society. Indeed, I argue throughout this book that documentaries seek to defeat this so-called 'collective numbing' mentioned by Hirsch by moving beyond atrocity and incorporating a wide range of affective images. Although the works explored in this book are chosen precisely because they are concerned with memories of this contested past, they are not confined to the horrors of it.

During this initial phase, which occurred roughly during the first decade (1990–2003), Chilean post-dictatorship documentary traces a *revelation of actual bodies*, an itinerary that is closely intertwined with the historical and political development of the early democratic era. If, since the mid-2000 onwards, documentaries have tended to engage predominantly in a formal exploration of the materiality of the image — its 'skin' as Laura U. Marks would have it — this first decade presents an emphasis on human bodies, notably through a revelation of images of atrocity. On the one hand, such revelations consist of the bodies of the disappeared — literally, their remains — as well as those of the people close to them, usually their female relatives. On the other hand, and later in time, the focus shifted to the revelation of tortured bodies, survivors marginalized from the public sphere who were only to appear on the screen at the turn of the twenty-first century.

The documentary landscape between 1990 and the early 2000s is therefore dominated by the voices of those directly affected by state violence, constituting a group of works that I identify under the umbrella term 'cinema of the affected'. In the Chilean context, a strict focus on the directly affected was imposed early on by the official initiative of the Rettig Report, which reduced its scope to what Steve Stern describes as the 'maximal victims', the executed and the disappeared.[11] Only since 2003 with the creation of the Valech Commission has the number of direct victims been officially expanded to include torture survivors. Significantly, post-dictatorship documentary followed a similar path to that described above; its initial and restrictive focus on the disappeared expanded later to include that of torture survivors.

Citing cultural critic Nelly Richard, I noted earlier that if the question 'Where are they?' had no place in the bleak post-dictatorship landscape, documentary has played a fundamental role in creating such a place, both with regard to the question of the disappeared and torture victims. In the post-dictatorial order in which the divisions between the vanquisher and the defeated have been so stark, documentary filmmakers have aligned without hesitation with the latter.

During this first phase of the trajectory, the documentaries I refer to as a 'cinema of the affected' for the most part:

i) seek to reveal the 'truth' about what happened;
ii) focus on the direct victims, particularly on the disappeared, their female relatives, and later on, torture survivors;
iii) rely heavily on onscreen testimony and other representational devices;
iv) avoid the usage of the first-person narrator in order to stress a sense of objectivity; and,
v) circulate images of past atrocities that may shock the spectator or effectively evoke this horror via reenactment.

These characteristics are present to varying degrees in the documentaries under analysis below and are by no means completely discarded in the following decade. Rather, what is at stake in this proposed trajectory is a shift of emphasis, as filmmakers will later engage more forcefully in wider affective accounts of the past.

The urgent cinema of the 1980s, largely characterized as one of *barricada*, was rapidly tamed after the restoration of civilian rule. Directors left the struggle of the streets to shift towards testimonial accounts. Testimony or *testimonio* has played a key role in Latin American countries in the reconstruction of the nation's historical past as well as of individual and national identity in the context of political conflicts.[12] Elizabeth Jelin assigns to the testimonies of repression an important political and instructive role. For her, the proliferation of testimonies of survivors and the relatives of the disappeared is a reflection of a desire to disseminate the collective dimension of political resistance and 'the horrors of repression, in an attempt to imagine desirable futures and to forcefully underline the notion of "never again"'.[13]

Testimonies of direct victims or witnesses dominate this long decade in which a sense of urgency remained latent; revelations were yet to be made, bodies were yet to be found, and crimes against humanity were yet to be judged and redressed. As discussed previously drawing on Steve Stern, the issue of memory in Chile is one of an 'unravelling impasse' in which achievements in terms of truth and justice have always been made against the odds. The comparison between *Huellas de sal*, produced in 1990, and *Nostalgia de la luz*, made twenty years afterwards, strikingly brings to the forefront Chile's 'unravelling impasse'. Constructed around the trope of absence and recovery of the bodies of the disappeared and the tireless quest of relatives against the backdrop of the Atacama Desert, this comparison allows me to illustrate that the trajectory I am proposing does not offer a teleological development of documentary. Furthermore, the comparative analysis makes clear that both a 'cinema of the affected' and a 'cinema of affect' may at times conflate.

There is another powerful reason to challenge the idea of a teleological development of documentary: productions dealing with human rights issues, atrocities, and torture existed under the military rule and even prior to the coup. Arguably, two of the most emblematic Chilean documentaries that dealt with the quest for justice of the relatives of the disappeared under the dictatorial regime are *Recado de Chile* (*Message from Chile*) (1979) by an anonymous collective constituted both by Chileans living in the country (who filmed it) and in exile (who edited it)[14] and *No olvidar* (1982) by Ignacio Agüero, who used the name Pedro Meneses out of concern for his safety.

According to Zuzana M. Pick, *Recado de Chile* is the first documentary to include the testimonies of those who had lost relatives and subsequently organized to claim for justice.[15] As the title suggests, the film is a message, a plea for help, and a denunciation of the crimes committed by the dictatorship, sent from these women to the international community. The approach to the female relatives of the disappeared in a particular sequence is one that persists over time: an endless litany of loss gathered collectively in a long take by a camera that stops briefly on each of these women's faces while they provide information about their missing ones. *No olvidar*, in turn, deals with the Lonquén's case and it includes testimonies of the relatives of the fifteen peasants who were murdered and abandoned in the limestone furnaces in 1978. This case became emblematic as the first evidence of the atrocities being committed by the regime, which were silenced and denied.

Likewise, testimonies of torture survivors began soon after the coup. In exile, their first appearance can be traced to *Je ne sais pas* (*I Don't Know*) (Marilú Mallet, 1974, credited originally as a 'collective realization'), a video that registered various testimonies of people subjected to torments, including that of director Patricio Henríquez, a young journalist back then.[16] Within the country, these voices go back at least to *Testimonio 1* (*Testimony 1*) (Hernán Fliman, 1979), an account of survivors' testimonies given during psychological treatment provided by a religious-based organization.[17] A distinct characteristic of these early documentaries dealing with torture is that although survivors refer to their experience, even describe it in detail, the works do not attempt to depict it; non-fiction seems to be able to talk about this horror but is largely hesitant to visualize it.[18]

Remarkably, the most explicit account of political torture appears in a documentary made before the coup called *No es hora de llorar* (*This is Not the Time to Cry*) (Pedro Chaskel and Luis Alberto Sanz, 1971).[19] Pablo Corro et. al have described 'un sentimiento apocalíptico, una conciencia catastrófica' ['an apocalyptic feeling, a catastrophic consciousness'][20] in pre-coup documentary; such consciousness is most palpable in this film. In *No es hora de llorar*, testimonies of Brazilian refugees in Chile alternate with the reenactment of the various modes of torture inflicted on them via actors assuming the roles of victim and perpetrator. These recreated methods include one where the person is forced to stand on two small cans and the Pau d'Arara (the 'parrot's perch') in which the victim is suspended by the back of his knees with his hands bound. Chaskel and Sanz render these torments mostly through tight framing and close-ups of a naked or barely dressed body, in a graphic, yet informative and non-dramatic way.

In 1990, only a few months after the inauguration of the first civilian administration led by Patricio Aylwin, the widespread circulation in the mass media of the remains of disappeared found in common graves shocked the country. The graves were initially found in Pisagua, in the Atacama Desert, so their mummified bodies bore clear traces of violence inflicted upon them. These corpses turned into undeniable evidence that the victims 'habían sido brutalizadas, atadas y fusiladas. Desde sus rostros momificados salían gritos silenciosos que perturbaron la conciencia y la comodidad nacional' [had been violently treated, tied up and executed. Quiet screams emerged from their mummified bodies, disturbing the nation's consciousness and comfort].[21] After their revelation, these ghastly images rapidly entered into the repertoire of post-dictatorship documentary films, persisting until today. As noted by Michael Lazzara, these and other bodies:

> [H]ave been particularly central to Chile's national drama since 1973. Allende, the *desaparecidos*, Patio 29, the exhumation and destruction of cadavers, the identification and archiving of bones at the Servicio Médico Legal, the human

remains that surfaced at Lonquén in December 1978: all of these cases speak to how the powerful have tried to keep bodies at bay, fragment them, silence them, or disappear them to avoid scandal or disrupt hegemony.[22] (emphasis in the original)

These corpses, as well as other atrocious images such as Allende's bloodstained body, or those of murdered victims lying in meadows, on the pavement, or by the riverbank of the Mapocho, are commonly found in early post-dictatorship documentary. Titles featuring such horrifying images include: *La verdadera historia de Johny* (sic) *Good* (*The True Story of Johny Good*) (Pablo Tupper and Patricia del Río, Grupo Proceso, 1990); *Raúl Silva Henríquez, el Cardenal* (*The Cardinal*) (Ricardo Larraín, 1996); *Patio 29: historias del silencio* [*Patio 29: Stories of Silence*] (Esteban Larraín, 1998); *Fernando ha vuelto* [*Fernando is Back*] (Silvio Caiozzi, 1998); *Chile, la herida abierta* (*Chile: The Open Wound*) (Orlando Lübbert, 1999); *El último combate de Salvador Allende* [*The Last Stand of Salvador Allende*] (1998) and *Imágenes de una dictadura* [*Images of a Dictatorship*] (1999), both directed by Patricio Henríquez; and a few years later, *Mi hermano y yo* [*My Brother and I*] (Sergio Gándara, 2002) (which reveals the remains of one of the youngest victims of the dictatorship unearthed in 1999). With the exception of Henríquez's latter work (the first is a careful reconstruction of Allende's last day in La Moneda via witness accounts, while the second is an outstanding compilation documentary), these documentaries draw heavily on testimonies, stressing content rather than form, and circulating images of atrocity as evidence of the crimes committed in order to create social awareness via shocking visuals. Two of these works deal at length with victims found in the so-called Patio 29: *Patio 29* and *Fernando ha vuelto*.

In 1991, 126 corpses were exhumed from a common grave in the Cementerio General located at a site known as Patio 29.[23] Since the late 1980s, the site was known to be a clandestine graveyard, yet only with the beginning of the transition to democracy did legal exhumations begin.[24] In some cases, two or even three bodies were found in the same grave. '¡Pero qué economía más grande! [What an economy!] was the appalling reply offered by Pinochet to journalists after being asked about his views on the discovery of the remains (this news footage is included in *Patio 29*). The Servicio Médico Legal (Medical Legal Service, herein SML) carried out the identification of the bodies and between 1993 and 2002 the names of ninety-six people were reported.[25] However, in April 2006 the SML acknowledged that their work was unreliable, confirming that errors had occurred in forty-eight cases, and that in thirty-seven of them the results were dubious.[26] The disappeared disappeared again, subjecting their relatives to a devastating saga of recognition and misrecognition.[27]

Long before the eruption of this painful scandal in 2006 and at the threshold of the 'Pinochet case', *Patio 29* and *Fernando ha vuelto* had already dealt with this topic in 1998, building their narratives around these corpses. Significantly, both documentaries are structured around the process of unearthing the bodies and their burial. This involves 'the loss', 'the search' and 'the encounter' in the case of *Patio 29*, and in the case of *Fernando ha vuelto*, 'the recognition', 'the waiting', 'homecoming', and 'goodbye'. While the latter focuses on the particular case of Fernando Olivares, tracking the forensic process by which Olivares's wife identifies the body of her husband before his burial, the former collects testimonies of several relatives (mostly female) as well as witness accounts, revealing a vast repertoire of images of atrocity. Both documentaries rely on the persuasiveness of their images and discard the use of a narrator, pointing to the directors' desire to stress objectivity. In both works, the aesthetic aspects are not prioritized in favour of a more immediate, even urgent, account, which is reflected in the use of handheld cameras, poorly lit testimonies, and loose framing. 'El tema era lo bastante importante como para no perderse en la forma' [The topic was important enough that it would not be lost in the cinematic form], asserts Esteban Larraín with regard to his *Patio 29*.[28] In fact, in 1997, when the director was a young journalism student, he explained the scope of his documentary in terms of its explicit political outcome: 'Queremos pues hacernos cargo de un pedacito de esa deuda y contribuir, al menos con *la verdad*, a combatir el enfermo olvido que hoy se impone. Y quizás, de paso, lograr un poco de *justicia*' (my emphasis) [we would like to take on a little part of the debt [that Chilean society and the state owes to the victims' relatives] by contributing, at least with the *truth*, against the sick forgetfulness that imposes itself today. And, maybe, along the way, achieve a bit of *justice*].[29]

Whereas Silvio Caiozzi seems more interested in depicting the persistence of state violence in the present via direct accounts (as its continuous effects unfold both in front of the wife and in front of the camera while *revealing* the remains), Larraín seeks to frame the unearthing of corpses within a broader historical context (via informative texts and archival materials which include news footage, photographs, and newspaper clippings). There is a certain formal quest in *Patio 29* which offers a modest textured account of the past as a traumatic one through the repeated insertion of black and white images filmed in 16mm of the N.N. memorial crosses above the graves (the acronym stands for 'No Name' or unknown graves), which have come to stand metonymically for the graveyard.

Unlike the rest of the works discussed above, *Fernando ha vuelto* has received considerable scholarly attention.[30] At the time of the documentary's release, Caiozzi was already a reputed fiction filmmaker, which probably contributed to the work's wider circulation abroad. Productive gendered and affective readings of *Fernando ha vuelto* have been prompted by the literal act of touching, notably by the radical act of caressing a corpse.[31] Moved by the intensity of Caiozzi's register of the bodily encounter between the cadaver of Olivares and his wife, Francine Masiello writes about the widow's gesture of touching her husband:

> The materiality of the body (and what greater density could give expression to the body than its weight in bone?) was thus unmistakably claimed; bone and personal identity, past history and current moment were linked in a single image, joining the visual presence of the skeleton to the highly unrepresentable aspects of physical and emotional pain.[32]

The particular qualities of the documentary — notably direct register, chronological order, and absence of archival material (except for a few family pictures) — are shaped by the fact that it was originally a private commission. Ágave Díaz, Olivares's wife, is Caiozzi's personal acquaintance, so she asked the director if he could register her visit to the SML. While recording the corpse on the examination table — an image with deep religious connotations as noticed by various authors[33] — Caiozzi realized that the footage he was capturing needed to be made public; this emotional urgency was inscribed in turn within the formal characteristics of the documentary.[34] Olivares's remains were thought to be part of those found in Patio 29, but the misidentification of the bodies prompted Caiozzi to add a coda to his DVD in 2006 with the title, *¿Fernando ha vuelto a desaparecer?* [Is Fernando Missing Again?] that includes a director's statement and an interview with Díaz. In this coda he questions media coverage of the misidentifications while foregrounding the persisting importance of his documentary.[35] Caiozzi explains in his statement that the discussion of to whom the human remains belong has occluded the truly important issues, which in his view are pain, torture, and the abuse of power. The director forcefully asserts that Olivares's case ought to be seen as exemplary, as a symbol, since 'los restos de Fernando, son los restos de todos los Fernando' [the remains of Fernando are the remains of every Fernando].

As for torture, the topic is present only in a few documentaries during the early 1990s such as *La verdadera historia de Johny Good* (1990), *Soy testigo* (*I am a Witness*) (Hermann Mondaca, Grupo Proceso, 1990), *Le Chili en transition* [*Chile in Transition*] (Gastón Ancelovici and Frank Diamand, 1991), *Correcto... o el alma en los tiempos de guerra* (Orlando Lübbert, 1993), and *La flaca Alejandra* (Carmen Castillo and Guy Girard, 1994). Torture's limited presence in non-fiction is undoubtedly related to the fact that this topic is one of the most ingrained taboos of Chilean post-dictatorial society. Though early examples such as those mentioned above can be found, documentaries began to openly address the experience of torture survivors only after 2001 (when the topic was raised by the 'Agüero-Meneses case', eventually triggering the release of the Valech Report, as discussed in the previous chapter).

Works concerned with unveiling the memories of survivors of former concentration camps or detention and torture centres go beyond the simple use of talking heads. They often use enactment, on occasion powerful reenactments, and draw on archival documents such as newspapers clippings, news reports, and photographs, as well as written texts that provide complementary historical information. The archival material functions as visible evidence of the crimes committed, largely underplayed — and even denied — by the military and conservative sectors during the 1990s. This footage largely derives from registers by foreign crews who were granted access to concentration camps by the military who carefully planned their visits, staging events with prisoners (parodies of music shows or artisanal workshops) in the hope that this would help to ease the international condemnation of the regime.[36] Post-dictatorship productions often use material extracted from films like *Septembre chilien* [*Chilean September*] (Bruno Muel, Théo Robichet, and Valérie Mayoux, 1973) (which includes footage of the Estadio Nacional) or from *Ich war, ich bin, ich werde sein* [*I Was, I Am, and I Shall Be*] (H&S, 1974) which registers the existence of the Pisagua and Chacabuco concentration camps and includes photographic proof of the horrors endured by prisoners in the Estadio Nacional.

Only from the late 1990s onwards, a series of documentaries emerged which were concerned with the memories of survivors of torture as well as with the centres and concentration camps in which the atrocities took place. These titles include *El derecho de vivir* [*Víctor Jara: The Right to Live in Peace*] (Carmen Luz Parot, 1999), *El muro de los nombres* (*The Wall of Names*) (Germán Liñero, 1999), *La venda* (*The Blindfold*) (Gloria Camiruaga, 2000), *Estadio Nacional* [*National Stadium*] (Carmen Luz Parot, 2001), *Chacabuco, memoria del silencio* [*Chacabuco: Memories of Silence*] (Gastón Ancelovici, 2001), *El caso Pinochet* [*The Pinochet Case*] (Patricio Guzmán, 2001), *Villa Grimaldi: Parque por la Paz* (*Villa Grimaldi: Park for Peace*) (Juan Pablo Zurita, 2002), *La cueca sola* (Marilú Mallet, 2003), *El lado oscuro de La Dama Blanca* [*The Dark Side of the White Lady*] (Patricio Henríquez, 2006), *La sombra de Don Roberto* [*Don Roberto's Shadow*] (Juan Diego Spoerer and Håkan Engström, 2007), and *Archaeology of Memory* (Quique Cruz and Marilyn Mulford, 2008).

Many of the aforementioned titles render visible sites that had been invisibilized during the redemocratization process and in which torture was carried out systematically as a state practice. These include locations such as the former Cuartel Ollagüe in *La flaca Alejandra* (in which Castillo literally takes the past by assault, sneaking through one of the windows of the closed down house); the Estadio Chile in *El derecho de vivir* (before the stadium was renamed in 2004 Estadio Víctor Jara, in memory of the renowned singer murdered there); Estadio Nacional in the homonymous documentary, a site which by 2001 was still not recognized as a National Monument (this only happened in 2003); and La Esmeralda in *El lado oscuro de La Dama Blanca*, which follows the struggle of human right activists (survivors and victim-relatives) to press the navy to recognize that this emblematic flagship, the so-called 'La Dama Blanca' (White Lady), was used as an improvised detention and torture centre. As these documentaries attest — and as noted by a number of scholars — it is mostly non-state actors that have succeeded in securing the official recognition of most of these places as protected sites of memory.[37]

Between 1988 and the inauguration of Patricio Aylwin's administration in 1990, a certain optimistic or perhaps expectant tone can be found in documentaries that deal with the country's shifting realities in the midst of the 1988 national plebiscite and the presidential elections of the following year. These include *Una vez más, mi país* [*Once Again, My Country*] (Claudio Sapiaín, 1989), *Canto a la vida* [*Song to Life*] (Lucía Salinas, 1990) and *No me amenaces* [*Don't Threaten Me*] (Andrés Racz, 1990). At the same time, however, the early redemocratization process also prompted less hopeful renderings. In 1990, *Vereda tropical* (*Tropical Pavement*) (Pablo Lavín) and *Imaginario inconcluso* (*Unfinished Imagery*) (Pablo Basulto and Colectivo Cámara en Mano), elaborated more critical views of the transitional process. Germán Liñero foregrounds these two works as he considers them to have reached a peak in the local video scene due to their formal exploration, distancing themselves from traditional witnessing accounts and realism at a time when these features were already distinguishable in Chilean documentary.[38] *Imaginario inconcluso* stands out for its focus on active militants — as it deals with the jailbreak of almost fifty members of the Frente Patriótico Manuel Rodríguez (Manuel Rodríguez Patriotic Front, FPMR, the armed branch of the Communist Party) which occurred in early 1990. The video offers interviews with some of the fugitives living underground, while reworking in a creative way the bombing of La Moneda. Basulto and the collective juxtapose a series of iconic moving and still images — Allende holding a sub-machine gun, La Moneda in flames, military members surrounding it, Pinochet with his sunglasses — which, originally in black and white, are coloured and altered as though a comic strip. *Vereda tropical* functions allegorically, showing the transformation of a little girl into a corrupted woman as an embodiment of the nation. This idea, together with the incorporation of testimonies of *desencanto* by young people as well as a rapid montage of archival images of the repression that occurred in the 1980s, alludes to Chile's traumatic modernization process as Liñero rightly remarks.[39] I would add that Lavín also furthers the idea of the democratic process as a *transvestite* one by including in the opening sequence images of a circus while the offscreen voice of a Spanish journalist overtly questions the presence of Pinochet in the political sphere. The idea of a political *transvestism* is also present in *La flaca Alejandra* through a woman in disguise who denounces the limitations of the Chilean transition. This idea of transvestism precedes the notion of political 'transformismo', which would go on to be theoretically discussed by Tomás Moulian in 1998 in his essay *Chile, actual: anatomía de un mito*.[40]

It is worth noting here that during this period directors also turned to biographical documentaries. They seem to have found in this genre a way to create veiled political discourses through which they could keep debates about the past alive by focusing on key figures that stood for political resistance like Cardinal Raúl Silva Henríquez or poet Pablo Neruda.[41] The tangential reference to the dictatorial past is particularly clear in *Neruda en el corazón* (*Neruda in the Heart*) (Jaime Barrios, Pedro Chaskel, and Gastón Ancelovici, 1993). In its closing scenes, the documentary includes a poignant sequence with footage from the communist poet's funeral — in slow motion and accompanied by Mikis Theodorakis' 'Neruda Requiem Aeternam' — with the military overlooking the scene at Santiago's Cementerio General. Though Neruda's burial occurred only a few days after the coup, a crowd accompanied his coffin to the cemetery and even sang the left-wing anthem 'The Internationale'; hence it is often seen as the first act of collective resistance against the dictatorship.[42] The documentary concludes with images of Neruda's remains being reburied at his house in Isla Negra in 1992, in line with the poet's will. Similarly, *Salvador Allende* (Gerardo Cáceres, Ictus, 1992) includes footage of Allende's official burial ceremony at the Cementerio General after he was exhumed from his original grave in Viña del Mar, an event that was also attended by large crowds.[43]

In 1990 there were only a handful of attempts to openly address the topic of the disappeared. That year the Grupo Proceso collective produced what they refer to as their human rights trilogy, consisting of *Soy testigo*, *La verdadera historia de Johny Good* and *Huellas de sal*. These works are deeply rooted in the so-called 'alternative video movement' of the 1980s, which flourished under the political and social reflections of numerous non-governmental organizations (NGOs), a legacy that, according to Liñero, persisted during most of the 1990s.[44] This tradition, entrenched in the fields of anthropology, ethnography, and sociology, granted visibility to the country's hidden face after years of silence, censorship, and repression, while at the same time helped people regain their voices and reconstruct their self-confidence.[45] In Liñero's view, this mandate translated audiovisually into onscreen testimonies, an absence of voiceovers, and the incorporation of topics considered marginal or excluded from society.[46] Grupo Proceso was an emblematic collective of this movement.[47] By the late eighties they defined their aims in the following terms: 'Proceso ha buscado trascender los límites del registro y la denuncia para validar los documentales en Video [sic] como expresión artística audiovisual' [Proceso has sought to transcend the limits of register and denunciation in order to validate documentaries produced on Video [sic] as an artistic audiovisual expression].[48] *La verdadera historia de Johny Good* and *Huellas de sal* have been described as being 'stylistically simple and rudimentary in terms of production', their force lying 'in the treatment of their content, namely, the *desaparecidos*'.[49] Released twenty years later, *Nostalgia de la luz* is the first of an ambitious trilogy begun by Guzmán to explore the intricate connections between the Chilean landscape and the country's history, consisting of *El botón de nácar* [*The Pearl Button*] (2015), which focused on water, and his recently released *La cordillera de los sueños* [*The Cordillera of Dreams*] (2019), which focuses on the Andes. A comparative analysis between *Huellas de sal* and *Nostalgia de la luz* will reveal that the two works share, rather unexpectedly, thematic and stylistic features. Both documentaries are concerned with the fate of the disappeared and the quest their female relatives undertake in the Atacama Desert to find their bodies, thus cinematically foregrounding the interactions between the women and the landscape. Although *Nostalgia de la luz* to a large extent goes beyond *Huellas de sal* in terms of its reflections on human rights issues, technical mastery, and engagement with the materiality of the image, I would argue that a poetic impulse is undoubtedly present in Vargas's modest video as well. These works' striking similarities and differences usefully illustrate the changes and continuities experienced by post-dictatorship documentary over two decades.

Huellas de sal and *Nostalgia de la luz*: The Search in the Atacama Desert

Several documentarians (as well as fiction film directors) have turned to the Atacama Desert due to its role as a silent custodian of the country's history and its dual status as a signifier of beauty and horror. The driest desert in the world, it played a part in the Pacific War, was an exploitation site for saltpetre mines, and was used by other authoritarian regimes throughout Chile's twentieth century as a prison. More recently, the Atacama Desert was where Pinochet located two emblematic concentration camps: Pisagua and Chacabuco. Since then it has been a virtually infinite space in which the bodies of countless disappeared were hidden by the military.[50]

Not by chance Guadalupe Santa Cruz describes Pisagua in cinematic terms. In her words, it is a site that 'a la inversa de la pasión operática nacional por el decoro y las apariencias, semeja el decorado en desuso de una película que ha sido abandonada a su suerte' [in a reverse operation as performed by the national opera-like inclination for decorum and appearances, looks like an abandoned set of a film that has been left to its fate].[51] A powerful visual trope, this arid landscape has been a regular setting between the twenty years that separate *Huellas de sal* and *Nostalgia de la luz* in numerous documentaries dealing with memories of the coup such as *La verdadera historia de Johny Good, Chacabuco, memoria del silencio, El caso Pinochet, Memoria desierta* [*Deserted Memory*] (Niles Atallah, Colectivo Diluvio, 2006), *El juez y el general* [*The Judge and The General*] (Elizabeth Farnsworth and Patricio Lanfranco, 2008), *La sombra de Don Roberto, La memoria herida* (*Wounded Memory*) (Francisco Casas and Yura Labarca, 2004), *Escucha Chile* [*Listen, Chile*] (Andrés Daie, 2008), *El soldado que no fue* [*The Soldier That Wasn't*] (Leopoldo Gutiérrez, 2010), *Mi vida con Carlos* [*My Life with Carlos*] (Germán Berger-Hertz, 2010), and *Abuelos* [*Grandparents*] (Carla Dávila, 2010).

This shift to the desert can also be explained due to its peculiar untamed characteristics as a 'site of memory'.[52] Landscape, according to Jens Andermann, 'always potentially contains a deterritorializing force, a line of flight which crosses and subverts disciplinary demarcations just as it works against monumental emplacement'.[53] Examining the figures of the sea, the mountains, and the desert in the literary work of Raúl Zurita, Andermann explains that the Chilean poet turns to them in their condition 'as surfaces that resist not just the marks of historical violence but *any kind of enduring inscription*' (emphasis in the original).[54] I believe that directors have looked to the desert in similar ways, for it allows them to constantly shape and reshape narratives about the nation and its past.

Huellas de sal and *Nostalgia de la luz* are constructed upon a complex dynamic of revelation and withholding of the bodies of the disappeared, underscoring the vastness of the desert and the David and Goliath-like struggle held between the female relatives of the victims against both landscape and impunity. Both documentaries turn to cases of 'La caravana de la muerte', the notorious deadly procession that crossed Chile in 1973 executing political prisoners. Moreover, the films foreground the testimonies of the same two women who have become emblematic figures of the struggle for human rights: Victoria Saavedra and Violeta Berríos, members of one of the associations for victims' relatives.

Notably, however, while in the first democratic decade documentaries tended to unveil the remains of the disappeared as they began to emerge in clandestine graves around the country, *Huellas de sal* operates by *subtraction*, withholding these bodies from the screen, as it is their radical absence that is underlined in this video. In contrast, while during the second decade documentary filmmakers tended to withhold these bodies as images of atrocity, *Nostalgia de la luz* functions by *excess*, emphasizing the visual presence of human remains; the calcium of their bones pervading the film as a whole, metaphorically and literally. If Vargas timidly essays the arid landscape as an allegory of disappearance, Guzmán creates, through his use of landscape, a powerful depiction of the revolutionary past as wreckage, taking it even further than in his homage to former president *Salvador Allende* (2004).[55] The radical differences between Vargas's and Guzmán's documentaries lie in the scope of their reflections and in terms of *intensity*; the latter advances dialectic readings with regard to Chile's recent past, whereas in the former a straightforward claim is made for justice and reparation for the relatives of the victims. Although both directors are aware of the poetic force of the cinematic form, the accent on the materiality of the image and the power of montage is unparalleled in Guzmán's documentary.

Huellas de sal is framed from its outset as a work of the video collective through the Grupo Proceso logo and not as an *auteur* documentary like Guzmán's post-dictatorship oeuvre. The radical absence of the bodies in this video is largely due to the fact that it began its shooting in 1989, *before* the shocking revelation of the mummified bodies in Pisagua took the country by storm in June 1990, when this documentary was already in post-production (indeed this is why *La verdadera historia de Johny Good* took on the task of putting into circulation the images of the common graves in Pisagua, as Vargas explains).[56] Shot in U-matic and building on the legacy of the 1980s video movement, the documentary uses devices commonly associated with this format, such as zoom outs, fade out effects, and even wipes to move from one interview to another. Despite some technical precariousness, such as the modest cinematography, loose framing in some interviews, and roughness of sound, a poetic impulse is undoubtedly present. The arid landscape is rendered chiefly through zoom outs used in a series of wide angle shots at the beginning of the documentary, which accompanied by the sound of the wind seek to convey the desert's immensity and desolation. The persistence of the violence — the presentness of the past — is suggested through archival sound via montage in the opening sequence. Together with images of the desert, the spectator hears one of the military proclamations (the *Bando nº 10*) as broadcast on the day of the coup.

The soundtrack of that day has been systematically revisited by Chilean cinema, both in fiction and documentary since the 1970s, becoming part of what Zuzana M. Pick has referred to as the 'emblematic set of *affective* and *political* codes through which the past could be safeguarded and preserved' (my emphasis).[57] Directors continuously return to the powerful sounds of the Hawker Hunters jets, the military *bandos*, radio broadcasts (including Allende's famous last speech), and the radio communications among the *golpistas*' armed chiefs. The expressive use of these sounds can be traced back to early fictional works such as *Il pleut sur Santiago* [*Rain over Santiago*] (Helvio Soto, 1975) and *La femme au foyer* (*The Housewife*) (Valeria Sarmiento, 1976), up until more recent ones such as *Post mortem* (Pablo Larraín, 2010). In documentaries, the creative treatment of this soundtrack can be traced from the emblematic *La batalla de Chile* to *Los niños de septiembre* (*September Children*) (Sergio Marras, 1989) and later works such as *Los escolares se siguen amando* [*Teenagers Keep on Loving*] (Paco Toledo, 2000), *Cofralandes I: hoy en día, rapsodia chilena* [*Cofralandes: Chilean Rhapsody*] (Raúl Ruiz, 2002), *El astuto mono Pinochet contra La Moneda de los cerdos* [*Clever Monkey Pinochet Versus La Moneda's Pigs*] (Bettina Perut and Iván Osnovikoff, 2004), *1973 Revoluciones por minuto* [*1973 Revolutions per*

Minute] (Fernando Valenzuela, 2008), and *El eco de las canciones* [*The Echo of Songs*] (Antonia Rossi, 2010), to name but a few. This is no coincidence; most Chileans experienced the coup, first of all, aurally, as Carmen Oquendo-Villar notes.[58] In her essay on the centrality of military radio broadcasts on the 11 September in the construction of power, she explains that the event was first of all heard, secondly seen, and thirdly read. Chileans were in this way, she says, gradually exposed to the coup's visuality. Until the members of the military *junta* appeared on television that same afternoon, the voices circulating on the radio were bodiless, their power emanating precisely from their 'visual indeterminación' [visual indetermination].[59] That is, the armed forces and their 'overwhelming scenographic display'[60] were first experienced as what Michel Chion has described as 'acousmatic' force.[61] Initially, the (bodiless) *junta* was able to see everything, knowing it all, having the power to act over events whenever desired, then was dramatically unveiled in a process of 'de-acousmatization' which anchored the sounds that Chileans had been hearing all day to the *golpistas*' bodies that appeared on the television screens.[62]

In *Huellas de sal*, a source-less military voice enumerates a list with the names of political leaders that had to 'voluntarily' present themselves to the Ministry of Defence, the voice heard as though still reverberating within the vastness of the landscape. The sound of this *bando* is then intercut with the voices of women giving testimony about how their relatives indeed presented themselves voluntarily to the authorities, only to never be released. Their testimonies are heard while their faces are shown in fixed medium shots superimposed against the details of the landscape and the northern houses, suggesting an incommensurable desolation; their witnessing accounts follow one after another, creating a sense of collective loss. Unlike Guzmán's distinctive voiceover (a signature of his post-dictatorial work), the male narrator of this video is not in the first-person and does not occupy a central role; rather, a journalistic and didactic tone is adopted to provide information. In one sequence, the narrator states:

> Hoy, lo fundamental es tratar de desentrañar *la verdad* de lo ocurrido con cada uno de estos hombres y mujeres, y de reparar el daño a sus esposas, madres e hijos que han debido vivir el calvario de una búsqueda incesante durante estos largos años.
>
> [Today the fundamental issue is to uncover the *truth* of what happened to each one of these men and women and to redress the harm brought to their wives, mothers and children who have endured the ordeal of this endless quest during these long years.] (my emphasis)

While these words may seem to openly align with the official discourse of the time based on 'truth and reconciliation' (tellingly, not justice), the camera zooms out of a mineral formation in the desert that dissolves into a photograph of one of the victims, a typical black and white photocopy, placed in the soil. It is this picture that demands more loudly for 'truth and justice' in large printed letters. This shot is clearly staged: the sand gradually covers the photograph of the victim, representing the bodies that remain missing. A closing text ends with a somehow optimistic note:

> Today hope blooms again, because neither man nor the desert can erase the "Salt Traces". In a short time, widows, brothers, and parents will have a place to put their carnations. Never again will they have to toss flowers into the air.[63]

Two decades later, Guzmán returns to the same visual trope — the photographic picture that stands for the disappeared in the midst of the desert. It is 2010 and still there is no place for the relatives to leave their carnations. Certainly, this return to the black and white portrait is not only due to the fact that these photographs have become the emblem of the struggle for human rights, but also because these bodies are yet to be found. As Nelly Richard writes:

> The drama of disappearance has been emblematized by the black-and-white photographs of the disappeared, which serve as reminders of a violent past worn on family members' chests. The photograph, as a technical medium, speaks of an absence through a presence-effect, within the temporally fractured register of the "living-dead".[64]

Nostalgia de la luz is a sophisticated tapestry that interweaves the infinitude of the cosmos, the vastness of the Atacama Desert, and the lost bones of the disappeared. In its most powerful montage sequence, the director goes from moving images of a galaxy to still close-ups of the moon that draw closer and closer to its surface. These series of cuts gently reveal changes of shape and colour to show via a slow panning shot that the moon is in fact a skull. *Nostalgia de la luz* constitutes, through a series of similar sequences, a deeply sensorial experience in which the gaze of the spectator seems to be touching the calcium of the dead bodies, the soil of the desert, and the dust of the stars. The multiple layers of resistant memory and political violence coexisting in the Chilean desert, a topic that has been studied in detail by Lessie Jo Frazier in her book *Salt in the Sand*, are poignantly exposed in Guzmán's work, particularly through the foregrounding of human remains. Multiple corpses are displayed here: the remains of former inhabitants of the saltpetre mines, whose bones can be seen through open coffins in the midst of the desert; the body of an indigenous mummy carefully preserved in a museum; the remains of the disappeared found in Pisagua in early 1990 (originally captured in video by Pablo Salas and Fernando Muñoz as credited by Guzmán); and the corpse of a disappeared whose remains were found during the shooting of the documentary. It is precisely through this excess of materiality that the director achieves the construction of what Patrick Blaine called the 'almost hyperbolic' emptiness of the film highlighted by the use of the desert as a backdrop.[65] Since the materiality of the bodies becomes the materiality of the cinematic image (the same is true the other way around), this work embodies in itself the trajectory of Chilean post-dictatorship documentary that I am proposing, which moves from literal bodies to haptic images.

Although it is true that Guzmán brings back the memories of horror that shocked Chilean society in early 1990, most notably by incorporating archival footage of the Pisagua exhumations, it is also certain that he goes beyond these atrocious images. Through a careful gaze he transforms multiple bodily remains into what Martine Beugnet describes as 'body-landscape'.[66] Beugnet quotes director Agnès Varda who explains that she films bodies through close-ups in long panoramic takes in order to transform these bodies into an 'immense landscape onto which one wanders'.[67] Like the 'cinema of sensation' Beugnet discusses, Guzmán's own 'regime of the close-up' also creates 'a different space for the camera to linger'.[68] In *Nostalgia de la luz* this space is only gradually revealed in some key sequences featuring lingering close-ups, such as when the moon becomes a skull or the desert sand becomes the bones of an indigenous mummy. Guzmán, however, foregrounds these different corpses not just as painful reminders and remainders of the state's political violence. Similar to Varda's 'body-landscapes', the corpses in *Nostalgia de la luz* are included as a 'repository of visual memory' and go beyond the representational realm through the temporal disruption provoked by the close-ups through which they are shown.[69] These bodies-as-landscapes create a 'temporal and spatial parenthesis', a certain 'stasis'[70] to borrow Beugnet's term, that affectively underscores the theme of Guzmán's documentary: the existence of multiple layers of the past coexisting in the — always vanishing — present.

The director had already explored other sensorial means to access the nation's past. For instance, in his famous opening sequence of *Salvador Allende*, Guzmán's hand rips a painting off a wall to uncover an ancient mural from the UP, a relic hidden under various layers of paint. The handheld camera exposes the rugged texture of the wall, which is touched and ripped in turn by his hand; thus unlike the haptic images described above (in which the images themselves are endowed with a tactile quality), the intensity of this sequence is mainly achieved by the literal act of touching along with Guzmán's poetic commentary. In *Nostalgia de la luz*, however, though he retreats from his oft-used trope of La Moneda being bombed, he returns to — as well as poetically rearticulates — other images of atrocity usually avoided in documentaries released towards the second phase of the period under analysis in this book. In addition, the director also returns to a device that has become one of his trademarks: the testimonies of female relatives of the disappeared. In this way, Guzmán's documentary epitomizes the tension that can be seen in the trajectory of the country's post-dictatorship documentary as well as that of Chilean society: the desire to move forward, while at the same time, the extreme difficulties that are involved with doing so. Thus *Nostalgia de la luz* clearly exposes the figure of memory's 'unravelling impasse' in Chile.

I mentioned above that *Huellas de Sal* and *Nostalgia de la luz* include testimonies of the same two women, Violeta Berríos and Victoria Saavedra, who are additionally shot in the same way with the desert as a backdrop. Moreover, Berríos appears in *Nostalgia de la luz* sitting in the exact same position as in *Huellas de sal*, legs crossed, as though she had become an indivisible part of the landscape. It is a common characteristic in Chilean post-dictatorship documentary to foreground women as the most emblematic face of the effects of state violence. They are often included as the embodiment of a traumatized nation: amnesiac, perplexed or speechless, wounded. In these accounts, women stand as victims.

Nonetheless, women have played a major active role in the struggles of memory that followed the fall of Latin American dictatorships and other state-led atrocities in the region, as has been widely documented by feminist scholarship.[71] Their participation and visibility in the Chilean national public sphere, notably after the election of Allende, has been significant and varied, ranging from spontaneous conservative political demonstrations such as the '*cacerolazos*' (protests with empty pots and pans) to political activism, from testimonial accounts to cutting-edge cultural and artistic manifestations. Yet, more often than not, women in documentary films are reduced to their role as witnesses. This is partly related to the fact that, as has been stressed by feminist scholars, gender played a fundamental part in how the repression was carried out in countries such as Chile and Argentina. This gendered dimension of violence shaped the struggle for justice and the ways in which the atrocities of the past are recalled and narrated today.

Jelin highlights the multifaceted role that women have acquired in post-authoritarian regimes, going beyond the stereotypical image of the suffering mother or grandmother of the disappeared.[72] Not only have women played a fundamental role in the organization of human rights movements, they have also continuously brought memory into the public sphere through different means as embodied 'mediators' and 'narrators', as Jelin asserts. It is mostly women who carry pictures of their missing relatives on their chests, and as Jelin rightly recalls, it is women also who appeared on television as the most fervent demonstrators during the detention of Pinochet in London, both for and against the dictator. In documentary, women have had a variety of functions, narrating the loss of loved ones and their experiences as survivors, while also taking on a crucial role behind the camera, as will be underscored in the next two chapters.

The attention placed on female relatives has also served the official desire to limit state violence to a private, familial problem, as a number of scholars have pointed out.[73] According to Carlos Casanova, the absence of justice meant that the figure of the relative took over that of the disappeared in a process of 'destitución sobre la destitución' [substitution of a substitution].[74] He argues that if the dictatorship had been concerned with the extermination of communism as an embodiment of evil ('the Marxist cancer'), the *Concertación* was concerned with emptying the image of victims of their political and ideological meaning, turning the entire issue into a familial, private affair, through the image of the relative.[75] However, the notion of the family has also been a destabilizing force during periods of repression, as feminist scholars have consistently argued.[76] According to Jean Franco, although it was motherhood that drove women into the political struggle as they staked claims for their sons and husbands,

> women never acted simply as mothers in the traditional sense, for they subverted the boundaries between public and private and challenged the assumption that mothering belonged to only the private sphere. They exploited the traditional view that mothers were the vessels of reproduction, but they also went beyond any essentialist definition of *mother* and thus demonstrated that it was possible to transform protest into a broader ethical position, one based on life and survival (emphasis in the original).[77]

If, during the dictatorship, these women pushed the boundaries of the family toward the public sphere, their broken families continued disrupting the official discourse. According to Kemy Oyarzún, 'La imagen de estas mujeres "solas" es por sí sola factor perturbador del mito conciliatorio' [The image of these women 'alone' is itself a disturbing element in the conciliatory myth].[78]

The powerful image of these women on their own has been symbolically staged by the dance of '*la cueca sola*', a performative act of loss undertaken by the women of the Agrupación de Familiares de Detenidos Desaparecidos (Association of Relatives of the Detained and Disappeared, AFDD) not only as an act of mourning but also as political denunciation. The image of one of them dancing as part of the massive ceremony performed in the Estadio Nacional to celebrate the restoration of democracy is included in *Huellas de sal*. In fact, it is through their radical desolation and loneliness that these women are depicted in both Vargas's and Guzmán's documentaries. This kind of representation perpetuates what psychologist Isabel Piper defines as 'la retórica de la marca' [the rhetoric of the scar].[79] Piper criticizes such a rhetoric constructed upon notions of trauma and redress, since although used strategically at some point in the struggle to achieve public recognition, it has eventually cast these individuals as marginal precisely in their essentialization of their identity as victims.[80] In the case of *Huellas de sal*, landscape is first introduced on its own, only to be later intervened by the presence of women walking across it. They appear as a group, in pairs, or on their own, but often adrift in the desert, shown through long shots (accompanied by zoom outs) taken at a significant distance that accentuates their minimal figures in relation to the monumental landscape. Tellingly, via fadeout transitions, Vargas juxtaposes the images of individual women wandering in the desert with that of collective struggles carried out elsewhere. The point — by 1990 — is to highlight that the struggle is not continued by them alone, as the images show and as the narrator explicitly says, but by society as a whole. I would also like to note here that images of direct clashes between demonstrators and the *carabineros* (policemen) seldom appear in early works; confrontation was to be avoided, this absence suggests, in order to support the frail transition. By 2010, there is no sign of collective struggle in *Nostalgia de la luz*; these women are now drastically shown on their own. Guzmán underscores the virtually endless quest of these women through long shots of them searching in the vastness of the arid landscape and through individual shots of them holding small shovels as they excavate the soil. His voice stresses the isolation of their persistent endeavour: 'las mujeres de Calama buscaron durante veintiocho años, hasta el 2002. Algunas continúan, pues las víctimas siguen apareciendo' [the women of Calama searched for twenty-eight years, until 2002. Some of them continue to search, as victims are still being found].[81]

The emphasis on males as the main targets of state repression (as in the cases examined here), problematically locates women in a 'reified [position] as sufferers and victims of the nation, and female revolutionary subjectivity is cast as marginal', as Macarena Gómez-Barris has argued.[82] This, however, was not always the case. Women as actively engaged political actors were common in video productions in the 1980s, as most evidently foregrounded in works like *Somos +* (Pedro Chaskel and Pablo Salas, Ictus, 1985) and *No me olvides* [Don't Forget Me] (Tatiana Gaviola, Ictus,

1988), both of which register major non-violent anti-dictatorial demonstrations convened by women's organizations, or *Días de octubre* (*Days of October*) (Hernán Castro, Colectivo Cine Ojo, 1989), which includes a sequence where a group of female relatives perform one of the first 'outings', directly challenging General Sergio Arellano Stark (who led the deadly flights of 'La caravana de la muerte'). A historical account of women's crucial role in Chilean politics (including under the UP, the dictatorship and in exile) can be found in the feminist documentary *Calles caminadas* (*Walked Streets*) (Eliana Largo and Verónica Quense, 2006), delivered mostly via testimonies of the protagonists — feminists, politicians, activists, and intellectuals — which are conventionally illustrated by archival footage. Further alternatives to the fixed position of women as victims can be found in other documentaries directed by women, as will be discussed in the following chapter. The next section will focus on the other major revelation performed by Chilean post-dictatorship documentary films in this first phase: the bodies of survivors of torture.

The Evocation of Torture: Uses of Reenactment

In *The Body in Pain: The Making and Unmaking of the World*, Elaine Scarry sets out to explore the resistance of physical pain to language.[83] If pain tends 'not simply to resist expression but to destroy the capacity of speech', Scarry argues that it is in torture that this trend 'is reenacted in overt, exaggerated form'.[84] The voice in torture 'either remains inarticulate or else the moment it first becomes articulate it silences all else: the moment language bodies forth the reality of pain, it makes all further statements seem ludicrous and inappropriate [...]. Nothing sustains its image in the world'.[85]

Idelber Avelar refers to this essential 'dilemma' of the torture survivor as 'always one of representability':[86] the experience needs a narrative in order to be elaborated and overcome, and yet it is language itself that appears insufficient to express it.[87] However, Avelar criticizes Scarry, as he believes that her contention that torture completely destroys language not only impedes the possibility of overcoming trauma but also acknowledges its success by fostering shame and self-hate.[88] Consequently, for him it is precisely in the realm of language that a collective struggle needs to be carried out, since 'to confront trauma is to conquer a space of narratability'.[89]

Within this debate, one might turn to Georges Didi-Huberman, who in opposition to the claims of the unrepresentability of the Holocaust, states that the image stands in *absolute solidarity* with language in testimonial accounts. According to Didi-Huberman, 'in each testimonial production, in each act of memory, language and image are *absolutely bound* to one another, never ceasing to exchange their reciprocal lacunae. An image often appears where a word seems to fail; a word often appears where the imagination seems to fail' (my emphasis).[90] Didi-Huberman's defence of the image is quite illuminating with regard to the cinematic representation of torture in Chilean documentary. The struggle over being able to name this horror — to represent it — is concerned with nothing less than the future trajectory of democracy, as Avelar asserts;[91] herein lies the fundamental importance of the ways in which non-fiction film began dealing with torture at the turn of the century. By 2001, these productions had begun to collaborate in bringing this taboo topic to the forefront, striving to defeat silence and giving victims a space in which to narrativize their experiences.

At the threshold of the twenty-first century, the suffering of thousands of people subjected to torture under Pinochet's regime had seldom been publicly acknowledged in Chile, as explained earlier. Hernán Vidal, taking a stance similar to Patricia Verdugo in her edited volume on the topic, contends that torture has an ambiguous status in the country in comparison with that of disappearance.[92] As he explains, during the 1970s torture seemed less important for human rights organizations than its consequences, death and disappearance. This was further emphasized by the fact that during the popular uprisings in the 1980s torture became widespread– beatings during demonstrations and inside police cars were a normal practice, for instance. With such 'saturación, frente al horror' [saturation in the face of horror], Vidal argues, torture 'perdió dramacidad' [lost its dramatic force].[93] This situation persisted well beyond the restoration of democracy. The Rettig Report focused solely on cases of torture which resulted in death, and the issue of survivors of torture would emerge only a decade later in the media with the 'Agüero-Meneses case' as well as other cases that began circulating at the time. As discussed in Chapter 1, torture as a systematic state practice came to the fore only with the release of the report by the Valech Commission in 2004. The commission verified over twenty-eight thousand cases of torture and documented the existence of over a thousand sites used as detention and torture centres across the country.

In this section I examine what I consider to be a second major revelation uncovered by post-dictatorship documentary over the first decade: the unveiling of tortured bodies. My focus is on the uses of reenactment and, to a lesser extent, enactment; Chilean documentary filmmakers frequently used these two cinematic strategies to address the topic of torture. Although it may be difficult to differentiate between reenactment and enactment, Janet Walker provides a useful distinction between these commonly utilized devices when rendering traumatic events. Enactment, she explains, refers to sequences that, although involving real people in real situations, would not have happened if the camera were absent; it is largely used as an 'act of returning' to the site of the traumatic event.[94] Conversely, reenactment functions *'as if a camera had been there'* when the event *'was originally taking place'* (emphasis in the original).[95] Enactment as an act of returning has been famously criticized by Dominick LaCapra in relation to Claude Lanzmann's *Shoah*.[96] LaCapra understands this return to sites as 'incarnation, actual reliving'; in psychoanalytic terms, it is an acting-out strategy that leads survivors to relive their traumatic past.[97]

In Chilean post-dictatorship documentary, enactment is often used in works dealing with the memories of survivors of concentration camps or torture centres such as in *La verdadera historia de Johny Good, Chacabuco, memoria del silencio* (featuring survivors returning to northern camps in Pisagua and Chacabuco, respectively), *El derecho de vivir, Estadio Nacional, El hombre de la foto* (*The Man in the Picture*) (María

José Martínez and Gonzalo Ramírez, 2006), and *GAP: Amigos Personales* (Claudia Serrano, 2008) (all of which interview survivors inside the former Estadio Chile and the Estadio Nacional); and *La flaca Alejandra* (in which former militant turned collaborator Marcia Merino is interviewed in the house that was once the detention and torture centre known as Cuartel Ollagüe). Nevertheless, it should be noted that documentaries do not just force survivors to conjure up their painful experiences, nor are they limited to the use of the specific mechanism of enactment. A number of these works turn significantly to reenactment, a strategy located on the brink of fiction.

Due to its extraordinary 'potential to evoke the past'[98] through fictive traits, reenactment has become a common strategy in contemporary documentaries.[99] A fascinating complex mechanism that presents multiple variations, its uses range from acting as proof of an event to precisely calling into question the evidentiary status of images. Scholars have understood reenactment to be a 'supplement'[100] to more traditional documentary strategies such as archival footage or interviews. For Bill Nichols, however, reenactment functions differently from illustrative footage since it may be seen as 'evidence of an iterative gesture but not evidence of that for which the reenactment stands. It is, in fact, not historical evidence but an artistic interpretation'.[101] Though Nichols agrees that in some particular uses reenactments do add to 'historical evidence', he argues that it often functions as a strategy of 'persuasiveness' since it fulfils, above all, an 'affective function'.[102] This affective role is achieved through reenactment's ability to recreate events vividly.[103] In Walker's account, its affective force emanates from its capability to reconstitute the past, as though a camera had witnessed the event while it unravelled.[104] She also significantly asserts that the issue at stake is the valuation of reenactment's 'historiographic properties' without forgetting its fictive traits.[105] According to Nichols, it is reenactment's particular relation to history that makes it such a powerful cinematographic device:

> Unlike the contemporaneous representation of an event — the classic documentary image, where an indexical link between image and historical occurrence exists — the reenactment forfeits its indexical bond to the original event. It draws its fantasmatic power from this very fact. The shift of levels engenders an impossible task for the reenactment: to retrieve a lost object in its original form even as the very act of retrieval generates a new object and a new pleasure. The viewer experiences the uncanny sense of a repetition of what remains historically unique. A specter haunts the text.[106]

Due to reenactment's capacity to essay a mise-en-scène of that which has been irretrievably lost, it has been favoured by Chilean documentarians who turn to it as a privileged device to convey emotional states, from fear to moments of joy. Scholars have indeed connected this practice to 'working through' trauma,[107] which becomes particularly relevant in the context of torture since this strategy 'can perform a liberating function, particularly to a historical subject for which no archive is readily available'.[108]

Film scholar Julia Lesage analysed a number of 'torture documentaries' that emerged in the context of the widespread circulation of the Abu Ghraib pictures, and the heated debates these prompted in the US about the use of this repressive technique. Lesage's intervention is particularly appropriate since she directly points to the limitations of understanding documentaries about torture within Nichols' framework of 'sobriety' and 'epistephilia' (which Nichols defines as a 'pleasure in knowing, that marks a distinctive form of social engagement'.)[109] In these films, Lesage states, 'knowledge and affect are not so neatly divided; all these documentaries elicit emotion and purvey knowledge and are structured to do so.'[110] Their affective dimension is not only inscribed in the documentary image in itself (as in photojournalism, she says), but also in the way they use interviews. Such accounts, which include testimonies of those who witnessed torture as well as the perpetrators and survivors, are able to prompt spectators' embodied responses. In her view, they implicitly call the spectator into action, while providing 'a viewing experience that elicits strong emotions and an empathetic body response'.[111]

Lesage's analysis points to the fact that 'torture documentaries' often turn to reenactment. Similarly, in Chilean documentary, reenactment is frequently used when dealing with the memories of torture survivors. Perhaps, the recurring use of this strategy in these documentaries is a response to the overtly dramatic features of torture, as Scarry has conceptualized it. In her view, torture is constructed upon repeated 'acts of display' and described as a practice that has as one of its aims the elaboration of 'a fantastic illusion of power', appearing as 'a grotesque piece of compensatory drama'.[112]

Early post-dictatorship documentaries dealing with torture such as *Soy testigo* and *Correcto... o el alma en tiempos de guerra* are concerned above all with creating social awareness of its existence as state practice. At the time, torture was considered an 'excess' carried out by individuals, thus these documentaries' primary goal is to inform the spectator and to denounce it as a widespread practice of state violence. In these two cases, directors rely extensively on interviews. In both accounts, however, survivor testimonies are included but not foregrounded, as their voices coexist with those of judges, politicians, psychologists, or journalists as well as the military and even local celebrities in the case of *Soy testigo*. In *Correcto...o el alma en tiempos de guerra* the documentary voice advances torture as a practice that extended to Chilean society as a whole since people were forced to live under uncertainty and fear.[113] *Soy testigo* deals with torture as a more targeted political crime by focusing on the role of judge René García Villegas, who courageously investigated this practice during the dictatorship. In this documentary only one torture survivor is interviewed, describing in detail how a rat was placed in his mouth. His testimony is partly 'illustrated' by the use of a reenactment sequence that consists of a long take with a handheld shaky camera — as though adopting the survivor's subjective point of view — in a sombre interminable corridor that evokes the sense of endless time he experienced in captivity. Against the graphic description rendered by the survivor through his testimony, the reenactment sequence remains silent. It appears as though a decision has been made not to depict this horror but instead only evoke it. The spectator then does not exactly relive the victim's experience, but the events narrated are given 'a sensory dimension'.[114] The camera soon decides to return to the victim's face to focus on his gestures while he describes his experience of torture.

With few exceptions — such as *El memorial* (*The Memorial*) (Andrés Brignardello, 2009), which includes a brief 'realist dramatization'[115] of a naked man being dragged and beaten in a dim space resembling a bathroom — post-dictatorship documentary eschews showing torture. Instead, since imprisonment and torture were once carried out in stadiums, the images of their basements (or similar places) have become a commonly used 'chronotope' in Chilean cinema, as Walescka Pino-Ojeda has rightly noted.[116] In documentary, depictions of sites of torture usually follow a common pattern that seeks to enhance the dramatic aspect of testimonies: a handheld shaky camera, long takes, dark basement-like locations, expressive lighting, and a subjective point of view that invites a process of identification between the survivor and the spectator.

La flaca Alejandra, a first-person account by Carmen Castillo, breaks away from several tacit social prohibitions such as the discussion of torture and the incorporation of traitors' and perpetrators' accounts, delivering an early and explicit critique of the neoliberal model as a legacy of Pinochet's dictatorship. The director engages with the task of facing Marcia Merino, better known as 'La flaca Alejandra' (hence the documentary's title), a former militant of the Movimiento de Izquierda Revolucionaria (Revolutionary Left Movement, MIR) who after 'breaking' under torture became a collaborator working with the secret police. Castillo and Merino return to the Cuartel Ollagüe, a site of horror from where over fifty people disappeared, many of whom were members of the MIR.[117] Castillo was also part of this radical left party founded by her partner, the legendary leader Miguel Enríquez. The house in which they lived in secrecy was discovered in 1974 and Enríquez was killed in the subsequent fight, while Castillo, pregnant at the time, was badly hurt (her cinematic returns to this house are discussed in the next chapter). The director stresses the difficulties of the context in which *La flaca Alejandra* was filmed: 'el rodaje era muy tenso, yo tenía mucho miedo' [the shooting was very tense, I was very scared].[118] The documentary denounces the names of numerous torturers, many of whom were free at the time, such as the criminal agent from the Dirección Nacional de Inteligencia (National Intelligence Agency, DINA) Miguel Krassnoff, who was still an active functionary and who refused to answer Castillo's persistent phone calls in the film.[119] The documentary engages cinematically with the visualization of traumatic experiences; as the director explains, she wanted to 'contar el miedo' [narrate the fear].[120] The experience of torture is initially rendered through Castillo's voice; she speaks over a long reenacted sequence depicting the process of capture, torture, and final 'breaking' under torture of Merino. The whole sequence is filmed in Super-8 footage, a format Castillo prefers as a means to lend cinematic texture to the revisited past (the next chapter will explore in more detail the uses of different film gauges to *touch* the past). The handheld mobile camera acts as a witness of Merino's horrific tour through the various sites of detention and torture in which she was kept, sometimes coinciding with her own point of view. Again, torture is not depicted; what the camera shows are the façades of three infamous sites — Londres 38, Cuartel Ollagüe, and Villa Grimaldi — accompanied with music that heightens the sequence's dramatic power. I would like to stress that when this documentary was under production *none* of these sites were officially recognized as centres formerly used for detention and torture. In another key sequence and in a stubborn act of memory, both Merino and Castillo trespass over the wall of the former Cuartel Ollagüe, which at that time was an abandoned house.[121] Merino relives her experience there, enacting with her body how she used to rest in those crammed rooms; Castillo pushes her to remember details of the house, the location of the furniture, and the methods of torture used. There are no archival images here, no reenactments whatsoever; it is the power of Merino's testimony that sustains this whole sequence. Additionally, Castillo adds her own voice to the interpretation of torture, imagining the experiences her militant friends might have lived there, while the camera lingers in the corners of the empty house so filled with horror.

After *La flaca Alejandra*, a heavy veil of silence regarding torture fell over the documentary scene until 2000, when Gloria Camiruaga directed *La venda*. Her work is a feminist project that features only women's testimonies, bringing to the fore the gendered dimensions of torture, while operating inversely as most documentaries about torture do. The director does not take these women to the sites where they lived their horrors; rather, she interviews them in their own domestic spaces which become imbued with the horrors they narrate. Camiruaga rejects the use of archival images, relying almost solely on these women's accounts. In an interesting parallel with Castillo's documentary project, Camiruaga avoids a reductionist depiction of women as victims, using the talking head as a feminist tool for resistance.[122] She also mobilizes similar uses of collective recall, as when survivors sit around a table while having '*once*' (Chilean tea), proudly remembering their strategies of resistance in the concentration camp.[123]

La venda, however, did not get the attention that Carmen Luz Parot's *Estadio Nacional* received, a work released a year later that pointed to the generational renewal that impacted the documentary scene at the threshold of the twenty-first century.[124] The interest prompted by Parot's documentary reflects the fact that it was released in the midst of a public debate about torture, as discussed in Chapter 1 in relation to the 'Agüero-Meneses case'.[125] *Estadio Nacional* is an in-depth investigation of the regime's largest concentration camp and it deals extensively with the memories of survivors, all of which are incarnated and relived at the stadium. The importance of the Estadio Nacional in the dictatorial symbolic repertoire has been described by Felipe Victoriano in these terms:

> El Estadio Nacional, el recinto deportivo más grande de Chile, se convirtió tempranamente en el día del golpe en el lugar que representó la imaginación concentracionaria que instauró la dictadura. Dicha imaginación había calculado el número de 'enemigos' con relación a la capacidad de público que El Estadio Nacional poseía (80.000 espectadores), convirtiéndolo aquel 11 de septiembre en el campo de concentración más grande en la historia del país.
>
> [The Estadio Nacional, the biggest sports centre in the country, early on, on the day of the coup, became the place that represented the concentrationary imagination installed by the dictatorship. That imagination had calculated the number of 'enemies' on the basis of the capacity of the Estadio Nacional (80,000

spectators), such that on that 11 September it became the biggest concentration camp in the nation's history].[126]

Parot uses extensive interviews and relies heavily on archival material, including both moving and still images of the stadium-turned-concentration camp, which the director productively uses to merge past and present. The photographs of the past, which show the stadium crowded with prisoners who are surrounded by soldiers, dissolve into the empty spaces of the site and its basements and corridors in the present. The juxtaposition of these images function both as evidence of the largely underemphasized use of the stadium as a concentration camp and to illustrate the survivors' testimonies. The spatial and temporal clashes between those images endow *Estadio Nacional* with a strong sense of the uncanny. The notion of the uncanny as developed by Sigmund Freud names that which is at once familiar and strange, 'that species of the frightening that goes back to what was once well known and had long been familiar'.[127] It 'applies to everything that was intended to remain secret, hidden away, and has come into the open'.[128] Following Freud, Victoriano attributes the stadium's deep uncanny status to its transformation from a sports centre into a concentration camp: 'se trata de una violencia que no expulsa el sentido, no lo exilia, sino que lo coopta, lo invade, lo habita' [it is a violence that does not get rid of its sense, does not exile it, but co-opts it, invades it, inhabits it].[129] Parot cinematically exploits the uncanniness of this site through the temporal and spatial superimpositions of archival material and contemporary images of the stadium, something that had already been effectively done by Guzmán in *Chile, la memoria obstinada*.

A significant amount of the archival material used by Parot comes from foreign documentaries such as *Septembre chilien* and *Ich war, ich bin, ich werde sein*, which have been mentioned earlier. The footage captured by the intrepid East German team of H&S in the latter film has circulated widely in Chilean post-dictatorship documentary since it contains early graphic evidence of the crimes perpetrated within the concentration camps.[130] H&S, though dealing mostly with the northern camps of Pisagua and Chacabuco, also managed to include in this particular film devastating photographic material captured secretly from a building located near the stadium with a long-distance lens as mentioned by the narrator of their 1974 documentary.[131] The pictures show a series of victims suffering abuses at the hands of the soldiers: a man holding up his hands as if surrendering or begging them to stop while being harassed, a prisoner half naked either arriving or being taken away, and several men with their heads covered by blankets, the now iconic blankets of the Estadio Nacional.[132]

These photographs can be considered today to be part of Chile's own 'concentrationary imagination', to borrow Victoriano's term, and Parot includes several of them in her documentary.[133] She does so by intervening them to various degrees; via panning shots or close-ups, for example, and uses them to illustrate different testimonial accounts from former prisoners. One could criticize the director for her reframing of these emblematic images. Parot erases the original source of these pictures, preserving them as a '*document* (the visible result, the distinct information)' but making them devoid of their value as 'an *event* (a process, a job, physical contact)' (emphasis in the original).[134] I am following here the discussion developed by Didi-Huberman with regard to the four well-known pictures smuggled out of the Nazi camps by someone known simply as Alex who remains unidentified. In *Estadio Nacional*, although one could easily imagine their clandestine source, there is no reference to the hidden photographic camera that granted these images their auratic power. Patricio Henríquez, however, maintains the value of this original event in his compilation documentary *Imágenes de una dictadura*, including the complete sequence of the H&S film, starting from the negatives of the original prints and inserting an explicative text that reads 'Photographs taken by an anonymous photographer' (in English in the original). Nonetheless, one could also argue that there is another operation at work in Parot's documentary.

It is worth recalling here that Scarry conceived of torture as a 'fiction of absolute power'.[135] The author remarks upon the common use of terms such as 'the production room', the 'cinema room' or 'the blue lit stage' within this practice, in order to emphasize the overly dramatic displays in which even perpetrators' language point to the deployment of a horrendous spectacle.[136] Parot brings precisely these cinematic displays of horror to the forefront, from the presence of the atrocious routine in which prisoners were summoned to 'El disco negro' [the Black Disc], which meant torture, to the fear provoked by 'El Encapuchado' [the Hooded Man],[137] a former Socialist who, concealed under a hood, toured the stadium led by a soldier on a rope, pointing out people, many of whom were killed. These sections include brief reenacted sequences inserted between the testimonies of survivors: medium close-ups in black and white of 'El Encapuchado' and depictions of 'El disco negro' filmed in 16mm create a textured account of this past and enhance their dramatic force. One of these sequences deserves further attention, because of the way in which *Estado Nacional* proposes a new treatment of the photographs included in the H&S film. The testimony of Adolfo Cozzi, a writer and former prisoner who sits inside the stadium and reads a section from his own book of memories, is illustrated by some of the photographs of prisoners covered by blankets included in the original H&S film. Next, however, the indexical power of these documents gives way to a fictive re-interpretation of them. A very brief, almost ghostly 16mm image functions as a reenactment by showing three men covered by blankets standing outside the Velodrome as if waiting to be tortured, or as if returning to haunt this place of horror in the present. A suspenseful tune accompanies the sequence, heightening its expressiveness. As in the previous cases under analysis, the torments are not visualized here; instead, the spectator is asked to imagine torture.

Henríquez's *El lado oscuro de La Dama Blanca*, released in 2006, relies more heavily on the power of reenactment while trying to convey the experience of two torture survivors of the Navy training vessel La Esmeralda, which was also turned into a centre for detention and torture in Valparaíso (though this lasted only a few days after the coup). The flagship continues today touring the world staffed by young Navy cadets as though nothing had happened within its walls.

Henríquez said on an interview that he was motivated by the contrasting images of the emblematic majestic ship as an emblem for Chile and its dark, hidden aspects.[138] 'Nunca se tortura en sitios que son bonitos, ¿verdad?' [Torture is never performed in beautiful places, right?] asks the sister of Father Miguel Woodward, an English priest who was killed after being tortured in La Esmeralda and whose body has never been found. Henríquez uses this powerful quote to introduce his highly stylized reenactment of torture aboard the training vessel, endowing it with a similar uncanny status as the Estadio Nacional. An early, albeit virtually unknown documentary from 1991 entitled *Le Chili en transition* includes an extensive section on La Esmeralda, unveiling precisely the violence that co-opts it (to paraphrase Victoriano) by overlapping testimonies of torture survivors over long shots of the flagship sailing away. In *El lado oscuro de La Dama Blanca*, the director seeks to stress torture's performative aspects through a powerful and expressive mise-en-scène. Each survivor's testimony (Sergio Vuskovic and María Elena Comené) is shot independently but staged in a similar way: in a dark studio, with only their bodies theatrically lit. Comené delivers the first testimony; she enters the frame as though entering a stage, and while she sits to read her account, one sees a hand installing a microphone. The spectator finds herself quickly inside La Esmeralda, *as if she were there*. White and black shots are inserted, as if they were flashes of lightning that enhance the sense of terror and uncertainty. Once on the deck, the camera adopts an improbable subjective point of view, soon to assume the victim's perspective as if descending a ladder. Henríquez then returns to the staged set to focus on Comené's face, the camera moving either via panning or zooms while the spectator hears her experience of torture and imprisonment inside the ship.

A similar staged sequence is constructed for Vuskovic, who reads fragments of his own testimonial book. Henríquez attempts no overt representations of torture here either; he turns instead to the sounds of steps and dramatic lighting, gloomy interior spaces, and odd framing mixed with subjective shots, conveying, above all, a state of fear and horror. Commenting on his decision to use reenactment but not attempting to depict torture, Henríquez explains:

> nunca me sentí [...] con la capacidad de recrear la tortura [...] creo que no tenía la capacidad para haber hecho algo pertinente y eficaz al mismo tiempo. Me parecía que la capacidad de evocación de un espectador es mejor que darle una imagen. A lo mejor darle una imagen que uno recrea, como que calma al espectador, él no tiene que hacerse su propia película.
>
> [I never felt [...] that I had the capacity to recreate torture [...] I think I lacked the ability to do something at once pertinent and effective. It seemed to me that the spectator's capacity to evoke is better than giving her an image. Perhaps providing the spectator with an image that has already been created soothes her, since she is not forced to make her own film.][139]

Indeed, Henríquez's reenactments force the spectator to imagine those experiences of torture and imprisonment affectively; almost to embody them.

As argued throughout this chapter, early post-dictatorship documentaries perform a trajectory built on the revelation of actual bodies; the initial uncovering of the disappeared and the women who have come to embody them, and subsequently, those of survivors of torture. These different revelations are intimately linked to the nation's own development with regard to struggles over memory. Since these works share a focus on direct victims and their female relatives, they belong to what I call a 'cinema of the affected'.

Although not as prolific as the bourgeoning amount of production in the 2000s, a number of significant documentaries were released between 1990 and the turn of the century. While the bulk of the works analysed here dates from the first post-dictatorial decade, I have also discussed documentaries from the second decade, underlining both recurring and shifting cinematic strategies to highlight the enduring effects of state violence on Chile's social body. Most of these works mobilize images of atrocity, namely the human remains of the disappeared (such as *La verdadera historia de Johny Good*, *Fernando ha vuelto* and *Patio 29*) or focus increasingly on testimonies of torture survivors (such as *Soy testigo*, *La flaca Alejandra* and *La venda*). In the early years of the transition to democracy, a few directors also engaged either in overt and sophisticated formal critiques of the recently restored civilian rule (such as *Imaginario inconcluso* and *Vereda tropical*) or more masked ones by turning to biography (such as *Neruda en el corazón*). The study of later works, such as *Estadio Nacional* and *El lado oscuro de La Dama Blanca*, helps us understand reenactment as a relevant strategy mobilized to evoke the experience of torture rather than directly visualizing it. The comparative analysis of documentaries made two decades apart, *Huellas de sal* and *Nostalgia de la luz*, allows us to explore formal strategies deployed to unearth and withhold corpses from the screen, while significantly complicating the trajectory I am proposing in this study.

As a matter of fact, the persisting interest in direct victims suggests that the trajectory of Chilean documentary is not a teleological one. In the following chapter, I further problematize any lineal readings of this itinerary as I engage in the creation of possible bridges between the exilic films of the early 1980s and the current shift to first-person accounts.

Notes to Chapter 2

1. I am paraphrasing, of course, the title of Alfredo Jocelyn-Holt's important essay *El Chile perplejo*.
2. On the topic of fear in the context of political violence in the region see *Fear at the Edge: State Terror and Resistance in Latin America*, ed. by Juan E. Corradi, Patricia Weiss Fagen, and Manuel Antonio Garretón (Berkeley: University of California Press, 1992).
3. Manuel Antonio Garretón, 'Fear in Military Regimes: An Overview', in *Fear at the Edge: State Terror and Resistance in Latin America*, ed. by Juan E. Corradi, Patricia Weiss Fagen, and Manuel Antonio Garretón (Berkeley: University of California Press, 1992), pp. 13–25 (p. 22).
4. Ibid., pp. 22–23.
5. Sofia Salimovich, Elizabeth Lira, and Eugenia Weinstein, 'Victims of Fear: The Social Psychology of Repression', in *Fear at the Edge: State Terror and Resistance in Latin America*, ed. by Juan E. Corradi, Patricia Weiss Fagen and Manuel Antonio Garretón (Berkeley: University of Calfornia Press, 1992), pp. 72–89.
6. Ibid., p. 89.
7. Hirsch, *Afterimage*, pp. 18–19 and 'Post-traumatic Cinema', pp. 100–02.

8. Hirsch, *Afterimage*, p. 19; 'Post-traumatic cinema', p. 102.
9. See Loveman and Lira, *El espejismo de la reconciliación política*, pp. 45–48; Stern, *Reckoning with Pinochet*, pp. 48–50 and Hite, 'La superación de los silencios', pp. 22–23.
10. Sorensen, p. 30.
11. Stern, *Reckoning with Pinochet*, p. 131.
12. See for instance, John Beverly, *Testimonio: On the Politics of Truth* (Minneapolis, University of Minnesota Press, 2004) and Jelin, *State Repression*, pp. 68–75.
13. Jelin, *State Repression*, p. 73.
14. The film has been recently credited to Guillermo Cahn, Carlos Flores del Pino, Alfonso Luco, Jaime Reyes, José Román, Raquel Salinas, and José de la Vega (the crew in Chile) and Fedora Robles, Pedro Chaskel, and Nelson Villagra (the crew in Cuba).
15. Pick, 'Cronología del cine chileno en el exilio 1973/1983', p. 18.
16. I thank José Miguel Palacios for pointing out the existence of Mallet's video to me.
17. Liñero, pp. 19–20.
18. A similar claim is made by Claudia Bossay in her study of fiction films and their depiction of violence. See her 'Remembering Traumatic Pasts: Memory and Historiophoty in Fiction and Factual Films from the 2000s that Represent the Chilean Popular Unity, Coup D'état, and Dictatorship (1970–1990)' (unpublished doctoral thesis, Queen's University Belfast, 2014), p. 121–22.
19. Earlier, Raúl Ruiz had directed *Militarismo y tortura* (*Militarism and Torture*) (1969), which was never shown, according to the director. It was 'a kind of parody lecture/demonstration on how to carry out torture', he recalls. Ian Christie and Malcolm Coad, 'Between Institutions: Interview with Raul Ruiz', *Afterimage*, 10 (1981), 103–14 (p. 108). Unfortunately, the negative and its copies are lost. Vega, p. 258.
20. Corro, Alberdi, Larraín, and Van Diest, p. 18.
21. Loveman and Lira, *El espejismo de la reconciliación política*, p. 49.
22. Lazzara, 'Pinochet's Cadaver as Ruin and Palimpsest', p. 121.
23. For details on the case see Javiera Bustamante and Stephan Ruderer, *Patio 29: tras la cruz de fierro* (Santiago: Ocho Libros, 2009), on which I base this brief account.
24. Corpses had begun to be illegally removed in the late 1970s but two judicial orders protected the site from further exhumations. Ibid., pp. 62–63.
25. Ibid., pp. 82–85.
26. Ibid., p. 105.
27. I am paraphrasing the title of a poignant column by Manuel Guerrero (son of one of the three victims of a notorious political crime carried out in 1985, known rather crudely as 'the case of the Slit Throats') written after the scandal went public. Manuel Guerrero, 'Desaparecer al Desaparecido', originally published in *La Nación*, 28 April 2006, and available online in the website of *Fortín Mapocho* <http://www.fortinmapocho.com/detalle.asp?iPro=727&iType=148> [accessed 2 November 2018].
28. Interview with Esteban Larraín, Santiago de Chile, 10 July 2013.
29. FONDART, *1992–96 FONDART: cultura tradicional y local, artes de la representación, patrimonio cultural, artes audiovisuales, literatura, plástica, música* (Santiago: Fondo de Desarrollo de las Artes y la Cultura, 1997), p. 33.
30. See, for example, Gómez-Barris, *Where Memory Dwells*, Chapter 4; Sarah Wright, 'Noli me tangere: Memory, Embodiment and Affect in Silvio Caiozzi's *Fernando ha vuelto* (2005); *Journal of Latin American Cultural Studies: Travesia*, 21:1 (2012), 37–48; Tomás Crowder-Taraborrelli, 'Exhumations and Double Disappearance: Silvio Caiozzi's *Fernando ha vuelto* and *¿Fernando ha vuelto a desaparecer?*', *Social Identities: Journal for the Study of Race, Nation and Culture*, 19: 3–4 (2013), 386–402; and Sorensen, pp. 59–68, which includes an analysis of the contested reception of this documentary in Chile.
31. See Wright and Gómez-Barris, *Where Memory Dwells*.
32. Francine Masiello, *The Art of Transition: Latin American Culture and Neoliberal Crisis* (Durham: Duke University Press, 2001), p. 1.
33. Gómez-Barris, *Where Memory Dwells*, p. 110; Wright, p. 40; and Masiello, p. 1.

34. Caiozzi explains: 'Y mientras yo apenas podía sostener mi cámara en mis manos, y me costaba muchísimo hacer foco por la emoción al ir registrando los detalles de las costillas que habían sido quebradas por golpes una a una, es en ese momento que yo pienso que esto no puede ser sencillamente un documento privado sino que debería ser un documento público, debería ser algo que todo el mundo viera.' [While I could barely hold my camera in my hands and I was barely able to focus it due to the emotion [I felt] while registering the details of the ribs that had been broken after being beaten one by one, in that moment I think that this cannot be simply a private document but must be a public one, something for everybody to see]. See Caiozzi, *¿Fernando ha vuelto a desaparecer?* Director's coda to *Fernando ha vuelto* (April 2006).
35. In early 2010, the Olivares family was informed that the remains that were thought to have belonged to Fernando Olivares were those of another young man, Francisco Zúñiga. See Verónica Torres, 'Patio 29: La doble tragedia de las familias obligadas a devolver sus muertos', *CIPER*, 3 August 2011 <http://ciperchile.cl/2011/08/03/patio-29-la-doble-tragedia-de-las-familias-obligadas-a-devolver-sus-muertos/> [accessed 2 November 2018].
36. See, for example, Carolina Amaral de Aguiar, 'Los prisioneros y la muerte del poeta: el Chile de la dictadura ante las cámaras extranjeras', *Archivos de la Filmoteca,* 73 (2017), 17–30.
37. See, for instance, Katherine Hite and Cath Collins, 'Memorial Fragments, Monumental Silences and Reawakenings in 21st-Century Chile', *Millennium: Journal of International Studies*, 38: 2 (2009), 379–400; Katherine Hite, 'Estadio Nacional: monumento y lugar de conmemoración', in *De la tortura no se habla: Agüero versus Meneses*, ed. by Patricia Verdugo (Santiago: Catalonia, 2004), pp. 213–27; and Michael J. Lazzara, 'Tres recorridos por Villa Grimaldi', in *Monumentos, memoriales y marcas territoriales*, ed. by Elizabeth Jelin and Victoria Langland (Madrid: Siglo XXI, 2003), pp. 127–47.
38. Liñero, pp. 165–69.
39. Ibid., pp. 165–66.
40. Moulian, esp. 141–43.
41. Other videos include *Conversaciones con el Cardenal Silva* (Conversations with Cardinal Silva) (Augusto Góngora, Ictus, 1990) and *Raúl Silva Henríquez* by Ricardo Larraín. The Catholic Church staunchly opposed the dictatorship from the very beginning, and one of the most visible faces was that of Cardinal Silva Henríquez.
42. See Alexander Wilde, 'Avenues of Memory: Santiago's General Cemetery and Chile's Recent Political History', *A Contracorriente*, 5: 3 (Spring 2008), 134–69 <http://www.ncsu.edu/project/acontracorriente/spring_08/Wilde.pdf> [accessed 20 October 2018] and Bruno Muel, 'Santiago en septiembre: la capital chilena a los ojos de un camarógrafo', trans. by Patricia Minarrieta, *Le Monde Diplomatique*, September 2013, p. 14 <http://www.lemondediplomatique.cl/IMG/pdf/Muel.pdf> [accessed 20 October 2018] as well as his own documentary *Septembre chilien*.
43. For more information on the symbolic importance of this ceremony for the redemocratization process and the overall role of the General Cemetery as a site of political memory for the Chilean nation, see Wilde, 'Avenues of Memory'.
44. Liñero, pp.193–96.
45. Ibid., p. 193.
46. Ibid..
47. Grupo Proceso began in 1983, producing over a hundred videos between then and 1997. For more information on this collective, see Liñero, pp. 48–53; Traverso and Liñero, pp. 167–84; Mondaca, pp. 56–60, and Alejandro de la Fuente and Claudio Guerrero, *El Grupo Proceso en los primeros años de la transición 1982–1993* (Santiago: Cineteca Nacional de Chile, 2015) <http://www.ccplm.cl/sitio/wp-content/uploads/2017/12/171107_Investigacion-archivo.pdf> [accessed 20 October 2018].
48. Grupo Proceso, *Grupo Proceso: Videos Televisión* (booklet) n.d. (p. 5).
49. Traverso, 'Dictatorship Memories', p. 183.
50. Jo Frazier traces the multiple layers of memory that coexist in the northern desert in her book *Salt in the Sand*.
51. Guadalupe Santa-Cruz, 'Capitales del olvido', in *Políticas y estéticas de la memoria*, ed. by Nelly Richard (Santiago: Cuarto Propio, 2000), pp. 105–12 (p. 106).

52. This term has been influentially developed by Pierre Nora, 'Between Memory and History: Les Lieux de Mémoire', trans. by Marc Roudebush, *Representations*, 26 (Spring 1989), 7–24. 'Sites of memory' in Nora's elaboration is 'where memory crystallizes and secretes itself', p. 7.
53. Jens Andermann, 'Expanded Fields: Postdictatorship and the Landscape', *Journal of Latin American Cultural Studies: Travesía*, 21:2 (2012), 165–87 (p. 166).
54. Ibid., p. 174.
55. On the uses of ruins in Guzmán's *Salvador Allende* from a critical stance see Federico Galende, 'Allende, Guzmán y la estructura mítica de los sueños', *Revista de Crítica Cultural*, 32 (November 2005), 48–51 and Carlos Pérez Villalobos, 'El irrecuperable Allende de Guzmán', *Revista de Crítica Cultural*, 32 (November 2005), 44–47. For an analysis of his earlier post-dictatorial documentaries and their treatment of the past as ruins, see Juan Carlos Rodríguez, 'Framing Ruins: Patricio Guzmán's Postdictatorial Documentaries', *Latin American Perspectives*, 40:1 (January 2013), 131–44.
56. Interview with Andrés Vargas, 1 April 2013 (via Skype).
57. Zuzana Pick, *The New Latin American Cinema: A Continental Project* (Austin: University of Texas Press, 1993), p. 164.
58. Carmen Oquendo-Villar, 'Chile 1973 — el Golpe y la Voz de la Ley', *E-misférica*, 3: 1 (June 2006) <http://hemisphericinstitute.org/journal/3.1/eng/en31_pg_oquendo_villar.html> [accessed 20 October 2018].
59. Ibid. On the sounds of the day, see also Diamela Eltit, 'The Two Sides of the Coin and the Two Faces of La Moneda', *Women's Studies*, 29:1 (2000), 82–91 and César Albornoz, 'Los sonidos del golpe', in *1973: La vida cotidiana de un año crucial*, ed. by Claudio Rolle (Santiago: Planeta, 2003), pp. 161–96.
60. Eltit, 'The Two Sides of the Coin', p. 83.
61. Michel Chion, *Audio-Vision: Sound on Screen*, trans. and ed. by Claudia Gorban (New York: Columbia University Press, 1994), pp. 129–31.
62. Ibid..
63. Slightly modified from the original text (in English in the copy I have).
64. Nelly Richard, 'Sites of Memory, Emptying Remembrance', trans. by Michael J. Lazzara, in *Telling Ruins in Latin America*, ed. by Michael Lazzara and Vicky Unruh (New York: Palgrave Macmillan, 2009), pp. 175–82 (p. 181).
65. Patrick Blaine, 'Representing Absences in the Postdictatorial Documentary Cinema of Patricio Guzmán', *Latin American Perspectives*, 40: 1 (January 2013), 114–30, (p. 128).
66. Beugnet, pp. 94–98.
67. Ibid. p. 95. Original quote from Agnès Varda, *Varda par Agnès* (Paris: Cahiers du cinéma, 1994) p. 279.
68. Beugnet, pp. 94–95.
69. Ibid., p. 95.
70. Ibid., p. 94.
71. See, *The Women's Movement in Latin America: Feminism and the Transition to Democracy*, ed. by Jane S. Jaquette, 2nd edn. (Boulder: Westview Press, 1994); *Gender Politics in Latin America: Debates in Theory and Practice*, ed. by Elizabeth Dore (New York: Monthly Review Press, 1997); and *Surviving Beyond Fear: Women, Children and Human Rights in Latin America*, ed. by Marjorie Agosín (Fredonia, NY: White Pine Press, 1993), among others.
72. Jelin, *State Repression*, pp. 76–88.
73. See, for instance, Carlos Casanova, 'Hay que hablar: testimonio de un olvido y política de la desaparición', in *Pensar en la post/dictadura*, ed. by Nelly Richard and Alberto Moreiras (Santiago: Cuarto Propio, 2001), pp. 155–73; Kemy Oyarzún, 'Des/memoria, género y globalización', in *Volver a la memoria*, ed. by Raquel Olea and Olga Grau (Santiago: LOM, 2001), pp. 21–38; Stern, *Reckoning with Pinochet*, pp. 131–32,194–95.
74. Casanova, 'Hay que hablar', p. 163.
75. Ibid., pp. 162–63.
76. Jean Franco, 'Gender, Death and Resistance: Facing the Ethical Vacuum', in *Fear at the Edge: State Terror and Resistance in Latin America*, ed. by Juan E. Corradi, Patricia Weiss Fagen and Manuel Antonio Garretón (Berkeley: University of California Press, 1992), pp. 104–18 (pp.

112–16); Patricia M. Chuchryk, 'Subversive Mothers: The Women's Opposition to the Military Regime in Chile', in *Surviving Beyond Fear: Women, Children and Human Rights in Latin America*, ed. by Marjorie Agosín (Fredonia, NY: White Pine Press, 1993), pp. 86–97 and Oyarzún, 'Des/memoria', pp. 21–38.
77. Franco, p. 116.
78. Oyarzún, p. 25.
79. Isabel Piper, 'La retórica de la marca y los sujetos de la dictadura', *Revista de Crítica Cultural*, 32 (November 2005), 16–19.
80. Ibid. 18.
81. Film's original English subtitles.
82. Gómez-Barris, *Where Memory Dwells*, p. 107.
83. Elaine Scarry, *The Body in Pain: The Making and Unmaking of the World* (New York: Oxford University Press, 1985).
84. Ibid., p. 54.
85. Ibid., p. 60.
86. Avelar, 'Five Theses on Torture', p. 260.
87. Ibid., p. 261.
88. Ibid., p. 260.
89. Ibid., p. 262.
90. Georges Didi-Huberman, *Images in Spite of All: Four Photographs from Auschwitz*, trans. by Shane B. Lillis (University of Chicago Press: Chicago, 2008), p. 26. 'Absolute solidarity' is the literal translation from the French original 'absolument solidaires', translated in the English edition as 'absolutely bound'. Didi-Huberman, Georges, *Images Malgré Tout* (Paris, Les Éditions de Minuit, 2003), p. 39.
91. Avelar, 'Five Theses on Torture', p. 262.
92. Hernán Vidal, *Chile: poética de la tortura política* (Santiago: Mosquito Comunicaciones, 2000), pp. 20–21.
93. Ibid., p. 21.
94. Walker, *Trauma Cinema*, p. 107.
95. Ibid., p. 110.
96. Dominick LaCapra, *History and Memory after Auschwitz* (Ithaca, NY: Cornell University Press, 1998), pp. 95–138.
97. Ibid., p. 102.
98. Walker, *Trauma Cinema*, p. 110.
99. See Bruzzi, *New Documentary*, pp. 43–46; Bill Nichols, 'Documentary Reenactment and the Fantasmatic Subject', *Critical Inquiry*, 35:1 (2008), 72–89; and Jonathan Kahana, 'Introduction: What Now? Presenting Reenactment', *Framework*, 50: 1–2 (Spring–Fall 2009), 46–60.
100. Bruzzi, *New Documentary*, p. 43; Kahana, p. 48.
101. Nichols, 'Documentary Reenactment', pp. 87–88.
102. Ibid., p. 88.
103. Ibid.
104. Walker, *Trauma Cinema*, p. 110.
105. Ibid., p. 110.
106. Nichols, 'Documentary Reenactment', p. 74.
107. Ibid.; Walker, *Trauma Cinema*, p. 110.
108. Bruzzi, *New Documentary*, p. 45.
109. Nichols, *Representing Reality*, p. 178.
110. Julia Lesage, 'Torture Documentaries', *Jump Cut,* 51 (2009) <http://www.ejumpcut.org/archive/jc51.2009/TortureDocumentaries/> [accessed 3 November 2018].
111. Ibid..
112. Scarry, pp. 27–28.
113. Interestingly, the documentary includes the 'expert voice' of Elizabeth Lira, a psychologist who has consistently fostered this interpretation.
114. Walker, *Trauma Cinema*, p. 113.
115. Nichols, 'Documentary Reenactment', p. 84.

116. Walescka Pino-Ojeda, 'Latent Image: Chilean Cinema and the Abject', trans. by Mariana Ortega Breña, *Latin American Perspectives*, 36 (September 2009), 133–46 (p. 140).
117. For more information on this site, see Laura Moya, *José Domingo Cañas 1367: más memoria* (Santiago: Colectivo José Domingo Cañas, 2007).
118. Interview with Carmen Castillo, Paris, 5 March 2011. Further details on the production of the film can be found in the book the director cowrote with her mother. Mónica Echeverría and Carmen Castillo, *Santiago–París: el vuelo de la memoria* (Santiago: LOM, 2002), pp. 272–79.
119. The DINA was the secret police that functioned under Pinochet's rule. Although officially created in June 1974, research carried out by the Truth and Reconciliation Commission demonstrated that it had been active at least since the day of the military coup. Stern, *Remembering Pinochet's Chile*, p. 45. It was replaced by the Central Nacional de Informaciones (National Intelligence Agency, CNI) in 1977.
120. Interview with Carmen Castillo, Paris, 5 March 2011.
121. The house was used by the DINA as an intensive torture centre between August and November in 1974. After the DINA's disarticulation it was used by the CNI as its headquarters until 1987. It was seemingly abandoned for over a decade and then sold by the state to a private owner in 2000 who demolished it. Moya, pp. 16–29. After a long struggle by the relatives of the victims and human rights activists, the house was declared a National Monument in 2002, but only managed to be bought from its owner in 2011, when it was transformed into a 'Casa-Memoria'. See Fundación 1367. Casa de Memoria José Domingo Cañas, *Recuperación del sitio* (Santiago: Fundación 1367. Casa de Memoria José Domingo Cañas) <http://josedomingocanas.org/historia/recuperacion-del-sitio/> [accessed 10 November 2018]
122. Julia Lesage, 'The Political Aesthetics of the Feminist Documentary Film', in *Issues in Feminist Film Criticism*, ed. by Patricia Erens (Bloomington: Indiana University Press, 1990) pp. 222–38 (p. 234).
123. For a gendered analysis of this documentary, see Bernardita Llanos, 'Memoria y testimonio visual en Chile: el documental *La venda* de Gloria Camiruaga', *Chasqui*, 39: 2 (November 2010), 42–53.
124. Claudia Bossay noted the growing interest of the local press in documentary since 2001 when Parot's production premiered. See Bossay, 'Cineastas al Rescate' (n.d).
125. For the media impact of this case, see Sebastián Brett, 'El caso en la prensa', in *De la tortura no se habla: Agüero versus Meneses*, ed. by Patricia Verdugo (Santiago: Catalonia, 2004), pp. 117–40.
126. Felipe Victoriano, 'La imaginación concentracionaria del golpe: el Estadio Nacional de Chile, lo siniestro y el fútbol', *Revista de Crítica Cultural*, 32 (November 2005), 34–43 (p. 39). For a detailed study about the Estadio Nacional as a concentration camp see Bonnefoy, Pascale, *Terrorismo de Estado: prisioneros de guerra en un campo de deportes* (Santiago: ChileAmérica CESOC, 2005). As she explains in her in-depth investigation there are no precise figures with regard to the number of prisoners apprehended during the two months in which the stadium functioned as a concentration camp (between September and November of 1973). Officially, the military *junta* stated that there were approximately seven thousand individuals detained, which increased to almost nine thousand after an incomplete listing was provided by former DINA Chief General Manuel Contreras in 2000. Bonnefoy challenges these numbers, suggesting a figure closer to twenty thousand (p. 14).
127. Sigmund Freud, *The Uncanny*, trans. by David McLintock (London: Penguin Modern Classics, 2003), p. 124.
128. Ibid., p. 132.
129. Victoriano, p. 41.
130. For details on the visits of Heywnoski and Scheumann and their team to Chile, see Villarroel and Mardones, pp. 131–46.
131. The origin of these pictures remains unclear. Patricio Henríquez, who also includes these images in *Imágenes de una dictadura*, as we shall see, believes that the photographs might have actually been taken by someone inside the stadium. Interview with Patricio Henríquez, 20 October 2012 (via Skype).
132. Besides the frequent use of these images in documentary, they have also been included in books.

One of these pictures is on the front cover of the testimonial account of poet Jorge Montealegre who as a very young man was taken prisoner at the stadium. Jorge Montealegre, *Frazadas del Estadio Nacional* (Santiago: LOM, 2003).
133. The concepts of 'concentrationary imaginaries' and 'concentrationary memories' have gained traction in the field of memory studies in recent years, as evidenced by the publication of a series of volumes edited by Griselda Pollock and Max Silverman, such as *Concentrationary Memories: Totalitarian Terror and Cultural Resistance* (London: I.B. Tauris, 2014) and *Concentrationary Imaginaries: Tracing Totalitarian Terror in Popular Culture* (London: I.B. Tauris, 2015).
134. Didi-Huberman, *Images in Spite of All*, p. 36.
135. Scarry, p. 27.
136. Ibid., p. 28.
137. 'The Hooded man' confessed his role to the Vicaría de la Solidaridad and was murdered weeks later, events which are also reported through newspaper clips and written texts in Parot's documentary.
138. Oscar Ranzani, 'El realizador chileno Patricio Henríquez en el DOCBSAS/07: Un buque escuela, de terror', *Página 12*, 18 October 2007 <http://www.pagina12.com.ar/diario/suplementos/espectaculos/5-7990-2007-10-18.html> [accessed 10 November 2018].
139. Interview with Patricio Henríquez, 20 October 2012 (via skype).

CHAPTER 3

Chilean Documentary Wanderings: Journeys of *Desexilio*

This chapter establishes continuities rather than ruptures in Chilean documentary through a focus on cinematic homecomings both before and after the democratic restoration. I examine the production of exilic directors, including works by a generation subjected to exile as a consequence of their parents' banishment. My emphasis is on documentaries by women directors in which the notion of political displacement is inscribed as a discursive and formal strategy incarnated in the travelling trope. Drawing on the influential neologism coined by Uruguayan writer Mario Benedetti, I conceive of these works of cinematic wanderings as documentaries of *desexilio* in order to stress that the experience of exile never comes to a halt, even after returning.[1]

I first analyse documentaries from the early 1980s, foregrounding key aesthetic features such as the act of return and the uncanny encounter with the city, the focus on intimate space, and performativity, all of which will be mobilized later by post-dictatorship productions. Before examining works from the post-authoritarian period, such as documentaries directed by Lucía Salinas, Carmen Castillo, Antonia Rossi, and Macarena Aguiló, I discuss the *burden of representation* carried by Chilean cinema after the military coup, a symbolic weight that crystallizes in the iconic images of La Moneda in flames.

In addition to the seminal work on Chilean cinema in exile developed by Zuzana M. Pick, my readings of these documentaries are influenced by Hamid Naficy and Laura U. Marks, who have distinguished cinematic accounts of displacement as having a strong emphasis on the senses. These affective cinematic homecomings contribute both to the building and complication of the trajectory proposed in this book, as the experience of exile cuts across several decades in national film history. The bridge enabled by the idea of *desexilio* illustrates that the itinerary undertaken by Chilean documentary from a 'cinema of the affected' to a 'cinema of affect' is not a teleological one.

Narratives of *Desexilio*: The Bridge Between the Past and the Present

After the military coup, Chilean cinema resumed quickly in exile, where documentary continued to be the dominant mode of production. In an interview published in 1979, director Raúl Ruiz, the most prolific and emblematic figure of Chilean exile cinema, referred to the 'paradoxical circumstance' of the thriving filmic production in exile, which he also believed 'unique in the history of film'.[2] According to Ruiz's explanation of this cultural phenomenon, this was 'not due only to the fertility of Chilean producers but also [to] the interest which Chile roused in the whole world as a *symbolic example of the universal political crisis*' (my emphasis).[3] The director claimed that Chilean filmmakers were producing quite heterogeneous works as a natural outcome of the fact that they were located in various countries, and hence they were impacted by the different social and economic characteristics of these places. Ruiz added that political divergences did exist and these particular differences were evident both in their films as well as in their interpretation of the political developments in Chile. He continued: 'We are trying to understand the significance of the crisis of Leninism on the one hand and the crisis of political cinema on the other; the disappearance of the whole symbolic system which was the basis of the political cinema during the 60's in the whole world, not only in Chile'.[4] In his interpretation, Ruiz is recognizing the heterogeneity of Chilean cinema in exile due to its particular conditions of production. Importantly, he also foregrounds the symbolic value that Chile, and by extension, its cinema, acquired in the fall of the socialist projects and the transformation of the notion of the political that followed this collapse.

Antonio Skármeta also refers to this 'undeniable paradox', stating 'that it was only with the exile of Chile's talents — both novices and the established — that Chilean cinema really began to develop. Previously it had operated on a makeshift, almost candlelit basis'.[5] This, as Skármeta stresses, was due to a lack of a proper film industry and to the limited available resources in Chile, a situation that was by no means exclusive to Salvador Allende's government but became critical during the UP because of the economic sanctions imposed by the US.[6] Therefore, I believe that the pivotal role that Chilean exile cinema played in the development of this country's film production and in its internationalization cannot be emphasized enough, as was argued early by scholars such as Zuzana M. Pick, Jacqueline Mouesca, John King, and Peter Schumann, among others. These authors have tackled the work carried out by Chilean directors in exile in helpful ways, in particular between 1973 and 1983. I aim to expand on the scholarship on this fertile period of production, providing some insights about the years that immediately followed with a focus on narratives of return from 1983 onwards.

Although democracy was officially reestablished in 1990, numerous people who had gone into exile had begun to return years before, motivated by the general social uprising that exploded in the context of the economic crisis that devastated the country in the early 1980s. Naturally, Chilean filmmakers wanted to come back 'home' and register the radical transformations of the social, political, and geographical landscape of the country they were forced to leave years before. From the end of 1982 onwards, when the first lists with the few names of the people allowed to return from exile began to be published by the dictatorship,[7] directors too began their homecomings. In some cases, however, they had to make use of several subterfuges to enter the country as they were still forbidden from returning.

The year 1983 is considered a turning point, not only in Chilean history (due to the popular uprisings that eventually led to Pinochet's defeat in the 1988 plebiscite) but also in Chilean cinema. According to Mouesca, the unique period of Chilean cinema in exile came to an end at this time.[8] For the film historian, one key work signals the end of this prolific period and the beginning of a new one: *Chile, no invoco tu nombre en vano* (*Chile, I Don't Invoke Your Name in Vain*) (1983) produced by Colectivo Cine-Ojo, which was anonymous at the time.[9] Mouesca argues that this documentary was the first to build a clear bridge between the two threads of Chilean cinema because it was shot in the country by local filmmakers and edited in Paris by those in exile. She also states that this was the first film to deal wholeheartedly with Chile's current affairs.

I also view 1983 as a turning point in Chilean cinema, but for reasons other than those given by Mouesca. First of all, earlier films had already brought together Chilean directors working in exile and in Chile, such as *Recado de Chile* (1978) (filmed in Chile and edited in Cuba through an anonymous collective effort) or *Gracias a la vida, o la pequeña historia de una mujer maltratada* [*Thanks to Life, or the Little Story of a Mistreated Woman*] (Angelina Vázquez, 1980) (a feature film that includes documentary footage of everyday life in Chile, that was smuggled out of the country).[10] Secondly, to state, like Mouesca does, that Chilean exile cinema comes to an end at this point — or any other date for that matter — presupposes that exile is an experience with an expiration date. The very experience of displacement calls this presupposition into question and the nature of how contemporary Chilean cinema has developed further challenges to this claim. Although a number of directors returned to the country, many others remained abroad. The fact that several of them have engaged in more than one cinematic homecoming, in most cases long after democracy was restored, bears witness to the endless experience of exile. In addition, I contend that Mouesca overlooks a crucial aspect of this particular historical juncture: the foregrounding of performativity in these cinematic returns, a consideration that serves more productively in understanding the early 1980s as a shifting point. Certainly, during that decade the so-called cinema *de barricada* was developed hand in hand with the riots and other collective actions. Yet, in parallel to the proliferation of this openly rebellious cinema, a less strident, tangential approach to the political struggle was also taking place.

According to Pick, it was the experience of exile that contributed to the development of a different approach to the revolutionary struggle and facilitated personal experience as a site for reflection. Exile, in her view,

> has been crucial to the production of a new political agency whereby community associations are relocated, cultural specificity is renegotiated, and cultural affiliations are reconstructed. Geographic and cultural displacement has fostered decentred views on identity and nationality, stressed the dialectics of historical and personal circumstance, and validated autobiography as a reflective site.[11]

Contact with Chilean reality provided returning directors with new possibilities to continue exploring what Pick calls the 'subjective paradox' of exile — a hybrid cinematic practice that oscillates between the directors' cultural origins and the foreign formations they adopted.[12] From the early 1980s onwards, Chilean directors have engaged in deeply affective and performative 'documentary journeys', to borrow a phrase from Stella Bruzzi. In her view, this journey is constructed around multiple encounters (not only between the director and her subject, but also between her and the spectator, with the director often being side-tracked by these encounters) and presents varying degrees of reflexivity (questioning the nature of non-fiction representation).[13]

As these early homecoming documentaries bear witness, exile did not come to a halt when it legally ended or when democracy was finally reinstated in 1990. Scholars examining Chilean exile have been quite emphatic on this point.[14] Loreto Rebolledo states in her article 'Memorias del des/exilio', a study of the memories of Chilean returnees (including second generation accounts), that the longed-for homecoming is never complete and adds yet another loss to what had already been experienced in banishment.[15] Rebolledo draws implicitly upon Benedetti's influential neologism to emphasize the impossibility of return. As Benedetti explains, he coined the term to stress the difficulties faced by Latin American returnees in their respective homelands.[16] To his mind, if nostalgia is a distinctive feature of exile, then one cannot discard that returnees experience *counter-nostalgia*.[17] Benedetti wonders, '¿hasta qué punto los que regresen comprenderán ese país distinto que van a encontrar?' [to what extent will those who return understand the different country they are due to encounter?].[18] Rebolledo, in turn, synthesizes the exile-return trajectory as one that remains unresolved, in which 'la escisión, el sentirse dividido en dos, no se logra resolver con el regreso, simplemente se invirte la nostalgia' [the split, to feel divided in two, is not resolved with the return; nostalgia is merely inverted].[19]

The notion of *desexilio* is useful to emphasize historical and political specificities as well as the permanence of such an experience of geographical and temporal dislocation. In addition, I draw on it not so much to linger on nostalgia, but because it usefully underscores the transformations brought about by the act of return.[20] It is in this sense that I conceive of the documentaries under analysis in this section as journeys of *desexilio*. I include within such a term the cinematic homecomings produced both prior to and after the democratic restoration, including films by directors who experienced exile directly and the works of directors whose parents were banished. Expatriation affected irrevocably the constitution of the nuclear family and that of the nation.[21] All the documentaries analysed in this chapter bring such reconfigurations of nation and family to the fore. Consequently, a reflection on Chilean exile cinema cannot ignore the voices of younger generations.

Before focusing on the specific aesthetic features present in documentary returns of the post-dictatorship period, it is necessary to go back to the homecomings of the 1980s, since the narratives of *desexilio* in this decade are key precedents of first-person documentary that would bourgeon in post-2000 Chile. As I see it, the autobiographical and performative dimensions that characterize these works offer possible points of encounter for the establishment of intergenerational continuities.

I engage in this task consciously aware of the fact that it goes against the grain. According to Chilean film critic Jorge Letelier:

> la dificultad de comprobar algún tipo de herencia estética perdurable dentro del cine chileno es un hecho indesmentible. La negación o el desconocimiento de su propia historia [...] ha sido un sello que ha acompañado los primeros cien años de la historia fílmica nacional [...] el gran fantasma al que se enfrentan las nuevas generaciones.[22]

> [the difficulty in verifying any kind of persisting aesthetic heritage within Chilean cinema is undeniable. The negation or ignorance of its own history [...] has been a hallmark that has accompanied the first hundred years of the national film history [...] the big phantasm which new generations need to face].

Letelier's account is devastating, and, I believe, not erroneous. Yet fortunately it can also be nuanced. The emphasis on discontinuities is itself taken to be part of a Latin American cultural tradition. Ruiz himself has defined Chilean cinema history as a headless one:

> To try to understand the history of Latin America as a continuing process of cause and effect is a mistake. It has to be understood through metaphor, as bodies which grow and are decapitated, followed by great voids. Chilean cinema is just this, founded four or five consecutive times, destroyed and re-created again, to start from zero.[23]

This sort of claim, as Doris Sommer remarks, is characteristic of the cultural history of the region.[24] Sommer also notes how writers of the literary 'boom' emphasized the apparent novelty of their generation by describing themselves as 'fatherless' (as Chilean writer José Donoso declared). Such claims, Sommer argues, locate the 'boom' in the whole literary tradition characteristic of the region; one that she describes as a 'counter-tradition of repeated denials'.[25] A similar 'fatherless' generational claim has also been brought forward by some younger film directors, who, as seen earlier, consider themselves to be part of an 'orphaned' generation as a result of the coup and its violent legacy.[26]

Despite the enduring break imposed by the coup — in fact, precisely because of it — I am interested in establishing possible bridges between younger generations and the rich exilic production. In a way, bringing these early documentaries of return into discussion is an attempt to make sense of my own encounter with some of these exilic films, which have been condemned to remain outside Chile for far too long.

As I see it, trying to create continuities between these productions is a political imperative. In this project, I draw upon the work of scholars such as Lessie Jo Frazier, who considers attempts to create historical connections as both strategic and necessary in the context of Chile's struggles over memory.[27] Frazier argues that attempts to elaborate the past as 'counter-memory' as famously theorized by Michel Foucault (who favours discontinuities and ruptures) must be tempered in the Chilean context.[28] Particularly, she claims that memories of the past have been subject to an official and 'homogenizing project of national reconciliation',[29] a context in which social actors 'have only a precarious hold on the power to organically connect "state" and "society", and thereby to forge a national memory'.[30] If the exilic condition is essentially 'a discontinuous state of being',[31] as defined by Edward W. Said, it is precisely by weaving through these exilic narratives, as paradoxical as it may seem, that intergenerational continuities might be established in my proposed trajectory.

In 1983, the same year that a number of mass demonstrations began to shake the pillars of the dictatorship, two exilic directors showed their groundbreaking returns to Chile on European television. Ruiz released his *Lettre d'un cinéaste ou le retour d'un amateur de bibliothèques* [*Letter from a Filmmaker or The Return of a Library Lover*] (1983) in France and Angelina Vázquez presented her *Fragmentos de un diario inacabado/ Otteita Keskenjääneestä Päiväkirjasta* [*Fragments from an Unfinished Diary*] (1983) in Finland. In the following years, Claudio Sapiaín would also return from Sweden in *Det var några som hade kommit från Chile...(They Were the Ones Who Came from Chile)* (1987) and Miguel Littin from Spain in *Acta general de Chile* [*General Statement on Chile*] (1986).

Ruiz's homecoming, most likely the first of these cinematic returns,[32] stands as an example of a 'reflexive journey' par excellence as defined by Bruzzi, in that it offers 'a commentary beyond the journey undertaken, frequently on the nature of filmmaking', in which the voyage itself does not follow a linear development.[33] Since talking about Ruiz's work is never a straightforward endeavour, his filmic return has been described as 'the documentary version of a Ruizian fiction'.[34] The director's dreamlike film letter is shot both on Super-8 and 16mm,[35] which seems to me an explicit attempt to explore both the materiality of film and the texture of memory (in Chile, at the time, the dominant medium was video). By using these two gauges, he is advancing at least two characteristics common in post-dictatorship documentary: the turn towards the domestic sphere (Super-8 has been long considered the privileged home movie format) and the merging of different formats in order to convey the past cinematically. Ruiz's homecoming, at once nostalgic and amusing, has been analysed elsewhere,[36] but here I would like to emphasize two points. Firstly, the director's return to his childhood home evidently does not refer to the present. As the narrator who 'dubs' Ruiz's voice explicitly says, he is moved by the desire to reconstruct his memories of the night preceding 11 September 1973. Secondly, I would stress that this is a strongly synaesthetic film; as Marks and Naficy underline, this is a salient feature of exilic and diasporic cinemas.[37] Ruiz's film is constructed around the mystery of a missing pink book that mirrors in turn Santiago's lack of colour, a distinctly chromatic aspect that has been emphasized in both fiction and documentary films dealing with the dictatorial period. The missing pink book points poignantly not just towards the failure of the revolutionary project but also to the fact that *el pueblo* has vanished: there is no trace of past or present collective action in Ruiz's wanderings.

In view of its particular conditions of production (it was filmed in Chile and completed in Finland), *Fragmentos de un diario inacabado*, like its contemporary, *Chile, no invoco tu nombre en vano*, also functions as a bridge between the two strands of Chilean cinema. In early 1983, Vázquez made a semi-clandestine entry into Chile to shoot a documentary. Although forbidden from returning, she managed to cross the border with her recently acquired Spanish passport, remaining undetected by the border police (Vázquez is the daughter of Spanish refugees who settled in Chile during the Civil War). A few weeks after her arrival, however, she was located by Pinochet's secret police and forced to leave. She had not yet filmed a single frame. Since Vázquez was confident she would be able to complete the film regardless of the outcomes of her underground entry, she directed it from Finland, naming it *Fragmentos de un diario inacabado*. The film resulted from a close collaboration between Vázquez and a team led by director Pablo Perelman in Chile. (Perelman had already returned to the country and would subsequently direct *Imagen latente* [*Latent Image*] (1987), a feature film with autobiographical traits that was censored by Pinochet's regime). Vázquez's documentary brings together elements of the diary and the epistolary film, and even of the travelogue. It is constructed around the poetic notes of the director's travel journal and it also includes footage gathered throughout the country. In addition, the film also stands as a message of resistance and survival sent both to the director and to the wider world. It features a female narrator who speaks in the first-person voice as though the director herself were speaking. But it was read in Finnish by her close friend and collaborator Anita Mikkonen, thus underscoring the director's exilic condition.[38]

These two seminal homecoming films anticipate a number of stylistic and discursive strategies that have become common in post-dictatorship documentary. These include a fragmented construction (emphasized in Vázquez's film by the inter-titles and the multiple testimonial voices, and in Ruiz's letter by the use of a disjointed voiceover); the autobiographical dimension and the use of the first-person narrator; the allegory of Santiago as a sick city (a 'schizophrenic' one, according to Vázquez, a colourless city, according to Ruiz) and the deeply affective, textured materiality of the past. Although these early returns do not disregard the radical transformations the country was going through, these are not mere homecomings in the present tense, as already suggested, but they also address the country the directors kept in their memories. This return to the past, both literal and metaphorical, will see a reemergence in post-dictatorship documentary. In all these productions, the trope of return appears as a fundamental narrative device and as a formal strategy in which the directors inscribe not just their subjectivity but prompt a more sensuous contact between the spectator and the images, while conveying the directors' own uncanny (dis)encounter with the recent past.

Littin's *Acta general de Chile* is arguably the most well known of these 1980s homecomings, as Gabriel García Márquez's book on the director's clandestine return contributed greatly to the documentary's visibility.[39] When compared with the aforementioned cinematic homecomings, this film seems to waver between being a four-hour epic coproduction saturated with information and an intimate reflection upon a rediscovered country by an exiled filmmaker in permanent danger. Littin's film could indeed be located in the antipodes of Ruiz's Super-8 cinematic return to his parents' house in Huelén Street and to a ghost-like country. Littin's *Acta general de Chile* is from the outset (even from its very title) an *orchestrated super-production*, whereas Ruiz's short film rejoices in its status as a *chamber film*.⁴⁰ Maya Deren's analogy is appropriate here. Her notion of *chamber* refers not only to the 'economy of means'⁴¹ of such productions but also points to the presence of an intimate space. Pick has characterized the filmic exploration of the exilic condition at its best as 'an inquiry into cinematic discourse capable of expressing a distinct sense of being in the world, as if in *a room of one's own*' (emphasis in the original).⁴² The fact that she is implicitly drawing on the work of feminist writer Virginia Woolf is no coincidence. Interior spaces, be they interstitial or transitional, are those inhabited by these *chamber films*, like the majority of documentaries directed during the post-dictatorship by exilic and diasporic female filmmakers, as will be discussed in the second section of this chapter.

While Michelle Bossy and Constanza Vergara posit Sapiaín's film as an important precursor of what they term the 'autobiographical' documentary in Chile,⁴³ local scholars tend to overlook these early productions, emphasizing the presence of first-person documentary in the post-dictatorship period as a novelty.⁴⁴ The focus on these early documentaries sheds new light on the ways that current production is often conceptualized. These early homecoming returns offer a fruitful entry point for approaching the most recent ways of addressing the past as well as for establishing continuities between different generations and historical periods. It can be seen from these works that the topic of the dictatorship had already begun to be construed from renewed angles, both thematically and formally, even when the country was under siege. In many cases, the raw material was aligned with that of the dominant documentary production (such as demonstrations, repression, and soup kitchens). Yet the treatment of such material was filtered through a greater degree of formal reflexivity and performativity, foregrounding the presence of the filmmakers and the constructedness of their works by which they fostered alternative political stances.

Not all of these returning directors, many of which sought to actively contribute to the fall of the dictatorship, inscribed their experiences of exile and return on an explicitly formal level in their works. *En nombre de Dios* [*In the Name of God*] (Patricio Guzmán, 1986) and *Dulce patria* [*Sweet Country*] (Andrés Racz, 1986) documented instead what was happening in the streets, taking an overtly activist and militant stance, merging numerous testimonies with images of both revolt and brutal repression.

After the democratic restoration, directors continued with their homecomings. Carmen Castillo, Patricio Guzmán, and Raúl Ruiz repeatedly returned to Chile from France, where they remained based, inscribing their displacements with different aesthetics. Two of the most relevant early returns in the 1990s are those of Lucía Salinas, who returns from Australia with *Canto a la vida* (1990) and Castillo's *La flaca Alejandra* (1994). Since 2003, these returns have blossomed: Marilú Mallet comes back with *La cueca sola* (2003), Emilio Pacull returns with *Héroes frágiles* [*The Conspiracy*] (2006), and Leopoldo Gutiérrez with *El soldado que no fue* (2010). Pacull sets out to reveal the active role of the US in the coup via expert testimonies; Mallet centres on the testimonies of four courageous Chilean women from different generations who challenge traditional representations of women-as-victims; and Gutiérrez gives voice to men like him who had once been young conscripts and were caught by the coup while doing their military service. These three documentaries are more concerned with understanding specific aspects of a less 'official' history rather than performativity or the filmmaker's 'subjective paradox'.

The children of people who were exiled also began to 'return' from 2003 onwards and would go on to inscribe their own multiple displacements. These include Alejandra Carmona in *En algún lugar del cielo* [*Somewhere in Heaven*] (2003), Antonia Rossi in *El eco de las canciones* [*The Echo of Songs*] (2010), Macarena Aguiló in *El edificio de los chilenos* [*The Chilean Building*] (2010, codirected by Susana Foxley), Germán Berger-Hertz in *Mi vida con Carlos* (2010), Rodrigo Dorfman in *Generation Exile* (2010), and Simón Bergman in *En resa till världens ände* [*A Trip to the End of the World*] (2011). However, the homecomings of these children seem, in a way, less straightforward than those of the generation that preceded them. Where is home for these children of exile? Germany, Italy, France, Cuba, Spain, the United States, Finland? Chile? For Rossi, it seems that images and sounds of Chile reverberated strongly for her in Italy; for Carmona, it is a rigid communist Germany where she experienced her rebel coming-of-age; for Aguiló, it is a communal family in Cuba. In the cases of Dorfman and Berger-Hertz, their own multiple geographical journeys are emotionally intertwined with those of their grandparents as Holocaust survivors. Likewise, in Bergman's case (Angelina Vázquez's son), his return from Finland to Chile is intricately entangled with his maternal grandparents' displacement as refugees from the Spanish Civil War and the travels of his grandfather, a Finnish cap-hornier. The fact that home radically changed and is no longer Chile also strikingly filters through the voice of director Camila Guzmán in a documentary set in Cuba titled *El telón de azúcar* [*The Sugar Curtain*] (2007). The film of Patricio Guzmán's daughter, who was raised on the island after the director's exile, is concerned with the memories of a generation of Cubans who grew up in the 1980s before the so-called 'Special Period'. It does not discuss the memories of the Chilean youth, but her Caribbean accent is a spectre that hovers the film as a whole, inscribing her exilic condition. Before entering into a discussion of some of these exiled directors' 'rooms of their own', it is necessary to expand on why approximations to Chilean contemporary cinema cannot ignore the tension around the forceful indexical images of the UP and the dictatorial period that followed. Some of this iconic footage has weighed heavily on cinematographic production, haunting, as it were, the cinematic landscape ever since 1973. I understand the first-person narratives analysed in this chapter as one of Chilean documentary's most distinctive responses to such a loaded imagery.

Symbolic Weight, or How to Deal with La Moneda in Flames?

Authors have described Chile as a country in which the weight of the dictatorial past is so utterly strong that it overdetermines the present.[45] If, as Joanna Page asserts, Latin American films 'are always overdetermined as national cultural products made at the periphery of a global culture industry',[46] in Chile, productions are also profoundly marked by the haunting presence of the authoritarian past. Contemporary Chilean cinema seems more often than not to be measured against the background of the dictatorship. It has been equally praised or criticized, by local and foreign audiences, as well as by film critics and directors themselves, for either being able to confront this painful past or for disregarding it. In an interview with *Sight and Sound*, Sebastián Silva, the director of the feature films *La nana* [*The Maid*] (2009) and *Magic Magic* (2013), elaborated the following impression when referring to the state of Latin American cinema:

> There are also many South American film-makers making political films because they know that speaking about the dictatorships or showing abuses of human rights sells best in Europe and helps them get their films into prestigious festivals. North America is not so receptive to this kind of cinema, because they are a little bit less condescending than Europe in that respect. In general, Europe enjoys Latin American suffering and misery in an aesthetic way.[47]

Although Silva avoids referring to the Chilean case, he is implicitly articulating a tension present in national cinema that is anything but new and can be traced back to before the coup; one that can be seen as *the burden of representation*.[48] Silva's words echo those of Colombian directors Luis Ospina and Carlos Mayolo in the late 1970s, who coined the term '*porno-miseria*' (poverty-porn) to complain about documentary's tendency to expose in an obscene way the socio-economic suffering of the country, particularly to foreign audiences.[49]

During the UP in Chile, Ruiz delivered a similar critique of what he used to call, with his characteristic wittiness, the 'Quilapayún culture'.[50] *Quilapayún* is one of the most representative bands of 'Nueva Canción Chilena' which developed in parallel with the so-called 'Nuevo Cine Chileno' in the 1960s and 1970s (they used traditional *ponchos* and embraced folk roots from the Andean region to the detriment of more hybrid forms of expression). For Ruiz, this trend came to represent in cinema the official history in that it substituted some 'official myths' for others based on purist and abstract aspects of the class struggle that, in addition to showing disrespect for reality, 'were also likely to prove politically ineffective, if not counter-productive'.[51] After the coup, Ruiz offered a similar critique of exilic production:

> I think there is a version of the 'official art' attitude which sets out to make 'history' exist. [...] there is an obvious point in making films to reveal this forgotten history and make known the secret massacres. But it is more difficult to accept when it becomes an imperative duty to follow the political line, showing even more massacres and creating a vast funeral ceremony.[52]

Ruiz's conception of cinema came to be understood in stark opposition to that of Littín's; the two directors being often located at two extreme poles of cinematic practice (as I do too, in fact, in the previous section).[53] Whereas Ruiz once famously described his own tangential approach to the Chilean revolutionary process as an 'irresponsible' one,[54] Littín's overtly militant stance made him largely known as 'the epic film-maker of Latin American resistance'.[55]

A similar debate continued through the 1980s in Chile.[56] In 1989, art critic Justo Pastor Mellado evaluated the state of video-art, which he saw as standing in stark opposition to documentary, expressing a critique similar to that articulated by Silva:

> nuestra particularidad nos condena. Más bien, la representación que los otros se hacen de nuestra particularidad. De partida, hemos tenido que luchar contra el imperialismo del video militante, que, desde las condiciones de represión cultural que compartíamos, intentó siempre dictarnos la línea. Las producciones de video militante pasaron a ser el 'Tío Tom' de los festivales europeos.

> [our particularity condemns us. Better said, the representation that others make of our particularity. To begin with, we have had to fight against the imperialism of the militant video, which, from the conditions of cultural repression that we shared, always attempted to dictate us the line. Militant video productions became the 'Uncle Tom' of European film festivals.][57]

Germán Liñero points out that the words of Mellado shed light on the burden that weighed upon Chilean artistic production, which persisted long after the dictatorship ended. In Liñero's view:

> La urgencia del proceso de resistencia era reforzada desde el resto de mundo por las lecturas de lo que debía o no ser financiado o financiable como producción cultural, en la medida que sirviese al proceso de recuperación de la democracia o no, cuestión que condicionó la producción cultural y la de videos incluso hasta bastante avanzada la década de los noventa.

> [The urgency of the process of resistance was enforced from the outside world by readings of what should be financed or not as cultural production, inasmuch as it served the process of democratic recovery. This issue conditioned cultural production and that of videos even well into the nineties.][58]

I quote these various voices because they all point to the conundrum faced by Chilean cinema after 11 September 1973: from that day onwards it would carry the weight of dealing with the coup and its aftermaths. This weight is epitomized most clearly by the recurring image of the bombing of the governmental palace La Moneda. The question that haunts documentary in the post-dictatorship era can thus be posed in the following terms: how to deal with such a *burden of representation*? In other words, how to deal with La Moneda in flames? As historian Alan Angell states, 'it is difficult to exaggerate the impact of the Chilean coup on the political consciousness of a wide variety of countries.'[59] The images of La Moneda being bombed, Pinochet behind dark glasses, the prisoners in the Estadio Nacional, and soldiers burning piles of books in the streets, all of which were broadly circulated around the world, virtually turned Allende's overthrow into the first televised military coup.[60]

Directors in exile would make extensive use of these iconic images together with the sounds of the period, such as revolutionary songs and radio transmissions, creating a veritable 'emblematic set of *affective* and *political* codes' to preserve the past, to return to Pick's idea cited in Chapter 2.[61] This cinematic repertoire continues to be drawn upon in contemporary productions while at the same time keeps expanding. It includes today images of social turmoil during the 1980s (mass demonstrations, police repression, helicopters overflying the city); images of atrocities in the 1990s (particularly of exhumed bodies); and, since the 2000s, the repertoire has opened up to include more personal, domestic archives (for example, home movies and family photographs).

Throughout the years, however, there is an image that has repeatedly been used in film productions: the bombing of La Moneda in black and white, as it appears in *La batalla de Chile*. Other images of the attack against the governmental palace have been unveiled in recent years, such as Juan Ángel Torti's raw footage filmed in 16mm and in colour. Torti captured the silent images of the jets and the smoke from a roof during the coup and, two days later, of La Moneda in ruins.[62] Nevertheless, it is the black and white sequence of La Moneda the one that has been subjected to unceasing repetition, reproduction, and remediation in various films, the media, photographs, and so on, becoming increasingly problematic. As César Barros writes, the historical value of it, 'its historical thickness, so to speak, has become thinner and thinner'.[63]

Arguably, memories of the coup will lose their intensity with the passing of time, with some 'irruptions of memory' in the national public sphere every now and then, as seen previously. Paradoxically, it will be another 9/11 that will awake a renewed interest in the international sphere in Chile's own 11 September. Lingering 'like a specter over the dominant narrative'[64] — that of the US as a victim of a terrorist attack — counter-narratives made by a number of intellectuals, such as Ariel Dorfman and Noam Chomsky, would touch on the uncanny parallelism of those dates,[65] not only critically referring to the so-called 'war on terror' but also evaluating the role that the US actively played in Chile's own September. In film, this critique would be undertaken by Ken Loach in his short documentary on this 'other' 9/11 through the experience of a Chilean refugee in the UK, included in the omnibus production *11'09"01 — September 11* (2002). Such an uncanny parallelism has also been drawn out in productions by Chilean directors such as *11 de septiembre* (Claudia Aravena, 2002), *I Wonder What You Will Remember of September* (Cecilia Cornejo, 2004) and *EEUU vs Allende* (Diego Marín and José Alayón, 2008). In her short video, Aravena chooses to split the screen to establish a direct parallel between those dates, while also evoking other historical catastrophes by including footage of *Hiroshima mon amour* (Alan Resnais, 1959); Cornejo uses both 9/11s in an essay addressed to her daughter raised in the US, while mobilizing her own sensorial memories of the 11 September as a child; and Marín and Ayalón begin their documentary with images of the attack on the Twin Towers before an analytical account of the US' active intervention in the military coup unfolds. These diverse works illustrate — through their return, once more, to the images of La Moneda under attack — that the old political and affective codes referred to by Pick continue to be extensively used. Yet some of them — as crystallized by the governmental palace in flames — have become increasingly challenging.

The turning point was the commemorative fever that arose in 2003. That 'memory must be created against the overabundance of information as well as against its absence',[66] as Jacques Rancière writes, was forcefully brought to the forefront in critical debates in the context of the commemorations of the thirtieth anniversary of the coup. Although, as seen earlier, scholars like Steve Stern praised such renewed interest in the past, others, such as writer Diamela Eltit, formulated a harsh critique against the flood of images on television. According to Eltit, their sudden and explosive emergence not only showed that the commemorations were 'enteramente bajo control' [entirely under control] but that the idea behind their release was to 'poner punto final a las imágenes. Las aniquilan a partir de un exceso' [put a final stop to the images. To annihilate them through excess].[67]

Drawing upon Eltit's view, Iván Pinto described such an overflow of images as a '*déficit* cinematográfico producido a causa de un *exceso* de imaginario' [a cinematographic *deficit* produced due to an *excess* of imagery] (emphasis in the original).[68] It is in this context that one has to read philosopher's Federico Galende's severe critique of *Salvador Allende*, which was released a year after this anniversary. Galende challenges Guzmán over what he sees as a:

> curiosa voluntad [...] por volver una vez más, siendo tan rica nuestra era en imágenes de la destrucción, a la *Moneda* (sic) bombardeada, un recurso que, naturalizando un tipo de percepción sensorial ya modificado por la reproducción técnica de la desgracia, le permite envasar el caleidoscopio de la historia en una imagen fetiche.[69]
>
> [curious determination [...] to return once more to the image of la *Moneda bombarded*, even with us living in a time so rich in images of destruction. This resource, which naturalizes a sensorial type of perception already modified for the technical reproduction of disgrace, allows him to encapsulate history's kaleidoscope within a fetish image.]

Documentary filmmakers have also expressed certain weariness with regard to this particular imagery of violence. Though not referring to Guzmán's oeuvre explicitly (certainly he is not the only one who has persisted in using the images of the bombardment of La Moneda), Pachi Bustos (codirector of *Actores secundarios*) notes:

> hay otras películas anteriores que en el fondo también abordan los '80, incluso los '70, pero siempre aparece la imagen de La Moneda, el bombardeo, el Golpe de Estado. Son como muy antiguos, en el fondo no avanzan a lo que está pasando hoy día. Yo creo que la gracia de nuestro documental o de *Malditos* [*Malditos: La historia de los Fiskales Ad-Hok* (*Damned: The History of the Fiskales Ad-Hok*) (Pablo Insunza, 2004)] es que tienen una mirada crítica respecto a la realidad que vivimos y al país que se ha construido a partir de los '90. *Nosotros nos sentimos orgullosos de no haber puesto ninguna imagen de La Moneda, del bombardeo a La Moneda.*
>
> [there are earlier films that also deal with the '80s, even the '70s, but there is always the image of La Moneda, of the bombing, of the military coup. It is as

though they are very old; in the end, they do not move forward towards what is happening today. I think that what distinguishes our documentary or *Malditos* is that they have a critical stance regarding the reality we are living in today and the country that has been constructed since the '90s. *We feel proud of not including a single frame of La Moneda, of the bombing of La Moneda.*] (my emphasis)[70]

Other voices from the post-dictatorship generation(s), such as Iván Osnovikoff, interpret this excess as being, in fact, a manifestation of a 'pobreza de imaginario' [deficient imagery].[71] Interestingly, some of these younger directors mobilize very similar terms as those used by Ruiz (with regard to the 'Quilapayún culture') to set their work against what they regard as dominant narratives. For instance, Paco Toledo, director of *Los escolares se siguen amando* (2000), set around the usual commemorative rituals and violent clashes of the 11 September, sees his documentary in direct opposition to what he describes as 'documental de llanto y música folklórica' [the weeping documentary with folk music].[72] It is not difficult to infer from these younger voices that what is at stake in this discussion is not only *how* to refer to this overwhelming past but also *who* gets to talk about it, a point to which I will return in the following chapters.

The aftermath of the thirtieth anniversary of the coup signalled a reconfiguration of the landscape of documentary, which in turn coincided with a more sustained appearance of these new voices. This turning point meant that the previous emblematic set of codes was either rearticulated or else directly replaced. Directors of different generations engaged in these tasks by different means: through a nostalgic turn towards the struggle of the 1980s (as in the case of *Actores secundarios* or *La ciudad de los fotógrafos* [*City of Photographers*] (Sebastián Moreno, 2006)), an emphasis on the intimate or the domestic sphere (such as the works of Castillo, Aguiló, or Rossi), the creation of discourses about memory (such as *Remitente: una carta visual* [*Postage: A Visual Letter*] (Tiziana Panizza, 2008) or *La quemadura* [*The Burn*] (René Ballesteros, 2009)), or else they turned their lenses toward unsettling voices such as Pinochet's supporters or accomplices (such as *La muerte de Pinochet* [*The Death of Pinochet*] (Bettina Perut and Iván Osnovikoff, 2011) and *El mocito* [*The Young Butler*] (Marcela Said and Jean de Certeau, 2011)). Ruiz, in his early response to this juncture, was quite *Ruizian* (in the absence of a better word). Against the images of corpses that dominated the previous long decade, Ruiz reacted by bringing — literally — those dead bodies back to life. In the first episode of his four part *Cofralandes* the iconic images of murdered bodies lying on the pavement covered by newspapers seen in the direct aftermath of the coup are reworked through a particularly theatrical reenactment; the dead bodies resurrect, raise the newspaper sheets that were covering them, and begin to read them. Although Guzmán's *Nostalgia de la luz* is certainly less playful, these wounded and missing bodies are still central. As discussed in the previous chapter, Guzmán refrains from showing once again footage of La Moneda under attack, offering instead the image of bodies-as-landscapes through the use of haptic sequences. In my view, *Nostalgia de la luz* is largely Guzmán's own reaction to the shift in the post-dictatorship documentary landscape in Chile.

As Valerio Fuenzalida et al. point out, the release of archival material by a number of institutions and national film archives and the circulation of available footage enabled by the historical juncture of the thirtieth anniversary (with the bicentennial celebrations on the horizon) contributed importantly to the reconfiguration of non-fictional and fictional discourses about the past.[73] Alongside this wider circulation of images, advances in the field of human rights also need to be considered when analysing the shifting face of the documentary landscape. The Valech Report, the numerous charges Pinochet was facing after 1998 in terms of violations of human rights, as well as the economic scandal that followed, as detailed in Chapter 1, undoubtedly granted directors more freedom so they could essay different responses to the not-so-recent past. By bearing this context in mind we can better understand the turn from what I call a 'cinema of the affected' towards a 'cinema of affect'.

Although one of the clearest trends of post-2004 production is the proliferation of first-person documentary, it is possible to trace this type of narrator at least back to the work of exilic directors in the early 1980s, as I would like to stress. Women filmmakers are central in this wider shift towards interior worlds, affective narratives and more tangential approaches to politics. B. Ruby Rich writes in her influential revision of the New Latin American Cinema that during the 1980s the production of the region undertook a turn from the 'revolutionary' to the 'revelatory'.[74] Within such a transformation, Rich argues, the focus on everyday life replaced the attention on the evidently political, bringing forth that which is 'implicitly political, at the level of banality, fantasy, and desire, and [involved] a corresponding shift in aesthetic strategies. Such a shift has also, not coincidentally, opened up the field to women'.[75] In the following section, I analyse how this turn towards the 'revelatory' and, more broadly, to the affective realm has seen a reemergence in post-dictatorship documentaries directed by women of different generations whose life and work have been marked by the experience of exile.

Travelling Women, Travelling Memories

Chilean women filmmakers have long been involved in the country's political struggles, as evident in the pioneering work of Valeria Sarmiento, Marilú Mallet, and Angelina Vázquez, who were only starting their careers when they were forced into exile.[76] During the 1980s, an important number of female documentarians, video artists, and photographers also actively engaged in the struggle against dictatorship. This section will explore *desexilio* documentaries made by women of different generations and their material exploration of displacement as inscribed in their narratives, particularly in the travelling shot. I will examine the work of directors who experienced the revolutionary period and/or the repression of Pinochet's dictatorship directly and went into exile, notably Salinas's film *Canto a la vida* and Castillo's *Calle Santa Fe*. I will also refer to the work of directors from a literal second generation who grew up or were born in exile, including Alejandra Carmona's *En algún lugar del cielo*, Macarena Aguiló's *El edificio de los chilenos* and Antonia Rossi's *El eco de las canciones,* to which I return in the next chapter.

Although these works may differ in many senses (mostly, though not exclusively, due to generational differences) my focus here is on their commonalities. All of them were produced after the official return to democracy and they deal with memories of exile and return. Because these documentary journeys are, above all, politically motivated by banishment and point towards 'home' — wherever this may be — I conceive of them as documentaries of *desexilio*. They share an autobiographical dimension conveyed through the use of a female voiceover (in the cases in which the director appears onscreen, the voice belongs to the filmmaker), are built around an intricate connection between the personal and the collective, and achieve powerful temporal blends between the past and the present. It is worth stressing that by using female commentary these women directors subvert the traditional use of the authoritative and patriarchal 'voice-of-God' while also highlight the subjective character of their works. As Bruzzi argues, the use of the female voiceover not only allows women to speak, but also helps emphasize documentary's inability to deliver an ultimate truth.[77] In her view, the woman's voice:

> is not the voice of universality but of specificity, and signals the impossibility and the lack that the single male voice-over frequently masks. [...] A female commentary is thus an overt tool for exposing the untenability of documentary's belief in its capacity for imparting 'generalised truths' faithfully and unproblematically.[78]

In addition, these documentaries are mostly *chamber* films constructed around memories of a lost home; those of the directors but also, in most cases, those of her interviewees, which turns these films into polyphonic narratives. In the case of the younger directors, they also share the use of childlike imagery and points of view, tending toward the use of collage and the incorporation of varying media and techniques, including found footage and animation in the cases of Rossi and Aguiló.

These documentaries seek to create a critical account of Chile's past atrocities and their legacies via what Rancière has called the 'splendor of the insignificant',[79] the details of everyday life. At the same time, they aim to elaborate discourses about memory itself. These filmmakers seek to aesthetically recreate the fragmented and irruptive nature of memory through various mechanisms, notably by the incorporation of images taken in Super-8 and 16mm, family pictures, letters, animation and reenacted sequences. Memories of the recent past assume in these works of exilic directors a profound tactility, as they largely draw upon what Laura Marks calls 'sense memories'.[80] Largely concerned with '[t]he fabric of everyday experience that tends to elude verbal or visual records',[81] these directors turn to their sensorial memories of childhood, from smell to touch. They convey cinematically these affective experiences, privileging haptic images, which are able in turn to trigger in the spectator a specific bodily response.[82] Marks recognizes the haptic properties shared both by film and video, notably 'changes in focus, graininess (achieved differently in each medium), and effects of under- and overexposure'.[83] Undoubtedly, Chilean documentarians are well aware of the possibilities of exploring the materiality of the medium, as many of them acknowledge that their use of 16mm or Super-8 is motivated by a desire to create a textured account of the past, which is most apparent in their reenactment sequences.

In addition to its particular materiality, the Super-8 film gauge bears strong domestic connotations as it is intrinsically linked with the home movie. Initially considered to be 'virtually by definition the documentary of the trivial, the personal and the inconsequential, events of interest only to the family involved',[84] the home movie has been swept into more creative practices, while maintaining a bond with the domestic sphere. The use of actual or reenacted home movies in almost all the works under analysis in this section, as well as the use of family pictures, seem to constantly blur the line between the private and the public realms while illustrating the feminist slogan that 'the personal is political'. Often, this dichotomy is questioned through the use of archival material such as news reportage and newspaper clippings that deal publicly with the tragic events that marked these directors' own experiences. In Castillo's case, this was the death of her partner, Miguel Enríquez, and in Aguiló's case it was her kidnapping as a child by the secret police and the separation from her militant parents; for Carmona, this event was the death of her father, Augusto Carmona, a journalist and also a committed activist. Interestingly, these three documentaries deal with the experience of MIR militants, the radical left-wing party located outside the UP and one of those that was most violently decimated by Pinochet's regime. These directors also use other strategies to highlight the political dimension of their personal experiences. For example, both Castillo and Aguiló perform the ritual of opening their own 'memory boxes' filled with letters and family pictures in front of the camera, and this is, in fact, the starting point of their documentaries. Similarly, Rossi explains that during the production process of making her film, when she was collecting home movies from various people, she felt as though she was entering into other people's memory boxes.[85]

I use the notion of travelling in various interconnected senses here. As explained in the introduction, I understand Chilean post-dictatorship documentary in general as cultural memories that are itinerant.[86] More specifically, since the works analysed here deal with memories of uprootedness, I refer to travelling memories to conceptualize the material experience of exile and dislocation endured by these female directors. The concept also refers to the distinctive use of travelling shots in these works. The documentaries in this section are itinerant in various ways: these accounts vary (are reworked) from generation to generation; this is strikingly evident in Rossi's experimental film that was compiled from assorted home movies, archival images from previous documentaries and excerpts of old animation films. The films also reference each other; for example, Castillo's *Calle Santa Fe* includes images of *El edificio de los chilenos* when it was a work-in-progress. Aguiló's documentary, in turn, incorporates footage from *Éramos una vez* (*Once We Were*) (1979) by exilic director Leonardo de la Barra. They also literally 'travel' from one country to another (some are international coproductions and/or have circulated abroad), yet remain historically and politically grounded, creating memories that are at once strongly local and transnational.

Again, the journeys are profoundly affective, since these women not only travel through the country's recent past but also through their own personal memories. It is the displaced condition of these directors that compels them to challenge the traditional and gendered dichotomy of dwelling and travelling, as well as to foreground the intimate connection between movement and emotion, as noted by Giuliana Bruno.[87] These women's documentaries embody a shift from what Bruno calls an 'old cinematic *voyeur*' to a 'moving vessel of a film *voyageuse*' (emphasis in the original)[88] in which both affection and movement become intricately woven. By journeying, these directors put the past on the move, set nostalgia into motion and challenge reified, monumental, and homogenous versions of the past. These films can be seen as '[a] place where nostalgia is replaced by *transito* — a mobile gap' (emphasis in the original).[89] The fact that motion produces emotion and 'that, correlatively, emotions contains a movement'[90] becomes explicit in the travelling shot, which leads me in fact to the more specific and material sense in which I use the idea of travelling, that of the moving image itself.

There is a recurring use of travelling shots in these works, often from cars, trains, or boats, what Naficy has termed 'thirdspace chronotopes' and in which the exiles' multiple displacements are inscribed.[91] Drawing on Bakhtin's concept of the 'chronotope' (which means literally the unity of time-space) and Edward Soja's notion of 'thirdspace', Naficy defines the particular time-space occupied by the exile as one of the 'thirdspace chronotope'.[92] He explains such temporal and spatial figures as a 'slipzone of simultaneity and intertextuality'[93] between homeland and exile in which everything is brought together (the subjective and the objective, history and the everyday life, sameness and difference, the imagined and the real, the past and the present, and so on). These 'thirdspace chronotopes', according to Naficy, 'are not just visual but also, and more important, synaesthetic, involving the entire human sensorium and memory.'[94] It is in the form of the tracking shot that this 'thirdspace chronotope' more clearly materializes in these *desexilio* documentaries.

The uses of the travelling shot and its connection to the elaboration of complex temporalities that seek to collapse or blend past and present times has a long tradition in the depiction of historical atrocities, which has been traced back to Alain Resnais' *Nuit et brouillard* [*Night and Fog*] (1955).[95] Thus it is not surprising that scholars such as Jens Andermann have similarly remarked upon the noticeable use of this strategy in Argentine post-dictatorship documentary.[96] For the Chilean case, there are at least four different recurring uses of travelling shots when dealing with issues of displacement and memories of the dictatorial past. There is the 'topographical' travelling, a tracking shot that conveys a rather straightforward geographical displacement that often seeks to depict the enormous social divide existing in the country. Examples of this can be found in *I Love Pinochet* (2001) in which director Marcela Said moves through Santiago depicting the obscene class divide to foreground the fact that Pinochet's supporters cut across lines of class, gender, and generation or in Mallet's *La cueca sola*, which similarly exposes the neoliberal transformations as inscribed in the cityscape. Another one is the 'flashback' travelling, which clearly indicates to the spectator that what she is looking at is a reenactment of past events often signposted through the use of a different format than the rest of the documentary (usually 16mm or Super-8). Consider, for example, the takes from inside the train in which Aguiló recalls her exile as a little girl with her mother in France or Castillo's bleak travelling shots in *La flaca Alejandra* depicting Marcia Merino's horrific tour through various detention centres from a subjective point of view. There are also examples of 'time-machine' travelling shots: this camera movement connotes at once a literal and metaphorical journey to the past and the homeland. This can be seen, for instance, in the arrival sequences when the directors return to Chile in *Volver a vernos* [*Pinochet's Children*] (Paula Rodríguez, 2003) or in *En algún lugar del cielo*. In addition to these sequences of arrival filmed on highways that lead to the city of Santiago, the directors explicitly state in their works that theirs is a double return; both to Chile and to the country's past. Finally, there is the 'time-image' travelling: here I draw on Gilles Deleuze's notion of the time-image which, he explains, exhibits a direct presentation of time. In it, 'we are plunged into time rather than crossing space'.[97] In the time-image, space and movement through space are subdued by time, a temporal succession that is no longer linear. The sequence 'past-present-future', as Deleuze explains, is called into question here; in the time-image, 'the sheets of past coexist in a non-chronological order'.[98] Such temporal disruptions, in which 'Time is out of joint' as Deleuze says, quoting Shakespeare's famous line,[99] are the most affective uses granted to the travelling shot in *desexilio* documentaries. Perhaps the most moving of these time-image sequences can be found in a fleeting sequence in Vázquez's homecoming, which I discuss below.

Even if documentaries of *desexilio* are structured precisely around the figure of return, a journey towards home (fleeting, interrupted, incomplete, but at least desired, and hence transformed into a film), the directors seem to engage in temporal digressions rather than just in spatial, geographical displacements. In this regard, their wandering sequences acquire a revelatory power, their films resembling the 'optical unconscious' elaborated by Walter Benjamin where that which is being captured reveals something that is not accessible to the gaze.[100] In the documentaries, the tracking shot points towards that which is not representable and has been lost, yet lingers like a ghostly presence. These travelling shots convey the uncanny experience that the directors encounter when rediscovering a landscape that appears at once strange and familiar. Through this camera movement spectators become involved in a 'mutual relation of recognition' between the image and themselves, in an 'intersubjective' relation, as defined by Marks, in which

> The viewer is called upon to fill in the gaps in the image, to engage with the traces the image leaves. By interacting up close with an image, close enough that figure and ground commingle, the viewer relinquishes her own sense of separateness from the image — not to know it, but to give herself up to her desire for it.[101]

As Edward Said explains, the difficulties of exile are not only about being forced to be away from home, but to be reminded in everyday life that home is so close;

the exile lives 'in constant but tantalizing and *unfulfilled touch* with the old place' (my emphasis).[102] Such impossibility of return is most poignantly inscribed in the truncated return to the country of Vázquez as depicted in her *Fragmentos de un diario inacabado*, which is why I return to this early example. A fleeting though deeply moving travelling sequence, in which the spectator sees the empty streets of a traditional Santiago accompanied by the voiceover of renowned actor and close friend of the director, Héctor Noguera (introduced as 'Tito'), is amongst one of the most affective sequences of Chilean *desexilio* documentaries. This moment is particularly striking, for in it the director's absence becomes explicit. It is true that the numerous testimonies she gathers from a plethora of voices (including survivors and activists) are delivered in the midst of a 'confessional' atmosphere, as Iván Pinto and José Miguel Palacios have rightly noted.[103] Yet, of all of them, Noguera is the only one who addresses his friend, Angelina Vázquez, directly. Through his testimony, whispered in the intimacy of a taxi, Noguera makes evident the filmmaker's absence and the insurmountable distance that lies between them. The window of the car — acting both as a sort of protective shield and as an element producing a separation from that which is beyond it — is the limit that exhibits the ceaseless, though impossible, allure to *touch*.

This travelling shot is a remarkable example of a 'thirdspace chronotope' in which everything is brought together. Here, history and everyday life merge, the intimate and the public are juxtaposed, as are the subjective with the objective dimensions, interiority and exteriority, past and present. Chilean poet Efraín Barquero wrote that exile is 'mirar a las personas como si fueran recuerdos' [to look at people as if they were reminiscences].[104] Movingly, in this travelling shot the city of Santiago emerges as a memory, an inaccessible city for the director exiled in Finland, and by extension, a city that is also inaccessible to us. As this sequence makes clear, these returns to the homeland — both metaphorical and literal — are not mere homecomings in the present tense, but also returns to the country that these directors have kept in their memories.

Canto a la vida is set right in the historical moment of the democratic restoration, and, similar to Vázquez's documentary, is narrated by a first-person female voice (in English in this case) as though it was the director speaking. Salinas's film is a tapestry of the voices of mostly emblematic women of different generations who fled the country after the military coup. Allende's wife Hortensia Bussi, writer Isabel Allende, and folksinger Isabel Parra are some of them. By using a reenacted sequence in black and white that continually irrupts during the narration and which shows the feet of a woman escaping from a soldier — an allegory of women's fear — Salinas carefully weaves these multiple testimonies and succeeds in creating a sense of shared traumatic experience. There is a particularly powerful montage sequence in which the director uses several travelling shots presumably taken from within a car in an Australian city at night. The images are strongly haptic; what is shown from the window are barely distinguishable shapes, lights, textures, all shown in slow motion, depicting virtually unrecognizable forms of a deep grainy quality. In fact, the footage was filmed in Super-8, projected and then filmed again in 16mm, in order to achieve, as Salinas explains, 'a feeling of isolation', of finding oneself suddenly estranged.[105] These images are accompanied by the juxtaposition of the disembodied voices of women who narrate their own stories of discrimination and alienation experienced in exile (voices that intertwine in accented English and Spanish) as though these multiple experiences were one. Salinas offers with it a forceful 'time-image' in which the frontiers of the subjective and the objective, past and the present, the inside and the outside, are collapsed.

Towards the end of her film, Salinas's narrator borrows a line from the also exiled Chilean writer and literary scholar Fernando Alegría to ask a fundamental question: 'Can the years we never lived be recalled?' While the director is referring here to the years under Pinochet's rule that herself and other women were not able to experience because they were living in exile, the question she poses here is one endowed with a profound ethical dimension: who has the right to talk; those who stayed behind or those who left? With this interrogation, Salinas also tackles the guilt that burdens those who left and survived — that of having been 'defeated', as folksinger Isabel Parra puts it in her testimony.

A similar question lies behind *Les murs de Santiago* [*Chile: Ten years of a Strong Man*] (1983), codirected by French filmmakers Fabienne Servan-Schreiber and Pierre Devert, and wrote by Carmen Castillo. This film is relevant as it anticipates many of the features of Castillo's future works such as the mise-en-scène of the exilic condition, the affective dimension of memory, and the use of the lyric first-person voice. Castillo was forbidden to enter the country at the time and that prohibition of return is inscribed through her poetically charged narration, directly addressing her father from Paris at the start of the film. Her voice intervenes intermittently throughout the film, commenting on the images filmed by the French crew. Made for television, the work oscillates between a televisual reportage that registers a portrait of Chilean society at the juncture of Pinochet's first decade in power, and a film letter. For Castillo, in *Les murs de Santiago* it is already possible to see

> esa búsqueda de las huellas, de interrogar desde lejos [...]. Esa necesidad de dialogar con un pasado que ya no es, con un presente que me sorprende, del cual soy expulsada. No tengo legitimidad moral, digamos, para hablar de ese presente, y la única que tengo es de hablar desde la emoción, del exilio.
>
> [a search for traces, of interrogating from afar [...]. That necessity for dialogue with a past that no longer is, with a present that surprises me, from which I am expelled. I do not have moral legitimacy, as it were, to speak about this present. The only one I have is that of speaking from emotion, from exile].

Castillo's post-dictatorship documentary oeuvre — *La flaca Alejandra, El país de mi padre* (*My Father's Country*) (2004) and *Calle Santa Fe* — all of which are *desexilio* documentaries, will further such endeavour. These works share a deep autobiographical and subjective dimension, given now by her onscreen presence, but most significantly, by her prevailing use of lyrical narration. Built around the tension between the public/political and the private/personal spheres, these films give attention to women's testimonies and collective remembering either through family, friends, or former militants.

I have expanded on some of these characteristics elsewhere, emphasizing how Castillo's post-dictatorial work illustrates the transformative potential of women's memories and their ability to challenge hegemonic discourses, not only those of reconciliation and consensus, but also those fostered by the left, dominated by masculine voices and epic accounts of revolution and resistance.[106] Here I would like to stress the affective dimension of her memory work, focusing on some sequences of *Calle Santa Fe*. This is a profoundly affective and polyphonic documentary that reconstructs the story of the MIR, taking as its starting point Castillo's memories of the house she used to share with her partner, Miguel Enríquez and their children (this is the house where Enríquez died in a combat, and where Castillo was badly hurt). It is affective because it is inhabited by the sound of children playing and by sensorial evocations such as the scent of the honeysuckle from her parent's garden. And it is collective because it features a wide-range of testimonies from the side of the 'defeated' as Castillo insists throughout, with an emphasis on the feelings of militant women and their daughters.[107] The director articulates an inquisitive and self-critical work on memory that deals with the painful decisions taken in the past and the consequences of those actions today in a collective way. As Nelly Richard asserts, *Calle Santa Fe* is a collective reflection constructed upon the 'auto-afirmación' [self-affirmation] of the 'Nosotros los miristas' [we, the MIR activists].[108]

Castillo's formal strategies to approximate this traumatic past have shifted over the years, something that comes to the fore when comparing the opening sequence of her first 'proper' homecoming documentary, *La flaca Alejandra*, with that of *Calle Santa Fe*, released over a decade later. In her 1994 film, Castillo returns to the house she shared with Enríquez, yet she is unable to enter to it. While standing outside the door, it is her voice that recalls the memories brought up by her former home. 'Como en una foto veo, pero no puedo pasar hacia adentro' [as with a photo, I can see, but I cannot get inside]. She remembers Enríquez working, their books, the music heard inside the house, the laughter of their children playing. Yet, she is only able to name these memories, not to visualize them. In *Calle Santa Fe*, however, she reenacts precisely such memories through an affective mise-en-scène of these same descriptions filmed on Super-8. In 2006 the director is able to evoke the images of this past cinematically and haptically, not just verbally. The 'content' of the memories, so to speak, are exactly the same (she references the books, the music, the laughter), yet the cinematographic form they acquire differs completely. The spectator is shown images inside a home, as though inside Santa Fe's house, featuring toys and books scattered on the floor, Castillo's hands writing rapidly on a typewriter, a curtain floating in the wind; the images being accompanied by children's laughter as well as by music. The director's shifting strategies in addressing her own memories further point to the itinerary undertook by Chilean documentary towards a 'cinema of affect'.

In my previous work on Castillo I have also stressed her rejection of a fixed identity as a survivor and how she contests the role of the 'heroic widow' that she was assigned by the party. She refuses such a role not only verbally, but also cinematically. Her voiceover describes her participation in 'solidarity tours' only a few months after Enríquez's and her child's death, describing them as 'andanzas sin visión, recorridos sin movimiento, la misma repetición de códigos, la viuda heroica se desplaza sorda, ciega y casi muda' [trajectories without movement, the same repetition of codes, the 'heroic widow' displaces herself, deaf, blind and nearly mute]. Castillo includes images of herself in one of those conferences, evidently detached and exhausted. The representation of her weariness is conveyed through the repetition of one of those images, as though the image was stuck due to a technical fault. I return to this segment since it is part of a wider montage sequence where she effectively stages her exilic condition and experience of loss, and which I see as another key example of a 'thirdspace chronotope'. The whole sequence starts with a reenactment scene shot in Super-8 of Castillo being expelled from the country after being taken by the militaries from the hospital from where she was recovering. The spectator sees iconic images of Alameda Avenue as perceived by Castillo through the blindfold that covered her eyes. The streets of Santiago, Havana, Toronto, and Paris become indistinguishable in a complex sequence while Castillo's grainy voice describes her own experience of exile:

> No hay un relato único del exilio, hay tantos exilios como exiliados y muchos exilios en el exilio de cada uno. Estoy en un espacio sin forma, cada imagen, cada olor, ruido o cadencia me remiten a otros más antiguos. Cada emoción me lleva a los ausentes, cada lucha a las que fueron interrumpidas. Recogimiento del tiempo, del cuerpo, del espacio.

> [There is no single story of exile, there are as many exiles as exiled people, and many exiles within one's own exile. I am in a formless space, and each image, each smell, each sound and cadence leads me to more remote ones. Each emotion takes me to the absent ones, each struggle to those that were interrupted. A recoil of time, of the body, of space].

The image track shows literally the shrinking of time and space to which the director is referring: the sequence ends with images of the Havana seafront that take the spectator via a panning shot, and an almost imperceptible cut, to the small Chilean fishing cove of Horcón. Castillo is able to convey in this sequence the characteristic temporal and spatial juxtaposition of exile, displaying a mournful contrapuntal consciousness, to paraphrase Said.[109]

The question 'Can the years we never lived be recalled?' would go on to be reformulated by a new generation of directors. Many of them belong to what I have been calling a literal second generation, though they are certainly not alone in exploring the possibilities of recalling a past that was not experienced, as I examine in the following chapter. As daughters of exile, Aguiló, Carmona, and Rossi explore, either verbally or more formally, the possibilities and limitations of recalling a traumatic event that was not experienced or not fully understood or remembered because they were so young.

In *El edificio de los chilenos,* Aguiló deals with the memories of the children of MIR militants. Her documentary centres on the experiences of these now adults who recall their coming-of-age in the 'Project Home' in the late 1970s. This project was a community centre in Cuba that sheltered around sixty children who were left in the care of twenty 'social parents' while their own biological parents returned to Chile to fight undercover against the dictatorship. The director was one of these children. Towards the beginning of *El edificio de los chilenos*, Aguiló narrates in voiceover her encounter with her mother in exile in Paris. In parallel, she crafts an exceptional sequence by merging material of a documentary nature and reenactment. The director opens her sequence with a close-up of the passport she used to leave the country, and then cuts to the common experience of exile by using black and white archive footage of groups of people in the airport fleeing the country. After that, she returns again to her own experience of exile, incorporating her own family pictures and drawings, but also reenacting her arrival to the country with footage of a particularly haptic quality. Through the window of a train we see Paris, the city that Aguiló recorded on 16mm film with a Bolex camera to formally convey the grainy texture of those past moments shared with her mother during her childhood (including the sense of taste through the image of colourful cupcakes in a shop, for example).

In *En algún lugar del cielo*, Carmona, raised in Berlin, arrives in Chile making explicit her return both discursively and formally, using several 'thirdspace chronotopes' (displacements in cars, trains, and airports) to inscribe her dislocation. While showing images of a Santiago she (dis)encounters via travelling shots, her voiceover says:

> A medida que me acerco más a la historia de este país me doy cuenta que aquí tuvo lugar un trauma, un cambio profundo y definitivo. El golpe militar destruyó la confianza de la gente [...]. Santiago me parece una ciudad de sobrevivientes.
>
> [As I get closer to this country's history I realize that a trauma occurred here, a profound and definitive change. The military coup destroyed the trust of people [...]. Santiago seems to me like a city of survivors].

Carmona constructs a montage sequence in which short captions of city inhabitants walking zombie-like are shown in slow motion and in a grey scale linked by white flashes (allow me to recall here the lack of colour in the city brought about by Ruiz's missing book). The director delivers the image of a city of survivors who are barely alive among the remains of the country's past.

In *El eco de las canciones*, Rossi deals with her and other peoples' memories of exile and return, moving back and forth between the past and the present, between here and there, aboard trains, cars, ships, crossing maps and times. On the brink of fiction, Rossi collects and interweaves in a poetic and an apparently non-hierarchical order documentary, fictional and animated images (some made for the film, others drawn from animated films such as, tellingly, *Gulliver's Travels*, from 1939). These images are woven together by the commentary of a fictive female narrator who speaks in the first-person. Rossi's nameless character is constructed from numerous testimonies gathered from second generation accounts from people who, like her, grew up or were born in exile in Italy, listening to their parents' songs and stories. The testimonies gathered together, along with the home movies she collected from different families, merge with Rossi's own personal material and are edited in such a way that the image track of the film stages precisely the complex ways in which personal memories interweave with history. Because of her particular material engagement with other people's memories, I see this work as a sort of 'hinge' production between a literal second generation and a broader one, as will be discussed in the next chapter.

Here I have examined homecoming documentaries, particularly by women from different generations who inscribe their memories of exile and return within their narratives, both as a formal and as a discursive strategy. I have drawn upon Benedetti's notion of *desexilio* to stress that the experience of exile never comes to a halt, even after returning. I looked to the early 1980s to seek commonalities between these productions and a number of post-dictatorship documentaries that share common issues of displacement, interest in domestic spaces, uncanny wanderings through a ghostly city, and the foregrounding of performativity. In addition, I discussed the debates that have developed around the recurring use of images of atrocity and of repression — as epitomized by the use of the iconic images of the bombardment of Chile's governmental palace — to suggest that these debates have played, for decades now, an important role in the refashioning of past and present accounts of the dictatorial experience.

In the final section I discussed the travelling memories of female directors who, through a creative and affective relationship both with the past and the documentary image, set out to recall the domestic side of history and put these memories on the move. Directors subjected to the experience of exile in the 1980s tend to develop a haptic cinema, foregrounding a wider affective experience of longing and multiple wanderings, anticipating a turn to the 'cinema of affect' of the last decade. The next chapter shall further take up the reemergence of first-person documentary with a focus on the post-dictatorship generation(s).

Notes to Chapter 3

1. The neologism *desexilio* was first coined by Benedetti in his novel *Primavera con una esquina rota* (1984). He later published a brief article in the Spanish newspaper *El País*, 18 April 1983, under the title of 'El desexilio' in which he further develops the concept. This article was reprinted in *El desexilio y otras conjeturas* (Madrid: El País, 1984). In the absence of a proper translation I have left the concept in Spanish.
2. Don Ranvaud, 'Interview with Raúl Ruiz', *Framework*, 10 (Spring 1979), 16–18 (p. 16).
3. Ibid., p. 16.
4. Ibid..
5. Antonio Skármeta, 'Europe: An Indispensable Link in the Production and Circulation of Latin American Cinema', in *New Latin American Cinema*, vol.1, ed. by Michael T. Martin (Detroit: Wayne State University Press, 1997), pp. 263–72 (first publ. in Third World Affairs 2 (1988), 169–72), p. 263.
6. Ibid., pp. 263–64.
7. Thomas C. Wright and Rody Oñate, *Flight from Chile: Voices of Exile*, trans. Irene Hodgson (Albuquerque: University of New Mexico Press, 1998), p. 172.
8. Mouesca, *Plano secuencia*, pp. 155–58.
9. Due to the complex production conditions, the definite formation of the collective has remained contested, but the members included Hernán Castro, Mario Díaz, Jaime Reyes, Gastón Ancelovici, and René Dávila.

10. The debate on this topic is clouded because until now, for the most part, exilic production has remained in 'exile', and the most authoritative catalogue of films produced in exile covers only until the year 1983. Pick, 'Cronología del cine chileno'. In 2008 the Cineteca Nacional de Chile published a large but incomplete inventory of productions of Chilean origin and films about Chile dispersed around the world. See Mónica Villarroel, and others, *Imágenes de Chile en el mundo: catastro del acervo audiovisual chileno en el exterior* (Santiago: Cineteca Nacional de Chile, 2008) <http://www.ccplm.cl/sitio/wp-content/uploads/2016/02/merged.pdf> [accessed 4 November 2018].
11. Pick, *New Latin American Cinema*, p. 195.
12. Pick, 'Chilean Cinema in Exile', p. 56.
13. Bruzzi, *New Documentary*, pp. 81–119.
14. See for example, Wright and Oñate, esp. Chapter 9 and Loreto Rebolledo, *Memorias del des/exilio*, in *Exiliados, emigrados y retornados: chilenos en América y Europa, 1973-2004*, ed. by José del Pozo (Santiago, RIL: 2006), pp. 167– 92.
15. Rebolledo, 'Memorias del des/exilio', pp. 167–92.
16. Benedetti, pp. 9–10.
17. Ibid., p. 41.
18. Ibid., p. 40.
19. Rebolledo, 'Memorias del des/exilio', p. 192.
20. For an analysis focusing on the politically enabling uses of nostalgia in documentaries of return, see Antonio Traverso, 'Nostalgia, Memory and Politics in Chilean Documentaries of Return', in *Dictatorships in the Hispanic World: Transatlantic and Transnational Perspectives*, ed. by Patricia L. Swier and Julia Riordan-Goncalves (Madison Lanham: Fairleigh Dikinson University Press, 2013), pp. 49–78.
21. As a matter of fact, Wright and Oñate notice that by 1994, when the short-lived governmental agency created by the Aylwin's administration to aid returnees in their settlement closed, a majority of exiles had not returned to the country. The Oficina Nacional de Retorno (National Office for Return, ONR) was created in 1990 and helped settle 56,000 returnees, as reported in their study. Wright and Oñate, p. 200.
22. Jorge Letelier, '¿De qué hablamos cuando hablamos de cine chileno?: la desmemoria obstinada', *Mabuse*, 6 October 2003 <http://www.mabuse.cl/cine_chileno.php?id=1790> [accessed 24 October 2018].
23. Ranvaud, p. 27. Verónica Cortínez and Manfred Engelbert challenge this standard version, offering a revision of Chilean cinema of the 1960s in light of a wider national film tradition, in *Evolución en libertad: el cine chileno de fines de los sesenta*, vol. 1 and 2 (Santiago: Cuarto Propio, 2014).
24. Doris Sommer, 'Irresistible Romance: The Foundational Fictions of Latin America', in *Nation and Narration*, ed. by Homi K. Bhabha (London: Routledge, 1990), pp. 71–98.
25. Sommer, p. 73.
26. Panizza, p. 7.
27. Frazier, p. 81–82.
28. See Michel Foucault, 'Nietzsche, Genealogy, History', in *Language, Counter-Memory, Practice: Selected Essays and Interviews*, ed. by Donald F. Bouchard, trans. by Donald F. Bouchard and Sherry Simon (Ithaca: Cornell University Press, 1977), pp. 139–64.
29. Frazier, p. 81.
30. Ibid., p. 82.
31. Edward W. Said, 'Reflections on Exile', in *Reflections on Exile and other Essays* (Cambridge, Mass.: Harvard University Press, 2000), pp. 173–86 (p. 177).
32. In a playful filmography published in *Cahiers du cinéma*, it was established that Ruiz returned to Chile around Christmas in 1982. Charles Tesson, 'Jeu de l'oie: un cauchemar didactique (ou la tentative hardie d'établir une bio-filmographie de Raoul Ruiz)', *Cahiers du Cinéma*, 345 (March 1983), 13–18 (p. 18).
33. Bruzzi, *New Documentary*, p. 109.
34. Charles Tesson, '*Letter from a Filmmaker, or The Return of a Library Lover (Lettre d'un cinéaste ou Le*

retour d'un amateur de bibliothèques, short, France, 1983)'. Raúl Ruiz: An Annotated Filmography. *Rouge*, 2 (2004) <http://www.rouge.com.au/2/letter.html> [accessed 10 November 2018].
35. *Ruiz: entrevistas escogidas–filmografía comentada*, ed. by Bruno Cuneo (Santiago: Universidad Diego Portales, 2013), p. 271.
36. See Andreea Marinescu, 'Raúl Ruiz's Surrealist Documentary of Return: *Le retour d'un amateur de bibliothèques* (1983) and *Cofralandes* (2002)', in *Rául Ruiz's Cinema of Inquiry*, ed. by Ignacio López-Vicuña and Andreea Marinescu (Detroit: Wayne State University Press: 2017), pp. 177–96; Valeria de los Ríos, 'La pregunta sobre el barroco en el cine de Raúl Ruiz', *Revista Chilena de Literatura*, 89 (2015), 113–31 (pp. 126–29); and José Miguel Palacios, 'Chilean Exile Cinema and its Homecoming Documentaries', in *Cinematic Homecomings: Exile and Return in Transnational Cinema*, ed. by Rebecca Prime (New York: Bloomsbury Academic, 2015) pp. 147–68.
37. See Marks, *The Skin of the Film* and Naficy.
38. Mikkonen also worked with her on *Gracias a la vida, Apuntes nicaragüenses* [*Notebook from Nicaragua*] (1982), and *Presencia lejana / Etällä ja läsnä: Kärsimyskertomus* [*Far Away and Yet so Near*] (1982).
39. Gabriel García Márquez, *Clandestine in Chile: The Adventures of Miguel Littin*, trans. by Asa Zats (New York: New York Review Books, 2010) [first publ. in Cambridge, England: Granta Books in association with Penguin, 1989].
40. Maya Deren, 'August 25, 1960', in *Essential Deren: Collected Writings on Film*, ed. with a preface by B. R. McPherson (Kingston: Documentext, 2005), pp. 241–44 (p. 243) (first publ. in *The Village Voice*, August 25, 1960).
41. Ibid.
42. Zuzana M. Pick, 'The Dialectical Wanderings of Exile', *Screen*, 30: 4 (1989), 48–65 (p. 57).
43. Bossy and Vergara, p. 8.
44. See, for example, Valeria Valenzuela, 'Yo te digo que el mundo es así: giro performativo en el documental chileno contemporáneo', *Doc On-line*, 1 (December 2006) 6–22. <http://dialnet.unirioja.es/descarga/articulo/4000485.pdf> [accessed 10 November 2018] and Claudia Barril, 'El yo en el documental chileno: una nueva forma de escritura política', in *El cine que fue: 100 años de cine chileno*, ed. by Claudia Barril and José María Santa Cruz (Santiago: Editorial ARCIS, 2011), pp. 162–69.
45. Loveman and Lira, *El espejismo de la reconciliación*, p. 247; Garretón, *Incomplete Democracy*, p. 151
46. Joana Page, *Crisis and Capitalism in Contemporary Argentine Cinema* (Durham: Duke University Press, 2009), p. 8.
47. Mar Diestro-Dópido, 'The View from Downstairs', *Sight and Sound*, 20: 9 (September 2010), 20. For a case study of European film festivals as a 'producer' of Latin American films see Miriam Ross, 'The Film Festival as Producer: Latin American Films and Rotterdam's Hubert Bals Fund', *Screen*, 52: 2 (2011), 261–67.
48. See Cortínez and Engelbert for an exploration of the tensions between local cinema and foreign critics in the 1960s, *Evolución en libertad*, vol.1, pp. 25–46.
49. See Michèle Faguet, 'Pornomiseria: or How Not to Make a Documentary Film', *Afterall*, 21 (Summer 2009) <http://www.afterall.org/journal/issue.21/pornomiseria.or.how.not.make.documentary.film> [accessed 11 November 2018].
50. See S. Salinas Acuña, R., Martinez, F., Said J.A, Soto, H. (sic), 'Entrevista a Raúl Ruiz: Prefiero registrar antes que mistificar el proceso chileno', *Primer Plano*, 1: 4 (Spring 1972), 3–21 (p. 9) and Malcolm Coad, 'Greats Events and Ordinary People', *Afterimage*, 10 (Autumn 1981), 72–77 (pp. 74–75).
51. Coad, p. 14.
52. Christie and Coad, p. 111
53. See Cortínez and Engelbert, *Evolución en libertad*, vol. 2, pp. 557–63.
54. Salinas, Martinez, Said, Soto p. 14.
55. King, p. 181.
56. Liñero, pp. 136–46.
57. Justo Pastor Mellado, 'Algunos aspectos polémicos de la producción chilena de video arte', in *Catálogo 9 Festival Franco-Chileno de Video Arte* (1989) quoted in Liñero, p. 145.

58. Ibid., p. 146.
59. Angell, p. 2.
60. Ibid., pp. 1–2.
61. Pick, *New Latin American Cinema*, p. 164. Claudia Bossay coined the term 'hyper-recording' to stress the vast amount of material filmed during the UP (in English in the original). See, Bossay, 'El protagonismo de lo visual en el trauma histórico: dicotomías en las lecturas de lo visual durante la Unidad Popular, la dictadura y la transición a la democracia', *Comunicación y Medios*, 29 (2014), 106–18 (p. 110) <http://www.comunicacionymedios.uchile.cl/index.php/RCM/issue/view/3271> [accessed 20 November 2018].
62. The 'revelation' of this valuable archival material is the subject of *La conciencia de golpe* (Manlio Helena-Urzúa, 2009), a documentary where Torti's footage is reproduced in its entirety. For a detailed analysis, see my article, 'La cámara que tiembla: sobre el bombardeo a La Moneda y algunas imágenes que nos mueven', *Savoirs en Prisme*, 9 (2019), <https://savoirsenprisme.com/numeros/09-dictature-et-image-absente-dans-le-cinema-de-non-fiction/la-camara-que-tiembla-sobre-el-bombardeo-al-palacio-de-la-moneda-y-algunas-imagenes-que-nos-mueven/> [accessed 24 April 2019].
63. César Barros, 'Declassifying the Archive: The Bombardment of *La Moneda* Palace and the Political Economy of the Image' in *Technology, Literature, and Digital Culture in Latin America: Mediatized Sensibilities in a Globalized Era*, ed. by Matthew Bush and Tania Gentic (New York: Routledge, 2016), pp. 127–45 (p. 129).
64. Patricia Keeton, 'Reevaluating the "Old" Cold War: A Dialectical Reading of Two 9/11 Narratives', *Cinema Journal*, 43: 4 (Summer 2004), 114–21 (p. 115).
65. See Ariel Dorfman, 'The Last September 11', in *Other September, Many Americas: Selected Provocations 1980–2004* (New York: Seven Stories Press, 2004) and Noam Chomsky, *9–11: Was There an Alternative?* (New York: Seven Stories Press, 2011) pp. 23–24.
66. Jacques Rancière, *Film Fables*, trans. by Emiliano Battista (Oxford: Berg, 2006), p. 158.
67. Eltit, 'La memoria pantalla', pp. 31–33.
68. Pinto, 'Cine, política, memoria' (n.d.).
69. Galende, p. 51
70. Toledo, (n.d.).
71. Interview with Iván Osnovikoff, Santiago de Chile, 2 January 2012.
72. Personal e-mail communication with Paco Toledo, 29 September 2012.
73. Fuenzalida, Corro and Mujica, pp. 220–21.
74. B. Ruby Rich, 'An/Other View of New Latin American Cinema', in *New Latin American Cinema*, vol.1, ed. by Michael T. Martin (Detroit: Wayne State University Press, 1997), pp. 273–97 (p. 282) (first publ. in *IRIS* 13 (1991), 5–27).
75. Ibid., p. 281.
76. On these filmmakers see Ramírez-Soto and Donoso.
77. Bruzzi, *New Documentary*, p. 66.
78. Ibid.
79. Rancière, p. 8.
80. On sense memory see Marks, *The Skin of the Film*, esp. pp. 110–14; 194–242.
81. Ibid., p. 130.
82. Ibid., p. 162.
83. Ibid., p. 172.
84. Stella Bruzzi, 'The Event: Archive and Imagination', in *New Challenges for Documentary*, ed. by Alan Rosenthal and John Corner, 2nd edn (Manchester: Manchester University Press, 2005), pp. 419–31 (p. 422).
85. Interview with Antonia Rossi, Santiago de Chile, 13 July 2011.
86. I draw upon scholars like Sturken, Erll, and Landsberg, for such understanding.
87. Giuliana Bruno, *Atlas of Emotion: Journeys in Art, Architecture and Film*, 2nd edn (London: Verso, 2007).
88. Ibid., p. 6.
89. Ibid., p. 86.

90. Ibid., p. 6.
91. Naficy, pp. 212–13; 153–54.
92. Ibid., p. 153; 212–13.
93. Ibid., p. 213.
94. Ibid., p. 153.
95. Hirsch, *Afterimage*, pp. 48–62.
96. Andermann, pp. 176–81.
97. Gilles Deleuze, *Cinema 2: The Time-Image*, trans. by Hugh Tomlinson and Robert Galeta (London: Athlone Press, 1989), p. xii.
98. Ibid.
99. Ibid., p. 41.
100. Benjamin, pp. 117–18.
101. Marks, *The Skin of the Film*, p.183.
102. Edward W. Said, 'Intellectual Exile: Expatriates and Marginals', *Grand Street*, 47 (Autumn 1993), 112–24 (p. 114).
103. Iván Pinto, 'Lo incompleto: desajuste y fractura en dos diarios fílmicos del exilio chileno', in *Prismas del cine latinoamericano*, ed. by Wolfgang Bongers (Santiago: Cuarto Propio, 2012), pp. 215–35, p. 221 and José Miguel Palacios, *Passages of Exile: Chilean Cinema 1973–2016* (unpublished doctoral thesis, New York University, 2014), pp. 174–76.
104. Efraín Barquero quoted in Loreto Rebolledo, *Memorias del desarraigo: testimonios de exilio y retorno de hombres y mujeres de Chile* (Santiago: Catalonia, 2006), p. 173.
105. Personal e-mail communication with Lucía Salinas, 29 March 2011.
106. Elizabeth Ramírez-Soto, 'Memoria y desobediencia: una aproximación a los documentales de Carmen Castillo', *La Fuga*, 12 (2011) <http://2016.lafuga.cl/memoria-y-desobediencia/450> [accessed 20 October 2018].
107. For a reading of Castillo's treatment of the bond between these militant mothers and their daughters, see Lisa Renee DiGiovanni, 'Memories of Motherhood and Militancy in Chile: Gender and Nostalgia in *Calle Santa Fe* by Carmen Castillo', *Journal of Latin American Cultural Studies: Travesia*, 21:1 (2012), 15–36, pp. 24–33.
108. Nelly Richard, 'Ir y venir', in *Crítica de la memoria (1990–2010)* (Santiago: Ediciones Universidad Diego Portales, 2010), pp. 146–64 (p. 160).
109. Said, *Reflections on Exile*, p. 148.

CHAPTER 4

On Glimpses of Childhood and Other People's Memories

When history was happening, or when our parents' 'novel' was taking place, as Chilean writer Alejandro Zambra puts it in his own novel *Formas de volver a casa*, the directors whose work I will be looking at here were learning to walk, to draw, to speak.[1] In this chapter I explore first-person documentary made by directors from the post-dictatorship generation(s) in terms of how they are constructed around the trope of the family, often drawing on childhood memories to deal with a past that they did not directly experience or could only witness through children's eyes.

First, I focus on documentaries directed by the children of direct victims of repression, partly expanding on some of the works mentioned previously. I argue that although these directors share the biographical fact of having been subjected to dictatorial violence as the children of those who were directly affected, their accounts of the past vary remarkably. Second, I extend the notion of 'second generation' — often restricted to the children of direct victims — to include the work of directors who, although not descendants of those directly affected, also use the trope of the family to elaborate discourses around memory, articulating an intrinsically affective cinema that privileges haptic and sensorial dimensions of memory. In doing so, I seek to move beyond a rather restrictive view of post-dictatorship responses as emerging solely *from the perspective of the parents* and *from the perspective of the sons and daughters* of direct victims as proposed by Ana Amado for the Argentine case.[2] This critical approach has been similarly adopted in Chile, focusing almost exclusively on filial bonds.[3] Such a perspective, this and the following chapters argue, is insufficient when dealing with the wide scope of state violence, the radical transformations of Chilean society experienced under the dictatorship, and the heterogeneous documentary responses that emerged in the post-dictatorial context.

The Rise of the Family, the Vanishing of *El Pueblo*

During the early transition to democracy the production of documentaries concerned with the country's recent past declined notably. Only with the turn of the new millennium did the documentary landscape begin to revitalize and new voices started to emerge. In this renewed scenario, the rise of first-person documentaries exploring the devastating effects of the dictatorship in the domestic sphere has been evident.[4] In Chile, as elsewhere, thanks to the 'lingua franca' status of the family, this trope has become a favoured vehicle in dealing with past atrocities.[5] One of the most visible strands examining the dictatorial period through the lens of family, or more broadly speaking through the personal sphere, is that of a literal second generation, understood as the daughters and sons of direct victims of repression (whose parents were executed, disappeared, tortured, and/or exiled). Such directors inscribe this bond explicitly in their works, usually through the use of voiceover and their onscreen presence. Among these productions (many of which were these directors' first films) are *Chile, los héroes están fatigados* [Chile, the Heroes are Tired] (Marco Enríquez-Ominami, 2002), *En algún lugar del cielo*, *I Wonder What You Will Remember of September*, *Min mors løfte* [My Mother's Promise] (Marianne Hougen-Moraga, 2007), *La realidad* [The Reality] (Andrés Lübbert, 2009), *El edificio de los chilenos*, *El eco de las canciones*, *Mi vida con Carlos*, *Generation Exile*, and *En resa till världens ände*. Less numerous, though equally important, are the works of directors who, although removed from this biological link with the dictatorial past, so to speak, adopt family detours to elaborate on discourses about memory that obliquely address Chile's past, developing a 'cinema of affect' — such as Tiziana Panizza's *Remitente* and René Ballesteros's *La quemadura*.

As argued in the previous chapter, the key precedents of first-person documentary emerged during the dictatorship, namely in the work of exilic filmmakers. These directors were trying to reckon with what Raúl Ruiz described as the loss of the complete symbolic system that was at the foundation of political cinema during the 1960s in the world as whole, not just in Chile.[6] The cinema of the region experienced within this context what has been described as a shift from the 'revolutionary' to the 'revelatory', a move from the epic to the domestic realm.[7] More broadly speaking, such a 'subjective turn', to use Beatriz Sarlo's famous formulation developed in *Tiempo Pasado*, has played a central role in the aftermath of Latin American dictatorships with the rise of *testimonio*. In Chile, the shift towards individual experience has been framed within the 'despolitización' [de-politization] of society, a process that began under the dictatorial regime and whose main objective has been the establishment and perpetuation of the neoliberal model, according to Tomás Moulian's bleak analysis. Throughout this transformation, which has pushed towards individualization, the notion of the consumer has replaced the central place formerly occupied by collective projects.[8]

In a similar vein, Francine Masiello argues in *The Art of Transition* that the once central category of *el pueblo*, or 'the popular subject' (which is comprised of subaltern, marginal, or delinquent subjects) acquires during transitions to democracy a highly conflictive connotation for intellectuals and artists of the Southern Cone.[9] Central to the 'critical imagination' of the 1960s as well as a 'sign of resistance against metropolitan places',[10] after the fall of the revolutionary projects *el pueblo* turned into an 'embarrassing archaism'.[11] In Masiello's view, the retreat of the popular subject from artistic practices and cultural discourses coincided with the decline of utopian thought and the radical instauration of a free-market economy perpetuated during the transitions: 'earlier utopian fantasies about the redemptive promise of lo popular now appears as a disembodied phantom. Lost is a plausible narrative about coalition and common rights; the material basis of communitarian ideas is dissolved'.[12] Gonzalo Aguilar's examination of the cinematographic treatment of *el pueblo* in the region since the 1970s (with a focus on New Argentine cinema) suggests a similar transformation on the big screen. According to Aguilar, there is 'una nueva lógica en la que el pueblo falta'[13] [a new logic in which el pueblo is missing], where the category notwithstanding remains haunting either as a lack or as a conceptual paradigm.[14]

These remarks contribute to a better understanding of the radical transformation of the mise-en-scène of *el pueblo* in Chilean post-dictatorship documentary, a transformation that is strikingly brought to the fore by the evident rise of the first-person in the 2000s. It is important to stress that although these documentaries emerge in a de-politicized context, this does not mean that they are apolitical texts, nor does it mean that they are only concerned with the individual. First-person documentary, as numerous scholars from Michael Renov to Alisa Lebow have forcefully argued, is never simply autobiographical, never just about the 'I', and is almost invariably imbricated with the collective.[15] In the Chilean case, moreover, most of these works are personal narratives that from the domestic realm contribute to a destabilization of official or dominant discourses about the dictatorial past.

The radical configuration of the popular subject will acquire several forms in post-dictatorship documentary. The overflowing images of *el pueblo* and of collective action were without a doubt the protagonists of documentary films both during the revolutionary period and during the uprisings of the 1980s. In post-dictatorship documentary, these images return as corpses: *el pueblo* is reduced to black and white archival footage and ghostly characters. In addition, domestic and deeply gendered narratives replace past images of epic and collective action. The rise of these gendered accounts can be seen most clearly after the turn of the century. It is then that first-person documentary, which had been developing intermittently since the early 1980s in the cinema of exilic directors as we have seen, reemerges with force. In fact, it is precisely filmmakers returning from exile who lead this endeavour in early post-dictatorship discourses. Explicitly inscribing their personae in their critiques of the neoliberal model, they contributed actively to the rare public debates about the recent past in the 1990s.

In this regard, the most emblematic figures are Carmen Castillo and Patricio Guzmán, who sought to build interconnections between their own individual memories and collective ones. Since their firsts post-dictatorship returns to the country with *La flaca Alejandra* and *Chile, la memoria obstinada*, respectively, a poignant nostalgia for *el pueblo* as a collective political actor prevails in their films. Nevertheless, both directors engage in the task of putting these static memories into motion, as Nelly Richard asserts when comparing their work. In her view, Castillo and Guzmán pursue 'la tarea crítica de desbloquear la memoria sedimentada de la nostalgia' [the critical task of unblocking the settled memory of nostalgia].[16] Both of them refer to Chilean society as being in a veritable state of love during the UP, an idea that finds a visual translation in archival footage of thousands of people taking part in a dream in black and white. In *Salvador Allende*, Guzmán states: 'era una sociedad entera en estado amoroso' [it was a whole society in a state of love]. Similarly, Castillo recalls in *Calle Santa Fe*, 'el recuerdo intenso del estado de enamoramiento que todos sentíamos' [the intense memory of those days when we all fell in love] (film's original English subtitles). In Guzmán's case, *el pueblo* is shown basically to emphasize that the collective actor is no longer present; in other words, to point to its radical absence.[17] In contrast, in Castillo's film, the old struggles are reconfigured into new modes of resistance by younger generations in the present — through artistic practices such as music or filmmaking, or through the rejection of a reified version of the past that attempts to turn it into a museum.

According to Pablo Corro, 'la masa' [the crowd] returns in 1990 after having been effectively eradicated as a significant symbol after the coup.[18] In his view, it does so as cinematic reconstruction, archival footage in a nostalgic mode,[19] or as inert masses.[20] He draws on the distinction elaborated by Peter Sloterdijk between the classic mass — the physical congregation of a multitude around a leader, as in the case of Nazi Germany — and the contemporary mass, an immobile congregation of people shorn of contact, usually gathered around a spectacle or informative source. In his view, the latter is the depiction of the inert mass found in some current Chilean documentaries, such as in *La muerte de Pinochet*, a documentary that I examine in the next chapter.[21] Corro, though rightly remarking on the major transformation in the cinematic treatment of *el pueblo* in post-dictatorship productions, overlooks the copious, if short-lived, return of the long shots of the crowds included in 1980s videos. Even though many of these images are mourning sequences — *el pueblo* accompanying its dead martyrs — this footage of collective images will be used insistently in numerous post-dictatorship documentaries. Arguably, the most emblematic of these long shots is the striking panning shot over the Plaza de Armas which shows large crowds accompanying the coffin of André Jarlan, a beloved priest murdered by the police in a typical raid on a shantytown, as included in the documentary *Andrés de La Victoria* (*Andrés from La Victoria*) (Claudio di Girólamo, Ictus, 1984). This funerary footage, just like that of Neruda's burial only a few days after the coup, has become a forceful image of political resistance. The persistence of this and similar footage in the cinematic imagery of the Chilean nation demonstrates that funerals 'could reverberate in many ways simultaneously — as lament for the dead and as political protest'.[22]

The image of *el pueblo* as an active political actor of a major epic as depicted in Chilean documentary of the 1960s and the 1970s would come to be replaced in post-dictatorship documentary by minimal stories of spectral, baffled, and forgetful figures. The post-dictatorial citizen acquires the form of a ghostly figure who bears the traces of an inconvenient past such as in *La sombra de Don Roberto* or in *Por sospecha de comunista* [*Under Suspicion of Being Communist*] (Cristóbal Cohen and Marcelo Hermosilla, 2008). A perplexed and powerless figure also emerges, one that is faced with the vertiginous changes of the city and society such as in *En defensa propia* [*In Self-defence*] (Claudia Barril, 2009) and *La batalla de la Plaza Italia* [*The Battle of Plaza Italia*] (Renato Villegas, 2008). A (mostly feminine) figure who has lost the ability to remember can be seen as well, such as in *Reinalda del Carmen, mi mamá y yo* [*Reinalda del Carmen, my Mother and Me*] (Lorena Giachino, 2007), *La quemadura* and *Remitente*.

In the case of the first-person documentaries analysed in this chapter, most of them are positioned as domestic and subjective narrations, yet at the same time complexly interwoven with the history of the nation that binds them. They share the explicit presence of a first-person who manifests either behind or in front of the camera as narrator or character. Through the use of cinematic mechanisms that often display memory's frailty and, at times, its unreliability, these documentaries stage both the impossibility of objectivity and of retrieving the past. As performative documentaries, in the sense developed by Stella Bruzzi, they demand the active and critical participation of the spectator, leaving questions without answers, building upon absences, and inviting reflection upon the possibilities and impossibilities of recovering the past while signalling a fragmented, rather mediated knowledge of it.

Most of these directors draw on childhood memories and inscribe their geographical (as well as temporal) displacements, since most of them have been marked by the experience of exile or other forms of migration. In this regard, they share many of the traits seen in the works of exilic filmmakers. However, they differ greatly from such films in the sense that these younger directors emphasize their generational bafflement, making explicit the gap between the experiences of their parents and their own, a confusion and perplexity that is inscribed not only verbally but also aesthetically (through drawings, reenactments, and/or through archival and sound footage).

Chilean scholarship examining the rise of the first-person documentary in the post-dictatorial period has favoured the notion of 'autobiographical documentary' (albeit often acknowledging the complexities and variations the term 'autobiography' entails).[23] I, however, prefer to use the notion 'first-person documentary'. As Lebow eloquently argues, 'first person film is not primarily, and certainly not always explicitly, autobiographical. Subjective as it may always be, the exploration of the filmmaker's own biography is a much less centrally important pursuit in these films than one might expect'.[24] Influenced by Jean-Luc Nancy's designation of the 'singular plural, wherein the individual "I" does not exist alone, but always "with" another', Lebow stresses that 'the "I" is always social, always already in relation'; it is, in fact, always 'the first person plural "we"'.[25] Previously, Annette Kuhn had coined the term 'revisionist autobiographies' to refer to literary texts that challenge the boundaries between the personal and the collective. For Kuhn, such narratives are 'not purely, nor arguably at all, about the lives and times of particular individuals'; on the contrary, they are 'about the relationship between the personal or the individual on the one hand and the social or the historical on the other — or to put it in another way, between experience and history'.[26] In light of the above, I favour a discussion of an autobiographical *dimension* of these works rather than categorizing them as autobiographical documentaries.

My readings of these documentaries both by a literal and broader second generation of directors are inspired particularly by Alison Landsberg's concept of 'prosthetic memory' and by Marianne Hirsch's notion of postmemory. Postmemory, initially conceptualized in terms of the children of Holocaust survivors (known as the 'second generation') has found important resonances in Latin America. This concept underlines the temporal gap that distances the memories of the second generation from the traumatic experience of an historical event while at the same time highlighting the affective dimension that links them to it.[27] 'Postmemory', Hirsch explains, 'characterizes the experience of those who grow up dominated by narratives that preceded their birth, whose own stories are evacuated by the stories of the previous generation shaped by traumatic events that can be neither understood nor recreated'.[28] The concept has been usually mobilized in the region in order to analyse documentaries by children of direct victims.[29] Its usage has not been free of critiques, most notably those from Argentine cultural critic Beatriz Sarlo who wondered whether the notion of postmemory was anything other than a 'inflación teórica' [theoretical inflation] that has attained its popularity due to the virtually undisputed legitimacy with which autobiographical narratives and subjectivity are bestowed.[30] However, Hirsch herself has clarified that postmemory should not be understood as 'an identity position, but as a space of remembrance [...]. It is a question of adopting the traumatic experience — and thus also the memories — of others as one's own'.[31] Therefore I see postmemory as a useful concept that helps to emphasize the ethical commitment to remember while also underscoring the differences in memory work among directors who lived through the revolutionary period and experienced Pinochet's tyranny directly, and those who were brought up under the repressive regime or felt the resonances of these stories from abroad.

Having said this, and since the majority of the documentarians I analyse in this chapter were born in the 1970s, it is tempting to consider their productions as works belonging to a generational cluster united by the fact of having been born and/or raised under Pinochet's rule. In fact, many of these voices consciously seek to break, or at least create a distance from, those narratives that preceded them. Yet, as helpful as it may seem, such an approach would be an oversimplification, not only because significant links can be established between directors of different generations, for instance, through the experience of political displacement, but also because there are important distinctions that need to be acknowledged within these children's accounts, and even among the sons and daughters of direct victims.[32]

This is clear if one considers, for example, the documentary responses of the children of MIR militants, such as Marco Enríquez-Ominami, Alejandra Carmona, and Macarena Aguiló in light of their own distinct experiences. Enríquez-Ominami fled into exile with his mother when he was only five months old (and hence was stripped of his nationality by the dictatorship) and has no memories of his father.[33] In contrast, Carmona was twelve years old when her father was murdered in 1977, and she had left for Berlin three years before with her mother. Aguiló, who was kidnapped as a child by the DINA as a ploy to get her father (thus becoming one of the youngest victims of the repression), has some 'vague memories' of that experience (as she indicates in her documentary). She was taken to Paris at the age of four, soon after being set free, and after several periods of displacement ended up living in a collective home in Cuba with other MIR children (both of her parents survived). Their divergent backgrounds make evident the complexities of dealing even with this narrower delimitation of a second generation, and demand nuanced readings to unpack the cinematic strategies deployed in their different personal works.

Children of the Revolution

Describing the practices of memory employed by the sons and daughters of Argentine victims of the Dirty War, Ana Amado notes that they reveal both a closeness and distance with their parents' generation:

> Concebidas como homenaje y a la vez puesta al día del vínculo genealógico, estas obras guardan, sin embargo, sea directamente o en sus desvíos, en su discurso explícito o en sus pliegues, una voluntad de distancia y afirmación generacional antes que una adhesión afectiva o ideológica incondicional.[34]
>
> [Though conceived as homage and actualisation of the genealogical bond, these oeuvres present, however, either directly or in their detours, in their explicit discourse or in their folds, a desire for distance and generational affirmation rather than an unconditional affective or ideological support.]

The documentaries directed by the Chilean descendants of direct victims are similarly conceived as being sceptical homages in which sons and daughters create elaborate mise-en-scènes in which they aim to bridge the lost parental bond, while at the same time inscribing their distance with the epic discourses that preceded them.

One of the earliest documentaries made by a son is *Chile, los héroes están fatigados*, directed by the son of the MIR leader Miguel Enríquez, Marco Enríquez-Ominami. In it, he touches explicitly upon what it means to be, as he says, 'el hijo de una leyenda' [the son of a legend], introducing his father rather playfully as 'una suerte de Che Guevera más austral' [a sort of more southern Che Guevara]. Some critics have read this documentary with distrust, seeing it as the director's calling card to the political world.[35] The fact that he ran for the last three presidential campaigns, and that his political career has been recently under scrutiny for alleged tax offenses, certainly ought to be acknowledged. His current position as a politician, however, should not be a reason for dismissing upfront his cinematographic work. On the contrary, this particular film (released in 2002, *before* his entrance into official politics) must be considered not only because it is one of the earliest documentaries by the son of a direct victim of repression, but also because it usefully serves to illustrate the heterogeneous ways in which these younger directors have dealt with the past. By using face-to-face interviews with former militants, now prosperous businessmen and politicians (including a failed interview with Ricardo Lagos, who was president at the time), the director compares the 'before' and 'after' via archival footage of their former revolutionary lives with their current positions of power, describing them as 'esclavos de la eficiencia' [slaves to efficiency]. Enríquez-Ominami explicitly conceived his documentary as a response against what he described as the expansive 'néo-romantisme nostalgique' [nostalgic neo-romanticism] for the Chilean revolution existent in Europe.[36] The director's stance is ironic, at times humorous, and overtly political (in that it is concerned with the partisan world). It is set to prove a hypothesis openly stated from the outset, and evident from its title; namely, that the old revolutionaries are tired.

However, he also sets to find out if his father's death was worth anything, and he poses this question directly to one of Enríquez's closest collaborators, who is shown working for a major corporation. Like other filmmakers facing the loss of their father — Carmona and Berger-Hertz, for example — Enríquez-Ominami also uses the moving image to connect to the parental figure, albeit without solemnity. Using *Forrest Gump*-like special effects, he travels through time and space to interview his father. Defeating time and death, he appears sharing the same space with the MIR leader in a television interview. The director intervenes the original black and white footage, occupying the place of the journalist; in this way, the materiality of the moving image is used as a bridge between the living and the dead. Although father and son share the same colourless cinematic space, the unbreachable gap is striking precisely because of this temporal collapse. Paraphrasing the journalist's original question, the director asks his father: 'Isn't it strange that you, who led the revolution, belong to the oligarchy?' The filmmaker also mimics the journalist's gestures, looking straight at the camera when Enríquez replies. He adds, however, other glances at the camera-spectator, most significantly after the MIR leader states: 'no defino a los hombres por la desgracia o gracia de quien son hijos' [I do not define men in terms of the grace or disgrace of who their parents are]. This particular gaze, which directly addresses the spectator, builds this moment with ironic intention rather than presenting it as a sequence of loss. However, the documentary is not completely devoid of mournful scenes. The director includes a visit to his father's tomb, a moment in which the heart-felt song 'Canto a Miguel' replaces the festive *cumbia* previously heard. Enríquez-Ominami addresses his father directly, saying: 'te embarcaste en una revolución generosa y te encontraste solo frente al enemigo' [You engaged in a generous revolution and found yourself alone against the enemy]. 'Me temo que tu muerte no sirvió de nada' [I'm afraid that your death was pointless], is the closing line of the documentary. These words are accompanied by footage recorded by an accusatory camera held towards the faces of those former 'heroes' while they sing the socialist party anthem at an assembly. After a cut, the camera follows the director leaving the meeting, turning his back to his father's generation to move towards something else; it is left ambiguous just what this is.

Unlike the 'opacity' of the documentaries analysed below in terms of presenting a more tangential approach to the political, Enríquez-Ominami's work still bears the 'transparency' characteristic of the previous decades in terms of rendering a clear and direct political message.[37] As such it differs largely from the rest of the productions examined in this chapter, which to varying degrees are works conceived and developed as a quest in which the directors stumble, hesitate, and present fissures that call into question categories like history, memory, and identity.

Similarly to the Argentine case, the majority of these sons and daughters of direct victims have 'chosen the discourse of the emotions instead of the strident political pronouncements that characterized their parents' generation'.[38] Carmona in *En algún lugar del cielo* and Aguiló in *El edificio de los chilenos* collect contested visions of the past, relying largely on emotional onscreen testimonies *from the perspective of the parents* and *from the perspective of the children* to return to Amado's theory.[39] Their works are deeply concerned with the construction of children's subjectivity and the experience of political displacement. To explore this construction cinematically, they rely both on materials of a fictional nature (namely, reenactment) and documentary sources (family pictures, home movies, letters, drawings). In these documentaries, akin to the literary works of children survivors of the Holocaust, one can clearly see 'both the child's helplessness and the adult's attempt to render that helplessness, retrospectively, in language'.[40] As seen previously, reenactment has been a privileged strategy to access the past as it 'replaces' the illustrative role of archival footage when there is no material available, while at the same time effectively conveying sensorial experiences ungraspable by explicit enunciations. Nevertheless, the reenactment sequences used by these directors differ significantly from those employed by the filmmakers described in Chapter 2 in that although they are not devoid of horror or fear, they seek to evoke a broader range of childlike perceptions often through haptic images.

Carmona, as we saw briefly in the previous chapter, returns to Chile motivated by a desire to reconstruct the figure of her father and 'para reconstruir los fragmentos dispersos de esta historia. Es como descifrar un acertijo, solo tengo preguntas y la memoria del dolor' [to try to rebuild the scattered pieces of this story. It is like deciphering a riddle. All I have are questions and the memory of pain] (This and following citations are from the film's original English subtitles). The director inscribes her presence both onscreen and offscreen through her voiceover. However, this first-person position is not consistent throughout the film, as she also uses the characteristic distance of televisual reporting. This is most baffling when her mother and a close friend give their onscreen testimony, as they refer to Carmona in the third person. The director explicitly acknowledges the difficulties of accessing a past indirectly experienced and in the voiceover says, 'comienzo a recolectar imágenes y recuerdos ajenos que hago míos en el afán de acercarme a mi padre' [I begin to collect other people's images and memories that I make my own out of eagerness to get closer to my father]. There is a particular haptic sequence in which the loss of her father is depicted in a powerful way. The very opening shot of the documentary is a reenactment sequence that immerses the spectator in the director's 'memoria del dolor' [memory of pain], as she calls it. It begins with a long take with a handheld camera which moves in slow motion inside the dark entrance of a building, presumably that of the flat in Berlin where Carmona lived as a child. The camera is positioned at the eye-level of a child, suggesting that this is her point of view when she was twelve years old. The camera's shaky movement mimics the child's anguish anticipating the news of her father's death, a premonitory feeling that is also stressed by the director's narration. Later in her documentary, Carmona returns to this initial reenacted scene to illustrate her mother's own offscreen account of this traumatic episode and how she delivered the news to her daughter. Immediately after the mother evokes this very moment — the mother is shown rendering her emotional testimony in a conventional 'talking head' — the illustrative reenactment that has been accompanying her account up until that point alters radically. The literal recreation of the girl's viewpoint arriving at her flat is now replaced by a highly stylized reenactment of the emotional impact that such a shattering event had in Carmona. Through a dissolve from her mother's interview, the spectator is now placed in a long, dim basement-like tunnel. At the end of the tunnel, out of focus, there is a figure that is barely distinguishable. The camera moves quickly towards the end of the tunnel through a tracking shot that finishes, after an almost imperceptible cut, in an extreme close-up of the director's eye (the figure was hers, as one can now distinguish). This image dissolves into a photograph of her father, who is shown smiling. The sequence is complemented by a soundtrack that builds up tension, notably through a ticking clock that merges with the sounds of heartbeats (Her father's? Hers?). Through a combination of blurry images, use of fast and slow camera movements, and rapid changes of focus, Carmona accomplishes in a few seconds a scene of profound affective force. Like Enríquez-Ominami, she also asks: '¿valió la pena morir o ser desterrado por unas ideas de las que hoy nadie se acuerda demasiado bien?' [Was it worth dying or being expatriated for ideas that no one really remembers?]. Carmona, however, wondering why her father returned to a house that was no longer secure while he was in hiding, says: 'lo quiero más por ese gesto descuidado que habla de su naturaleza inocente' [I love him more for that careless gesture that shows his innocent nature'] thus downplaying, unlike Enríquez's son, the epic dimension of the parental figure.

The return to Chile of Germán Berger-Hertz, like that of Carmona, manifests a common desire of these children of victims 'not just to feel and know, but also to re-member, to re-build, to re-incarnate, to re-place, and to repair'.[41] *Mi vida con Carlos* is, from its very opening sequence — a breathtaking tracking shot of the Atacama Desert — inscribed within a framework of loss and absence, as well as within a highly aestheticized cinematic discourse. Through his film, Berger-Hertz tries to reconstruct the figure of his father, Carlos Berger, a communist journalist executed by 'La caravana de la muerte', whose body was still among those of the disappeared until early 2014.[42] The journalist was also the husband of the famous human rights lawyer Carmen Hertz, who, as we find out from the film, spoke very little of Berger to her son.[43]

After the opening shot of the desert, the documentary turns to vanishing Super-8 images of the director's father as a boy running towards the sea. These images are shown in slow motion, while the director says, 'La primera vez que te vi, fue en esta imagen de Super-8' [The first time I saw you was in this Super-8 image] (the father, as a matter of fact, will be the addressee throughout the documentary, in an epistolary mode). Soon after this sequence, the spectator is faced with a Super-8 montage sequence in which black and white stills of the director's father holding him as a baby are intercalated with coloured moving images of a man performing the same action. Unaware of the temporal gap, because of the same grainy, blurry quality of the different images, the spectator is drawn to assume that both are the same man, that is, the filmmaker's father, holding him as a baby. Yet, the man in the colour footage is the director holding his own daughter, as we soon realize when his voice talks over more contemporary footage of the same texture. Berger-Hertz plays and replays the few seconds of footage of him with his father when he was a child as a way to seek a connection with him, not metaphorically but materially; a bond sought precisely through the film's body. As it emerges from these sequences, it is not just photography (the photographs of the director's father are re-filmed on Super-8) but specifically, this specific film gauge — the Super-8 — associated with home movies that acts as the 'umbilical cord' which ties the son to his father, subverting somehow the maternal metaphor used by Roland Barthes to refer to the power of photography to link us to the dead.[44] It is also Super-8 that weaves the family's histories of displacements together (a whole sequence on Berger's grandparents who came from Europe in the context of the Holocaust is narrated through home movies).

As daughters and sons of notable figures, these directors often have to deal explicitly with the public personae of their parents, which they continue to incarnate. Many of these documentaries directed by the children themselves include archival material from other media to inscribe the public dimension of their life. Such is the case of Berger-Hertz, who includes a montage of several images of his mother in the news (as the courageous and determined human rights lawyer) as well as of himself being interviewed when he was nine years old for an Ictus video production (footage that also points to the symbolic position he occupied as a child victim compelled to act as an adult during the dictatorship).[45] This is also the case for Aguiló, who opens her documentary *El edificio de los chilenos* with footage taken from a national television programme in which she was interviewed as one of the youngest victims of repression. Aguiló, however, emphasizes the distance from this 'official' discourse by shooting the television monitor that shows her images on the screen, from the intimacy of her home. She conveys instead this experience evocatively, inscribing both visually and verbally her sensory recollections from those twenty days in captivity; a slow panning of autumn leaves in Santiago from the present day are matched by the memories she keeps of that autumn in the city, the dry air, the heat under her woollen clothes. And, rather than dwelling on that episode, she goes on to narrate the story of the 'Chilean building' in Cuba.

In the previous chapter I discussed Aguiló's mise-en-scène of memories of displacement as depicted through the window of a train in Paris. This is part of a wider montage sequence in which the director also exposes the generational gap between herself and her parents while developing a poignant critique of their privileging of revolutionary ideals — a choice that led to her childhood separation from them. Soon after a series of brief shots taken from the train, the spectator is positioned within a domestic space, looking onto an exterior urban landscape, as images filmed with a handheld 16mm camera pointing out from a window of a building in Paris (apparently her flat) are shown. The director's voiceover locates the spectator: 'Yo iba a la escuela y ella trabajaba. La acompañaba a reuniones donde se fumaba mucho y donde escuchaba cosas que a veces yo entendía'. [I went to school and she [her mother] worked. I went along to her meetings, where they smoked a lot, and sometimes I would understand something' (This and following citations are from the film's original English subtitles). Images of the city landscape as seen through the flat's window are juxtaposed with the offscreen voice of a man talking about military tactics and revolutionary strategies: '¿Qué significa una estrategia de guerra popular? No significa que haya que estar disparando siempre [...]' [What is the 'Popular War Strategy'? It doesn't mean we have to be shooting all the time (...)] His voice is interrupted by that of the director's, recorded when she was five years old: '¿y yo?...uy! quiero hacer pipí!' [and me? ...Oh! I need to pee!']. Here, the director depicts her confusion as a child and her limited understanding of the world of adults, making evident the complexities of relating to their political experiences while also challenging the boundaries between documentary and fiction.

This scene creates an intense temporal collapse; although the recording of the girl's voice dates back to Aguiló's childhood years, the recording of the man's voice is recent. The voice belongs to one of the historical leaders of the MIR, Andrés Pascal, and dates from a speech he made at a gathering in 2004 that was organized to commemorate the thirtieth anniversary of the death of Miguel Enríquez.[46] Via Pascal's speech, the voices of Aguiló's parents and their fellow militants are thus replaced 'por la voz de la autoridad del grupo político, por la jerarquía, la orden de partido' [with the voice of the authority of the political group, with hierarchy, the party's order].[47] This is a remarkable sequence where the blending of fictional and non-fictional sources, as well as the temporal collapse created by their encounter, stress, as Rancière claims, that 'memory is the work [*oeuvre*] of fiction' (emphasis and translation in the original).

Aguiló turns to drawings and letters to convey the child's vantage point from which she examines the past, as well as several reenactments through which she depicts everyday life in the communal home where she was raised in Cuba. This past, then, is not only her own, but also that of her numerous 'social' brothers and sisters. She creates a collective portrait in which these children inscribe not only their losses, but also their joy of finding themselves surrounded by numerous siblings overnight, or savouring their first feelings of freedom. The director also conveys how powerful the memories — and the images — of repression were for children growing up in exile. One of Aguiló's sisters recalls that they would receive videotapes from Chile and all the kids would gather around the television monitor to watch the images of the dictatorial repression. Her account is illustrated with faded black and white video images of the social revolt and the violence unleashed against it as though seen from a television monitor, while her sister affirms 'sabíamos todo lo que pasaba' [we knew what was going on].

This travelling imagery of violence and resistance arriving from Chile also makes its way into *El eco de las canciones*. Similarly to Aguiló, Rossi does not limit herself to images of catastrophe (though these are certainly vast and varied, ranging from the atomic bomb to hurricanes, from footage of Chile's repression to natural disasters), exploring other forgotten fragments of this history. However, Rossi's quest is not to reconstruct these fragments; she is not interested in suturing these scattered glimpses of childhood into a coherent narrative, but on the contrary, to expose them precisely in their condition as remnants. She moves even further away from the realm of reason to the affective one. Despite being the daughter of Chileans driven to exile, she is not interested in singling out her own experience as such. Rather, she attempts to create a more radical polyphonic quilt in which many stories, her own and that of other children like her, commingle, dissolve and merge. Because of the particular aesthetic characteristics of *El eco de las canciones*, which heavily draws upon the haptic dimensions of the moving image, I think of it as a sort of bridge between the literal and the broader second generation.

Haptic Memories in the 'Cinema of Affect'

If the aforementioned documentaries include profoundly affective sequences, the works I will deal with in this section are intrinsically haptic. Rossi's *El eco de las canciones*, Panizza's *Remitente* and Ballesteros's *La quemadura* constitute remarkable examples of an 'aesthetic of sensation' as described by Martine Beugnet.[48] As previously explained, this 'cinema of sensation' is characterized by a continual passage from an optical regime of perception to a haptic visuality, with the materiality of the image often superseding its representational force. It features the use of unfamiliar frames and angles, variations in focus, combinations of varying formats from 8mm to high definition digital footage and alternations from close-ups to long shots.[49] The works of Rossi, Panizza, and Ballesteros are constituted upon such strategies, and thus I see them as powerful examples of the 'cinema of affect'. To recall, by a 'cinema of affect' I refer to documentaries that:

i) aim to reveal the materiality of the image rather than a certain 'truth';
ii) feature other voices aside from those of the direct victims, including those of younger generations that did not experience the coup or the UP first hand, and unsettling voices such as Pinochet's collaborators or supporters;
iii) rather than onscreen testimony or direct forms of address, favour other creative strategies, including non-representational ones;
iv) embrace a subjective point of view, endorsing the use of a first-person narrator;
v) occlude images of past atrocities in order to elicit more affective responses from the audience.

As I have insisted, although the differences between the 'cinema of the affected' and the 'cinema of affect' are largely a matter of degree, the directors who craft a 'cinema of affect' are not too interested in revealing any particular truth or in raising consciousness-awareness, at least not in such a straightforward manner as those who engage with a 'cinema of the affected'. Unlike the emphasis on the revelation of literal bodies taken up by directors in the previous decade, these filmmakers turn to unveil the film's *skin*. The temporal distance from the historical event of the coup makes itself felt in these sensorial productions.

By the time these productions were released, Chilean society had made important advances in the field of human rights, albeit in its characteristic 'unravelling impasse' fashion. In fact, these documentaries emerged in the aftermath of the death of the dictator in 2006 as both Panizza and Rossi make clear by including images of the polarized reactions of Chilean citizens to this event. Rossi's film even offers a furtive glimpse of the dictator's body inside the coffin in a shuddering, blurry close-up. For the most part, however, these post-Pinochet documentaries eschew images from the archives of atrocities that haunted the post-dictatorial scene. Their cinema is one of affect, perceptions, out-takes, stories disregarded, materials discarded. If there is a revelation at stake here, it is the unveiling of the materiality of the image.

El eco de las canciones, *Remitente*, and *La quemadura* differ largely from the documentaries of directors like Carmona or Aguiló, who, although they include some sequences deeply haptic in nature, rely widely on the use of onscreen testimony. Furthermore, although they insert their experiences into a broader collective framework, both Carmona and Aguiló ground their narratives in the personal experience of loss and as direct victims of the dictatorship. Because of the subjected position from which these directors address the spectator, they risk fostering a response of simple identification, which is intensified by these works' tendency to depict children as victims. As Marianne Hirsch asserts, the dangers of mobilizing the image of the child victim is that 'it facilitates an identification in which the viewer can too easily become a surrogate victim'.[50] The spectatorial identification prompted by the figure of children 'risks the blurring of important areas of difference and alterity: context, specificity, responsibility, history'.[51]

On the contrary, in the cases of Rossi, Panizza, and Ballesteros, despite drawing upon the trope of the family and childhood memories, their disembodied and fragmented narrators, and most significantly, the emphasis they place on materiality, hinder character identification. The identification these documentaries trigger is of a different nature, involving the materiality of the image itself, which Beugnet has defined as a 'primary' one.[52] Rather than an identification with characters, the 'cinema of sensation' fosters one with the 'film as event', relying 'on the material qualities of the medium to construct a space that encourages a relation of intimacy or proximity with the object of the gaze'.[53] This primary identification goes beyond the one established with the camera's point of view to include issues such as framing, tone, and rhythm.[54]

Pablo Corro has coined the notion of 'poéticas débiles' [feeble poetics] to explain Chilean cinema's growing tendency (in fiction and non-fiction) to reject an epic treatment of historical events and to privilege the insignificant story, the undetermined, and the offscreen space to the detriment of action and information, among other characteristics.[55] These features in fact are constitutive of the 'cinema of affect' that I take up in this section. I would like to insist, however, that in my view, an understanding of cinema as a sensorial experience does not mean that these works are unconcerned with history or that they fail to present a political stance. As Beugnet asserts, 'synaesthetic, embodied evocation may be one of the ways by which film can 'think' its way concretely through the most burning of contemporary issues, tackling strategies of historical amnesia and exclusion through its own operations.'[56]

In a similar vein, examining the transformation of the notion of the political in Argentine contemporary cinema, Aguilar suggests that there emerged a group of films characterized by a certain 'opacity', in which no overtly political message was to be found.[57] As he explains, this is not to say that these films are apolitical or depoliticizing, but that they may trigger political readings, largely through their formal operations. In Aguilar's words:

> Film aesthetics, these movies seemed to be telling us, cannot access action or political consciousness directly without first reflecting on its own form. But not only this: it is in its form that film, unfailingly and without recognizing an obligation from without, should find its own political justification, one not given beforehand. [...] Because this function is not previously ascribed, every response is a political option in and of itself. [...] Rather than film being something that reaches us in the form of a message, the screen is a surface on which both director and spectators inscribe a meaning that may or may not be political.[58]

Aguilar describes what is at stake in the three Chilean post-dictatorship documentaries I discuss in this section. All three were released at the end of the decade, but the formal reflection on how to deal with the past within a broader second generation can be traced back at least to *Los escolares se siguen amando,* produced in 2000. Due to its characteristics — haptic images, recourse to an aural historical archive instead of a visual one, and the absence of 'talking heads' (of direct *testimonio*) — this documentary is an important early example of a 'cinema of affect' that developed more clearly by the end of the first decade of the twenty-first century. Paco Toledo's work was filmed in 16mm and 35mm from material that some production companies offered to the crew (again, one might think of discarded material), as they were part of the advertisement world. Hence the particular haptic images offered by this film are partly due to budget restrictions, but also reflect the fact that the documentary was filmed at varying, sometimes very slow, rates of speed (for the most part 4, 6, and 12 FPS).[59] As mentioned in my discussion of the *burden of representation* carried by Chilean cinema since the coup, Toledo sought to move away from what he describes as 'el documental de llanto y música folklórica', and decided to experiment with less common audiovisual strategies in political documentary.[60] *Los escolares se siguen amando* registers the events commemorating 11 September in Santiago in 1999, when Pinochet was detained in London. There are no archival images, no interviews or commentary (the director appears onscreen only once to briefly change the film in the camera). In Toledo's film, history enters aurally through the use of short fragments of the aural repertoire of the military coup (such as Allende's last speech, the radio communications between Pinochet and other commanders during the fatidic morning, and the military *bandos* that followed); these sounds of the past are layered against Chile's backdrop of the end of the century. The director goes to the same places where the commemorative public rituals take place: La Moneda, the Cementerio General, the Estadio Nacional.

However, the camera is located either below or above the subjects he registers in those locations, never from within, and the images are always in fast or slow motion. Through these gestures, similar to other documentarians' work almost a decade later (such as that of Panizza, or Perut and Osnovikoff), he distances formally both from hegemonic discourses and the figure of *el pueblo*, which are here personified by a crowd composed of journalists, policemen, and demonstrators. Toledo includes, intermittently throughout the film, almost undistinguishable images of the brutal folkloric tradition of cockfighting, as though they were brushstrokes of colour. These persistent abstract images of violence function as a metaphor for the notorious clashes that repeatedly erupt in Chile's largely polarized society each 11 September. The documentary ends with images of teenagers in love, oblivious to the commemorative fever, countered by extracts of the coup's 'soundtrack'. As I read it, this ending signals that the past still hovers over the present, despite the obliviousness of youth. What Toledo also seems to suggest with this closure is a call for the past to be addressed differently, in terms of discursive forms and violent repetitions. After all, he seems to say, the youth are not to blame.

I would like to recall at this point the question raised by Lucía Salinas in her 1990 documentary, *Canto a la vida*: 'Can the years we never lived be recalled?'. How can a past not experienced directly, but which has inevitably marked an individual's own experience, be appropriated? I believe that Rossi, Panizza, and Ballesteros aesthetically engage with the challenge posed by this question. Rossi takes part in this quest as a child of Chilean parents born in exile, and Panizza and Ballesteros do the same as members of a broader second generation. All of them inscribe their own diasporic identities in their works, Rossi as Chilean-born and raised in Italy, Panizza as a Chilean-Italian who studied abroad in Cuba and the UK, and Ballesteros as a director who trained in France, where he is currently based. Although they adopt different strategies, they share the use of a first-person narrator/character who does not seem to have the legitimacy provided by direct experience (Rossi, who is nonetheless a child of exiled parents, did not experience the dictatorship *en carne y hueso* so to speak, as she was born and raised abroad), and they reflect on identity and memory while obliquely evoking the dictatorial period and its remnants. These works not only foreground their constructedness, in the way performative documentaries as theorized by Bruzzi do, but also significantly incline towards what Bill Nichols has defined as performative: they deflect the spectator's focus away from the indexical status of the image, favouring instead documentary's more expressive, evocative, and affective potential.[61]

Interestingly, these three filmmakers reflect on the 'prosthetic' character of memories, questioning the notions of authenticity and ownership that surround them, while interrogating the documentary image as a straightforward index of the past. The notion of prosthetic seeks to foreground the itinerant character of memory, as Alison Landsberg has proposed, since memories are not necessarily grounded in an experience lived directly, but may also be incorporated and turned into a constitutive part of identity.[62] In *El eco de las canciones*, as mentioned earlier, the director brings together various kinds of footage, from fiction to documentary, from news reports to home movies, all interwoven by a disembodied and nameless fictive narrator. Rossi's female character is constructed around the testimonies she gathered from children who, like her, were raised in exile in Italy. Her film emerges directly from these interviews. The questions she posed to her interviewees were articulated precisely around affect; Rossi was interested in capturing the perceptions, dreams, and smells they recalled, moving the testimonies away from the realm of reason.[63] One might say then that her work seeks to stage the whispers or reverberations of a history only heard through other people's voices, as she explains: 'empecé a recolectar trozos [...] retazos de todas estas historias y a construir un personaje ficcionado, o sea, es mi historia y la historia de todos estos personajes' [I gathered remnants from all these stories and began constructing a fictive character, so this is my story, but it is also the story of all these characters].[64] The nameless and disembodied woman who recalls, and the broad range of footage through which Rossi builds the childhood memories of her fictional character dilute the boundaries between the individual experience and the collective one. The director incorporates myriad reminiscences of the experience of exile, collecting sounds and images from other people's childhoods or youth (children's games, family dinners, holidays) as though they belonged to her. Through the montage of this recovered material the director is able to construct both beautifully and wittily the process of growing up (from childbirth via the inclusion of home movies taken in hospital rooms to footage of graduation parties), effectively constructing an allegory of the displaced individual. Her narrator embodies the collective experience of exile; the fact that she is nameless adds to such an allegorical function. It is precisely the mixture of different visual materials and their juxtaposition with the elaborate soundtrack (both fictional and documentary in nature) that constitutes the particular haptic qualities of the film.

Remitente is the second part of Tiziana Panizza's *Cartas visuales* [*Visual Letters*] trilogy; the first is constructed around a letter sent from London to Chile, *Dear Nonna: A Film Letter* (2004), the second, about a letter sent from Chile to Italy, and the third one, *Al final: la última carta* [*In the End: The Last Letter*] (2012), is addressed to her son. In these epistolary works, all of which are filmed in Super-8, the director merges her own images with found footage, graphic animations, and handwritten texts, intermingling, without hierarchical order, the materiality of everyday life (for instance, her grandmother's loss of memory, the sound of organ grinders, her maternity) and history (notably, Pinochet's death).

Rossi and Panizza enact the same gesture towards the past: they literally and materially borrow other people's images and make them their own. This political and aesthetic gesture is two-fold. On the one hand, by including other people's domestic footage these two directors suggest that it is possible to incorporate other people's memories. By doing so, they avow that memories are not necessarily anchored to a subject, that there is no possible exclusive 'ownership' of the past. They stage via their material operations that 'Cultural memories no longer have exclusive owners; they do not "naturally" belong to anyone.'[65] On the other hand, the images they borrow are not historically significant images; these are, in Rossi's words, 'imágenes escupidas por la historia' [images spat out by history].[66]

The materials these directors rescue have been previously discarded, not only by official discourses, but also by people themselves, either by dumping them into their memory boxes or discarding them at flea markets. Panizza rescues the memories of anonymous people, buying their domestic remembrances in the form of Super-8 films at a popular flea market. What Panizza rescues from oblivion are other people's instants: 'Son recuerdos de otros' [They're other people's memories], she states on handwritten notes set against a black screen; 'Son *mis* recuerdos' [They're *my* memories] (film's original English subtitles, my emphasis), she amends afterwards. The spectator sees the transformation of these memories from commodities into a poetic montage of amateur filmmakers holding their own cameras (she is those men *now*; she will be an image like those men in the *future*), a woman knitting a baby's cardigan, families on the beach — all of them juxtaposed by the director's own list of things she does not want to forget (a piece of orange peel in her pocket, the smell of her father's pillow, the first time she heard her own baby's heartbeat). These images' affective force are derived not only from the 'feelings of intimacy' triggered by their domestic origin, as Beugnet explains, but also by 'the material and aesthetic characteristics of the medium itself that endow its images with a specific corporeal and synaesthetic appeal'.[67] The fleetingness of the Super-8 footage links its specific materiality to the 'episodic and contemplative' instead of a structured narrative.[68] Beugnet goes on to note: 'The aim is simply to document a moment, the memory of an instant or a particular atmosphere. Moreover, the footage often shows the marks of repeated manipulation — scratches that are, to paraphrase the title of Marks' book, like scars on the "skin of the film".'[69] In addition to the use of Super-8 to create her textured account on the nature of memory, Panizza also interrogates the notion of a fixed identity, addressing the spectators as a wandering tourist, as she describes herself in her film. Her self-inscription is always fragmented, as though in transit. Not only does she mix several media, thus playing with the limits of the documentary film, but she also utilizes multiple languages (English, Mapudungun, Italian).

La quemadura by René Ballesteros interconnects the search of the director and his sister for their mother, who abandoned them almost thirty years before, with the country's past via the lost books of Quimantú (the publishing house created during Allende's government that sought to massively expand book production). Like Rossi and Panizza, Ballesteros also seems to suggest that there is no exclusive ownership of the past and stresses that there is no direct link whatsoever between the documentary image and truth. Unlike Rossi and Panizza, however, the director performs an inverse operation in *La quemadura*. Rather than incorporating other people's memories as his own, Ballesteros calls into question the authenticity of his own family pictures, exposing them as a fabrication; a sort of memory implant. During one of the extensive telephonic conservations between the director and his mother, she tells Ballesteros how her body, when she first arrived in Venezuela, used to feel Chile's seasonal changes. He explains to her that what she describes is similar to what is called the 'phantom limb' syndrome: the feeling experienced by someone who has lost a body part and is nevertheless able to perceive the member as though it were still there. This sequence can be linked to a later one in which the artifices of memory are highlighted. The two siblings look at Polaroid pictures of their childhood, which their mother has just given them. The stills are shown in extreme close-ups; they cannot be seen in their entirety, as the silhouette of one of the siblings partially covers them, making the original Polaroid seem even more diffuse, thus emphasizing the documentary's tactile qualities. In the pictures, the two children are smiling, walking around and sitting on the bonnet of a car. They look happy. Yet, the director believes these pictures to be scenarios staged by their mother just before her departure: 'parecen como de mentira [...] Es como una ficción' [they are so far from the truth [...] It's like a fiction'], he says to his sister (this and following citations are from the film's original English subtitles). This particular sequence refers to a couple of points highlighted by Annette Kuhn, such as that family pictures can be a battlefield and that the 'use' one gives to photographs places them in a tense relationship with the past and present.[70] This also seems to suggest that, just as one can feel a body part that it is no longer there as 'phantom limb', one can also create memories in their absence as though they were prosthetic. These three documentaries are linked then, not only by their material qualities but also by their itinerant understanding of memory; in these works memories circulate, can be bought, implanted, even rejected. They seem to align with Landsberg's claim: 'authenticity is no longer considered a necessary element of memory. Where memories come from matters less than how they enable a person to live in the present'.[71]

It is important to underscore yet again the fact that none of these directors dismiss history from their works; rather, history enters their discourses obliquely. In Rossi's film for instance, the dictatorial past enters via extensive archival material that is both aural and visual. The historically significant materials included here are varied and the period covered is vast, ranging from the infamous radio broadcasts by the military during the 11 of September to images of Pinochet in his coffin in 2006. Yet history is always mediated, as if heard or seen from radio or television, or through a window; these events are inscribed as 'subjectivized' episodes, as Rossi describes them.[72] Take, for instance, the sequence in *El eco de las canciones* where Rossi's narrator remembers her father yelling from his room: '¡Noticias de Chile!' [News from Chile!]. An animation of a young boy who cleans a fogged up window dissolves into the demonstrations of the 1980s. In distinctive U-matic quality the documentary shows bloodstains on the floor next to a leaflet calling for mobilization and women being attacked by police water cannon. The images of the protests are further mediated by the voiceover of a news narrator who speaks in Italian about the repression in Chile. Though Rossi is drawing here from a repertoire of images systematically revisited in Chilean contemporary cinema, as will be seen in the next chapter, she goes further than many of these revisions in its self-reflexive treatment. Rather than functioning in an illustrative way, or as evidence of an argument, Rossi puts this footage in circulation not to say 'this is what happened' but to forcefully state that 'this is how I recall that it happened' (an 'I' that is for Rossi necessarily collective).

In *Remitente*, history seems to have caught the director, pulling her into filming Pinochet's death. Panizza's work is constructed upon an elaborate soundtrack (the sound of water, birds, buildings in construction, radio transmissions, music) and fragmented images (the flag, the Andes, yellow buses, Providencia's neighbourhood buildings, citizens in a state wavering between perplexity and euphoria) which seek to build through association and repetition not only the texture of memory and oblivion but also a poetic proposal of the nation's imagery. Hence, like Rossi, despite the obvious significance of Pinochet's death, Panizza does not privilege these fragments over others. She nonetheless decides to go out into the streets and film the polarized reactions of Chilean society to this event. Throughout this action she nods to the militant documentary tradition of the previous decades. Handwritten words inform the spectator of this event. 'Pinochet is dead' appears on the screen. 'I was there with my camera', she writes, paying tribute to Jonas Mekas. Through the pointed montage of this sequence, the director addresses the uncertainty and confusion that infused Chilean society as it faced this event as well as the impossibility of accessing this past. Glimpses of a baffled woman who peers out from a bus window, a mannequin of a nurse that holds a banner that reads 'tenemos todo para su enfermo' [we have everything for your sick one] and several broken audio recordings that seem to be talking about mathematical formulas merge with images of Pinochet's supporters. The images of these supporters bring the past into the present, reminding the spectator of the hatred that divided the country under Salvador Allende, and in particular we see one of them who confronts the filmmaker violently but we cannot hear his words. 'He called me "communist bitch... get out of here"', Panizza writes in English on the screen while she places the camera at a significant distance between her and the demonstrators, stating that she is filming as an outsider. With this move she not only distances herself from Pinochet's supporters but also stages her detachment from *el pueblo* and emphasizes her own relationship with history. It is she who is there with her camera. She will continue filming Chile's social transformations from an intimate standpoint in her last letter, *Al final*, by merging textured images of the Estadio Nacional today (explicitly stressing the violence which occurred there) with glimpses of everyday life, seeking to bring to a halt the passage of time.

Lastly, the title of Ballesteros's documentary *La quemadura* points both to the wound caused by the disappearance of the director's mother and to a bonfire in which the military destroyed the Quimantú books in the days that followed the coup. Numerous books were burnt as part of what has been called the regime's 'operación limpieza' [cleansing operation] of the cultural traces of the UP.[73] These books, which the mother used to collect but has now forgotten, embody metonymically the phantom of Allende's government and build a bridge between personal, familiar, and cultural memories. This link is explicitly made at the site where the publishing house used to stand, an area now facing destruction where the director interviews two former employees of the publishing house who talk about the burning of the books. Though a deeply personal work, the dictatorial past weighs heavily on *La quemadura*. Ballesteros sees this complex personal and historical weaving 'tal vez como muestras, en el sentido de las muestras médicas, como un análisis microscópico de un momento en la historia de una familia que pudiera iluminar un fragmento de la historia de la censura y destrucción de libros en Chile' [like a microscopic analysis of a particular moment shared by a family that may shed light on a fragment of the history of censorship and of the destruction of books in Chile].[74]

This documentary may be more narrative than the other two analysed in this section, but it is just as haptic. An interest in exploring the affective quality of memory is revealed at the outset of the film, the title of which, *La quemadura* — *The Burn* — already suggests a tactile sensation. The haptic qualities achieved by the documentary are partly brought about by the use of four different cameras (of varying resolutions), which Ballesteros explains was initially a question of budget restrictions.[75] Only later he realized that the distinct textures and sounds they provided worked in a synaesthetic way that allowed him to convey senses like smell:

> Yo podía oler la página con ese sonido y no con el otro [...] tu puedes restituir otros sentidos que no están presentes a la base en el cine [...] la memoria, el olfato, las sensaciones táctiles que puedas tener [...] yo creo que el trabajo con la materia te puede dar eso [...] hay que buscar un poco como restituir las cosas que no están en la película directamente.[76]

> [I could smell the page with that sound and not with the other [...] in cinema you can restore the senses that are not present from the outset [...] memory, smell, the tactile sensations that one might have [...] I believe that the work with the materiality [of the image] allows you to do that [...] you have to look a little, to restore what is not directly in the film.]

In *La quemadura*, tightly fixed frames of long duration, combined with unstable close-ups taken with handheld low-resolution cameras (usually in closed spaces), prompt the immersion of the spectator in a suffocating atmosphere. Occasionally, Ballesteros is seen taking swimming lessons, which only increases the asphyxiating sensation. This is most remarkably achieved in a sequence in which the spectator sees the director's fragmented body moving awkwardly underwater, the camera placed inside the pool in a medium long shot; the lens abruptly zooms to his chest and then cuts to various shots of the director's fragmented body which appears headless throughout the whole sequence. The images of the body under water are juxtaposed with the telephone conversation between Ballesteros and his mother about the Quimantú books. He asks her if she remembers the publishing house, which she does not. He insists: 'era una editorial del gobierno de Allende' [It was a publisher under the socialist government of Allende]. 'Nada, no me acuerdo nada de esa época' [I don't remember anything from that era], she replies. These books, he insists, are the only things that remain from the period they lived together. But she has no memories of it. The dialogue continues in this circular fashion, with Ballesteros insisting on bringing his mother's memories back while she struggles, in vain, to do so. Forcefully, the images filmed underwater, like those that traverse the library archives and its corridors, are all threaded together by the disembodied voice of the mother over the telephone, exteriorizing an interior landscape of 'sense memories', as defined by Jill Bennett. In Bennett's interpretation,

> a sense memory is about tapping a certain kind of process; a process experienced not as a remembering of the past but as a continuous negotiation of a present with indeterminable links to the past. The poetics of sense memory involve not so much *speaking of* but *speaking out of* a particular memory or experience — in other words, speaking from the body *sustaining sensation*.[77] (emphasis in the original)

Ballesteros's body is submerged in the deep waters of memory, and the spectator's body is invited to plunge alongside it. What Bennett writes about contemporary artworks' engagement with extreme bodily exposure is illuminating here. Ballesteros seems not just to be staging his own body's enduring sensation, but also to be seeking an affective reaction from the spectator, since 'to engage with it is always in some sense to feel it viscerally'.[78] Ballesteros' documentary is circular, elliptical, it presents lacunae; his work cinematically embodies memory's vicissitudes. The Quimantú books were their only link to their mother and to the dictatorial past; they have disappeared not only from their own house, but also from the history of the nation, leaving only traces. Likewise, in his family no one wants to, or simply cannot, testify about the past (his mother is unable to recall anything, as if in 'shock', she says, while his grandmother cannot remember anything because of old age and his father refuses to talk about it). In return, it is as if the senses are remembering when no one else does.[79] The historical past is depicted here through its absence; there are no archival images of the publishing house or of political repression. Ballesteros includes only his own family pictures, marking a significant difference in this regard from Rossi's and Panizza's work. His multiple geographical displacements exhibit no trajectories (he moves from Chile to France to Venezuela, and when in Chile he moves from Santiago to the southern city of Temuco, yet the spectator remains largely unaware of all these journeys). Similarly to both Rossi's and Panizza's project, however, *La quemadura* is also constructed from interstices, narrated from the periphery — from a dysfunctional family, from a generation without major epics to narrate, from non-metropolitan places — and also from a mainly feminine universe (the main characters are women: his mother, his sister, his grandmother, the *machi*),[80] which accentuates the documentary's location on the outskirts of hegemonic discourses.

In this chapter I have explored the context in which the first-person documentaries of a second generation of directors emerged. For lack of more adequate terms, I use literal second generation to refer to the work of directors whose parents were direct victims of state violence and broader second generation to talk about the work of directors who did not experience it directly. My rationale for this move is to facilitate a recognition of the difficulties entailed in discussing generational differences in the context of the Chilean dictatorship, particularly regarding its long duration, the scope of violence, the structural transformations enacted by the military rule, and its authoritarian remnants.

By drawing on the concepts of postmemory and prosthetic memory I have stressed the affective features mobilized by these directors to address a past they did not experience or, because of their young age, they only remember through glimpses of childhood. Focusing on a number of brief sequences from several documentaries I have explored the cinematic mechanisms through which these directors affectively engage with the past. On the one hand, I have explored how the children of direct victims use the materiality of the image in order to breach the gap that separates them from their fathers who died at the hands of the regime. On the other hand, I have examined how a broader generation develops discourses around the prosthetic quality of memory, thus cinematically exploring the possibilities of making other people's memories one's own.

While some of the documentaries of the children of those who were directly affected include haptic moments, usually in the form of reenactments and/or through the use of Super-8 or 16mm, the documentaries analysed in the last section constitute inherently sensorial works. They constitute remarkable examples of the shift in post-dictatorship documentary towards a 'cinema of affect'. In the next chapter, I continue exploring the way this shift was taken up by a broader second generation during the 2000s, focusing both on nostalgic accounts from the 1980s and on two of the most challenging documentaries confronting the 'memory question' in Chile.

Notes to Chapter 4

1. Alejandro Zambra, *Formas de volver a casa* (Barcelona: Anagrama, 2011), p. 57.
2. Ana Amado, *La imagen justa: cine argentino y política, 1980–2007* (Buenos Aires: Colihue, 2009), pp. 145–203.
3. See, for example, Johansson and Vergara; María José Bello, 'Documentales sobre la memoria chilena: aproximaciones desde lo íntimo', *Cinémas d'Amérique latine* 19 (2011), 77–79; and Bernardita Llanos, 'Caught Off Guard at the Crossroads of Ideology and Affect: Documentary Films by the Daughters of Revolutionaries', in *Latin American Documentary Film in the New Millenium*, ed. by María Guadalupe Arenillas and Michael J. Lazzara (New York: Palgrave, 2016), pp. 243–58.
4. See, for instance, Bossy and Vergara.
5. Marianne Hirsch, 'The Generation of Postmemory', *Poetics Today*, 29 (Spring 2008), 103–28 (p. 115). For the Latin American case with a focus on Argentina, see Ana Amado and Nora Domínguez, *Lazos de familia: herencias, cuerpos y ficciones* (Buenos Aires: Paidós, 2004).
6. Ranvaud, p. 16.
7. Rich, p. 282.
8. Ibid., pp. 83–122.
9. Masiello, pp. 14–15.
10. Ibid., p. 28.
11. Ibid., p. 23.
12. Ibid., pp. 23–24.
13. Gonzalo Aguilar, 'El pueblo como lo "real": hacia una genealogía del cine latinoamericano', in *Más allá del pueblo: imágenes, indicios y políticas del cine* (Buenos Aires: Fondo de Cultura Económica, 2015), pp. 179–94 (p. 190)
14. Ibid., p. 193
15. Renov, *The Subject of Documentary* and Alisa Lebow, 'Introduction', in *The Cinema of Me: The Self and Subjectivity in First Person Documentary*, ed. by Alisa Lebow (London: Wallflower Press, 2012), pp. 1–11.
16. Richard, 'Ir y venir', p. 148. See also my analysis focused on Castillo, 'Memoria y desobediencia'.

17. For a critique of such striking representational absence in Guzmán's post-dictatorial work, see Klubock; for a more celebratory stance on the director's emphasis on absence, see Blaine.
18. Pablo Corro, *Retóricas del cine chileno: ensayos con el realismo* (Santiago: Cuarto Propio, 2012), p. 74.
19. Ibid., pp. 74–75.
20. Ibid., pp. 227–40.
21. Ibid..
22. Frazier, p. 230.
23. See, among others, Bossy and Vergara; Johansson and Vergara; and Paola Lagos, 'Ecografías del "yo": documental autobiográfico y estrategias de (auto) representación de la subjetividad', *Comunicación y Medios*, 24 (2011), 60–80.
24. Lebow, ibid., p. 2.
25. Ibid., p. 3.
26. Kuhn, p. 151.
27. Hirsch, *Family Frames*, p. 22.
28. Ibid..
29. See, for example, Gabriela Nouzeilles, 'Postmemory Cinema and the Future of the Past in Albertina Carri's Los Rubios', *Journal of Latin American Cultural Studies: Travesia*, 14: 3 (2005) 263–78; Michael J. Lazzara, 'Filming Loss: (Post-) Memory, Subjectivity, and the Performance of Failure in Recent Argentine Documentary Films', *Latin American Perspectives*, 36:5 (2009), 147–57; and Beatriz Tadeo-Fuica, 'Memory or postmemory? Documentaries directed by Uruguay's second generation', *Memory Studies*, 8:3 (2015), 298–312.
30. Sarlo, p. 134. For her extended critique see pp. 125–57.
31. Marianne Hirsch, 'Projected Memory: Holocaust Photographs in Personal and Public Fantasy', in *Acts of Memory: Cultural Recall in the Present*, ed. by Mieke Bal, Jonathan Crewe and Leo Spitzer (Hanover: University Press of New England, 1999), pp. 5–23 (pp. 8–9).
32. Such difficulties have been provocatively addressed in the context of child survivors in the context of the Holocaust by Susan Rubin Suleiman, 'The 1.5 Generation: Thinking About Child Survivors and the Holocaust', *American Imago*, 59:3 (Fall 2002), 277–95. For a similar nuanced discussion of the Uruguayan case, see Tadeo-Fuica.
33. La Nación, 'Marco Enríquez-Ominami: La sorpresa de la campaña chilena', *La Nación*, 27 September 2009 <http://www.lanacion.com.ar/1179066-marco-enriquez-ominami-la-sorpresa-de-la-campana-chilena> [accessed 15 October 2018].
34. Ana Amado, 'Órdenes de la memoria y desórdenes de la ficción', in *Lazos de familia: herencias, cuerpos y ficciones*, ed. by Ana Amado and Nora Domínguez (Buenos Aires: Paidós, 2004), pp. 43–82 (p. 51).
35. Jorge Morales, 'Vine a decirles que me quedo: el cine de Marco Enríquez-Ominami', *Mabuse* (2004) <http://www.mabuse.cl/cine_chileno.php?id=86432> [accessed 15 October 2018].
36. ARTE, 'Programmation Spéciale Chili' (n.d.). <http://download.pro.arte.tv/archives/fichiers/01676297.pdf> [accessed 15 October 2018]. The film was indeed coproduced by ARTE (a French-German channel) and aired on a special season commemorating the thirtieth anniversary of the military coup.
37. These terms are explored by Gonzalo Aguilar in his *Other Worlds: New Argentine Film*, trans. by Sarah Ann Wells (New York: Palgrave Macmillan, 2008). I will return to them later in this chapter.
38. Ana Amado, 'Memory, Identity and Film: Blending Past and Present', *ReVista Harvard Review of Latin America* (Fall 2009/Winter 2010), 38–41 (p. 38).
39. Amado, *La imagen justa*, pp. 145–203.
40. Rubin Suleiman, p. 292.
41. Hirsch, *Family Frames*, p. 243.
42. Only in January 2014 recent investigations were able to identify Berger's remains. See Ivonne Toro, 'Carmen Hertz y censura a obituario de Carlos Berger: "Es indecente e inmoral. Voy a emprender acciones legales contra El Mercurio"', *The Clinic*, 9 April 2014 <http://www.theclinic.cl/2014/04/09/carmen-hertz-y-censura-a-obituario-de-carlos-berger-es-indecente-e-inmoral-voy-a-emprender-acciones-legales-contra-el-mercurio/> [accessed 10 November 2018].

43. The struggle of Carmen Hertz to pursue truth and justice has been depicted in a major television fiction series directed by celebrated Chilean director Andrés Wood, *Ecos del desierto* (*Echoes of the Desert*) (2013). The four episode series was released in Chilevision in September 2013 in the context of the commemorations of the fortieth anniversary of the coup. Hertz recently published her memoirs under the telling title *La historia fue otra* (Santiago: Penguin Random House, 2017).
44. Barthes's words were: 'A sort of umbilical cord links the body of the photographed thing to my gaze: light, though impalpable, is here a carnal medium, a skin I share with anyone who has been photographed'. See his *Camera Lucida: Reflections on Photography*, trans. by Richard Howard (New York: Hill and Wang, 1981), p.81. I have been inspired by Hirsch's reading of Barthes, who remarks upon the maternal metaphor offered by the philosopher. See Hirsch, *Family Frames*, p. 20.
45. Johansson and Vergara, p. 102.
46. Personal e-mail communication with Macarena Aguiló, 22 April 2011.
47. Donoso, p. 27.
48. Beugnet, Chapter 2.
49. Ibid., pp. 67–68.
50. Hirsch, 'Projected Memory', p. 17.
51. Ibid.
52. Beugnet, pp. 6–7 n. 8; 68.
53. Ibid., p. 68.
54. Ibid., p. 7 n. 8.
55. Corro, *Retóricas*, pp. 217–25.
56. Beugnet, p. 83.
57. Aguilar, *Other Worlds*, pp. 120–21.
58. Ibid., pp. 122–23.
59. Personal e-mail communication with Paco Toledo, 26 September 2012.
60. Ibid.
61. Bill Nichols, *Blurred Boundaries: Questions of Meaning in Contemporary Culture* (Bloomington: Indiana University Press, 1994), pp. 92–116.
62. Landsberg, pp. 25–26.
63. Interview with Antonia Rossi, Santiago de Chile, 13 July 2011.
64. Ibid.
65. Landsberg, p. 18.
66. Interview with Antonia Rossi, Santiago de Chile, 13 July 2011.
67. Beugnet, p. 133.
68. Ibid., p. 133.
69. Ibid., pp. 133–34.
70. Kuhn, p. 19.
71. Landsberg, p. 42.
72. Interview with Antonia Rossi, Santiago de Chile, 13 July 2011.
73. Luis Hernán Errázuriz, 'Dictadura militar en Chile: antecedentes del golpe estético-cultural', *Latin American Research Review* 44:2 (2009), 136–57 (p. 139).
74. Personal e-mail communication with René Ballesteros, 29 April 2010.
75. Interview with René Ballesteros, Paris, 12 March 2012.
76. Ibid.
77. Bennett, p. 38.
78. Ibid..
79. Marks, *The Skin of the Film*, p. 110.
80. *Machi* is the name given to sage indigenous Mapuche women.

CHAPTER 5

Extending the Circle: Nostalgia for the 1980s and Unsettling Accounts

This chapter focuses on documentaries that emerged in the aftermath of the thirtieth anniversary of the coup, when a significant number of productions dealing with the experience of direct victims had already been released and important cultural and political transformations were taking place in Chile. Created by a broader second generation, in the sense that the filmmakers do not inscribe in their texts an explicit familial bond with a direct victim, these works continue to expand the idea of the directly affected by inserting into history previously disregarded stories as well as rather unsettling voices.

In the first section I look at documentaries that, instead of focusing on the UP or the early years of the repression, shift their lenses to the political struggles of the 1980s. After examining the main features of these productions, particularly their distinct nostalgic stance and their mobilization of archival footage of those struggles, the second section analyses two documentaries that further complicate debates about the recent past. In both of them, concealed bodies are revealed. However, unlike the bodies of the directly affected unearthed by early post-dictatorship productions, these works expose abject bodies that disturb the traditionally dominant polarized discourses about the past. *El mocito* (Marcela Said and Jean de Certeau, 2011) and *La muerte de Pinochet* (Bettina Perut and Iván Osnovikoff, hereafter P+O, as they also call themselves, 2011) do so through an ambiguous character that worked as a butler for Pinochet's secret police, and through Pinochet's supporters, respectively. Despite the radical differences that can be found between documentaries that return to the 1980s and those that reveal abject bodies, all of them share the need to broaden the position from which to speak, moving away, more or less explicitly, from a restrictive focus on the direct victims.

Beyond Family Ties

In 2013, *No* (Pablo Larraín, 2012) made an — until then — unparalleled successful circuit for a Chilean feature film at international festivals, obtaining several awards, securing the country's first Academy Award nomination for Best Foreign Film, and appearing on the front pages of major international journals such as *Sight and Sound*. The film is based on actual facts pertaining to the backstage of the cheerful marketing campaign elaborated by Pinochet's opposition which aired nationwide on the eve of the national referendum in 1988. In this historical poll, Chileans voted 'Yes' for Pinochet to remain in power (for eight more years) or 'No' for Pinochet to resign; as is known, the 'No' option triumphed.

Larraín's *No* is shot on U-matic (a format widely used during the 1980s), which allows him to 'approximate'[1] factual and fictive footage, seamlessly merging past and present material. It includes extensive fragments of the television campaign as well as many of its original protagonists and creators performing as themselves in front of the camera today, strikingly exposing the passage of time through the bodies on the screen.[2] Despite its formal achievements and in stark opposition to the enthusiastic international responses, the film's local reception was deeply contested due to its reductionist historical interpretation of Chile's democratic opening. As it emerges from the film, the 'No' option triumphed thanks to the appealing television campaign that knew how to 'sell' democracy as just another product of consumption, radically downplaying the active role that civil society played in the democratic restoration. Reactions within the country were harsh and were voiced by a broad array of scholars, politicians, and even people actively involved in the 'No' campaign: sociologist Manuel Antonio Garretón described it as 'basura ideológica' [ideological rubbish],[3] feminist literary scholar Raquel Olea called it a 'perversión' [perversion] of history,[4] and journalist Augusto Góngora, a central figure from the 1980s audiovisual scene (including the referendum campaign), critiqued the underlying principle of the film as it negates the enormous efforts made by grassroots movements.[5] Which buttons did *No* push to trigger such heated reactions? Larraín touches upon nothing less than the powerful heroic memories of the social uprising against the dictatorship, which have attained an even mythic character across widespread sectors of Chilean society.[6]

Memories of the struggles undertaken during the 1980s have found their way into numerous Chilean post-dictatorship documentaries, many of which have been made by directors of this broader second generation: *Volver a vernos* (2002), *Malditos, la historia de los Fiskales Ad-Hok* (hereinafter *Malditos*) (Pablo Insunza, 2004), *Actores secundarios* (2004), *Con el ojo en el visor* (*With the Eye Behind the Camera Lens*) (Sebastián Larraín, 2004), *La ciudad de los fotógrafos* (2006), *80s: el soundtrack de una generación* (*80s: The Soundtrack of a Generation*, hereinafter *80s*) (Eduardo Bertrán, 2006), *Ruidos molestos* (*Annoying Noises*) (Viviana Sepúlveda, 2007), and *Electrodomésticos: el frío misterio* [*Electrodomésticos: The Cold Mystery*, hereinafter *Electrodomésticos*] (Sergio Castro San Martín, 2010).

These productions speak about the so-called *desencanto* characteristic of the Chilean transition, particularly in the arresting opposition they exhibit between the present-day and the collective awakening experienced in the past, when these directors and the subjects they focus on were children, teenagers, or young adults. The rage and frustration of a generation raised under a state of siege was channelled during the 1980s through mass mobilization and artistic practices that were seen as cultural and political resistance. These documentaries perform a revelation of archival material often relegated from the screen; they put into circulation discarded stories and images — notably of video footage — of both the collective resistance and the vibrant countercultural scene that developed in the context of the anti-dictatorial struggle. That is, they reveal filmic bodies that had been kept away from the public eye; they bring back to life video footage that had been, until then, dormant. Even when assuming the first-person narration of their productions, the directors aim to construct a collective portrait of actors who claim to have been active participants in the forging of a history that has seemingly obliterated them. Therefore, these works actively extend what Steve Stern has called the 'symbolic circle' of victims of the dictatorship.

In Stern's view, the country had reached by the end of the 1990s 'a cultural endpoint'.[7] A restrictive understanding of who the victims of repression were had crystallized in Chilean society at the time, exacting significant costs in terms of cultural awareness.[8] This was not always the case, however, as indicated by the mass demonstrations held periodically between 1983 and 1984 which continued with varying degrees of stridence throughout the decade.[9] In the 1980s, although the disappeared and their relatives remained a powerful social force, the circle broadened to include people who had gone into exile, students, shantytown dwellers, and middle-class women.[10] During those years of collective awakening, 'a social majority had turned into "victims of dictatorship" to some degree'.[11] In that everyday battle, responsibility was not assigned to a few or a single hero. Instead, resistance was carried on different fronts, including what Javier Martínez has described as 'nonheroic' actions (such as staying at home and beating empty pots and pans); through these and similar acts ordinary citizens managed to overcome perceptions of helplessness in the face of the dictatorship.[12] Nonetheless, this extended awareness rapidly changed with the arrival of the first civilian administration, which drastically tapered — most clearly through the Rettig Report — the 'symbolic circle' of what it meant to be a victim of the dictatorship.[13]

The new 'season of memory' (to return to Wilde's expression) that began at the threshold of the new century managed to create a renewed atmosphere regarding the human rights scene.[14] This context — set into motion by the multiple resonances of Pinochet's detention — facilitated the arrival of many different voices in documentary production, not merely of the children of direct victims, but also of other figures who began asserting more or less overtly their place in this extended 'symbolic circle'.

In light of these transformations, a critical approach based solely on familial bonds is insufficient for understanding the trajectory of post-dictatorship documentary during the 2000s. As a matter of fact, one has to be careful when emphasizing narratives of kinship and direct experience in the context of Latin American post-authoritarian regimes. Beatriz Sarlo, while recognizing that relying on victims' testimonies is a necessary stage for the restoration of democracy and the pursuit of justice and reparations, argues that this does not mean that these narratives should remain protected or unchallenged, as they too are discourses.[15] Victims' accounts should also be open to interpretation, she asserts, especially because other narrations have emerged in parallel with these testimonies which are not protected by the same right or untouchability endorsed by experience.[16] Sociologist Elizabeth Jelin points out that one of the dangers entailed by a restricted focus on the directly affected is that it risks undermining the involvement of the rest of civil society, affecting a more inclusive construction of the past.[17] Furthermore, she argues that an emphasis on kinship in Argentina has established

> a distance in public mobilization between those who are the 'actual' carriers of suffering, and therefore of 'truth', and those motivated by political, humanitarian, or citizen-based reasons. The latter came to be seen as not equally transparent or legitimate. Therefore, in the public sphere of debate and denunciation, participation became stratified according to the public exposure of family ties with the victims.[18]

As this paragraph suggests, this discussion is largely about who has the right to speak about the past, and how. Documentaries by a broader second generation in Chile, whose productions began to be released mostly after 2004, usefully illustrate and nurture this debate as it developed within the country. The proliferation of narratives of the direct victims or their children, and of stories relying on memories of the lived experience of militants, have fostered varied reactions from post-dictatorial directors.

Some documentarians have chosen to openly expose their blood connection to this past, so to speak. For example, in *La ciudad de los fotógrafos*, Sebastián Moreno stresses in voiceover the filial bond he has with one of the photographers — his father — who played a fundamental role registering the last years of repression. Used almost as a triggering device, his unobtrusive personal narration (along with personal childhood pictures that open and close the documentary) emphasizes this kinship despite the fact that his work is above all a well-crafted collective portrait of committed photographers who vigorously engaged in the struggle of the 1980s with their cameras. Similarly, *EEUU vs Allende* features the voice of one of the codirectors, Diego Marín, who opens this investigation of the role played by the US on Allende's fall by openly positioning himself as the son of renowned activist journalist, Patricia Verdugo (Marín does so both aurally and in written form, as the investigation is based on a book she wrote and the documentary is dedicated to her). Lorena Giachino, in *Reinalda del Carmen, mi mamá y yo*, constructs her narration based on the strong bond that her mother had with one of the victims of the regime, Reinalda del Carmen Pereira. Pereira's case is emblematic for human rights organizations because she disappeared while pregnant (the protagonist of *El mocito* was one of the last people who saw her in one of the detention centres). Interestingly, Giachino's strategy is to broaden the notion of family, going beyond a direct bloodline or genetic bond to the victims that Jelin calls into question. In her stubborn quest to discover the destiny of her mother's best friend, she appears to become Pereira's daughter. This extended and alternative conception of family can be seen in the work of other female directors who deal with the experiences of motherhood of revolutionary women as well as that of their children, as previously seen in the case of *Calle Santa Fe* and *El edificio de los chilenos*.

Two other stances go beyond the emphasis on kinship that largely relies upon the legitimacy provided by blood ties or, in Nelly Richard's words, by 'la categoría moral de la experiencia' [the moral category of experience].[19] As seen in the previous chapter, directors from this broader second generation, such as Tiziana Panizza and René Ballesteros, have opted to engage more formally on the exploration of the (im)possibilities of recalling a past that was not directly experienced, thereby elaborating on discourses about the prosthetic qualities of memory. Another of the strategies deployed by these younger directors is to radically invert the focus on the directly affected to other social actors, most polemically towards Pinochet's supporters and collaborators. Documentarians taking these two alternative stances position themselves against narratives constructed around direct victims; that is against what I conceive as a 'cinema of the affected'. They broaden the position from which to speak, shifting the focus away from direct victims and, in cases, even from the wider symbolic circle toward other social actors, further challenging the 'categorical oppositions between official and dissident forces'[20] fostered by the dictatorial scenario. For instance, René Ballesteros situates his work almost in contrast to films that in his view either monumentalize or victimize memory (in the sense of speaking on behalf of the victims),[21] and Iván Osnovikoff sees the P+O documentary project as a rebellion against conventional historical discourses of both the right and the left. [22]

Both *El mocito* and *La muerte de Pinochet* elaborate unsettling narratives that drastically distance themselves from the works analysed so far. As a matter of fact, P+O's project explicitly calls into question what they consider to be the standard human rights discourse and its manifestation in documentary, which Osnovikoff describes as the hegemonic tendency to idealize people and even to sacralize them.[23] The duo thus sets out to deconstruct what Richard has described elsewhere as 'the mythologization of the historical past', visualized as an emblem of pure political ideals which led to 'a sanctification of the victims'.[24] Before focusing on these last two documentaries of the trajectory proposed by this book, I analyse the work of directors who forcefully vindicate the role of collective action and thus actively extend the symbolic circle of victims of the dictatorship by looking at the 1980s through a lens of nostalgia.

The 1980s or Longings for the 'Sacrificial *Fiesta*'

Paradoxically, it is through fiction film and primetime television that archival footage from the 1980s has gained unprecedented visibility in recent years. Films such as Larraín's *No* (turned also into a four episode series shown on TVN in 2014 with extended material) and the popularity of television programmes such as the fiction series *Los 80* or *Chile, las imágenes prohibidas* contributed significantly to the visibilization of this 'other' — unofficial — archive.[25] Before these productions reached a wider audience, however, documentary filmmakers had already started looking back to those turbulent years.

In fact, many of the images and sounds captured by the prolific production of video in the 1980s have been systematically revisited by post-dictatorship documentary. The vast amount of footage, which was captured with courage and conviction, has effectively enlarged the cinematic repertoire through which Chilean documentarians have persistently safeguarded the past. Some of the emblematic sounds and images that are now part of this extended repertoire include the threatening sounds of helicopters, police water cannons (in Chilean slang called *guanacos*) unleashed on defenceless citizens, breathtaking shots of people accompanying the body of a beloved priest murdered during a mass raid, a young student violently held by a policeman who holds a shotgun against his face, and countless other examples of similar footage.

Documentaries that return to the 1980s usually foreground the heroic dimensions of the quotidian struggle and adopt a chronological perspective on past events, although directors always locate their stance as an explicit exercise of looking back from present-day Chile. Besides relying extensively on archival material of the street struggles, they also depend on onscreen testimonies as witness accounts or 'expert' voices: musicians and journalists when dealing with the thriving music scene (such as *Malditos, Ruidos molestos, Electrodomésticos, 80s*); former high school or university students involved in political activism (such as *Actores secundarios* and *Volver a vernos*); and the work of independent photographers or cameramen (such as *La ciudad de los fotógrafos* or *Con el ojo en el visor*). Whether dealing with students, photographers, or musicians, these productions favour a linear narration of historical events. They begin with the emergence of these movements in relation to the social and political upheaval in the midst of a virtually barren cultural landscape, and they continue by showing their ebullition and subsequent decline. Either explicitly or more subtly, such decline coincides with the perplexity and even the *desencanto* that assaulted these collective actors with the arrival of the civilian rule. This common narrative structure can be explained due to the fact that, as Pachi Bustos and Jorge Leiva note regarding *Actores secundarios*, the dramatic structure of the documentary was given by the dramatic denouement of historical events themselves: 'la estructura dramática, ahí sola, no había nada que hacer: Presentación, Desarrollo, Desenlace y Final' [there was nothing to do, the order was given [by the events]: introduction, development, dénouement and ending].[26]

The fact that many productions turn to music to talk about this period, or perhaps more accurately, the fact that history so vehemently emerges in works concerned with the music scene, can be explained via the conception of music as a rebellious artistic practice carried out in direct opposition to the regime.[27] The role that music played in the shaping of a 'counter-hegemonic culture' by the mid-1980s has been explained in the following terms by musicologist Juan-Pablo González:

> The revival of the early forms of *rock* during the 1980s is associated with the rise of a generational movement. [...] The growth and modernization of Chilean cities have augmented their pollution, violence, materialism, and insecurity. The repressive practices of the military government have created a tremendous feeling of frustration and rebellion among young people. This situation has shaped the new *rock* in Chile (emphasis in the original).[28]

The heterogeneous 1980s soundtrack, which ranged from the revival of folk roots through the *Canto Nuevo* ['New Song'] movement to punk, is therefore intricately woven together with the anti-dictatorial struggle.[29]

Historians and sociologists have remarked upon both the festive and ritualistic aspects of these mobilizations in the 1980s especially in an early stage, before repression increased.[30] In the words of Alfredo Jocelyn-Holt, these mass demonstrations were a '*fiesta* sacrificial' [sacrificial *party*] (my emphasis), a notion the historian uses to foreground not just the violence and the struggle as collective ritual, but also its festive aspects.[31] Drawing on this description (without its implied sarcasm), I would say that the most distinctive aspect of a number of these documentaries, such as *Actores secundarios*, *Malditos*, *Ruidos molestos*, or *80s*, is their stress on the festive rather than the sacrificial. Stern, in fact, has described the years of 1983–86 as 'times of fury' but also of desire and love:

> Times of protests, persecution, and emergency produced strong experiences within communities of dissenters. The brew of loyalty, solidarity, and caring could catalyse rapid bonding and friendship, in some instances affection and protectiveness. Memory of bonds forged under dictatorship even produced a certain nostalgia in the mid-1990s as persons recalled and idealized the clear lines of 'we' versus 'they' and the intense solidarities of caring and friendship provoked by dictatorship. The ambiguities and limits of democratic transition fostered a common remark, meant more as irony than a literal description. 'We were better in dictatorship'.[32]

These documentaries engage precisely in depictions of the rise and decline of these 'communities of dissenters' involved in the political front, as photographers or students, or as members of the music scene. This nostalgic turn stands in stark contrast with depictions of these mobilizations in earlier works from the 1990s. In *Conversaciones con el Cardenal Silva* (Augusto Góngora, Ictus, 1990) or Esteban Larraín's *Patio 29*, what is foregrounded instead is the struggle carried out by the relatives of the victims, notably their female kin, who are included with their portraits of their beloved ones asking 'Where are they?' in order to emphasize their quest. In Góngora's early transition documentary, the depiction of these mobilizations acquires an almost pristine look in that no images of clashes or repression are included (people seem even to protest in an orderly way, as though unwilling to upset the incipient process of redemocratization). Larraín chooses instead to include a montage of moving and still images of women demonstrating either in despair or being subjected to a disproportionate display of violence. He further underscores the liturgical (that is, sacrificial) aspects of the struggle, by removing the original sound of the demonstrations and replacing it with the singing of a religious choir in the soundtrack of this sequence. At the threshold of the new millennium, however, the uses of archival images depicting the struggles of the 1980s start to differ significantly. Directors begin to highlight the multifaceted composition of the resistance; no longer limited to relatives, documentaries begin foregrounding people's agency and stubborn resistance rather than their helplessness in the face of repression. Illustrative of this turn is Patricio Henríquez's witty archival documentary *Imágenes de una dictadura* (1999), which was constructed from material recorded by Henríquez's close collaborator, independent cameraman Raúl

Cuevas. Henríquez developed this project with the explicit aim of putting into circulation this footage; he said to himself 'no puede seguir durmiendo eso en las bibliotecas' [this [material] cannot continue sleeping in libraries].[33] In one sequence, the director dwells on images of the incessant clashes between common citizens, the police and their *guanacos*. However, the use of one of Händel's compositions (tellingly titled *Water Music Suite 2*), endows these images of repression with certain playfulness, the clashes depicted as a peculiar choreography. Later works, perhaps most remarkably *Actores secundarios*, *Malditos* and *Electromésticos*, engage further in offering a celebratory depiction of this period of political resistance.

In my view, these works exhibit nostalgia's most productive face, as described by Svetlana Boym in her oft-cited book *The Future of Nostalgia*, as an intermediary between individual and cultural memory through which these collective remembrances 'can be seen as a playground, not a graveyard of multiple individual recollections'.[34] Boym's conceptualization of nostalgia distinguishes between what she calls 'restorative' and 'reflective' nostalgia in order to foreground the positive dimensions of this notion that has become tainted with negative views.[35] While restorative nostalgia manifests a desire to return to a supposedly original, fixed, and complete past, 'its perfect snapshot' as she puts it, reflective nostalgia lingers on the passage of time and the impossibility of returning to that past or any given truth.[36] Antonio Traverso has criticized Boym's dichotomic understanding of the term since he argues that it reproduces at the same time the difference between a 'good' (reflexive) nostalgia and 'bad' (restorative) nostalgia.[37] He suggests instead an understanding of nostalgia 'as an "emotion" attached to either the subjective experience or textual representation of remembering. Considered this way [...] nostalgia concedes affect and embodiment to the critical activity of remembering and working through a traumatic past.'[38] Traverso is right in pointing out the importance of going beyond a dichotomic view of the term and underlining the politically enabling uses of nostalgia. Boym's gesture towards the liberation of nostalgia from its negative weight remains, however, a valuable tool as it usefully sheds light on some of the more playful or even less traumatic approaches to the past that exist in these documentaries. Moreover, Boym fosters an understanding of the term that is not merely concerned with the past but also with the future, as she argues that the views one elaborates about the past modelled by present needs will impact directly on the construction of the future.[39] Borrowing from her analysis, I believe that documentaries like *Actores secundarios* or *Malditos* exhibit nostalgia 'as a double-edged sword: it seems to be an emotional antidote to politics, and thus remains the best political tool'.[40] If the post-dictatorial climate has been described as more grieving than festive,[41] it may not come as a surprise that many of these directors have set out to rescue the celebratory aspect of past struggles.

Documentaries dealing with memories of the struggles of the 1980s heavily rely on their protagonists' testimonies from which much of their affective force emanates. Declamations like this abound: 'En esta plaza hice más que una foto, en esta plaza me enfrenté con la dictadura, en esta plaza vi un niño con un ojo vaciado, me enfrenté con la violencia más absoluta y con un pueblo levantado'

[In this square I did more than take a picture, in this square I confronted the dictatorship, in this square I saw a boy whose eye was gouged out, I was confronted with the most absolute violence and with a *pueblo* aroused] (photographer Óscar Navarro in *La ciudad de los fotógrafos*). Consider this example as well: 'te sentíai que habíai participado en un acto colectivo humano, de cierta importancia... es como triste decir, chucha, o sea tenemos que estar en un régimen así... pa' que aflore la expresión artística de la gente... uno no quiere decir eso'. [You felt as though you have been part of a collective human act of certain importance... it is sort of sad to say, oh shit, we have to be in a regime like this... so that the artistic expression of people flourishes... People do not want to say that...] (musician Carlos Cabezas in *Malditos*). Or, 'por el hecho de ser jóvenes a nosotros nos movía fundamentalmente el amor' [Because we were young, we were fundamentally moved by love] (Dago Pérez, musician and former MIR militant, in *Actores secundarios*).

In addition, as I proposed earlier, these works perform another revelation alongside the stories of these 1980s rebels: they unearth the images of these past struggles, mostly shot in U-matic, which until the release of these documentaries had rarely circulated. When they had, they had often been used to illustrate the incessant struggle of female relatives. Arguably, the most remarkable exception is *Recuerdos del futuro: Raúl Pellegrín* (*Memories of the Future: Raúl Pellegrín*) (Colectivo Audiovisual Rodriguista, CARO, 1994), which deals with the life (and actions) of 'Comandante José Miguel' (Raúl Pellegrín) who was tortured and murdered in 1988 with his partner 'Comandante Tamara' (Cecilia Magni) — both of them were upper level leaders of the FPMR, responsible for the failed attempt to kill Pinochet in 1986. The anonymous collective documentary includes archival material of the redistribution of food (through the assault of a truck carrying chicken) carried out by the FPMR in La Victoria, an emblematic shantytown with a strong tradition of political struggle. Legendary independent cameraman Pablo Salas originally recorded this footage.[42]

Laura U. Marks has described the haptic characteristics of video images in open contrast with the view popularized by Marshall McLuhan who regarded video as a 'cool' and distancing medium.[43] Marks argues instead that the tactile features intrinsic to video — image composition from a signal and not from a material source as in cinema, the contrast of ratio and pixel density, its ease of electronic manipulation, its rapid deterioration — make it 'a warm medium'.[44] Following Marks's reassessment of video images, I believe that besides the affective force of the testimonies offered in these accounts, an important part of the *intensity* emanating from these works is based on the utilization of video footage. This archival material fosters a certain proximity with the spectator because of its inherently 'warm' characteristics, which usually stand in contrast to the sharper quality of interviews made in present-day Chile or the rest of the directors' own material. In addition, due to the sheer danger that capturing this footage entailed back in those years and the difficulties of obtaining a copy of these documentaries (both the older and more recent ones), we are invited to emotionally identify with these images, as Marks argues in 'Loving a Disappearing Image'.[45] These documentaries, though very distinct from the cases she examines, similarly invite the spectator

> to build an emotional connection with the medium itself. We are not asked to reject their images on their surfaces, themselves precious indexes of long-ago events, but to understand them to be inextricable from another body whose evanescence we witness now, the body of the medium.[46]

In my view, by circulating these highly precious audiovisual materials (relegated, almost forgotten, in danger of disappearing), these nostalgic documentaries also 'borrow the aura of the disappearing images in which they meditate';[47] in this case, images which comment not only on the frailty of the material itself, but also on the collective action which they long for.

Following Jaimie Baron, the extensive footage of these past struggles are able to produce what she refers to as the 'archive affect',

> When we are confronted by these images of time's inscription on human bodies and places, there is not only an epistemological effect but also an emotional one based in the revelation of temporal disparity. In other words, not only do we invest archival documents with the authority of the real past, but also with the feeling of loss.[48]

The affective force of this archive material is perhaps most salient in *La ciudad de los fotógrafos*, above all through the montage by María Teresa Viera-Gallo. Although a sacrificial rather than a festive tone prevails, there is a particularly remarkable sequence at the beginning of the documentary introduced by the director's voiceover. Moreno asks: '¿Dónde está la ciudad que mi padre fotografió? ¿Qué cosas vio en ella que ya no existen? ¿Qué desapareció?' [Where is the city that my father photographed? What things did he see in it that no longer exist? What has disappeared?]. His voice then retreats in order to let the images he puts into circulation speak. The juxtaposition created between abundant photographic, moving, and aural archival material reveals an entangled web of 'endangered gazes', a concept Vivian Sobchack uses to refer to filmmakers coexisting in 'proximity' to death and violence.[49] Within this sequence there is a powerful segment that reveals this symbiotic web including the lenses of cameramen and photographers, who are seen both as recording and contributing actively to the human rights struggle. The spectator sees video footage as captured from a corner of Alameda Avenue, the camera pointing directly towards a police water cannon in a long shot: the camera does not move, one might say that it does not even blink; intrepid it stands there, staring directly at the *guanaco*. When the powerful stream of water is about to reach the camera, the cameraman swiftly covers the lens with his hand to protect it. After a seemingly invisible cut, through the now wet lens we see in a medium close-up the hands of a photographer who is in turn cleaning the lens of his own wet camera. By carefully selecting the footage in which the photographers were recorded in action, the montage sequence also brings to the fore the 'film' as a 'perceiving subject'.[50] This is not just a record of the events deployed in front of the camera, not merely the literal body of the cameraman that enters the frame with his hand. What the spectator sees in this sequence as a whole — the camera moving, running, shaking, getting wet — is the film's body. As Jennifer Barker explains in her description of the filmic body, what one watches is '*the film seeing*: we see its own (if humanly enabled) process of perception and expression unfolding in space and time' (emphasis in the original).[51] These 'endangered gazes' that bring to the fore the film's body (or more precisely, in this case, the video's body) are a common feature in the 1980s productions, such as in *Somos +* by Pedro Chaskel and Pablo Salas or *En nombre de Dios* by Patricio Guzmán, where camera lenses get wet, or the film crew is also seen being attacked by the police.

It is important to note that directors who revisit these archival documents use them above all as visible evidence to back up their subjects' testimonies. Perhaps because this past has been — and continuous to be — so contested, the material these narratives incorporate does not raise questions regarding the evidentiary status of the image (as later post-Pinochet documentaries would do, as in the cases of Rossi or Ballesteros, for instance). These images are deployed precisely in their status of proof, as evidence of everyday violence and courageous collective actions. Such is the status, for instance, of the shaky images of a yellow Citroën also by Salas. In the footage, two individuals start shooting from the yellow car, presumably at the demonstrators (who remain offscreen); this material is included both in *Actores secundarios* and *Malditos*. This forceful register reflects precisely the ways in which Salas sees his work both as inserted within a common project of struggle and as an effective weapon, which he explains in the following terms: 'salía a filmar yo porque era interesante que alguien lo hiciera, nunca tuve ningún problema con compartir, estábamos en contra de los milicos y *les disparábamos* con materiales audiovisuales' (my emphasis). [I went out to film because I thought it was an interesting thing for someone to do. I never had any trouble sharing [images], we fought against the military and we *shot* them with our audiovisual materials].[52] The footage mobilized by these directors aims to authenticate the testimonies of violence and resistance delivered by the subjects, students, and musicians. As Bill Nichols explains:

> The indexical image authenticates testimony now about what happened then. With historical footage from the time recounted appended to it, indexicality may guarantee an apparent congruity between what happened then and what is said now. (The historic footage enjoys the legitimating power of indexicality while the spoken testimony determines its meaning.)[53]

Testimony and archival footage are therefore closely integrated in these productions, the material guaranteeing the 'truthfulness' of the events told by the documentaries' protagonists. In other cases, these archival images acquire a more affective function, which Nichols has described as 'emotional proof', a rhetoric device that triggers feelings in a predisposed audience in order to push forward a certain argument.[54] This is clear in *Actores secundarios*, which is constructed upon enactment sequences in which former high school students return to their respective schools to recall together, collectively, the emblematic *tomas* (actions in which buildings are occupied by force as a form of political pressure). In the absence of a narrator, the documentary 'voice'[55] tells us from the outset that this work is an act of retrieving this past struggle. It is framed as a nostalgic take on the student movement of the 1980s in order to advance an open critique of the present democracy (this is clearly stated by many of the former students, who at the time of the documentary shooting were in their mid-30s). This nostalgia emerges more forcefully after an opening sequence that strikingly exposes the continuation of authoritarian constraints. Through it, spectators learn (via radio news, collective interviews, press clippings, and a press conference) that in 2004 a group of high school students were driven out of school for reenacting as an assignment one of the *tomas* held in the 1980s. After this scene, the aural archive of the title sequence '*Hasta la victoria compañeros!*' merges with a song from one of the representative bands of the *Canto Nuevo*, whose lyrics also perform a nostalgic revision of this past.[56] Whereas the archival footage stresses the students' agency and their brief ownership of the streets, the song clearly utters the documentary voice, namely: What happened to the poster of the *Che* you once had on your wall? The documentary therefore addresses its intended spectator directly: What happened to *your own* revolutionary ideals? The material is edited following the beat provided by the nostalgic song; images of the young students showed in slow motion dissolve quickly one after the other. This past footage intercalates with shots taken today of the quiet and empty façades of the previously mobilized high schools, exposing the arresting passage of time but above all the stagnation of post-dictatorial society.

Likewise, *Malditos,* also disposing of a voiceover narrator and foregrounding the sense of community, tells the story of the punk band Fiskales Ad-Hok, known for its politically charged lyrics (both before and during the post-dictatorial era). In this case, the documentary depicts the musical front, which is presented as inseparable from anti-dictatorial struggle. Alvaro España, the lead singer, says 'en vez de tomar una metralleta y salir a matar milicos, era tomar una guitarra y usarla como metralleta' [Instead of grabbing a machine gun and going out into the street to kill the soldiers [the point was to] grab a guitar and use it as a machine gun]. Tellingly, the interview with the band takes place on the street, underscoring both the combative character of the musical front and the relevance of recalling in a collective way a period in which society went, collectively as well, into the streets.[57] Here the archival material is used to reconstruct the convulsive historical moment in which the band emerges. Macarena Urzúa has remarked on the symbolically significant stills in which the band is shown playing behind bars inside an art gallery, through which the 'simulacro de la prisión deviene en realidad' [simulacrum of the prison becomes reality].[58] These images and the lyrics of the song that accompany them, 'mucha sangre corre Chile', ['a lot of blood covers Chile'] provide the cue for a montage sequence that powerfully deploys both the violence of the period and the heterogeneous composition of the anti-dictatorial resistance front. Televisual footage shows former Minister Secretary-General of the Government, Francisco Javier Cuadra, during a press conference in which the country was declared to be under a 'state of siege'. Cuadra grimly enumerates a list of things which the government is henceforth entitled to do: arrest people in their own houses, exile individuals from the country, restrict freedom of transport, suspend or restrict the right to gather, and so on. The minister's litany is heard first as seen in television, but soon the director turns to 'un-official' archival material to illustrate the effects of such measures on everyday life. Images of a seemingly endless army of policemen are contrasted with those of young people wearing handkerchiefs and throwing stones, women being dragged on the streets, a medium shot of a young student with a gun to his head being pushed violently against a wall, and a policeman destroying a man's glasses; in short, people of different ages, from school girls to elderly women, from young students to men. After this sequence, instead of returning to the band, the director gives voice to musician Carlos Cabezas from Electrodomésticos, another emblematic band of the time. He explains that during the dictatorship Chilean people were divided between the military and civic society, and whatever one did was done in relation to this order, including artistic practices. Archival images seem to change radically — the images of protests are replaced by images from a concert of Cabeza's band at the legendary Garage Matucana where many underground events took place. This footage is used at this stage precisely to equate both the street protests and the underground musical scene. It works metonymically as an extension of the other side of struggle, which is the cultural front. Music is thereby equated to resistance. A similar construction can be found in the documentary devoted precisely to Electrodomésticos, in which an 'expert' voice explicitly describes participation in both fronts as political acts while the footage of street resistance illustrates his claim. Photographer (and journalist) Esteban Cabezas says:

> ir a sacar fotos a Matucana o a El Trolley era súper parecido a ir a sacar fotos de protestas, era lo mismo...era manifestar que vivíamos en un estado de dictadura, y al mismo tiempo, ir a recitales o armar una serie de recitales, era igual de político que sacar fotos de protestas
>
> [going to take pictures of [Garage] Matucana or El Trolley was very similar to going to take pictures of protests, it was the same.... it was demonstrating that we were living under a dictatorship. And at the same time, going to concerts or organizing a series of concerts was just as political as taking pictures of protests.]

The same is true for the more modest *Ruidos molestos*, which explores Valparaíso's rock music scene of the late 1980s and early 1990s. Although the musicians of thrash and metal bands interviewed here appear less politically articulated and foster a less epic vision of this period as it emerges from *Malditos*, for example, some of the testimonies also long for collective action, while the director also puts into circulation rare footage of the communal struggle as experienced in the port. Overall, these works offer 'un recuerdo de una resistencia que se instala en este doble movimiento entre resistir y apuntar al futuro, que ya ha sido perdido y frente el cual sólo es posible el resistir' [the memory of a resistance set between a double movement: that of resisting and that of pointing towards the future, a future which has already been lost and against which one can only resist], as Urzúa asserts in her text.[59]

Bertrán's *80s* depicts the more popular and commercial side of the musical front, taking up the development of the local music scene. He does so mostly through 'talking heads' with its leading figures including journalists, music managers, and members of emblematic bands, such as Los Prisioneros or Electrodomésticos, or even with more commercial bands which came into being, as the documentary reveals, as a result of the dictatorial machinery, such as Engrupo. Notably, this production does not discuss more independent bands, which *Malditos* or *Ruidos molestos* posit as being central to this period (given the fact that this work was coproduced by a major music label, however, this absence should not come as a surprise). Unlike most of the previous examples, this documentary transmits a fair amount of information through extensive use of the director's voiceover. *8os*, instead of being a reconstruction of an era, as the director rather grandiloquently describes it at the outset, consists above all of the televisual memories of a 'fortunate' child, as Bertrán admits he was, since he is the son of a famous television director of the time. It is from this privileged position that the work is constructed; history appears through the point of view of a child deeply immersed in the televisual culture. Thus, in contrast to the documentaries examined above, which rely largely on material recorded by independent photographers and cameramen, Bertrán includes abundant 'official' footage of the time: advertisements, music videos, TV shows, and news reports. For example, he includes a long sequence of the news coverage of the bombing of La Moneda as reported by Canal 13 via a pro-government journalist reporting from the inside of what is left of the palace (it should be noted that this is rather unusual footage in post-dictatorship documentary). Bertrán also insists that these are the memories of a child raised under the shadow of Pinochet's dictatorship, illustrating, for example, the role of the 'Chicago Boys' (the name by which the ideologists of Chile's neoliberal model are known) in a witty stop-motion sequence in which technocrats are shown as small play dough figures. Interestingly, it is in this similar childlike vein that he includes images of the protests. Rather than stressing their significance in terms of collective political resistance or depicting their festive aspects, Bertrán refers to the demonstrations of this period as they appeared in the news, describing them as terrorist actions against state violence. In his opinion, the situation was 'pa' cagarse de susto' [enough to scare you shitless]. In another sequence, he depicts these incessant clashes between the youth and police forces in the form of a brief animation sequence. Despite the fact that a sense of collectiveness does emerge in some of the accounts of musicians, the documentary overall deflects the political struggle, the last image being illustrative of this: home movies of the destruction of Bertrán's beloved childhood home stand less as a metaphor for the end of the period than as a nostalgic account of his own childhood.

Abject Bodies, Abject Documentaries

In this last section, I examine two of arguably the most challenging documentaries regarding the 'memory question' made during the last decade covered by this study, which radically differ from the works I have dealt with up to this point. I focus on Marcela Said and Jean de Certeau's *El mocito* and P+O's *La muerte de Pinochet*, in which history appears as inscribed in abject bodies, elaborating discourses that further complicate the two ideological poles of the left and the right. P+O's documentary is constructed around the memories of four individuals concerning the day on which the dictator died; two of these are fervent Pinochet supporters, another is a former conscript who despises him, and the last an alcoholic who found himself swept into the street celebrations of the dictator's death. Said and de Certeau's camera accompanies Jorgelino Vergara in his daily endeavours; Vergara arrived as a boy to work as a butler for Pinochet's secret police. His everyday duties ranged from activities as varied as serving coffee (which explains the title, 'The young butler') to cleaning up the remains of tortured and executed bodies at detention centres well-known for the violence that was perpetrated there: the Cuartel de la Brigada Lautaro (which no longer exists and was converted into a condominium) and Villa Grimaldi (now a memorial park). His collaboration with justice in 2007 facilitated the discovery of the only headquarters used solely as centre for executions and hence led to the prosecution of seventy-four agents, the largest number in any human rights case in the country.[60]

These two 'unsettling accounts', to borrow the title of Leigh A. Payne's book, advance what the author describes as a 'contentious coexistence', that is, a 'conflictual dialogic approach to democracy in deeply divided societies.'[61] In her study, which includes an examination of the confessions of two notorious Chilean agents of repression (civil agent Osvaldo Romo and General Manuel Contreras), she explains that this model lies between 'cautionary and utopian extremes of conflict resolution' and 'embraces democratic dialogue, even over highly factious issues, as healthy for democracies'.[62] Discarding 'infeasible official and healing truth' it favours instead 'multiple and contending truths that reflect different political viewpoints in society'.[63] Rather than requiring sophisticated institutional instruments, she explains, this model 'is stimulated by dramatic stories, acts or images that provoke widespread participation, contestation over prevailing political viewpoints, and competition over ideas. Contentious coexistence, in other words, is democracy in practice'.[64] In Vergara's case, his confession became an important contribution to judicial cases, as he gave the names — on and off the screen — of former secret police agents that were previously unknown. This contribution brings to the fore the performative character of these types of confessions as elaborated by Payne: they 'are more than mere political talk: they not only *say* something, they *do* something' (emphasis in the original).[65] By shifting their lenses to these polemic subjects — Pinochet supporters and a collaborator of the secret police — these directors reflect on the place these abject figures occupy in narratives about the past, actively shaking the discourses around memory struggles.

If, as I have been arguing all along, post-dictatorship documentary follows Chile's own 'unravelling impasse', mirroring the almost imperceptible accomplishments of the struggle for human rights, these two documentaries demonstrate that this impasse has indeed been unravelling, albeit in complex ways. These two examples of a 'cinema of affect', concerned with abject bodies and inconvenient truths, shed further light on the country's long trajectory towards democracy. So far I have shown how documentaries have been mimicking to some extent the expansion of the symbolic circle of victims of Chilean society. However, at this stage of the trajectory undertaken by post-dictatorship documentary, what the emergence of these two films indicates is not a mere widening of this circle, but a radical 'redefinition of victimhood'.[66] As Michael J. Lazzara explains, the eruption of the figure of Vergara as a civil 'accomplice' illustrates the shifting public discourse that by the fortieth anniversary of the military coup would readily acknowledge the active role that civilians played during the dictatorship.[67] At the same time, Vergara's unsettling account, together with the voices of military conscripts and other Pinochet collaborators who in many cases considered themselves victims, would point to the post-dictatorship 'tendency to produce a generalized notion of victimhood'.[68]

Due to the subjects chosen by these documentaries and their formal approach, I examine them through Julia Kristeva's influential description of the abject as that which 'disturbs identity, system, order. What does not respect borders, positions, rules. The in-between, the ambiguous, the composite'.[69] Although for Kristeva the corpse is the utmost concrete expression of this figure, the abject, as she explains, acquires many forms. It is 'the traitor, the liar, the criminal with a good conscience, the shameless rapist, the killer who claims he is a savior [...] it is immoral, sinister, scheming, and shady: a terror that dissembles, a hatred that smiles'.[70] While *El mocito* foregrounds a subject who dwells in what Primo Levi has influentially described as the 'gray zone',[71] *La muerte de Pinochet* focuses on subjects who appear to be ethically dubious (most evidently, though not exclusively, through Pinochet's supporters) but who are *constituted as abject* by the directors' treatment of their bodies. As Kristeva notes, 'abjection is above all ambiguity'.[72] I view these documentaries themselves as deeply disturbing works in that they are consciously and deliberately crafted as ambiguous; it is as though through the mise-en-scène of these contentious subjects the directors have managed to create matching abject cinematic bodies.

Despite that such controversial productions are uncommon in Chilean post-dictatorship documentary, these are not the sole cases. Said herself had previously turned to the conservative right in *I Love Pinochet* (2001, original title in English), in which she gathered often virulent testimonies of mostly female defendants of the dictator during his imprisonment in London. She performed a similar move in *Opus Dei: una cruzada silenciosa* [*Opus Day: A Silent Crusade*] (codirected by de Certau, 2006), which examines the hold on power wielded by this fundamentalist Catholic group. The most remarkable antecedent that seeks to approximate the 'gray zone' is *La flaca Alejandra*, which deals with the memories of a former MIR militant who turned collaborator after being 'broken' in torture, a film discussed earlier in this study. Documentaries indeed have often included accounts from the 'other' side of the human rights struggle: conscripts, members of the military, and agents from the secret police, such as *Correcto... o el alma en los tiempos de guerra*, and even present encounters between victims and perpetrators such as *La sombra de Don Roberto*. Seldom, however, are these subjects granted the role of a protagonist. More recently, *El soldado que no fue* (2010), a peculiar homecoming documentary of director Leopoldo Gutiérrez (who is based in Canada), gathers individual and collective testimonies of former conscripts who, like him, were doing their compulsory military service at the time of the coup. Although some avow their eager participation in the coup, many see themselves as having had no choice, describing themselves explicitly as victims; the director, in fact, returns with a group of them to a so-called 'prisoner camp' where conscripts, as we find out, were subjected to torments as part of their training.

El mocito and *La muerte de Pinochet* can also be seen as examples of a 'cinema of affect', though in radically different ways than the documentaries examined heretofore. First of all, they do not draw on archival footage; rather, they are composed almost entirely of material recorded by the directors themselves. In fact, only a few personal pictures of Vergara are included in *El mocito,* whereas P+O return to their own footage of the events that surrounded Pinochet's death that they recorded while shooting *Noticias* [*News*] (2009). Both documentaries were shot in high definition video (HDV and HDcam, respectively), so their construction as haptic works differs significantly in terms of their focus on the materiality of the image, as discussed in previous chapters. In the case of *El mocito*, the affective dimension is conveyed above all by the use of long takes, while in *La muerte de Pinochet* the highly textured images are delivered by the mise-en-scène of the bodies themselves, particularly through the use of extreme close-ups. Though *El mocito* and *La muerte de Pinochet* are observational documentaries, they differ in numerous ways. Indeed, even if both refrain from using voiceover narration, *El mocito* moves closer to what Nichols has defined as an observational mode.[73] Since the emphasis is on Vergara's everyday life (the camera follows him in his peculiar daily endeavours), the frequent use of long takes and synchronous sounds in *El mocito* appears to convey 'a sense of unmediated and unfettered access to the world'.[74] Having said this, however, Jorge Arriagada's disturbing music and Arnaldo Rodríguez's careful cinematography challenge a conventional understanding of such observational mode since the very opening of the documentary, as seen below. In the case of *La muerte de Pinochet*, also deeply observational and indeed truly interested in the microscopic, the directors' gaze might be described as thanatological, following scholar Pablo Corro.[75] I would add that due to the directors' insistence on the extreme close-up, their work seems to invert what Nichols has referred to as documentary's distinctive 'epistephilia' (the pleasure in knowing), aligning instead with that of 'scopophilia' (the pleasure in looking).[76] Martine Beugnet describes the close-up as a key element in what she terms a 'cinema of sensation', explaining that it is precisely from this scopophilic drive that this device derives its disturbing effect.[77] According to Beugnet, 'The repulsive/compulsive paradox is no better illustrated than in the experience of being presented with the relentless reality of the abject in close-up — the magnified image of the body deformed or metamorphosing that suddenly fills one's field of vision'[78] (I will return to this connection between the abject and the close-up below). In the alternation of this device between two different poles, the examination of the imperceptible and the body under transformation, she argues that the close-up 'offers nourishment for the haptic eye rather than psychological information or narrative linkages'.[79] In effect, there is no actual information delivered in *La muerte de Pinochet*; the documentary is above all about the memories of these non-authoritative characters around a major historical event, but it is certainly not about the event itself. Since the directors do not seem to take sides, they have been accused of holding an ambiguous political discourse. Indeed, some critics have harshly criticized P+O's ethical approach, claiming that their gaze shows no compassion for the subjects they film.[80] Other scholars, however, such as Corro (probably their most fervent advocator), have praised them precisely because they have altered the landscape of post-dictatorship documentary by going against the dominant trend of what he calls 'construcciones edificantes' [edifying narratives], thus effectively destabilizing traditional accounts of the dictatorship.[81] He suggests that what *La muerte de Pinochet* does is an 'inversión diabólica' [evil inversion] of the consensus rhetoric, by literally going against the conventional frameworks of representation of the political poles.[82] By doing so, he claims, the documentary challenges the expectations of those spectators who demand 'la representación simétrica de buenos y malos respecto del Golpe, comunistas y fascistas, víctimas y victimarios' [a symmetric representation of the goods and the bads of the coup, communists and fascists, victims and perpetrators]. It is these spectators, he argues, who 'ven en *La muerte de Pinochet* un cuadro desequilibrado hacia el platillo de los pinochetistas adorables, una película fascista' [see in *La muerte de Pinochet* a fascist film, an unbalanced work in favour of adorable Pinochet supporters].[83]

Indeed, as Osnovikoff recognizes, they were self-consciously avoiding balance, and playing with 'indeterminación política' [political indeterminacy]:

> Yo estoy de acuerdo que nosotros jugamos con la ambigüedad política, pero no veo por qué sea malo [...]. Dudo que haya alguien que no se ha sentado a comer con un pariente pinochetista y haya tenido un momento agradable [...] también creo que hay una riqueza en buscar la complejidad.[84]
>
> [I do agree that we play with political indeterminacy, but I do not see why this should be a bad thing [...]. I doubt there is anyone who has not sat down to eat with a *pinochetista* (Pinochet supporter) relative and had a pleasant time [...] I think that there is richness in approaching this in more complex ways].

Similarly, Said notes that, in the case of *El mocito*, they too were guided by the idea of leaving the spectator in a state of certain 'desamparo' [abandonment], forcing viewers to create their own opinion regarding Vergara.[85] Indeed, spectators feel unease when confronted with this character, an indeterminate figure whose actual actions as a functionary of the DINA are never concretely pinned down.

The emergence of these documentaries at this particular historical juncture (after Pinochet's death and on the eve of the widespread social outburst in 2011) attests to the shifting strategies drawn upon by documentary filmmakers to refer to the dictatorship. These are not precisely accounts that deal with the past; they address its painful legacies from the present, exposing, so to speak, the *abject* side of Chile's social body. And, rather than ignoring the existence of these voices, they acknowledge them. This is not to say that they do so in a condescending or empathetic way, however. They do so mainly through ambiguity. I am interested in exploring how this ambivalence is achieved cinematically.

Notably, despite the contested reactions the works of P+O have received, local scholars and critics similarly describe their cinema in medical or surgical terms: an 'estética de la disección' [aesthetics of dissection], an 'aproximación tanatológica' [thanatological approximation], a 'cirujía a tajo abierto' [an open surgery], an 'examen clínico' [clinical exam] of the subjects they film.[86] Evidently, these descriptions point to the central role that both the literal and filmic body occupy in their oeuvre. The human bodies unfolded in their works are, according to Corro, euphoric or deformed bodies through which history circulates abnormally.[87] Their project, concerned with exhibiting the weight of history as inscribed in the post-dictatorial citizen's body, was evident in their first documentary, *Chi-Chi-Chi, le-le-le, Martín Vargas de Chile* (2000), as seen in the aging body of a retired boxer. This was intensified in their documentary *El astuto mono Pinochet contra La Moneda de los cerdos* [*Clever Monkey Pinochet Versus La Moneda's Pigs*] (2004), in which violence is depicted via children's and youths' own imagery of the coup. Two of the figures in *La muerte de Pinochet*, as discussed above, are staunched Pinochet supporters (a woman who sells flowers at the Plaza de Armas and the aging president of a feeble pro-Pinochet institution), while the other two are a former conscript who despises the dictator and an alcoholic who parks cars for a living and is unable to clearly articulate his ideas on the topic. Although P+O do indeed use Pinochet's death to construct their narration, rather than dwelling on an examination of his cadaver (which, although included, is gradually occluded by a shadow), the directors focus instead on these four characters. In effect, they are not interested in the event in itself, as Osnovikoff explains, but in taking advantage of the event to explore how individuals relate to it.[88] In contrast with the restless handheld camera in *El astuto mono Pinochet contra La Moneda de los cerdos*, they use in *La muerte de Pinochet* a static and ecstatic gaze that shifts between long shots and extreme close-ups of bodily details, notably their interviewees' mouths, a strategy that evidently foregrounds the constructedness of their discourse. Although they reject the use of voiceover, which in more conventional observational works points to the creation of seemingly non-intrusive situations, P+O make it clear that their interventions run deep. They do so by various means but most obviously by the particularly kitsch setting in which they register the florist's testimony. Surrounded by the colourful paper flowers she used to sell in her little shop, she is presented in a medium shot, posing silently and waiting uneasily for the directors to start shooting. Suddenly, an intrusive hand breaks the perfectly framed shot to arrange the flowers (it is the hand of cinematographer Pablo Valdés); this is an intentional strategy which seeks to eliminate any remaining doubts about the possible transparency of their discourse.

These euphoric bodies, as Corro calls them, are subjected to what I would refer to as a process of 'abjectivization' through their repeated incisions (to continue with the surgical metaphors) via the use of the close-up. It is precisely P+O's extreme approximations to these bodies that turn them into deeply haptic and profoundly disrupting surfaces. I return here to Beugnet's illuminating discussion of the close-up and its relation to the abject. In her view:

> In the way it orchestrates a passage or a rupture from optical vision into haptic visuality, the close-up epitomises how cinema's incessant processes of metamorphosis ultimately entail a sense of radical desubjectivation. It is here,

at the point where the boundary between subject and object of the gaze appears to dissolve, that cinema most powerfully evokes a sense of loss of self, where the cinematic experience offers itself most strikingly as an exultant combination of pleasure and terror.[89]

By emphasizing what she calls the paradoxical nature of the close-up, the pleasure/ terror or repulsion/compulsion it triggers, Beugnet explicitly stresses the connection between the close-up and Kristeva's notion of the abject. The rough surfaces of these radically magnified bodies onscreen, the fluids of their mouths, both fascinate and repel in their delivery as haptic images. The bodies tend to be so close that their fluids on occasion even spatter the lens, reminding the spectator of her own frail human condition. As Kristeva points out, 'refuse and corpses *show me what I permanently thrust aside in order to live. These body fluids, this defilement, this shit are what life withstands, hardly and with difficulty, on the part of death*' (emphasis in the original).[90] Mary Ann Doane has also described the close-up as 'a lurking danger, a potential semiotic threat'.[91] The transformation of these bodies into something abject through the directors' gaze is more evidently achieved by the fact that the four characters often pose for the camera while their voices are continuously juxtaposed over still images of their bodies. As Corro notices, through such mise-en-scène their bodies acquire an air similar to that of corpses: 'el espectador tiene a ratos la sensación que se trata de remedos de cuerpos de taxidermia, de animales embalsamados' [the spectator feels at times that these bodies imitate those of taxidermy, of embalmed animals].[92] He adds that the use of the close-up is an operation that seeks, via the insistence of the characters' mouths, to strip them of their ideological discourses, preventing the spectator from acquiring an understanding of them as a social unity or as part of any collective.[93] Furthermore, Corro remarks that what becomes evident in *La muerte de Pinochet* is that there is simply no possibility of there being a collective associated with the dictator, much less after his death.[94] This passivity is not only suggested by the immobile mass of people who gathered outside the hospital for instance, but also by the detailed focus on the four characters, whose bodies 'representa[n] dramáticamente una operación que inhibe la figura del conjunto social uniforme' [dramatically represent an operation that inhibits the figure of a uniformed social body].[95] Through the particular gaze by which they approximate these characters, P+O manage to create a grotesque and painful vision of the post-dictatorial citizen.

Like *La muerte de Pinochet*, *El mocito* is also anchored in a significant historical event, in this case the testimony delivered by Jorgelino Vergara, which triggered one of the most important judicial processes of the redemocratization process. His confession made it possible for Judge Víctor Montiglio to indict seventy-four people involved in crimes committed at the centres where Vergara worked as a butler of sorts. Said and de Certeau's emphasis however, is on the current everyday life of this highly disturbing figure. In her director statement, Said describes their documentary both as a psychological portrayal and explicitly as a reflection on 'the banality of evil', thus drawing on Hannah Arendt's well-known phrase.[96] Said explains:

> Our purpose in making this film is to get to know the 'monster', to confront my own fears, and those of a whole society. To get to know the 'monster', not in order to judge him, but to try to understand [him]. To get to know his surroundings, his family, his daily life. To tell his story from the present, the banal. I hope to help people reflect on these complex realities. (In English in the original)[97]

Such desire to know, to understand the 'why' and yet, the *failure* of doing so, is what lies behind the elaboration and readings of perpetrator's narratives according to Robert Eaglestone. In his view, this does not mean that '"there is no why" but that evil [...] is not open to a foundational answer'.[98] Perhaps, he states, 'the attempt to "penetrate", to understand the evil is doomed to failure, because, simply, there is nothing to understand.'[99] The impossibility of accessing a 'why' behind the role performed by Vergara at the Brigada Lautaro (that is, the impossibility of understanding him), assumes in *El mocito* the form of hesitation. As Said explains, the directors wanted to be able to make the spectator experience what they themselves felt while interacting so closely with Vergara. They wanted to convey cinematically 'esta especie de duda, de vaivén de sensaciones' ['this sort of doubt, of swings of sensations] to make the spectator constantly wonder: is Vergara telling the truth or not?[100] For me, such a *swinging of sensations* is achieved through the recurring use of long takes that both approximate and create a distance from Vergara, and in doing so, this audiovisual hesitation contributes to an effective transmission of this uncertainty. So, rather than considering *El mocito*'s portrait to be overall generous, as Lazzara has described it, I read it as a portrait that is profoundly ambiguous.[101]

Exploring the use of the long take as a key component in contemporary world cinema, Tiago de Luca coins the notion of a 'realism of the senses' to describe the 'contemplative approach' of fiction film directors who share a desire to foreground the materiality of the bodies and landscapes while clearly challenging the boundaries between fiction and documentary.[102] The long take in these productions 'ceases to serve dramatic purposes. In their turn, characters are often devoid of psychological traits: they are laconic, listless, impassive. More than their psychology, it is their psychical characteristics and physiology which is on display.'[103] Although I am hesitant to characterize the use of the long takes in *El mocito* as 'hyperbolic', which de Luca considers to be distinctive of this contemplative cinema (the longest shot here lasts slightly over three minutes), there is an abundance of considerably long takes which bring to the fore the material quality of the landscape and its complex relationship with the character. These long takes in *El mocito* are certainly able to invite 'a sensory mode of spectatorship'[104] similar to the one described by the author, through which the directors' effectively manage to immerse the spectator in the same uncomfortable cinematic space with Vergara.

El mocito's longest take presents, via an enclosed, static medium shot, an encounter between renowned human rights lawyer Nelson Caucoto and Vergara. The former butler asks Caucoto if he has the right to economic reparation by the state, as he considers himself to be 'un actor involuntario' [an involuntary actor], and not just that, but 'un preso más' [one more prisoner]. This encounter is one of the few occasions in which the spectator sees Vergara interacting with other individuals, as the documentary consists largely of long takes of Vergara in his radical solitude, shots that force the spectator to experience his abandonment. This sequence (divided into two long takes shown at different moments) is particularly important since it provides additional information about his role while also revealing the documentary voice through the figure of the lawyer who seems in disbelief of what he hears.

El mocito opens with Vergara's confession. In a medium close shot, directly addressing Said (and hence, the spectator), he claims:

> Yo soy el tipo más honesto que pisa la tierra, aunque tú no me lo creas. Aunque fui partícipe involuntariamente de secuestros y asesinatos y de todo el atado… oye, yo lo vi, pero nada más… o sea yo no participé, o sea, no podrías tú acusarme a mí de asesino ¿sí o no? No podrías acusarme de asesino, porque de hecho, en los hechos, yo no fui asesino. Pero sí te digo una cosa: asesinaron, mataron tanta gente, comadre, mira, mira sin escrúpulos, la mataron… puta, pero pa' que te digo más, pa' que te digo… la mataron tan sin escrúpulos, que a mí me dolía, siendo un adolescente. Ese es mi cuento ¿Qué más quieres?

> [I am the most honest man on earth, even if you don't believe me. Even though I participated involuntarily in kidnappings and murders and all that stuff… hey, I saw it, but that's all… I mean, I didn't participate. I mean, you can't accuse me of being a murderer, right? Because actually, in light of the facts, I was not a murderer. But I will tell you one thing: they murdered so many people, *comadre*. Look, look, with no qualms they killed… shit, but why tell you more, why tell you… they killed people with no qualms at all, and it hurt me, I was just a teenager. That's my story. What else do you want?]

From the first moment, therefore, uncertainty is established — is he telling the truth or not? In this initial sequence, Said effectively includes her presence, capturing the tension between her and the character (her suspicious gaze easily imagined behind the camera). 'El mocito' is depicted from the outset as someone unreliable, not merely because of his manner of speaking but because he is obviously drunk and seems to doubt his own words while uttering them. Significantly, this opening scene grabs the spectator's attention precisely through the promise (unfulfilled, in the end) of getting to know Vergara's 'true' story. The next sequence takes the spectator into the woods, and through this, an equivalence is established between savagery and Vergara. As suggested above, this is done through the use of the long take and the external display of Vergara's psychic characteristics as though embodied in the landscape. The camera follows his journey into a forest and, forced by the irregularity of the terrain, both Vergara and the camera swing back and forth between approximation and distance (along with it, the spectator moves closer or further away from him). The documentary is filled with such oscillations; the camera at times stands quite close to character, shifting from the intimacy of his bedroom to move as far away as it can, particularly when in open spaces. Although there is no access to his interiority, there is an intricate connection between him and the bleak landscape. Said explains that indeed they sought to undo the idealization of the Chilean rural landscape, and in turn they aimed to convey the sense that its precarious and gloomy conditions mirrored Vergara's own mental and economic state.[105] The image that emerges from their encounter is as if there were no differences between interiority and exteriority; the landscape becomes Vergara and Vergara becomes the landscape. At the beginning of the documentary, after the opening monologue quoted above, there is a highly aestheticized sequence reinforced by Rodríguez's camera and Arriagada's chilling score that seems to belong to a scene from a thriller or a horror movie. Inside a forest, Vergara moves confidently among the trees like a predator. The camera's presence is brought to the fore, never letting Vergara escape the frame, as though Vergara himself was being followed by someone. There are a couple of almost imperceptible cuts as trees literally stand in the way. After the second cut, the camera shows the man engaged in some kind of activity (now from a significant distance, shown via a long shot in the woods), his body bent towards the ground. It is unclear what he is doing until one sees — and hears — an animal thrashing in his grip. The subject is shown lifting a rabbit (one is able to distinguish now) and killing it with a single blow, the animal dying in front of the camera, its tail trembling after the precise blow; after a cut, he is seen placing the animal in a plastic bag. Then there is another cut and the spectator is faced with the body of the rabbit hanging from its feet while Vergara, impassive, skins it. Unlike the rabbit's death in *La règle du jeu* [*The Rules of the Game*] (Jean Renoir, 1939) discussed by Vivian Sobchack, which 'violently, abruptly, punctuates fictional space with documentary space',[106] the death of the rabbit occurs already within the documentary space. And it exceeds, in my opinion, the already excessive death of Renoir's rabbit stretching and folding its paws, because of the horrific resonances prompted by the onscreen death of the animal and its subsequent skinning at the hands of a former agent involved (how actively and willingly is unclear) in countless crimes. These images are certainly able to trigger associations with tortured bodies and not just through the extra-cinematic knowledge that the spectator brings with her. These associations are further provoked by a following sequence taken at a former detention and torture centre. There, Vergara engages in embodied descriptions of the tortures he saw while serving coffee, which included hanging the bodies of prisoners from their legs (he incarnates his memories in a similar fashion to that of Merino in *La flaca Alejandra*). As the original centre was demolished and is now a condominium, Vergara enacts these scenes of torture in Londres 38, the first torture centre occupied by the DINA and an emblematic site of struggles over memory, which itself barely escaped being demolished in 2005.[107] As discussed earlier, post-dictatorship documentary is often characterized by an overall refusal to represent scenes of torture. To this unwillingness, documentaries of the late 2000s add a hesitance to show images of atrocities. *El mocito* also eschews images of this sort, functioning instead metonymically or by association: Vergara practicing with a *nunkachu* (weapon associated with the fascist faction of the country during the UP), a scene of him picking up a gun at a flea market and then straight away a shot of him playing with a rifle at a fair with his daughter (in a sequence in which the directors also inscribe their distance from him, as they are, like the spectator, unable to hear the intimate dialogue Vergara establishes with the girl). There is also a scene that shows Vergara extremely drunk, wearing a black beret (again, a symbol of his military past) and mumbling to himself almost unintelligibly as he looks in the mirror. The mute associations triggered by these images call into question the veracity of Vergara's words, adding to the complex and 'gray' constitution of his character. There are other sequences in which this gray zone is brought to the forefront in more overt ways, as for example during his encounter with former coronel Juan Morales Salgado, who was in charge of the Brigada Lautaro.[108] At this almost fraternal meeting, which is still strongly marked by a difference in class and military hierarchy, Vergara states that he regards other agents of repression with whom he worked with as veritable 'fathers' and 'mothers' to him.

Said refers to their documentary as a sort of coming-of-age story in which the spectator is able to see somehow Vergara's 'toma de conciencia' [personal awareness] by seeing him go from hunting in precarious conditions to sitting at a table with the relatives of one of the disappeared.[109] Said is referring to the final sequence in which Vergara sits down with the descendants of Daniel Palma, a former member of the Communist Party. Significantly, this scene shows both the performative character of these kinds of confessions (they 'do' something), as well as the transformative capacity of documentaries. Said explained to me that originally they tried to create an encounter between Vergara and Viviana Díaz, one of the most representative figures of the human rights movement (her father was a leader of the Communist Party who disappeared in 1976). Díaz, however, refused to participate. The directors waited until one of Palma's sons approached the production team, as he wanted to be able to speak to Vergara. In the film, Vergara agrees to give to Palma's sons and daughter the names of the individuals involved in their father's death (he writes them on a piece of paper, but the spectator is unable to see them). Vergara claims he had never done that before; through this action, the performative character of this unsettling account is revealed onscreen.

The documentaries examined in this chapter belong to a broader second generation of directors who have actively expanded the discourses about the past by exploring diverse forms to address its memories and legacies today. While the last examples focused on directors who revealed abject bodies, an important number of documentarians revisited the 1980s to recover untold stories of collective action. By doing so, they have unearthed a vast archive of sounds and images from a decade in which political activism and music were deeply intertwined. Taking up the period as a 'sacrificial *fiesta*', I have discussed documentaries that emphasize the festive rather than the sacrificial when recalling this period of social upheaval. These nostalgic, yet lively memories of collective action function as a critique of Chile's disenchanted and demobilized present, at least until 2011, when a new outbreak of social upheaval shook the country.

In the final section of this chapter I shifted the focus to deal with the work of two teams of directors, Said and de Certeau and P+O, whose works have deeply challenged dominant accounts of the past, including those articulated from the left. I drew both on the notion of the abject and the contentious yet productive dimensions of unsettling accounts to analyse *El mocito* and *La muerte de Pinochet*. These works helpfully illustrate the trajectory of bodies that I have proposed throughout this book. Unveiling abject bodies that effectively disturb the documentary landscape as well as the status quo, these ambiguous films constitute further examples of a 'cinema of affect'. *La muerte de Pinochet*, through a hyperbolic use of close-ups, and *El mocito*, through the use of long takes, challenge the spectator with images that are both affective and disturbing. These documentaries also point to further trajectories undertaken by Chilean documentary in the years to come, as will be discussed in the conclusion.

Notes to Chapter 5

1. I borrow this term from Stella Bruzzi, 'Approximation: Documentary, History and the Staging of Reality', *Moving Image Review & Art Journal*, 2:1 (April 2013), 38–52 (p. 15) <http://dx.doi.org/10.1386/miraj.2.1.38_1>
2. For an interpretation of the film's exposition of the Concertación as a 'living cadaver', see José Miguel Palacios, 'Nothing is Happier than Happiness', *The Brooklyn Rail*, 4 March 2013 <http://www.brooklynrail.org/2013/03/film/nothings-happier-than-happiness-pablo-larrans-no> [accessed 17 October 2018].
3. Emol, '"No" según M.A. Garretón: es la basura ideológica más grande que he visto', *El Mercurio*, 23 August 2012 <http://www.emol.com/noticias/magazine/2012/08/23/557085/manuel-antonio-garreton-contra-la-pelicula-no.html> [accessed 22 October 2018].
4. Raquel Olea, 'No... la perversión de la verdad en la película', *Radio Tierra*, 13 August 2012 <http://www.radiotierra.cl/node/4741> [accessed 22 November 2018].
5. Augusto Góngora made this declaration without having yet seen the film, as he disclaimed at a panel, 'Cine documental de resistencia en dictadura', which was held a day before the release of *No* in Chile. The panel was part of the activities of the first *Festival Itinerante de Cine de Derechos Humanos* organized by the Museo de la Memoria on 8 August 2012. For an eloquent critique of the film as a 'sátira vacía' [empty satire] see Nelly Richard, 'Memoria contemplativa y memoria crítico-transformadora', *La Fuga*, 16 (2014) http://2016.lafuga.cl/memoria-contemplativa-y-memoria-critico-transformadora/675 [accessed 22 October 2018]
6. Nelly Richard, 'Cites/Sites of Violence: Convulsions of Sense and Official Routines', in *Cultural Residues: Chile in Transition*, trans. by Alan West-Durán and Theodore Quester (Minneapolis: University of Minnesota Press, 2004), pp. 15–29, p. 22.
7. Stern, *Reckoning with Pinochet*, p. 194.
8. Ibid., p. 132.
9. For more on the 1980s protests and cultural transformations in the Chilean nation, see Stern, *Battling for Hearts,* esp. pp. 249–333; 383–88. See also Moulian, pp. 261–314, and Javier Martínez, 'Fear of the State, Fear of Society: On the Opposition Protests in Chile', in *Fear at the Edge: State Terror and Resistance in Latin America*, ed. by Juan E. Corradi, Patricia Weiss Fagen, and Manuel Antonio Garretón (Berkeley: University of California Press, 1992), pp. 142–60. For a history from 'below' see Gabriel Salazar, *La violencia política popular en las 'Grandes Alamedas'*, 2nd edn (Santiago: LOM, 2006), esp. pp. 277–308.
10. Stern, *Reckoning with Pinochet*, p. 131.
11. Ibid.
12. Martínez, pp. 144–55.
13. Stern, *Reckoning with Pinochet*, pp. 68–69; 131–32.
14. Wilde, 'A Season of Memory', pp. 39–51.
15. Sarlo, pp. 62–64.
16. Ibid., p. 62.
17. Jelin, 'Victims, Relatives and Citizens', p. 200.
18. Jelin, p. 183.
19. Richard, 'Ir y venir', p. 159.
20. Richard, 'Cites/Sites of Violence', p. 23.

21. Interview with René Ballesteros, Paris, 12 March 2012.
22. Interview with Iván Osnovikoff, Santiago de Chile, 25 January 2012.
23. Ibid.
24. Richard, 'Cites/Sites of Violence', p. 23.
25. See my study of *Los 80* and the circulation of this 'unofficial' footage in Ramírez-Soto, 'Reflections on the *Other* Archive on Television: Chilean Fiction Series and Approximations to the Dictatorial Past', *New Cinemas: Journal of Contemporary Film*, 13: 1 (2015), 9–22 <doi: 10.1386/ncin.13.1.9_1>
26. Toledo, (n.d.).
27. A number of these documentaries dealing with the music scene have been recently labelled as 'nostalgia rockumentary'. See Susana Díaz, '¡Ruido, vanguardia, desacato y subversión! Un recorrido por los rockumentales chilenos más representativos del dos mil', in *Suban el volumen: 13 ensayos sobre cine y rock*, ed. by Ximena Vergara, Iván Pinto and Álvaro García (Santiago: La calabaza del diablo, 2016), pp. 281–300.
28. Juan-Pablo González, 'Hegemony and Counter-Hegemony of Music in Latin-America: The Chilean Pop', *Popular Music and Society*, 15: 2 (1991), 63–78 (p. 68).
29. See González; Fabio Salas, *La primavera terrestre: cartografías del rock chileno y la Nueva Canción chilena* (Santiago: Cuarto Propio, 2003), pp. 153–73; and Marisol García, *Canción valiente, 1960–1989. Tres décadas de canto social y político en Chile* (Santiago: Ediciones B, 2013). For a vibrant account of 1980s Chilean culture under the dictatorship see Óscar Contardo and Macarena García, *La era ochentera: tevé, pop y under en el Chile de los ochenta* (Santiago: Ediciones B Chile, 2009).
30. See Moulian, p. 275; Jocelyn-Holt, *El Chile perplejo*, pp. 196–97; Joignant, *El gesto y la palabra: ritos políticos y representaciones sociales de la construcción democrática en Chile* (Santiago: Universidad ARCIS-LOM, 1998), pp. 36–37; and Stern, *Battling for Hearts*, p. 253.
31. Jocelyn-Holt, *El Chile perplejo*, p. 196.
32. Stern, *Battling for Hearts*, p. 330.
33. Interview with Patricio Henríquez, 20 October 2012 (via Skype).
34. Boym, p. 54.
35. Ibid. On the differences between these two nostalgias, see esp. pp. 41–56.
36. Ibid., p. 49.
37. Traverso, 'Nostalgia, Memory and Politics', pp. 56–57; 67–78.
38. Ibid., pp. 68–69.
39. Boym, p. xvi.
40. Ibid., p. 58.
41. Moreiras, p. 27.
42. This rare documentary was presumably directed by members of the FPMR. It also includes clandestine footage taken from the Cárcel de Alta Seguridad (High Security Prison) and testimonies of active members of the FPMR whose faces are concealed. Some information about the video was found in '"Recuerdos del futuro": así se explicaba el FPMR en los 90,' published on 2 April 2013 on the website *El Dínamo*. <http://www.eldinamo.cl/tumblr/videos-recuerdos-del-futuro-asi-se-explicaba-el-fpmr-en-los-90/> [accessed 20 July 2013]. Unfortunately this piece is no longer available online.
43. Marks, *The Skin of the Film*, pp. 175–76.
44. Ibid., p. 176.
45. Laura U. Marks, 'Loving a Disappearing Image', in *Touch: Sensuous Theory and Multisensory Media* (Minneapolis: University of Minnesota Press, 2002). pp. 91–110.
46. Ibid., p. 109.
47. Ibid., p. 94.
48. Jaimie Baron, *The Archive Effect: Found Footage and the Audiovisual Experience of History* (London: Routledge, 2013), p. 21.
49. Vivian Sobchack, 'Inscribing Ethical Space: Ten Propositions on Death, Representation, and Documentary', in *Carnal Thoughts: Embodiment and Moving Image Culture* (Berkeley: University of California Press, 2004), pp. 226–57 (pp. 251–52) (first publ. in *Quarterly Review of Film Studies* 9:4 (1984), 283–300).

50. Barker, p. 164 n. 17.
51. Ibid. p. 9.
52. Pablo Salas cited in Mondaca, p. 69.
53. Nichols, *Blurred Boundaries*, p. 4.
54. Ibid., pp. 135–36; *Representing Reality*, p. 135.
55. Bill Nichols, 'The Voice of Documentary', in *New Challenges for Documentary*, ed. by Alan Rosenthal and John Corner (Manchester: Manchester University Press, 2005), pp. 17–33.
56. The song was written by Luis Le-Bert, 'Qué pasó con el afiche del Che en la pared?', Santiago del Nuevo Extremo. In addition to music, the directors draw upon a number of significant objects such as books, posters, cassettes, and clothes of the time to recreate the 'materialidad cultural' [cultural materiality] of the period, as highlighted by Claudia Bossay, 'Astutos chascones secundarios: el trauma histórico chileno visto desde la adolescencia', *Cinémas d'Amérique latine*, 23 (2015), 122–33 (128) <http://cinelatino.revues.org/1939> [accessed 25 June 2017].
57. Macarena Urzúa, 'Cartografías disidentes: punk y nostalgia en el documental de la postdictadura chilena', *La Fuga*, 11 (2010) <http://www.lafuga.cl/cartografias-disidentes-punk-y-nostalgia-en-el-documental-de-la-postdictadura-chilena/404> [accessed 20 October 2018].
58. Ibid.
59. Ibid.
60. For a detailed investigation of this case, see Javier Rebolledo, *La danza de los cuervos: el destino final de los detenidos desaparecidos* (Santiago: Ceibo, 2012). The journalist worked closely with the directors of *El mocito* as an assistant director before publishing this book.
61. Leigh A. Payne, *Unsettling Accounts: Neither Truth nor Reconciliation in Confessions of State Violence* (Durham: Duke University Press, 2008), p. 3.
62. Ibid., p. 281.
63. Ibid.
64. Ibid.
65. Ibid., p. 13.
66. Lazzara, *Civil Obedience*, p. 123
67. Ibid.,p. 120–47
68. Ibid. p. 140
69. Julia Kristeva, *Powers of Horror: An Essay on Abjection*, trans. by Leon S. Roudiez (New York: Columbia University Press, 1982), p. 4.
70. Ibid.
71. Levi described the 'gray zone' in the following terms: 'the hybrid class of the prisoner-functionary constitutes its armature and at the same time its most disquieting feature. It is a gray zone, poorly defined, where the two camps of masters and servants both diverge and converge'. Primo Levi, *The Drowned and the Dead*, trans. Raymond Rosenthal (New York: Vintage International, 1989), p. 42.
72. Kristeva, p. 9.
73. Nichols, *Representing Reality*, pp. 38–44.
74. Ibid., p. 40.
75. Corro, *Retóricas*, pp. 227–28.
76. Nichols, *Representing Reality*, p. 178.
77. Beugnet, p. 91.
78. Ibid.
79. Ibid., p. 89.
80. See Jorge Morales, 'En los límites del documental: Mentiras verdaderas', *Mabuse* (4 August 2004). This article was originally published in this online journal, and can be found now on P+O's official website: <http://perutosnovikoff.com/wp/wp-content/uploads/2009/01/mabuse_jorgemorales.pdf> [accessed 16 October 2018].
81. Pablo Corro, 'El astuto mono Pinochet y La Moneda de los cerdos, Perut + Osnovikoff, 2004', *Una vuelta*, 14 September 2004. Similarly, this article was originally published in this online journal, and can be found now on P+O's official website: <http://perutosnovikoff.com/wp/wp-content/uploads/2009/01/unavuelta_pablocorro.pdf> [accessed 16 October 2018].

82. Corro, *Retóricas*, pp. 230–31.
83. Ibid., pp. 230–31.
84. Interview with Iván Osnovikoff, Santiago de Chile, 25 January 2012.
85. Interview with Marcela Said, Santiago de Chile, 29 July 2011.
86. See, respectively, 'La estética de la disección en el filme "Noticias" (Chile, 2009)', in III Congreso Internacional de la Asociación Argentina de Estudios de Cine y Audiovisual, Universidad Nacional de Córdoba 10–12 May 2012 <http://www.asaeca.org/aactas/parada__marcela_-_ponencia.pdf> [accessed 16 October 2018]; Corro, *Retóricas*, p. 227; Morales, 'En los límites', and Iván Pinto, 'Welcome to New York: Dispositivos', *La Fuga*, 4 (2007) <http://www.lafuga.cl/welcome-to-new-york/337> [accessed 16 October 2018].
87. Pablo Corro, 'Silencio, cuerpo, e historia en dos referentes del documental chileno', in II Congreso Internacional de la Asociación Argentina de Estudios de Cine y Audiovisual, Universidad de Buenos Aires and Universidad Nacional de General Sarmiento 19–23 October 2010 <http://www.asaeca.org/aactas/corro_pablo.pdf> [accessed 16 October 2018]
88. Interview with Iván Osnovikoff, Santiago de Chile, 25 January 2012.
89. Beugnet, p. 89.
90. Kristeva, p. 3.
91. Mary Ann Doane, 'The Close-Up: Scale and Detail in the Cinema', *A Journal of Feminist Cultural Studies*, 14:3 (Fall 2003), 89–111 (p. 90).
92. Corro, *Retóricas*, p. 232.
93. Ibid., p. 231.
94. Ibid., p. 230.
95. Ibid. p. 231.
96. Hannah Arendt, *Eichmann in Jerusalem*, rev., enlarged edn. (New York: Penguin, 1992) p. 252.
97. Icalma, *El mocito / The Young Butler* (Press Kit) <http://www.icalmafilms.com/prensa.html> [accessed 10 January 2012] (no longer available online).
98. Robert Eaglestone, 'Reading Perpetrator Testimony', *The Future of Memory*, ed. by Richard Crownshaw, Jane Kilby and Anthony Rowland (New York: Berghan Books, 2014), pp. 123–34 (p. 132).
99. Ibid., p. 132.
100. Interview with Marcela Said, Santiago de Chile, 20 July 2011.
101. See Lazzara, *Civil Obedience*, p. 12; 129 and 'El fenómeno Mocito (Las puestas en escena de un sujeto cómplice)', *A Contracorriente*, 12: 1 (Fall 2014), 89–106 (p. 94–95) <https://acontracorriente.chass.ncsu.edu/index.php/acontracorriente/article/view/1301> [accessed 16 October 2018].
102. Tiago de Luca, 'Realism of the Senses: A Tendency in Contemporary World Cinema', in *Theorizing World Cinema*, ed. by Lucia Nagib, Chris Perriam and Rajinder Dudrah (London: I.B.Tauris, 2012), pp. 183–205 (p. 197).
103. Ibid.
104. Ibid., p. 198.
105. Interview with Marcela Said, Santiago de Chile, 29 July 2011.
106. Sobchack, *Inscribing Ethical Space*, p. 247.
107. On the long memory struggle over this 'strategic' site of memory, see Stern, *Reckoning with Pinochet*, pp. 318–23. After several years of uncertainty, in 2010 Londres 38 became the first site of its kind to receive support from the state to keep it thriving and functioning. In 2011, civil society activists managed to secure a concession for the use of the building after the state's recuperation of the site. See Londres 38. Espacios de Memoria, *La recuperación de Londres 38* (Santiago: Londres 38, 2013) <http://www.londres38.cl/1937/w3-printer-91128.html> [accessed 14 September 2013]
108. Said's own encounter with Morales Salgado inspired her second feature *Los perros* [The Dogs], premiered at the Critics' Week during the 2017 Cannes Film Festival.
109. Interview with Marcela Said, Santiago de Chile, 29 July 2011.

CONCLUSION

In 2010, journalist Juan Ángel Torti donated to the Cineteca Nacional de Chile the raw footage he registered on the 11, 13, and 14 September 1973, which was shot with a 16mm Paillard Bolex camera and with no sound. In thirteen minutes, these images document the jets overflying the city on the day of the coup, the smoke that covered the sky, the people walking rapidly through a ghostly cityscape surveyed by military forces. Two days later, they record La Moneda in ruins. Torti's images of the morning of 11 September (always taken from afar of the governmental palace), the striking ellipsis of the footage (no images of the immediate aftermath whatsoever), the film's fading colour and the *scars* on the celluloid do not deliver much information, but constitute today a profoundly affective experience of the past. The recent *revelation* of Torti's images (available now online on different websites and platforms) almost four decades after they were originally shot, point to the fact that filmic bodies like this keep emerging. In 2015 the catalogue published by the Museo de la Memoria y los Derechos Humanos listed over 2,500 holdings of audiovisual materials of different nature (documentary, feature films, raw footage, reportages, interviews, and oral testimonies, among others), including Torti's material, all of which deal with the dictatorship and the struggle for human rights.[1] The museum's ever expanding audiovisual collection has made images and sounds — both *from* and *about* the past — increasingly accessible. Chilean documentary filmmakers keep enlarging such archive of memories with their own narratives of the coup and its legacies today.

This book has provided a narrative for this vast array of responses to the military coup elaborating a broad understanding of the post-dictatorship documentary landscape from the restoration of civilian rule from 1990 until 2011. It was guided by the need to make sense of this elusive corpus. The two decades under examination suggest that Chilean documentary traces a trajectory marked by a *revelation of bodies* — from that of direct victims to that of the body of the film itself — in intimate connection with the country's historical, political, and cultural transformations. The revision of nearly a hundred documentary films of various duration and formats, as well as close readings of selected sequences, signalled this transit. I have approached these works with caution, avoiding the imposition of any theoretical model upon them, leaving the collected material to illuminate its own route. What emerged from this path was that documentary shifted from elaborating a 'cinema of the affected' to crafting a 'cinema of affect'. The trajectory of a *revelation of bodies* traced by Chilean documentary indicated an initial and urgent concern for unearthing actual bodies, which later shifted towards the unveiling of the materiality of the cinematic image. In other words, it showed that non-fiction film moved from a cinema concerned with the unveiling of atrocious images and irrefutable truths to a cinema less preoccupied with truthfulness and more interested in revealing the subjective and affective texture of the past. In doing so, it took up not just traumatic memories, but memories of a past in which a wide range of emotions, affects, and textures converge.

By and large, the diverse responses to the military coup prove that remaining within a trauma studies framework prevents a more comprehensive understanding of the complexities of the post-dictatorship documentary landscape from 1990 onwards. Furthermore, Chilean documentary's shifting cinematic strategies to address the military coup and its aftershocks underscore the fact that it is not enough to look at works concerned merely with direct victims of state repression. Such an approach occludes the broad scope of the violence unleashed by the regime and the radical and enduring transformations it imposed on Chilean society.

Notwithstanding, post-dictatorship documentary's itinerary has proved not to be a straightforward one. The route it traces, as I have insisted throughout, does not suggest a teleological development. Rather, the trajectory of the *revelation of bodies* performed by these documentaries intimately mirrors Chile's particular 'unravelling impasse', as Steve Stern describes the gradual if at times imperceptible accomplishments by the struggle for human rights.

The initial comparative reading between *Huellas de sal* and *Nostalgia de la luz* illustrates precisely the complexities of such unravelling. Separated by two decades, both works focused on the same female relatives of the victims and are set against the same location of the Atacama Desert. However, whereas the first stressed the radical absence of the corpses, the latter created a profoundly affective film based on excess in which the corpses themselves are exposed through haptic images. Overall, documentaries from the first long decade (1990–2003) followed Susan Sontag's political imperative to 'let the atrocious images haunt us'.[2] These documentaries circulated images of atrocity, namely of human remains (from *La verdadera historia de Johny Good* to *Fernando ha vuelto*) and focused increasingly on testimonies of torture survivors (from *Soy testigo* to *La venda*). When dealing with the experience of torture, however, filmmakers have retreated from direct representations, favouring instead reenactment in order to evoke such experience (such as in *Estadio Nacional* or more evidently in *El lado oscuro de La Dama Blanca*).

The shift from a 'cinema of the affected' to a 'cinema of affect' emerged more clearly in the aftermath of the thirtieth anniversary of the coup, when the documentary landscape presented important transformations: new voices forcefully entered the scene and responses to the dictatorial past expanded remarkably. This is not to say that the atrocious images stopped haunting Chilean society. In fact, these images have never stopped doing so. The missing bodies continue to be central to the struggle for human rights and truths are yet to be told. It would be wrong to suggest that documentary filmmakers have left aside their commitment to revelations of truth and missing and wounded bodies. What happened, however, was a shift of emphasis in which other stories began to be told alongside those of the disappeared, their female relatives, and those of torture survivors; in this process, new non-fiction images and sounds were unearthed and began to circulate. These included footage from the anti-dictatorial struggle of the 1980s as well as more personal archives from the domestic sphere.

Documentaries from the second decade (2003–2011) saw the emergence of narratives from children of direct victims and from a broader second generation of filmmakers. The itinerary demonstrated that the clearest post-2000 trend of first-person documentaries has its key precedents in the cinematic returns of exilic directors to the country in the 1980s. By analysing early homecomings such as *Fragmentos de un diario inacabado* as well as more recent ones such as *Calle Santa Fe* and *El edificio de los chilenos* through the notion of *desexilio*, I emphasized both continuities and divergences in the work of different generations of documentarians. In some cases, younger directors engaged in the construction of an intrinsically haptic cinema, such as in *El eco de las canciones* or *La quemadura*. These works, illustrative cases of a 'cinema of affect', tend to conceal former images of atrocity, bringing to the fore instead the *film's skin* by various means, including the use of Super-8, the merging of low and high video resolutions, and archival footage from different sources including home movies.

In the last chapter, I analysed heterogeneous responses from what I have called a broader second generation of directors. Some of them elaborate nostalgic responses to the anti-dictatorial struggle of the 1980s, a decade characterized by a revival of collective action and the development of a vibrant counter-cultural scene. Documentaries such as *Actores secundarios* and *Malditos* set into motion archival material of that same struggle, which had for years been gathering dust on the shelves of some of the many collectives and independent cameramen who took extensive footage of that time. I concluded this chapter by examining *El mocito* and *La muerte de Pinochet,* two works that further widen these choruses of voices, featuring disturbing accounts of Pinochet's collaborators and supporters, respectively. Somehow aesthetically matching the abject subjects on which they focus, these documentaries do not fit into more traditional polarized accounts about the past; yet evidently attest to Chile's 'unravelling impasse'.

This trajectory of *revelation of bodies* is the most significant transit undertaken by documentary film since the official restoration of democracy. I do not claim, however, that this is the sole itinerary possible to be traced in Chilean post-dictatorship documentary. Other routes can certainly be followed, most of which, or perhaps all of which, remain closely attached to that of the bodies of direct victims. Beyond case studies, further research could adopt a similar broad historical approach focusing on documentary's shifting strategies to deal with sites of memory, the biographical treatment of contested figures (such as Pinochet or Allende) or the transformations endured by the cityscape.

Chilean documentary and its intimate connection to the memory struggles will continue to be a challenging and fruitful terrain for exploration. This book concludes in 2011, but since then, many documentaries have been released. First-person narratives continue to thrive: Marcia Tambutti filmed a documentary about her grandfather, Salvador Allende, entitled *Allende, mi abuelo Allende* [*Beyond my Grandfather Allende*] (2015); Álvaro de la Barra, the son of two MIR militants murdered by the dictatorship, sought to reconstruct his parents' story and his own identity in *Venían a buscarme* [*They Were Coming to Get Me*] (2016); and unsettling accounts became more troublesome as Lissette Orozco, the niece of a former DINA agent, turned her camera to her aunt in *El pacto de Adriana* (2017) and Andrés Lübbert in *El color del camaleón* [*The Color of the Chameleon*] (2017) interrogated the secretive past of his father Jorge Lübbert, who fled to Europe after receiving training to become part of the secret police, an experience that deeply traumatized him.

El pacto de Adriana and *El color del camaleón* continue to expand the disruptive voices that were brought to the forefront of public discourse with Jorgelino Vergara in *El mocito*. The implications that these recent personal narratives will have in Chilean society's long quest for truth and justice are yet to be explored. What their emergence already indicates though is that these previously invisibilized abject voices have already begun to reshape the nation's memory struggles and the trajectory of Chilean post-dictatorship documentary in ways that are still unforeseen. It seems as though these unsettling accounts are here to stay; documentary will necessarily grapple with different strategies to deal with them.

Emphasizing the current tribulations of the country, although undoubtedly bound to the dictatorship's neoliberal legacy, recent documentaries have also set out to address the generalized climate of social unrest triggered by the student protests in 2011. Emerging from this social malaise, Sebastián González, Vanja Munjin, and Iván Pinto have distinguished a group of documentaries that formally interrogate the notion of '*lo político*', such as *El vals de los inútiles* [*The Waltz*] (Edison Cajas, 2013), which deals with the student movement; *Propaganda* (Colectivo Mafi, 2014), which registers the 2013 presidential campaign; *Crónica de un comité* [*A Committee Chronicle*] (José Luis Sepúlveda and Carolina Adriazola, 2014), which follows a political committee created to pursue justice for the assassination of a student during one of the demonstrations; and *Si escuchas atentamente* [*If You Listen Carefully*] (Nicolás Guzmán, 2015), which centres on a group of high school students reflecting about their future.[3] The two significant transformations I have signalled above — the rise of these abject voices and the reformulation of the notion of the political after the 2011 protests — mark the end of this study and clearly demonstrate that Chilean documentary continues to develop in close dialogue with the country's own historical and cultural trajectory.

Undoubtedly, the readings I have undertaken of post-dictatorship documentary are influenced by my own experiences as a child raised in the shadow of Pinochet's dictatorship and as a young student in Santiago de Chile whose eyes were opened and whose body was moved by the images that circulated in the screening room of the Goethe Institute where the first editions of FIDOCS took place. I engaged in the book the reader holds in her hands with a desire to make sense of all the contradictions and ambivalences, as well as all the silences and fears of growing up in a society in state of perplexity.

I remember that before travelling to the UK where I undertook the bulk of this research, while I was struggling to pack into my suitcases dozens of books with titles including the words dictatorship, Pinochet, human rights and the like, my grandfather, who was standing by the door to my room, whispered in bewilderment to my mother: 'Won't she get in trouble carrying all that?' This was in 2009, the dictator had died a few years before, and yet, *mi tata*, a modest man who was quite sympathetic to the dictatorship, talked as though it was only yesterday when people actually did 'get in trouble' for carrying books. Of course, I did not get into trouble. Chile had changed — imperceptibly at times, perhaps — but it had changed. The unprecedented social outcry of 2011, led by what came to be known as the 'generation without fear', highlighted the transformations that had been unravelling within the country, as well as those changes that urged to be undertaken. Bleak recent readings about the concrete outcomes of this particular juncture suggest that Chilean society somehow missed the opportunity offered by this major turning point in history to finally overcome the ingrained dictatorial legacies.[4] I have no doubt then that Chilean documentary will persevere in its desire to register, shape, and forge these transformations with courage, conviction, and *afecto*.

Notes to the Conclusion

1. Museo de la Memoria y los Derechos Humanos, *Archivo audiovisual: colección del Museo de la Memoria y los Derechos Humanos* (Santiago: Ocho Libros / Museo de la Memoria y los Derechos Humanos, 2015).
2. Susan Sontag, *Regarding the Pain of Others* (New York: Picador, 2003), p. 115.
3. Sebastián González, Vanja Munjin, and Iván Pinto, 'Figurar la comunidad: cine chileno en tres tiempos 1990–2017', *Cinémas d'Amérique latine*, 26 (2018), 102–17.
4. Daniel Hopenhayn, 'Manuel Antonio Garretón: "Tenemos una ciudadanía muy poco empoderada con la ilusión narcisista de que tiene poder"', *The Clinic*, 14 June 2017 <http://www.theclinic.cl/2017/06/14/manuel-antonio-garreton-tenemos-una-ciudadania-poco-empoderada-la-ilusion-narcisista-poder/> [accessed 15 June 2017].

BIBLIOGRAPHY

AGOSIN, MARJORIE, ed., *Surviving Beyond Fear: Women, Children and Human Rights in Latin America* (Fredonia NY: White Pine Press, 1993)

AGUILAR, GONZALO, 'El pueblo como lo "real": hacia una genealogía del cine latinoamericano', in *Más allá del pueblo: imágenes, indicios y políticas del cine* (Buenos Aires: Fondo de Cultura Económica, 2015), pp. 179–94

—— *Other Worlds: New Argentine Film*, trans. by Sarah Ann Wells (New York: Palgrave Macmillan, 2008)

ALBORNOZ, CÉSAR, 'Los sonidos del golpe', in *1973: la vida cotidiana de un año crucial*, ed. by Claudio Rolle (Santiago: Planeta, 2003), pp. 161–96

ALTAMIRANO, JUAN CARLOS, 'The Audio Visual Battle of Chile', in *Internal Exile: New Films and Videos from Chile*, ed. by Coco Fusco (New York: Third World Reels, 1990), pp. 18–22

—— *¿TV or not TV?: una mirada interna de la televisión* (Santiago: Planeta, 2006)

AMADO, ANA, *La imagen justa: cine argentino y política, 1980–2007* (Buenos Aires: Colihue, 2009)

—— 'Memory, Identity and Film. Blending Past and Present', *ReVista Harvard Review of Latin America* (Fall 2009/Winter 2010), 38–41

—— 'Órdenes de la memoria y desórdenes de la ficción', in *Lazos de familia: herencias, cuerpos y ficciones*, ed. by Ana Amado and Nora Domínguez (Buenos Aires: Paidós, 2004), pp. 43–82

—— and NORA DOMÍNGUEZ, eds., *Lazos de familia: herencias, cuerpos y ficciones* (Buenos Aires: Paidós, 2004)

AMARAL DE AGUIAR, CAROLINA, 'Los prisioneros y la muerte del poeta: el Chile de la dictadura ante las cámaras extranjeras', *Archivos de la Filmoteca*, 73 (2017), 17–30

ANDERMANN, JENS, 'Expanded Fields: Postdictatorship and the Landscape', *Journal of Latin American Cultural Studies: Travesia*, 21: 2 (2012), 165–87

ANGELL, ALAN, *Democracy after Pinochet: Politics, Parties, and Elections in Chile* (London: Institute for the Study of the Americas, 2007)

ARENDT, HANNAH, *Eichmann in Jerusalem*, rev., enlarged edn. (New York: Penguin, 1992)

ARENILLAS, MARÍA GUADALUPE, and MICHAEL J. LAZZARA, eds., *Latin American Documentary Film in the New Millenium* (New York: Palgrave, 2016)

ARIAS, ARTURO and ALICIA DEL CAMPO, 'Introduction: Memory and Popular Culture', *Latin American Perspectives*, 36: 5 (2009), 3–20

ARTE, 'Programmation Spéciale Chili' (n.d.) <http://download.pro.arte.tv/archives/fichiers/01676297.pdf> [accessed 10 October 2018]

AVELAR, IDELBER, 'Five Theses on Torture', *Journal of Latin American Cultural Studies*, 10:3 (2001), 253–71

—— *The Untimely Present: Postdictatorial Latin American Fiction and the Task of Mourning* (Durham: Duke University Press, 1999)

BARKER, JENNIFER M., *The Tactile Eye: Touch and the Cinematic Experience* (Berkeley: University of California Press, 2009)

BARON, JAIMIE, *The Archive Effect: Found Footage and the Audiovisual Experience of History* (London and New York: Routledge, 2013)

BARRIL, CLAUDIA, 'El yo en el documental chileno: una nueva forma de escritura política', in *El cine que fue: 100 años de cine chileno*, ed. by Claudia Barril and José M. Santa Cruz (Santiago: Editorial ARCIS, 2011), pp. 162–69

BARROS, CÉSAR, 'Declassifying the Archive: The Bombardment of *La Moneda* Palace and the Political Economy of the Image' in *Technology, Literature, and Digital Culture in Latin America: Mediatized Sensibilities in a Globalized Era*, ed. by Matthew Bush and Tania Gentic (New York: Routledge, 2016), pp. 127–45

BARTHES, ROLAND, *Camera Lucida: Reflections on Photography*, trans. by Richard Howard (New York: Hill and Wang, 1981)

BELLO, MARÍA JOSÉ, 'Documentales sobre la memoria chilena: aproximaciones desde lo íntimo', *Cinémas d'Amérique latine*, 19 (2011), 77–79

BENEDETTI, MARIO, *El desexilio y otras conjeturas* (Madrid: El País, 1984)

BENJAMIN, WALTER, 'The Work of Art in the Age of its Technological Reproducibility (Second Version)', in *Walter Benjamin: Selected Writings, vol.3, 1935–1938*, trans. by Edmund Jephcott and others, ed. by Howard Eiland and Michael W. Jennings (Cambridge, Mass: Harvard University Press: 2002) pp. 101–40

BENNETT, JILL, *Empathic Vision: Affect, Trauma, and Contemporary Art* (Stanford: Stanford University Press, 2005)

BETTATI, BRUNO, *Why Not?: política industrial para el audiovisual chileno* (ebooks Patagonia, 2012)

BEUGNET, MARTINE, *Cinema and Sensation: French Film and the Art of Transgression* (Edinburgh: Edinburgh University Press, 2012)

BEVERLY, JOHN, *Testimonio: On the Politics of Truth* (Minneapolis, University of Minnesota Press, 2004)

BLAINE, PATRICK, 'Representing Absences in the Postdictatorial Documentary Cinema of Patricio Guzmán', *Latin American Perspectives*, 40:1 (January 2013), 114–30

BONNEFOY, PASCALE, *Terrorismo de estadio: prisioneros de guerra en un campo de deportes* (Santiago: ChileAmérica-CESOC, 2005)

BOSSAY, CLAUDIA, 'Cineastas al rescate de la memoria reciente chilena', *Imagofagia*, 4 (2011) <www.asaeca.org/imagofagia > [accessed 4 June 2017]

——'Astutos chascones secundarios: el trauma histórico chileno visto desde la adolescencia', *Cinémas d'Amérique latine*, 23 (2015), 122–33 (128) <http://cinelatino.revues.org/1939> [accessed 25 June 2017]

——'El protagonismo de lo visual en el trauma histórico: dicotomías en las lecturas de lo visual durante la Unidad Popular, la dictadura y la transición a la democracia', *Comunicación y Medios*, 29 (2014) 106–18. <http://www.comunicacionymedios.uchile.cl/index.php/RCM/issue/view/3271> [accessed 20 November 2018]

——'Remembering Traumatic Pasts: Memory and Historiophoty in Fiction and Factual Films from the 2000s that Represent the Chilean Popular Unity, Coup D'état, and Dictatorship (1970–1990)' (unpublished doctoral thesis, Queen's University Belfast, 2014)

BOSSY, MICHELLE, and CONSTANZA VERGARA, *Documentales autobiográficos chilenos* (Santiago: Fondo de Fomento Audiovisual del Consejo Nacional de la Cultura y las Artes, 2010)

BOYM, SVETLANA, *The Future of Nostalgia* (New York: Basic Books, 2001)

BRETT, SEBASTIÁN, 'El caso en la prensa', in *De la tortura no se habla: Agüero versus Meneses*, ed. by Patricia Verdugo (Santiago: Catalonia, 2004), pp. 117–40

BRUNO, GIULIANA, *Atlas of Emotion: Journeys in Art, Architecture and Film*, 2nd edn (London: Verso, 2007)

BRUZZI, STELLA, 'Approximation: Documentary, History and the Staging of Reality',

Moving Image Review & Art Journal 2:1 (April 2013), 38–52 <http://dx.doi.org/10.1386/miraj.2.1.38_1>

—— 'The Event: Archive and Imagination', in *New Challenges for Documentary*, ed. by Alan Rosenthal and John Corner, 2nd edn (Manchester: Manchester University Press, 2005), pp. 419–31

—— *New Documentary: A Critical Introduction*, 2nd edn (London: Routledge, 2006)

BUCK-MORSS, SUSAN, 'Aesthetics and Anaesthetics: Walter Benjamin's Artwork Essay Reconsidered', *October*, 62 (Autumn 1992), 3–41

BUTLER, JUDITH, 'Introduction to the Paperback Edition', in *Frames of War: When Is Life Grievable?*, ed. by Judith Butler (London: Verso, 2010), pp. ix–xxx

BURNS, ROB, 'Turkish-German Cinema: From Cultural Resistance to Transnational Cinema?', in *German Cinema: Since Unification*, ed. by David Clarke (London: Continuum, 2006), pp. 127–34

BUSTAMANTE, JAVIERA, and STEPHAN RUDERER, *Patio 29: tras la cruz de fierro* (Santiago: Ocho Libros, 2009)

CALOGUEREA, ALEJANDRO, 'El cine en Chile en el 2010', in *Panorama del audiovisual chileno*, ed. by Valerio Fuenzalida and Pablo Julio (Santiago: Dirección de Artes y Cultura de la Pontificia Universidad Católica de Chile, 2011), pp. 28–51. <http://www.accionaudiovisual.uc.cl/prontus_accion/site/artic/20111029/asocfile/20111029013029/panorama_corregido_22_noviembre___11.pdf> [accessed 30 October 2018]

CARUTH, CATHY, 'Introduction', in *Trauma: Explorations in Memory*, ed. by Cathy Caruth, (Baltimore: Johns Hopkins University 1995), pp. 3–12

—— ED., *Trauma: Explorations in Memory* (Baltimore: Johns Hopkins University Press, 1995)

—— *Unclaimed Experience: Trauma, Narrative, and History* (Baltimore: Johns Hopkins University Press, 1996)

CASANOVA, CARLOS, 'Hay que hablar: testimonio de un olvido y política de la desaparición', in *Pensar en la post/dictadura*, ed. by Nelly Richard and Alberto Moreiras, (Santiago: Cuarto Propio, 2001), pp. 155–73

CAVALLO, ASCANIO, PABLO DOUZET, and CECILIA RODRÍGUEZ, *Huérfanos y perdidos: relectura del cine chileno de la transición 1990–1999* (Santiago: Uqbar, 2007)

CINECHILE: ENCICLOPEDIA DEL CINE CHILENO, *Documentales* <http://www.cinechile.cl/documentales.php> [accessed 5 June 2017]

CHANAN, MICHAEL, 'El documental y la esfera pública en América latina: notas sobre la situación del documental en América latina (comparada con cualquier otro sitio)', *Secuencias*, 18 (2003), 22–32

—— ED., *Chilean Cinema* (London: BFI, 1976)

CHILEDOC, 'Comienzo del despegue: estado de la distribución y comercialización de documentales en Chile entre 2000 y 2010' (Santiago: Fondo de Fomento Audiovisual del Consejo del Arte y la Industria Audiovisual, 2014), p. 13 <http://www.chiledoc.cl/web/wp-content/uploads/2014/10/COMIENZO_DESPEGUE_25OCT_FINAL.pdf> [accessed 11 November 2018]

CHIGNOLI, ANDREA, and CATALINA DONOSO, *(Des)montando fábulas: el documental político de Pedro Chaskel* (Santiago: Uqbar, 2013)

CHION, MICHEL, *Audio-Vision: Sound on Screen*, trans. and ed. by Claudia Gorban (New York: Columbia University Press, 1994)

CHRISTIE, IAN, and MALCOLM COAD, 'Between Institutions: Interview with Raul Ruiz', *Afterimage*, 10 (1981), 103–14

CHOMSKY, NOAM, *9–11: Was There an Alternative?* (New York: Seven Stories Press, 2011)

CHUCHRYK, PATRICIA M., 'Subversive Mothers: The Women's Opposition to the Military Regime in Chile', in *Surviving Beyond Fear: Women, Children and Human Rights in Latin America*, ed. by Margorie Agosín (Fredonia, NY: White Pine Press, 1993), pp. 86–97

CinemaChile, *Chilean Films 2010/2011* (n.d.) http://issuu.com/media.cinemachile/docs/cinemachile2010> [accessed 11 November 2018]
Cinedirecto Producciones — Todo por las Niñas, 'My Life with Carlos: A Film by Germán Berger-Hertz' (Press book) (n.d.). <http://www.gebrueder-beetz.de/produktionen/mein-leben-mit-carlos> [accessed 18 November 2017]
Coad, Malcolm, 'Greats Events and Ordinary People', *Afterimage*, 10 (1981), 72–77
Collins, Cath, 'The Moral Economy of Memory', in *Accounting for Violence: Marketing Memory in Latin America*, ed. by Ksenija Bilbij and Leigh A. Payne (Durham: Duke University Press, 2011), pp. 235–63
——Katherine Hite, and Alfredo Joignant, eds., *The Politics of Memory in Chile: From Pinochet to Bachelet* (Colorado: Firstforum Press, 2013)
Comisión Nacional sobre Prisión Política y Tortura, *Informe de la Comisión Nacional sobre Prisión Política y Tortura* (Santiago: 2004) <http://www.memoriaviva.com/Tortura/Informe_Valech.pdf> [accessed 30 October 2017]
Constable, Pamela, and Arturo Valenzuela, *A Nation of Enemies: Chile under Pinochet* (New York: W.W. Norton, 1991)
Contardo, Óscar, and Macarena García, *La era ochentera: tevé, pop y under en el Chile de los ochenta* (Santiago: Ediciones B Chile, 2009)
Cooperativa, 'Finalmente TVN estrenará "El diario de Agustín" este sábado', 4 July 2014: <https://www.cooperativa.cl/noticias/entretencion/television/television-nacional/finalmente-tvn-estrenara-a-el-diario-de-agustina-este-sabado/2014-07-04/194235.html> [accessed 22 October 2018]
Corradi, Juan E., Patricia Fagen Weiss and Manuel Antonio Garretón, eds., *Fear at the Edge: State Terror and Resistance in Latin America* (Berkeley: University of California Press, 1992)
Corro, Pablo, 'El astuto mono Pinochet y La Moneda de los cerdos, Perut + Osnovikoff, 2004', *Una vuelta*, 14 September 2004 <http://perutosnovikoff.com/wp/wp-content/uploads/2009/01/unavuelta_pablocorro.pdf, 14th September 2004> [accessed 16 October 2018]
——*Retóricas del cine chileno: ensayos con el realismo* (Santiago: Cuarto Propio, 2012)
——'Sergio Bravo y tendencias del montaje', *Aisthesis*, 47 (July 2010), 83–99
——'Silencio, cuerpo, e historia en dos referentes del documental chileno', in II Congreso Internacional de la Asociación Argentina de Estudios de Cine y Audiovisual, Universidad de Buenos Aires and Universidad Nacional de General Sarmiento 19–23 October 2010 <http://www.asaeca.org/aactas/corro_pablo.pdf> [accessed 16 October 2018]
Corro, Pablo and others, *Teorías del cine documental chileno, 1957–1973* (Santiago: Pontificia Universidad Católica de Chile, Facultad de Filosofía, Instituto de Estética, 2007)
Cortínez, Verónica, and Manfred Engelbert, *Evolución en libertad: el cine chileno de los sesenta*, vol 1 and 2 (Santiago: Cuarto Propio, 2014)
——*La tristeza de los tigres y los misterios de Raúl Ruiz* (Santiago: Cuarto Propio, 2011)
Crowder-Taraborrelli, Tomás, 'Exhumations and Double Disappearance: Silvio Caiozzi's *Fernando ha vuelto* and *¿Fernando ha vuelto a desaparecer?*', *Social Identities: Journal for the Study of Race, Nation and Culture* 19: 3–4 (2013), 386–402
Cuneo, Bruno, ed., *Ruiz: entrevistas escogidas-filmografía comentada* (Santiago: Universidad Diego Portales, 2013)
Cvetkovich, Ann, *An Archive of Feelings: Trauma, Sexuality, and Lesbian Public Cultures* (Durham: Duke University Press, 2003)
De los Ríos, Valeria, 'La pregunta sobre el barroco en el cine de Raúl Ruiz', *Revista Chilena de Literatura*, 89 (2015), 113–31
——and Catalina Donoso, *El cine de Ignacio Agüero: el documental como la lectura de un espacio* (Santiago: Cuarto Propio, 2015)

—— and IVÁN PINTO, eds., *El cine de Raúl Ruiz: fantasmas, simulacros y artificios* (Santiago: Uqbar, 2010)

DE LUCA, TIAGO, 'Realism of the Senses: A Tendency in Contemporary World Cinema', in *Theorizing World Cinema*, ed. by Lucia Nagib, Chris Perriam, and Rajinder Dudrah (London: I. B. Tauris, 2012), pp. 183–205

DEL VALLE, IGNACIO, *Cámaras en trance: el Nuevo Cine Latinoamericano, un proyecto subcontinental* (Santiago, Cuarto Propio, 2014)

DELEUZE, GILLES, *Cinema 2: The Time-Image*, trans. by Hugh Tomlinson and Robert Galeta (London: Athlone Press, 1989)

DEREN, MAYA, 'August 25, 1960', in *Essential Deren: Collected Writings on Film*, ed. with a preface by B. R. McPherson (Kingston and New York: Documentext, 2005) pp. 241–44 (p. 243) (first publ. in The Village Voice, 'August 25, 1960')

DÍAZ, SUSANA, '¡Ruido, vanguardia, desacato y subversión! Un recorrido por los rockumentales chilenos más representativos del dos mil', in *Suban el volumen: 13 ensayos sobre cine y rock*, ed. by Ximena Vergara, Iván Pinto and Álvaro García eds. (Santiago: La calabaza del diablo, 2016), pp. 281–300

DIDI-HUBERMAN, GEORGES, *Images in Spite of All: Four Photographs from Auschwitz*, trans. by Shane B. Lillis (Chicago: University of Chicago Press, 2008)

—— *Images Malgré Tout* (Paris, Les Éditions de Minuit, 2003)

DIESTRO-DÓPIDO, MAR, 'The View from Downstairs', *Sight and Sound*, 20: 9 (September 2010), 20

DIGIOVANNI, LISA RENEE, 'Memories of Motherhood and Militancy in Chile: Gender and Nostalgia in *Calle Santa Fe* by Carmen Castillo', *Journal of Latin American Cultural Studies: Travesia*, 21:1 (2012), 15–36

DINAMARCA, HERNÁN, *El video en América latina: actor innovador del espacio audiovisual* (Santiago: ArteCien and Canelo de Nos, 1991)

DOANE, MARY ANN, 'The Close-Up: Scale and Detail in the Cinema', *A Journal of Feminist Cultural Studies*, 14:3 (Fall 2003), 89–111

DONOSO, CAMILA JOSÉ and, SANGIORGI, EVA, eds., *Ignacio Agüero: dos o tres cosas que sabemos de él* (Ciudad de México, Universidad Nacional Autónoma de México, 2017)

DONOSO, CATALINA, 'Sobre algunas estrategias fílmicas para una propuesta de primera persona documental', *Comunicación y Medios*, 26 (2012), 22–30

DORE, ELIZABETH, ed., *Gender Politics in Latin America: Debates in Theory and Practice* (New York: Monthly Review Press, 1997)

DORFMAN, ARIEL, 'The Last September 11', in *Other September, Many Americas: Selected Provocations 1980–2004* (New York: Seven Stories Press, 2004)

DRAKE, PAUL W., and IVÁN JAKSIĆ, 'Introduction: Transformation and Transition in Chile, 1982–1990', in *The Struggle for Democracy in Chile 1982–1990*, ed. by Paul W. Drake and Iván Jaksić, revised edn (Lincoln: University of Nebraska Press, 1995), pp. 1–17

ECHEVERRÍA, MÓNICA and CARMEN CASTILLO, *Santiago-París: el vuelo de la memoria* (Santiago: LOM, 2002)

ROBERT EAGLESTONE, 'Reading Perpetrator Testimony', *The Future of Memory*, ed. by Richard Crownshaw, Jane Kilby, and Anthony Rowland (New York: Berghan Books, 2014), pp. 123–34

EL DÍNAMO, '"Recuerdos del futuro": así se explicaba el FPMR en los 90', 2 April 2013 <http://www.eldinamo.cl/tumblr/videos-recuerdos-del-futuro-asi-se-explicaba-el-fpmr-en-los-90/> [accessed 20 July 2013]

EL MOSTRADOR, 'ARTV saca de su programación: "El diario de Agustín" y realizadores acusan nueva censura', *El Mostrador*, 24 April 2013 <http://www.elmostrador.cl/pais/2013/04/24/artv-saca-de-su-programacion-el-diario-de-agustin/> [accessed 22 October 2018]

—— 'Renuncia la directora de ARTV por censura a documental "El diario de Agustín"', *El Mostrador*, 1 May 2013 <http://www.elmostrador.cl/noticias/pais/2013/05/01/renuncia-la-directora-de-artv-por-censura-a-documental-el-diario-de-agustin/> [accessed 22 October 2018]

ELSAESSER, THOMAS, and HAGENER, MALTE, *Film Theory: An Introduction through the Senses* (New York: Routledge, 2010)

ELTIT, DIAMELA, 'La memoria pantalla (acerca de las imágenes públicas como políticas de desmemoria)', *Revista de Crítica Cultural*, 32 (November 2005), 30–33

—— 'The Two Sides of the Coin and the Two Faces of La Moneda', *Women's Studies*, 29: 1 (2000), 82–91

EMOL, '"No" según M.A. Garretón: es la basura ideologica más grande que he visto', *El Mercurio*, 23 August 2012 <http://www.emol.com/noticias/magazine/2012/08/23/557085/manuel-antonio-garreton-contra-la-pelicula-no.html> [accessed 22 October 2018]

ENG, DAVID L., and DAVID KAZANJIAN, 'Introduction: Mourning Remains', in *Loss: The Politics of Mourning*, ed. by David L. Eng and David Kazanjian (Berkeley: University of California Press, 2003), pp. 1–25

ERIKSON, KAI, 'Notes on Trauma and Community', in *Trauma: Explorations in Memory*, ed. by Cathy Caruth (Baltimore: John Hopkins University Press, 1995), pp. 183–99

ERLL, ASTRID, 'Travelling Memory', *Parallax*, 17:4 (2011), 4–18

ERRÁZURIZ, LUIS HERNÁN, 'Dictadura militar en Chile: antecedentes del golpe estético-cultural', *Latin American Research Review*, 44: 2 (2009), 136–57

ESTÉVEZ, ANTONELLA, *Luz, cámara, transición: el rollo del cine chileno de 1993 al 2003* (Santiago: Radio Universidad de Chile, 2005)

FAGUET, MICHÈLE, 'Pornomiseria: or How Not to Make a Documentary Film', *Afterall*, 21 (Summer 2009) <http://www.afterall.org/journal/issue.21/pornomiseria.or.how.not.make.documentary.film> [accessed 11 November 2018]

FELMAN, SHOSHANA, and DORI LAUB, ed., *Testimony: Crisis of Witnessing, Testimony in Literature, Psychoanalysis and History* (New York: Routledge, 1992)

FIDOCS, *Catálogo Primer Festival Internacional de Cine Documental* (Santiago: FIDOCS, 1997)

—— *Catálogo II Festival Internacional de Cine Documental en Santiago de Chile* (Santiago: FIDOCS, 1998)

—— *Catálogo 16° Festival Internacional Documentales Santiago Chile* (Santiago: FIDOCS, 2012)

FONDART, *1992–96 FONDART: cultura tradicional y local, artes de la representación, patrimonio cultural, artes audiovisuales, literatura, plástica, música* (Santiago: Fondo de Desarrollo de las Artes y la Cultura, 1997)

FOUCAULT, MICHEL, 'Nietzsche, Genealogy, History', in *Language, Counter-Memory, Practice: Selected Essays and Interviews*, trans. by Donald F. Bouchard and Sherry Simon, ed. by Donald F. Bouchard (Ithaca: Cornell University Press, 1977), pp. 139–64

FRANCO, JEAN, 'Gender, Death and Resistance: Facing the Ethical Vacuum', in *Fear at the Edge: State Terror and Resistance in Latin America*, ed. by Juan E. Corradi, Patricia Weiss Fagen and Manuel Antonio Garretón (Berkeley: University of California Press, 1992), pp. 104–18

FRAZIER, LESSIE JO, *Salt in the Sand: Memory, Violence, and the Nation-State in Chile, 1890 to the Present* (Durham: Duke University Press, 2007)

—— 'Subverted Memories: Countermourning as Political Action in Chile', in *Acts of Memory: Cultural Recall in the Present*, ed. by Mieke Bal, Jonathan Crewe, and Leo Spitzer (Hanover: University Press of New England, 1999), pp. 105–19

FREUD, SIGMUND, 'Mourning and Melancholia', in *The Standard Edition of the Complete Psychological Works of Sigmund Freud*, vol. 14, trans. and ed. by James Strachey (London: Hogarth Press, 1957), pp. 243–58

—— *The Uncanny*, trans. by David McLintock (London: Penguin Modern Classics, 2003)

FRIEDLÄNDER, SAUL, 'Introduction', in *Probing the Limits of Representation: Nazism and the 'Final Solution'*, ed. by Saul Friedländer (Cambridge: Harvard University Press, 1992), pp. 1–21

FUENZALIDA, VALERIO, PABLO CORRO, and CONSTANZA MUJICA, *Melodrama, subjectividad e historia en el cine y televisión chilenos de los 90* (Santiago: Pontificia Universidad Católica de Chile-Fondo de Fomento Audiovisual del Consejo Nacional de la Cultura y las Artes, 2009)

DE LA FUENTE, ALEJANDRO, and CLAUDIO GUERRERO, *El Grupo Proceso en los primeros años de la transición 1982–1993* (Santiago: Cineteca Nacional de Chile, 2015) <http://www.ccplm.cl/sitio/wp-content/uploads/2017/12/171107_Investigacion-archivo.pdf> [accessed 20 October 2018]

FUNDACIÓN 1367. CASA DE MEMORIA JOSÉ DOMINGO CAÑAS, *recuperación del sitio* (Santiago: Fundación 1367. Casa de Memoria José Domingo Cañas) <http://josedomingocanas.org/historia/recuperacion-del-sitio/> [accessed 10 November 2018]

GÓMEZ-BARRIS, MACARENA, *Where Memory Dwells: Culture and State Violence in Chile* (Berkeley: University of California Press, 2009)

GÓNGORA, AUGUSTO, *Video alternativo y comunicación en democracia* (working paper) (Santiago, ILET:1984)

GAINES, JANE M., 'Political Mimesis', in *Collecting Visible Evidence*, ed. by Jane M. Gaines and Michael Renov (Minneapolis: University of Minnesota Press, 1999), pp. 84–102

GALENDE, FEDERICO, 'Allende, Guzmán y la estructura mítica de los sueños', *Revista de Crítica Cultural*, 32 (November 2005), 48–51

GALLO, MACARENA, 'El director de TVN le tiene miedo a Agustín Edwards', *The Clinic*, 26 December 2012 <http://www.theclinic.cl/2012/12/26/el-directorio-de-tvn-le-tiene-miedo-a-agustin-edwards/> [22 October 2018]

GARCÍA MARISOL, *Canción valiente, 1960–1989: tres décadas de canto social y político en Chile* (Santiago: Ediciones B, 2013)

GARCÍA-MÁRQUEZ, GABRIEL, *Clandestine in Chile: The Adventures of Miguel Littín*, trans. by Asa Zats (New York: New York Review Books, 2010) [first publ. in Cambridge, England: Granta Books in association with Penguin, 1989]

GARRETÓN, MANUEL ANTONIO, 'Fear in Military Regimes: An Overview', in *Fear at the Edge: State Terror and Resistance in Latin America*, ed. by Juan E. Corradi, Patricia Weiss Fagen, and Manuel Antonio Garretón (Berkeley: University of California Press, 1992), pp. 13–25

——*Incomplete Democracy: Political Democratization in Chile and Latin America*, trans. by R. Kelly Washbourne and Gregory Horvath (Chapell Hill: University of North Carolina Press, 2003)

GONZÁLEZ, SEBASTIÁN, VANJA MUNJIN and IVÁN PINTO, 'Figurar la comunidad: cine chileno en tres tiempos 1990–2017', *Cinémas d'Amérique latine*, 26 (2018), 102–17

GONZÁLEZ, JUAN-PABLO, 'Hegemony and Counter-Hegemony of Music in Latin-America: The Chilean Pop', *Popular Music and Society*, 15: 2 (1991), 63–78

GRUPO PROCESO, *Grupo Proceso: videos televisión* (booklet) (n.d.)

GUERIN, FRANCES, and ROGER HALLAS, 'Introduction', in *The Image and the Witness: Trauma, Memory and Visual Culture*, ed. by Frances Guerin and Roger Hallas (London and New York: Wallflower Press, 2007), pp. 1–20

GUERRERO, MANUEL, 'Desaparecer al desaparecido', *La Nación*, 28 April 2006 <http://www.fortinmapocho.com/detalle.asp?iPro=727&iType=148> [accessed 2 November 2018]

GUZMÁN, PATRICIO, 'Carta abierta de Patricio Guzmán a Mauro Valdés, director ejecutivo de TVN', *CULDOC*, 31 July 2013 <http://corporacionculdoc.wordpress.com/2013/08/01/carta-abierta-de-patricio-guzman-dirigida-al-senor-mauro-valdes-director-ejecutivo-de-tvn/> [accessed 22 October 2018]

Guzmán, Patricio, and Pedro Sempere, *Chile: el cine contra el facismo* (Valencia: Fernando Torres, 1977)
Haddu, Miriam, and Joanna Page, eds., *Visual Synergies in Fiction and Documentary Film from Latin America* (New York: Palgrave Macmillan, 2009)
Hardt, Michael, 'Foreword: What Affects are Good for', in *The Affective Turn: Theorizing the Social*, ed. by Patricia Ticineto Clough and Jean Halley (Durham: Duke University Press, 2007), pp. ix–xiii
Hertz, Carmen, *La historia fue otra* (Santiago: Penguin Random House, 2017)
Henebelle, Guy, and Alfonso Gumucio Dragón, eds., *Les cinemas de l'Amérique Latine* (Paris: L' Herminier, 1981)
Hirsch, Joshua, *Afterimage: Film, Trauma, and the Holocaust* (Philadelphia: Temple University Press, 2004)
—— 'Post-Traumatic Cinema and the Holocaust Documentary', in *Trauma and Cinema: Cross-Cultural Explorations*, ed. by E. Ann Kaplan and Ban Wang (Hong Kong: Hong Kong University Press, 2008), pp. 93–122
Hirsch, Marianne, *Family Frames: Photography, Narrative, and Postmemory* (Cambridge: Harvard University Press, 1997)
—— 'The Generation of Postmemory', *Poetics Today*, 29 (Spring 2008), 103–28
—— 'Projected Memory: Holocaust Photographs in Personal and Public Fantasy', in Mieke Bal, Jonathan Crewe and Leo Spitzer, ed., *Acts of Memory: Cultural Recall in the Present* (Hanover: University Press of New England, 1999), pp. 5–23
Hite, Katherine, 'Estadio Nacional: monumento y lugar de conmmemoración', in Patricia Verdugo, ed., *De la tortura no se habla: Agüero versus Meneses* (Santiago: Catalonia, 2004), pp. 213–27
—— 'La superación de los silencios oficiales en el chile posautoritario', trans. by Horacio Pons, in *Historizar el pasado vivo en America latina*, ed. by Anne Pérotin-Dumon (Santiago: Universidad Alberto Hurtado, 2007), pp. 1–41 <http://www.historizarelpasadovivo.cl/downloads/hite.pdf> [accessed 24 October 2013]
—— *Politics and the Art of Commemoration: Memorials to Struggle in Latin America and Spain* (London: Routledge, 2012)
—— and Cath Collins, 'Memorial Fragments, Monumental Silences and Reawakenings in 21st-Century Chile', *Millennium: Journal of International Studies*, 38: 2 (2009), 379–400
Hopenhayn, Daniel, 'Manuel Antonio Garretón: "Tenemos una ciudadanía muy poco empoderada con la ilusión narcisista de que tiene poder"', *The Clinic*, 14 June 2017 <http://www.theclinic.cl/2017/06/14/manuel-antonio-garreton-tenemos-una-ciudadania-poco-empoderada-la-ilusion-narcisista-poder/> [Accessed 15 June 2017]
Huneeus, Carlos, and Sebastián Ibarra, 'The Memory of the Pinochet Regime in Public Opinion', in *The Politics of Memory in Chile: From Pinochet to Bachelet*, ed. by Cath Collins, Katherine Hite and Alfredo Joignant (Boulder: First Forum Press, 2013), pp. 197–238
Hurtado, María de la Luz, *La industria cinematográfica: límites y posibilidades de su democratización*, 2nd edn (Santiago: Ceneca, 1986)
Huyssen, Andreas, *Present Pasts: Urban Palimpsests and the Politics of Memory*, (Stanford: Stanford University Press, 2003)
Icalma, *El mocito / The Young Butler* (Press Kit) <http://www.icalmafilms.com/prensa.html> [accessed 10 January 2012]
Jaquette, Jane S., ed., *The Women's Movement in Latin America: Feminism and the Transition to Democracy*, 2nd edn (Boulder: Westview Press, 1994)
Jelin, Elizabeth, *State Repression and the Struggles for Memory*, trans. by Judy Rein and Marcial Godoy-Anatavia (London: Latin American Bureau, 2003)

—— 'Victims, Relatives, and Citizens in Argentina: Whose Voice is Legitimate Enough?', in *Humanitarianism and Suffering: The Mobilization of Empathy*, ed. by Richard Ashby Wilson and Richard D. Brown (Cambridge: Cambridge University Press, 2009), pp. 177–201

JOCELYN-HOLT, ALFREDO, *El Chile perplejo*, 3rd edn (Santiago: Planeta-Ariel, 1999)

JOIGNANT, ALFREDO, 'Pinochet's Funeral: Memory, History, and Immortality', trans. by Cath Collins, in *The Politics of Memory in Chile: From Pinochet to Bachelet*, ed. by Cath Collins, Katherine Hite, and Alfredo Joignant (Boulder: First Forum Press, 2013), pp. 165–95

—— *El gesto y la palabra: ritos políticos y representaciones sociales de la construcción democrática en Chile* (Santiago: Universidad ARCIS-LOM, 1998)

—— *Un día distinto: memorias festivas y batallas conmemorativas en torno al 11 de septiembre en Chile, 1974–2006* (Santiago: Editorial Universitaria, 2007)

JOHANSSON, MARÍA TERESA, and CONSTANZA VERGARA, 'Filman los hijos: nuevo testimonio en los documentales *En algún lugar del cielo* de Alejandra Carmona y *Mi vida con Carlos* de Germán Berger-Hertz', *Meridional*, 2 (2014), pp. 89–105

KAES, ANTON, *Shell Shock Cinema: Weimar Culture and the Wounds of War* (Princeton, NJ: Princeton University Press, 2009)

KAHANA, JONATHAN, 'Introduction: What Now? Presenting Reenactment', *Framework*, 50:1–2 (Spring–Fall 2009), 46–60

KAPLAN, E. ANN, *Trauma Culture: The Politics of Terror and Loss in Media and Literature* (New Brunswick: Rutgers University Press, 2005)

—— and BAN WANG, 'Introduction: From Traumatic Paralysis to the Force of Modernity', in *Trauma and Cinema: Cross-Cultural Explorations*, ed. by E. Ann Kaplan and Ban Wang (Hong Kong: Hong Kong University Press, 2004), pp. 1–22

KEETON, PATRICIA, 'Reevaluating the "Old" Cold War: A Dialectical Reading of Two 9/11 Narratives', *Cinema Journal*, 43:4 (Summer 2004), 114–21

KING, JOHN, *Magical Reels: A History of Cinema in Latin America*, 2nd edn (London: Verso, 2000)

KLEIN, KERWIN LEE, 'On the Emergence of Memory in Historical Discourse', *Representations*, 69 (Winter 2000), pp. 127–50

KLUBOCK, THOMAS MILLER, 'History and Memory in Neoliberal Chile: Patricio Guzmán' Obstinate Memory and the Battle of Chile', *Radical History Review*, 85 (Winter 2003), 271–81

KRISTEVA, JULIA, *Powers of Horror: An Essay on Abjection*, trans. by Leon S. Roudiez (New York: Columbia University Press, 1982)

KUHN, ANNETTE, *Family Secrets: Acts of Memory and Imagination*, new edn (London: Verso, 2002)

LABANYI, JO, 'Doing Things: Emotion, Affect, and Materiality', *Journal of Spanish Cultural Studies*, 11: 3–4 (2010), 223–33

LA NACIÓN, 'Marco Enríquez-Ominami: la sorpresa de la campaña chilena', *La Nación*, 27 September 2009 <http://www.lanacion.com.ar/1179066-marco-enriquez-ominami-la-sorpresa-de-la-campana-chilena> [accessed 15 October 2018]

LACAPRA, DOMINICK, *History and Memory after Auschwitz* (Ithaca, NY: Cornell University Press, 1998)

LAGOS, CLAUDIA, *El diario de Agustín* (Santiago: Lom, 2009)

LAGOS, PAOLA, 'Ecografías del "yo": documental autobiográfico y estrategias de (auto) representación de la subjetividad', *Comunicación y Medios*, 24 (2011), 60–80

LANDSBERG, ALISON, *Prosthetic Memory: The Transformation of American Remembrance in the Age of Mass Culture* (New York: Columbia University Press, 2004)

LARRAÍN, CAROLINA, 'Nuevas tendencias del cine chileno tras la llegada del cine digital', *Aisthesis*, 47 (July 2010) 156–71

LAZZARA, MICHAEL J., *Chile in Transition: The Poetics and Politics of Memory* (Gainesville, FL: University Press of Florida, 2006)

—— *Civil Obedience: Complicity and Complacency in Chile since Pinochet* (Madison: University of Wisconsin Press, 2018)

—— 'El fenómeno Mocito (Las puestas en escena de un sujeto cómplice)', *A Contracorriente* 12: 1 (Fall 2014) 89–106 (94–95). <https://acontracorriente.chass.ncsu.edu/index.php/acontracorriente/article/view/1301>[accessed 16 October 2018]

—— 'Filming Loss: (Post-)Memory, Subjectivity, and the Performance of Failure in Recent Argentine Documentary Films', *Latin American Perspectives*, 36: 5 (2009), 147–57

—— 'Pinochet's Cadaver as Ruin and Palimpsest', in *Telling Ruins in Latin America*, ed. by Michael J. Lazzara and Vicky Unruh (New York: Palgrave Macmillan, 2009), pp. 121–34

—— 'Tres recorridos por Villa Grimaldi', in *Monumentos, memoriales y marcas territoriales*, ed. by Elizabeth Jelin and Victoria Langland (Madrid: Siglo XXI, 2003), pp. 127–47

LEBOW, ALISA, 'Introduction', in *The Cinema of Me: The Self and Subjectivity in First Person Documentary*, ed. by Alisa Lebow (London: Wallflower Press, 2012), pp. 1–11

LECHNER, NORBERT, and PEDRO GÜELL, 'Construcción social de las memorias en la transición chilena', in *Subjetividad y figuras de la memoria*, ed. by Elizabeth Jelin and Susana Kaufman (Madrid: Siglo XXI, 2006), pp. 17–44

LEIGHTON, CRISTIÁN, 'La elipsis del documental', *EAC Magazine*, 2 (n.d.) <http://jhcnewmedia.org/eacmagazine/> [accessed 28 August 2016] (first publ. in *Patrimonio Cultural, Dibam* 25 (2002))

LESAGE, JULIA, 'The Political Aesthetics of the Feminist Documentary Film', in *Issues in Feminist Film Critiscism*, ed. by Patricia Erens (Bloomington: Indiana University Press, 1990), pp. 222–38

—— 'Torture Documentaries', *Jump Cut*, 51 (2009) <http://www.ejumpcut.org/archive/jc51.2009/TortureDocumentaries/> [accessed 3 November 2018]

LETELIER, JORGE, '¿De qué hablamos cuando hablamos de cine chileno?: la desmemoria obstinada', *Mabuse*, 6 October 2003 <http://www.mabuse.cl/cine_chileno.php?id=1790> [accessed 24 October 2018]

LEVI, PRIMO, *The Drowned and the Dead*, trans. by Raymond Rosenthal (New York: Vintage International, 1989)

LIÑERO, GERMÁN, *Apuntes para una historia del video en Chile* (Santiago: Ocho libros, 2010)

LIRA, ELIZABETH, and BRIAN LOVEMAN, 'Torture as Public Policy, 1810–2011', in *The Politics of Memory in Chile: From Pinochet to Bachelet*, ed. by Cath Collins, Katherine Hite, and Alfredo Joignant (Boulder: First Forum Press, 2013), pp. 91–132

LLANOS, BERNARDITA, 'Memoria y testimonio visual en Chile: el documental *La Venda* de Gloria Camiruaga', *Chasqui*, 39: 2 (November 2010), 42–53

—— 'Caught Off Guard at the Crossroads of Ideology and Affect: Documentary Films by the Daughters of Revolutionaries', in *Latin American Documentary Film in the New Millenium*, ed. by María Guadalupe Arenillas and Michael J. Lazzara (New York: Palgrave, 2016), pp. 243–58

LONDRES 38. ESPACIOS DE MEMORIA, *La recuperación de Londres 38* (Santiago: Londres 38, 2013) <http://www.londres38.cl/1937/w3-printer-91128.html> [accessed 14 September 2013]

LÓPEZ, ANA M., '*The Battle of Chile*: Documentary, Political Process and Representation', in *The Social Documentary in Latin America*, ed. by Julianne Burton (Pittsburgh: University of Pittsburgh Press, 1990), pp. 267–87

LOVEMAN, BRIAN, 'The Transition to Civilian Government in Chile, 1990–1994', in *The*

Struggle for Democracy in Chile, ed. by Paul W. Drake and Iván Jaksić, revised edn (Lincoln: University of Nebraska Press, 1995)
—— and ELIZABETH LIRA, *El espejismo de la reconciliación política Chile 1990–2002* (Santiago: LOM, 2002)
—— 'Truth, Justice, Reconciliation, and Impunity as Historical Themes: Chile, 1984–2006', *Radical History Review*, 97 (Winter 2007), 43–76
MALIK, SARITA, 'Beyond "the Cinema of Duty"? The Pleasures of Hybridity: Black British Film of the 1980s and 1990s', in *Dissolving Views: Key Writings on British Cinema*, ed. by Andrew Higson (London: Cassell, 1996), pp. 202–15
MARINESCU, ANDREEA, 'Raúl Ruiz's Surrealist Documentary of Return: *Le retour d'un amateur de bibliothèques* (1983) and *Cofralandes* (2002)', in *Raúl Ruiz's Cinema of Inquiry*, ed. by Ignacio López-Vicuña and Andreea Marinescu (Detroit: Wayne State University Press: 2017), pp. 177–96
MARKS, LAURA U., 'Loving a Disappearing Image', in *Touch: Sensuous Theory and Multisensory Media* (Minneapolis: University of Minnesota Press, 2002), pp. 91–110
—— *The Skin of the Film: Intercultural Cinema, Embodiment, and the Senses* (Durham: Duke University Press, 2000)
—— *Touch: Sensuous Theory and Multisensory Media* (Minneapolis: University of Minnesota Press, 2002)
—— 'Video Haptics and Erotics', in *Touch: Sensuous Theory and Multisensory Media* (Minneapolis: University of Minnesota Press, 2002), pp. 1–20
MARTÍNEZ, JAVIER, 'Fear of the State, Fear of Society: On the Opposition Protests in Chile', in *Fear at the Edge: State Terror and Resistance in Latin America*, ed. by Juan E. Corradi, Patricia Weiss Fagen, and Manuel Antonio Garretón (Berkeley: University of California Press, 1992), pp. 142–60
MASIELLO, FRANCINE, *The Art of Transition: Latin American Culture and Neoliberal Crisis* (Durham: Duke University Press, 2001)
MASSUMI, BRIAN, 'The Autonomy of Affect', *Cultural Critique*, 31 (Autumn 1995), 83–109
MAYOL, ALBERTO, *El derrumbe del modelo: la crisis de la economía de mercado en el Chile contemporáneo* (Santiago: LOM, 2012)
MONDACA, HERMANN, 'Las imágenes de un país invisible: historia del movimiento de video alternativo en Chile en el período 1980 a 1990 y su relación con los medios de comunicación' (unpublished bachelor thesis, Universidad Pedro de Valdivia, 2009)
MONTEALEGRE, JORGE, *Frazadas del Estadio Nacional* (Santiago: LOM, 2003)
MORALES, JORGE, 'En los límites del documental: mentiras verdaderas', *Mabuse* (4 August 2004) <http://perutosnovikoff.com/wp/wp-content/uploads/2009/01/mabuse_jorgemorales.pdf> [accessed 16 October 2018]
—— 'Vine a decirles que me quedo: el cine de Marco Enríquez-Ominami', *Mabuse* (2004) <http://www.mabuse.cl/cine_chileno.php?id=86432> [accessed 15 October 2018]
—— and GONZALO MAZA, *Idénticamente desigual: el cine imperfecto de Carlos Flores*, 2nd edn. (Santiago: FIDOCS, 2014)
MOREIRAS, ALBERTO, 'Postdictadura y reforma del pensamiento', *Revista de Crítica Cultural*, 7 (1993), 26–35
MOUESCA, JACQUELINE, 'Cine: un largo camino de ilusiones', in *100 años de cultura chilena 1905–2005*, ed. by Juan Andrés Piña (Santiago: Zig-Zag, 2006), pp. 331–80
—— *El documental chileno* (Santiago: LOM, 2005)
—— *Plano secuencia de la memoria de Chile: veinticinco años de cine chileno (1960–1985)* (Santiago: Ediciones del Litoral, 1988)
MOULIAN, TOMÁS, *Chile actual: anatomía de un mito*, 3rd edn (Santigo: LOM, 2002)
MOYA, LAURA, *José Domingo Cañas 1367: más memoria* (Santiago: Colectivo José Domingo Cañas, 2007)

MUEL, BRUNO, 'Santiago en septiembre: la capital chilena a los ojos de un camarógrafo', trans. by Patricia Minarrieta, *Le Monde Diplomatique*, September 2013, p. 14. <http://www.lemondediplomatique.cl/IMG/pdf/Muel.pdf> [accessed 20 October 2018]

MUSEO DE LA MEMORIA Y LOS DERECHOS HUMANOS, *Archivo audiovisual: colección del Museo de la Memoria y los Derechos Humanos* (Santiago: Ocho Libros / Museo de la Memoria y los Derechos Humanos, 2015)

NAVARRO, VINICIUS, and JUAN CARLOS RODRÍGUEZ, eds., *New Documentaries from Latin America* (New York: Palgrave Macmillan, 2014)

NAFICY, HAMID, *An Accented Cinema: Exilic and Diasporic Filmmaking* (Princeton, NJ: Princeton University Press, 2001)

NICHOLS, BILL, *Blurred Boundaries: Questions of Meaning in Contemporary Culture* (Bloomington: Indiana University Press, 1994)

——'Documentary Reenactment and the Fantasmatic Subject', *Critical Inquiry*, 35:1 (2008), 72–89

——*Representing Reality* (Bloomington: Indiana University Press, 1991)

——'The Voice of Documentary', in *New Challenges for Documentary*, ed. by Alan Rosenthal and John Corner, 2nd edn (Manchester: Manchester University Press, 2005), pp. 17–33

NORA, PIERRE, 'Between Memory and History: Les Lieux de Mémoire', trans. by Marc Roudebush, *Representations*, 26 (Spring 1989), 7–24

NOUZEILLES, GABRIELA, 'Postmemory Cinema and the Future of the Past in Albertina Carri's *Los Rubios*', *Journal of Latin American Cultural Studies: Travesia*, 14: 3 (2005), 263–78

OBILINOVIC, DUSANKA, 'Entre aplausos y bajo rating: Los archivos del cardenal llega a su final', *La Tercera*, 26 May 2014 <http://www.latercera.com/noticia/entre-aplausos-y-bajo-rating-los-archivos-del-cardenal-llega-a-su-final/> [accessed 22 October 2018]

OLAVARRÍA, PATRICIO, 'Ignacio Agüero, documentalista: "La ley antiterrorista es una provocación a la dignidad de los cineastas, aunque la mayoría de ellos ni lo sepan"', *El Mostrador*, 4 June 2017 <http://www.elmostrador.cl/cultura/2017/06/04/ignacio-aguero-documentalista-la-ley-antiterrorista-es-una-provocacion-a-la-dignidad-de-los-cineastas-aunque-la-mayoria-de-ellos-ni-lo-sepan/> [accessed 22 October 2018]

OLEA, RAQUEL, 'No... la perversión de la verdad en la película', *Radio Tierra*, 13 August 2012 <http://www.radiotierra.cl/node/4741> [accessed 22 October 2012]

OQUENDO-VILLAR, CARMEN, 'Chile 1973-el golpe y la voz de la ley', *E-misférica*, 3: 1 (June 2006) <http://hemisphericinstitute.org/journal/3.1/eng/en31_pg_oquendo_villar.html> [accessed 20 October 2018]

——'Dress for Success', in *Accounting for Violence: Marketing Memory in Latin America*, ed. by Ksenija Bilbija and Leigh A. Payne (Durham: Duke University Press, 2011), pp. 265–85

OYARZÚN, KEMY, 'Des/memoria, género y globalización', in *Volver a la memoria*, ed. by Raquel Olea and Olga Grau (Santiago: LOM, 2001), pp. 21–38

PAGE, JOANNA, *Crisis and Capitalism in Contemporary Argentine Cinema* (Durham: Duke University Press, 2009)

PALACIOS, JOSÉ MIGUEL, 'Chilean Exile Cinema and its Homecoming Documentaries', in *Cinematic Homecomings: Exile and Return in Transnational Cinema*, ed. by Rebecca Prime (New York: Bloomsbury Academic, 2015), pp. 147–68

——'Nothing is Happier than Happiness', *The Brooklyn Rail* (4 March 2013) <http://www.brooklynrail.org/2013/03/film/nothings-happier-than-happiness-pablo-larrans-no> [accessed 17 October 2018]

——'Pasagges of Exile: Chilean Cinema 1973–2016' (unpublished doctoral thesis, New York University, 2017)

PANIZZA, TIZIANA, 'Por mí y por todos mis compañeros', *Filmonauta*, 6 (April 2010) <http://issuu.com/filmonauta/docs/filmonauta_06> [accessed 8 July 2017]

Parada, Marcela, 'El estado de los estudios sobre cine en Chile: una visión panorámica 1960–2009', *Razón y Palabra*, 77 (2011) <http://www.razonypalabra.org.mx/varia/77%205a%20parte/67_Parada_V77.pdf> [accessed 27 August 2016]

——'La estética de la disección en el filme "Noticias" (Chile, 2009)', in III Congreso Internacional de la Asociación Argentina de Estudios de Cine y Audiovisual, Universidad Nacional de Córdoba 10–12 May 2012 <http://www.asaeca.org/aactas/parada__marcela_-_ponencia.pdf> [accessed 16 October 2018]

Paranaguá, Paulo Antonio, ed., *Cine documental en América latina* (Madrid: Cátedra, 2003)

——'Orígenes, evolución y problemas', in *Cine documental en América latina*, ed. by Paulo Antonio Paranaguá (Madrid: Cátedra, 2003), pp. 13–78

Payne, Leigh A., *Unsettling Accounts: Neither Truth nor Reconciliation in Confessions of State Violence* (Durham: Duke University Press, 2008)

Peirano, María Paz, 'FIDOCS y la formación de un campo de cine documental en Chile en la década de 1990', *Cine Documental* 18 (2018), 62–89. <http://revista.cinedocumental.com.ar/indice-18/> [accessed 28 October 2018]

——'Connecting and Sharing Experiences: Chilean Documentary Film Professionals at the Film Festival Circuit', in *Documentary Film Festivals*, ed. by Aida Vallejo and Ezra Winton (London: Palgrave MacMillan, 2018, 2019)

Pérez Villalobos, Carlos, 'El irrecuperable Allende de Guzmán', *Revista de Crítica Cultural* 32 (2005), pp. 44–47

Pequeño, Pamela, 'Catastro: nuestro universo documental' (January 2007) <http://www.adoc-chile.org/cat/?page_id=125> [accessed 20 October 2013]

——'Catastro virtual de la producción documental chilena', *ADOC* (January 2007) <http://www.adoc-chile.org/cat/?page_id=125> [accessed 23 December 2013]

——*Productora Ictus TV, Videoteca: memoria histórica 1978–1992* (Santiago: 2005)

Pick, Zuzana M., 'Chilean Cinema in Exile (1973–1986). The Notion of Exile: A Field of Investigation and its Conceptual Framework', *Framework*, 34 (1987), 39–57

——'Chilean Cinema: Ten Years of Exile (1973–83)', *Jump Cut*, 32 (1987) 66–70. <http://www.ejumpcut.org/archive/onlinessays/JC32folder/ChileanFilmExile.html.> [accessed 23 July 2016]

——'Chilean Documentary Continuity and Disjunction', in *The Social Documentary in Latin America*, ed. by Julianne Burton (Pittsburgh: University of Pittsburgh Press, 1990), pp. 109–30

——'Cronología del cine chileno en el exilio 1973/1983', *Literatura Chilena, Creación y Crítica*, 10:27 (January–March, 1984), 15–21

——'The Dialectical Wanderings of Exile', *Screen*, 30: 4 (1989), 48–65

——*The New Latin American Cinema: A Continental Project* (Austin: University of Texas Press, 1993)

Pino-Ojeda, Walescka, '*Latent Image*: Chilean Cinema and the Abject', trans. by Mariana Ortega Breña, *Latin American Perspectives*, 36 (September 2009), 133–46

Pinto, Iván, 'Cine, política, memoria: nuevos entramados en el documental chileno', *La Fuga*, 4 (2007) <http://2016.lafuga.cl/cine-politica-memoria/341> [accessed 4 junio 2016] [accessed 4 June 2017]

——'Formas expandidas: límites y entre-lugares del documental chileno 2004- 2016', *Cine Documental*, 4 (2016), <http://revista.cinedocumental.com.ar/formas-expandidas-limites-y-entre-lugares-del-documental-chileno-2004–2016/> [accessed 4 junio 2017]

——'Lo incompleto: desajuste y fractura en dos diarios fílmicos del exilio chileno', in *Prismas del cine latinoamericano*, ed. by Wolfgang Bongers (Santiago: Cuarto Propio, 2012), pp. 215–35

―― 'Welcome to New York: Dispositivos', *La Fuga*, 4 (2007) <http://www.lafuga.cl/welcome-to-new-york/337> <http://www.lafuga.cl/welcome-to-new-york/337> [accessed 16 October 2018]

PIPER, ISABEL, 'La retórica de la marca y los sujetos de la dictadura', *Revista de Crítica Cultural*, 32 (November 2005), 16–19

PODALSKY, LAURA, *The Politics of Affect and Emotion in Contemporary Latin American Cinema: Argentina, Brazil, Cuba, and Mexico* (New York: Palgrave Macmillan, 2011)

GRISELDA POLLOCK and MAX SILVERMAN, eds., *Concentrationary Memories: Totalitarian Terror and Cultural Resistance* (London: I.B. Tauris, 2014)

―― *Concentrationary Imaginaries: Tracing Totalitarian Terror in Popular Culture* (London: I.B. Tauris, 2015)

RAMÍREZ-SOTO, ELIZABETH, 'Impertinent Interventions: On Raúl Ruiz and an Emerging Field', *Journal of Latin American Cultural Studies: Travesia*, 21:1 (2012), 49–59

―― 'La cámara que tiembla: sobre el bombardeo a La Moneda y algunas imágenes que nos mueven', *Savoirs en Prisme*, 9 (2019) <https://savoirsenprisme.com/numeros/09-dictature-et-image-absente-dans-le-cinema-de-non-fiction/la-camara-que-tiembla-sobre-el-bombardeo-al-palacio-de-la-moneda-y-algunas-imagenes-que-nos-mueven/> [accessed 24 April 2019]

―― 'Memoria y desobediencia: una aproximación a los documentales de Carmen Castillo', *La Fuga*, 12 (2011) <http://2016.lafuga.cl/memoria-y-desobediencia/450> [accessed 20 October 2018]

―― 'Reflections on the *Other* Archive on Television: Chilean Fiction Series and Approximations to the Dictatorial Past', *New Cinemas: Journal of Contemporary Film*, 13:1 (2015), 9–22

―― and CATALINA DONOSO PINTO, eds., *Nomadías: el cine de Marilú Mallet, Valeria Sarmiento y Angelina Vázquez* (Santiago: Metales Pesados, 2016)

RANCIÈRE, JACQUES, *Film Fables*, trans. by Emiliano Battista (Oxford: Berg, 2006)

RANVAUD, DON, 'Interview with Raúl Ruiz', *Framework*, 10 (Spring 1979), 16–18

RANZANI, OSCAR, 'El realizador chileno Patricio Henríquez en el DOCBSAS/07: un buque escuela, de terror', *Página 12*, 18 October 2007 <http://www.pagina12.com.ar/diario/suplementos/espectaculos/5-7990-2007-10-18.html> [accessed 10 November 2018]

RASCAROLI, LAURA, *The Personal Camera: Subjective Cinema and the Essay Film* (London and New York: Wallflower Press, 2009)

REBOLLEDO, JAVIER, *La danza de los cuervos: el destino final de los detenidos desaparecidos* (Santiago: Ceibo, 2012)

REBOLLEDO, LORETO, 'Memorias del des-exilio: chilenos en América y Europa, 1973–2004', in *Exiliados, emigrados y retornados*, ed. by José del Pozo Arias (Santiago: RIL, 2006), pp. 167–92

―― *Memorias del desarraigo: testimonios de exilio y retorno de hombres y mujeres de Chile* (Santiago: Catalonia, 2006)

RENOV, MICHAEL, 'Introduction: The Truth About Non-Fiction', in *Theorizing Documentary*, ed. by Michael Renov (New York: Routledge, 1993), pp. 1–11

―― *The Subject of Documentary* (Minneapolis: University of Minnesota Press, 2004)

RICCIARELLI, CECILIA, *El cine documental según Patricio Guzmán* (Santiago: FIDOCS, 2010)

RICH, B. RUBY, 'An/Other View of New Latin American Cinema', in *New Latin American Cinema*, vol.1, ed. by Michael T. Martin (Detroit: Wayne State University Press, 1997), pp. 273–97 (first publ. in *IRIS* 13 (1991), 5–27)

RICHARD, NELLY, 'Cites/Sites of Violence: Convulsions of Sense and Official Routines', in *Cultural Residues: Chile in Transition*, trans. by Alan West-Durán and Theodore Quester (Minneapolis: University of Minnesota Press, 2004), pp. 15–29

—— 'Con motivo del 11 de septiembre: notas sobre *La memoria obstinada* (1996) de Patricio Guzmán', in *Escrituras, imágenes y escenarios ante la represión*, Elizabeth Jelin and Ana Longoni, ed., (Madrid: Siglo XXI, 2005) pp. 121–29 (first publ. in Revista de Crítica Cultural, 15 (1998))

—— ed., *Crítica de la memoria (1990–2010)* (Santiago: Ediciones Universidad Diego Portales, 2010)

—— *Cultural Residues: Chile in Transition*, trans. by Alan West-Durán and Theodore Quester (Minneapolis: University of Minnesota Press, 2004)

—— 'Memoria contemplativa y memoria crítico-transformadora', *La Fuga*, 16 (2014) <http://2016.lafuga.cl/memoria-contemplativa-y-memoria-critico-transformadora/675>[accessed 22 October 2018]

—— 'Ir y venir', in *Crítica de la memoria (1990–2010)* (Santiago: Ediciones Universidad Diego Portales, 2010), 146–64

—— 'The Reconfigurations of Post-Dictatorship Critical Thought', *Journal of Latin American Cultural Studies*, 9:3 (2000), 273–82

—— 'Sites of Memory, Emptying Remembrance', in *Telling Ruins in Latin America*, ed. by Michael J. Lazzara and Vicky Unruh (New York: Palgrave Macmillan, 2009), pp. 175–82

RODRÍGUEZ, JUAN CARLOS, 'Framing Ruins: Patricio Guzmán's Postdictatorial Documentaries', *Latin American Perspectives*, 40:1 (January 2013), 131–44

ROHT-ARRIAZA, NAOMI, *The Pinochet Effect: Transnational Justice in the Age of Human Rights* (Philadelphia: University of Pennsylvania Press, 2005)

ROS, ANA, *The Post-Dictatorship Generation in Argentina, Chile, and Uruguay: Collective Memory and Cultural Production* (New York: Palgrave MacMillan, 2012)

ROSS, MIRIAM, 'The Film Festival as Producer: Latin American Films and Rotterdam's Hubert Bals Fund', *Screen*, 52: 2 (2011), 261–67

RUBIO, ROBERTO, 'Chilean documentaries and their multiplication within the industry', in *Documentary Pathways*, ed. by ChileDoc (Santiago: ChileDoc, 2014), <http://www.chiledoc.cl/web/wp-content/uploads/2015/08/Documentary-pathways1.pdf> [accessed 22 October 2018]

RUFFINELLI, JORGE, *El cine de Patricio Guzmán: en busca de las imágenes verdaderas* (Santiago: Uqbar, 2008)

SALINAS, S., ACUÑA, R., MARTINEZ, F., SAID J.A, SOTO, H. (sic), 'Entrevista a Raúl Ruiz: Prefiero registrar antes que mistificar el proceso chileno', *Primer Plano*, 1: 4 (Spring 1972), 3–21

SAID, EDWARD W., 'Intellectual Exile: Expatriates and Marginals', *Grand Street* 47 (Autumn 1993), 112–24

—— 'Reflections on Exile', in *Reflections on Exile and other Essays* (Cambridge, Mass: Harvard University Press, 2000) pp. 173–86

SALAS, FABIO, *La primavera terrestre: cartografías del Rock chileno y la Nueva Canción chilena* (Santiago: Cuarto Propio, 2003)

SALAZAR, GABRIEL, *La violencia política popular en las 'Grandes Alamedas'*, 2nd edn (Santiago: LOM, 2006)

SALEH, FELIPE, 'Las esquirlas de "El diario de Agustín" salpican ahora al Museo de la Memoria', *El Mostrador,* 12 December 2013 <http://www.elmostrador.cl/pais/2013/03/12/las-esquirlas-de-el-diario-de-agustin-salpican-ahora-al-museo-de-la-memoria/> [accessed 22 October 2018]

SALIMOVICH, SOFIA, ELIZABETH LIRA, and EUGENIA WEINSTEIN, 'Victims of Fear: The Social Psychology of Repression', in *Fear at the Edge: State Terror and Resistance in Latin America,* ed. by Juan E. Corradi, Patricia Weiss Fagen, and Manuel Antonio Garretón (Berkeley, Los Angeles: University of Calfornia Press, 1992), pp. 72–89

SALINAS, CLAUDIO, and HANS STANGE (with the collaboration of Sergio Salinas), *Historia del cine experimental en la Universidad de Chile 1957–1973* (Santiago: Uqbar, 2008)

SANTA-CRUZ, GUADALUPE, 'Capitales del olvido', in *Políticas y estéticas de la memoria*, ed. by Nelly Richard (Santiago: Cuarto Propio, 2000), pp. 105–12

SARKAR, BHASKAR, and JANET WALKER, eds., *Documentary Testimonies: Global Archives of Suffering* (New York: Routledge, 2010)

—— 'Moving Testimonies', in *Documentary Testimonies: Global Archives of Suffering*, ed. by Bhaskar Sarkar and Janet Walker (New York: Routledge, 2010), pp. 1–34

SARLO, BEATRIZ, *Tiempo pasado: cultura de la memoria y giro subjetivo. Una discusión* (Buenos Aires: Siglo XXI, 2005)

SEGOVIA, CAROLINA, and RICARDO GAMBOA, 'Chile: el año en que salimos a la calle', *Revista de Ciencia Política*, 32: 1 (2012), 65–85

SCARRY, ELAINE, *The Body in Pain: The Making and Unmaking of the World* (New York: Oxford University Press, 1985)

SCHUMANN, PETER B., *Historia del cine latinoamericano*, trans. by Oscar Zambrano (Buenos Aires: Editorial Legasa, 1987)

SHAVIRO, STEVEN, *The Cinematic Body* (Minneapolis: University of Minnesota Press, 1993)

SKÁRMETA, ANTONIO, 'Europe: An Indispensable Link in the Production and Circulation of Latin American Cinema', in *New Latin American Cinema*, vol.1, ed. by Michael T. Martin (Detroit: Wayne State University Press, 1997), pp. 263–72 (first publ. in *Third World Affairs 2* (1988), 169–72)

SMAILL, BELINDA, *The Documentary: Politics, Emotion, Culture* (New York: Palgrave Macmillan, 2010)

SOBCHACK, VIVIAN, *The Address of the Eye: A Phenomenology of Film Experience* (Princeton, NJ: Princeton University Press, 1992)

—— 'Inscribing Ethical Space: Ten Propositions on Death, Representation, and Documentary', in *Carnal Thoughts: Embodiment and Moving Image Culture* (Berkeley: University of California Press, 2004), pp. 226–57 (first publ. in *Quarterly Review of Film Studies*, 9: 4 (1984), 283–300)

—— 'What My Fingers Knew: The Cinesthetic Subject, or Vision in the Flesh', in *Carnal Thoughts: Embodiment and Moving Image Culture* (Berkeley: University of California Press, 2004), pp. 53–84

SOMMER, DORIS, 'Irresistible Romance: The Foundational Fictions of Latin America', in *Nation and Narration*, ed. by Homi K. Bhabha (London: Routledge, 1990), pp. 71–98

SONTAG, SUSAN, *Regarding the Pain of Others* (New York: Picador, 2003)

SORENSEN, KRISTIN, *Media, Memory, and Human Rights in Chile* (New York: Palgrave Macmillan, 2009)

STANGE, HANS, and CLAUDIO SALINAS, 'La incipiente literatura sobre cine chileno', *La Fuga*, 7 (2008) <http://www.lafuga.cl/la-incipiente-literatura-sobre-cine-chileno/302> [accessed 27 August 2016]

—— 'Hacia una elucidación del campo de estudios sobre cine en Chile', *Aisthesis*, 46 (December 2009), 270–83

STEPHENS, ELIZABETH, 'Sensation Machine: Film, Phenomenology and the Training of the Senses', *Continuum*, 26:4 (2012), 529–39

STERN, STEVE, *Battling for Hearts and Minds: Memory Struggles in Pinochet's Chile, 1973–1988*. Book Two, *Memory Box of Pinochet's Chile* (Durham: Duke University Press, 2006)

—— 'Introduction to the Trilogy', p. xxi–xxxiv, in *Reckoning with Pinochet: The Memory Question in Democratic Chile, 1989–2006*. Book Three, *Memory Box of Pinochet's Chile* (Durham: Duke University Press, 2010)

—— *Reckoning with Pinochet: The Memory Question in Democratic Chile, 1989–2006*. Book Three, *Memory Box of Pinochet's Chile* (Durham: Duke University Press, 2010)

—— *Remembering Pinochet's Chile: On the Eve of London 1998*. Book One, *Memory Box of Pinochet's Chile* (Durham: Duke University Press, 2004)
STURKEN, MARITA, *Tangled Memories: The Vietnam War, the Aids Epidemic, and the Politics of Remembering* (Berkeley: University of California Press, 1997)
SULEIMAN, SUSAN RUBIN, 'The 1.5 Generation: Thinking About Child Survivors and the Holocaust', *American Imago*, 59: 3 (Fall 2002), 277–95
TADEO-FUICA, BEATRIZ, 'Memory or postmemory? Documentaries directed by Uruguay's second generation', *Memory Studies*, 8:3 (2015), 298–312
TESSON, CHARLES, 'Jeu de l'oie: un cauchemar didactique (Ou la tentative hardie d'établir une bio-filmographie de Raoul Ruiz)', *Cahiers du Cinéma*, 345 (March 1983), 13–18
—— 'Letter from a Filmmaker, or The Return of a Library Lover (*Lettre d'un cinéaste ou Le Retour d'un amateur de bibliothèques*, Short, France, 1983)'. Raúl Ruiz: An Annotated Filmography. *Rouge*, 2 (2004) <http://www.rouge.com.au/2/letter.html> [accessed 10 November 2018]
THE CLINIC, 'Realizador de "El diario de Agustín" sobre "censura" en ARTV: "es extraño que esa mano negra sea tan larga"', *The Clinic*, 24 April 2013 <http://www.theclinic.cl/2013/04/24/realizador-de-el-diario-de-agustin-sobre-censura-en-artv-es-extrano-que-esa-mano-negra-sea-tan-larga/> [accessed 22 October 2018]
TOLEDO, PATRICIO, 'Entrevista a Patricia Bustos y Jorge Levia: Actores secundarios', *Revista Chilena de Antropología Visual*, 6 (2005) <http://www.antropologiavisual.cl/actores_secundarios.htm> [accessed 23 October 2017]
TORO, IVONNE, 'Carmen Hertz y censura a obituario de Carlos Berger: "Es indecente e inmoral. Voy a emprender acciones legales contra El Mercurio"', *The Clinic*, 9 April 2014 <http://www.theclinic.cl/2014/04/09/carmen-hertz-y-censura-a-obituario-de-carlos-berger-es-indecente-e-inmoral-voy-a-emprender-acciones-legales-contra-el-mercurio/> [accessed 10 November 2018]
TORRES, VERÓNICA, 'Patio 29: La doble tragedia de las familias obligadas a devolver sus muertos', *CIPER*, 3 August 2011 <http://ciperchile.cl/2011/08/03/patio-29-la-doble-tragedia-de-las-familias-obligadas-a-devolver-sus-muertos/> [accessed 2 November 2018]
TRAVERSO, ANTONIO, 'Dictatorship Memories: Working through Trauma in Chilean Post-Dictatorship Documentary', *Continuum*, 24:1 (2010), 179–91
—— 'Nostalgia, Memory and Politics in Chilean Documentaries of Return', in *Dictatorships in the Hispanic World: Transatlantic and Transnational Perspectives* ed. by Patricia L. Swier and Julia Riordan-Goncalves (Madison Lanham: Fairleigh Dikinson University Press, 2013), pp. 49–78
—— 'Working through Trauma in Post-Dictatorial Chilean Documentary: Lorena Giachino's Reinalda del Carmen', ed. by Dawn Bennett, Jaya Earnest, and Miyume Tanji, *People, Place, and Power: Australia and the Asia Pacific* (Perth: Black Swan Press, 2009), pp. 208–29
—— and MICK BRODERICK, 'Interrogating Trauma: Towards a Critical Trauma Studies', *Continuum*, 24: 1 (2010), 3–15
—— and GERMÁN LIÑERO, 'Chilean Political Documentary Video of the 1980s', in *New Documentaries in Latin America*, ed. by Vinicius Navarro and Juan Carlos Rodríguez (New York: Palgrave Macmillan, 2014), pp. 168–84
TREJO, ROBERTO, *Cine, neoliberalismo y cultura: crítica de la economía política del cine chileno contemporáneo* (Santiago: Editorial ARCIS, 2009)
ULLOA, YÉSSICA, *Video independiente en Chile* (Santiago: Ceneca, 1985)
URIBE, ARMANDO, and MIGUEL VICUÑA, *El accidente Pinochet* (Santiago: Sudamericana Chilena, 1999)

URZÚA, MACARENA, 'Cartografías disidentes: punk y nostalgia en el documental de la postdictadura chilena', *La Fuga*, 11 (2010) <http://www.lafuga.cl/cartografias-disidentes-punk-y-nostalgia-en-el-documental-de-la-postdictadura-chilena/404> [accessed 20 October 2018]

VALENZUELA, VALERIA, 'Yo te digo que el mundo es así: giro performativo en el documental chileno contemporáneo', *Doc On-line*, 1 (December 2006) 6–22. <http://dialnet.unirioja.es/descarga/articulo/4000485.pdf> [accessed 10 November 2018]

VEGA, ALICIA, *Itinerario del cine documental chileno, 1900–1990* (Santiago: Centro EAC, Universidad Alberto Hurtado, 2006)

VENKATESH, VINODH and MARÍA DEL CARMEN CAÑA JIMÉNEZ, 'Affect, Bodies, and Circulations in Contemporary Latin American Film', *Arizona Journal of Hispanic Cultural Studies*, 20 (2016), 175-181.

VERDUGO, PATRICIA, *De la tortura no se habla: Agüero versus Meneses* (Santiago: Catalonia, 2004)

——'Los protagonistas', in *De la tortura no se habla: Agüero versus Meneses*, ed. by Patricia Verdugo (Santiago: Catalonia, 2004), pp. 19–44

——'Prólogo', in *De la tortura no se habla: Agüero versus Meneses* (Santiago: Catalonia, 2004), pp. 11–16

VERGARA, CAROLINA, 'La producción y exhibición del documental', in *Panorama del audiovisual chileno*, ed. by Valerio Fuenzalida and Pablo Julio (Santiago: Dirección de Artes y Cultura de la Pontificia Universidad Católica de Chile, 2011), pp. 80–91

——'La producción y exhibición del documental', in *II Panorama del audiovisual chileno*, ed. by Valerio Fuenzalida and Pablo Julio (Santiago: Dirección de Artes y Cultura de la Pontificia Universidad Católica de Chile, 2012), pp. 107–23

——'Producción y exhibición del documental', in *III Panorama del audiovisual chileno*, ed. by Valerio Fuenzalida and Johanna Whittle (Santiago: Dirección de Artes y Cultura de la Pontificia Universidad Católica de Chile, 2013), pp. 55–62

——'La producción y exhibición del documental en 2013', in *IV Panorama del audiovisual chileno*, ed. by Pablo Julio, Sebastián Alaniz and Francisco Fernández (Santiago: Dirección de Artes y Cultura de la Pontificia Universidad Católica de Chile, 2015), pp. 58–64

VICTORIANO, FELIPE, 'La imaginación concentracionaria del golpe: el Estadio Nacional de Chile, lo siniestro y el fútbol', *Revista de Crítica Cultural*, 32 (November 2005), 34–43

VIDAL, HERNÁN, *Chile: poética de la tortura política* (Santiago: Mosquito Comunicaciones, 2000)

VILLAGRÁN, FERNANDO, '¿Por qué "El diario de Agustín" no puede exhibirse en la TV chilena?', *The Clinic*, 19 March 2013 <http://www.theclinic.cl/2013/03/19/por-que-el-diario-de-agustin-no-puede-exhibirse-en-la-tv-chilena/> [accessed 22 October 2018]

VILLARROEL, MÓNICA, *La voz de los cineastas: cine e identidad chilena en el umbral del milenio* (Santiago: Cuarto Propio, 2005)

VILLARROEL, MÓNICA and ISABEL MARDONES, *Señales contra el olvido: cine chileno recobrado* (Santiago: Cuarto Propio, 2012)

VILLARROEL, MÓNICA, and OTHERS, *Imágenes de Chile en el mundo: catastro del acervo audiovisual chileno en el exterior* (Santiago: Cineteca Nacional de Chile, 2008) <http://www.ccplm.cl/sitio/wp-content/uploads/2016/02/merged.pdf> [accessed 4 November 2018]

WALKER, JANET, *Trauma Cinema: Documenting Incest and the Holocaust* (Berkeley: University of California Press, 2005)

——'Trauma Cinema: False Memories and True Experience', *Screen*, 42: 2 (2001), 211–16

——'The Traumatic Paradox: Documentary Films, Historical Fictions, and Cataclysmic Past Events', *Signs*, 22: 4 (1997), 803–25

WALLIS, VICTOR, and BARLOW, JOHN D., 'Documentary as Participation: The Battle of Chile', in *'Show Us Life': Toward a History and Aesthetics of the Committed Documentary*, ed. by Thomas Waugh (London: Scarecrow Press, 1984), pp. 403–16

WHITE, HAYDEN, 'The Modernist Event', in *The Persistence of History: Cinema, Television, and the Modern Event*, ed. by Vivian Sobchack (New York: Routledge, 1996), pp. 17–38

WILDE, ALEXANDER, 'A Season of Memory: Human Rights in Chile's Long Transition', in *The Politics of Memory in Chile: From Pinochet to Bachelet*, ed. by Cath Collins, Katherine Hite and Alfredo Joignant (Boulder: First Forum Press, 2013), pp. 31–60

—— 'Avenues of Memory: Santiago's General Cemetery and Chile's Recent Political History', *A Contracorriente* 5:3 (Spring 2008), 134–69 <http://www.ncsu.edu/project/acontracorriente/spring_08/Wilde.pdf> [accessed 23 October 2018]

—— 'Irruptions of Memory: Expressive Politics in Chile's Transition to Democracy', *Journal of Latin American Studies*, 31: 2 (May 1999), 473–500

WILLIAMS, LINDA, 'Mirrors without Memories: Truth, History, and the New Documentary', *Film Quarterly*, 46: 3 (Spring 1993), 9–21

WRIGHT, SARAH, 'Noli me tangere: Memory, Embodiment and Affect in Silvio Caiozzi's *Fernando ha vuelto* (2005) ', *Journal of Latin American Cultural Studies: Travesia* 21: 1 (2012), 37–48

WRIGHT, THOMAS C., and OÑATE, RODY, *Flight from Chile: Voices of Exile*, trans. by Irene Hodgson (Albuquerque: University of New Mexico Press, 1998)

ZAMBRA, ALEJANDRO, *Formas de volver a casa* (Barcelona: Anagrama, 2011)

ZAVALA, FERNANDO, 'Actores secundarios: el filme que consolidó a los nuevos documentalistas', *El Mercurio*, 22 August 2005 <http://diario.elmercurio.com/detalle/index.asp?id=%7B9ca462e5-8605-4099-96b4-1f7fbed9478f%7D> [accessed 8 July 2017]

ZERÁN, FARIDE, 'Premio Nacional de Periodismo denuncia grave censura del Museo de la Memoria', *DiarioUChile*, 7 March 2013 <http://radio.uchile.cl/2013/03/07/grave-censura-del-museo-de-la-memoria/> [accessed 22 October 2018]

FILMOGRAPHY

11 de septiembre, dir. by Claudia Aravena (2002)
11'09"01–September 11, dir. by Ken Loach and others (2002)
80s: el soundtrack de una generación (80s: The Soundtrack of a Generation), dir. by Eduardo Bertrán (2006)
Abuelos [*Grandparents*], dir. by Carla Dávila (2010)
Acta general de Chile [*General Statement on Chile*], dir. by Miguel Littin (1986)
Actores secundarios (Supporting Actors), dir. by Pachi Bustos and Jorge Leiva, Colectivo Viridiana Audiovisual (2004)
Al final: la última carta [*In The End: The Last Letter*], dir. by Tiziana Panizza (2012)
Allende, mi abuelo Allende [*Beyond my Grandfather Allende*], dir. by Marcia Tambutti (2015)
Andrés de La Victoria (Andrés from La Victoria), dir. by Claudio di Girólamo, Ictus (1984)
Apuntes nicaragüenses [*Notebook from Nicaragua*], dir. by Angelina Vázquez (1982)
Archaeology of Memory, dir. by Quique Cruz and Marilyn Mulford (2008)
Calles caminadas (Walked Streets), dir. by Eliana Largo and Verónica Quense (2006)
Calle Santa Fe [*Santa Fe Street*], dir. by Carmen Castillo (2006)
Canto a la vida [*Song to Life*], dir. by Lucía Salinas (1990)
Chacabuco, memoria del silencio [*Chacabuco: Memories of Silence*], dir. by Gastón Ancelovici (2001)
Chi-chi-chi, le-le-le, Martín Vargas de Chile, dir. by Bettina Perut, David Bravo Nuñez, and Iván Osnovikoff (2000)
Chile, la herida abierta (Chile: The Open Wound), dir. by Orlando Lübbert (1999)
Chile, la memoria obstinada [*Chile, Obstinate Memory*], dir. by Patricio Guzmán (1997)
Chile, los héroes están fatigados [*Chile, the Heroes are Tired*], dir. by Marco Enríquez-Ominami (2002)
Chile, no invoco tu nombre en vano (Chile, I Don't Invoke Your Name in Vain), dir. by Colectivo Cine-Ojo (1983)
Chile, las imágenes prohibidas (Chile, the Forbidden Images), dir. by Claudio Marchant, Chilevisión (2013)
Cien niños esperando un tren [*One Hundred Children Waiting for a Train*], dir. by Ignacio Agüero (1988)
Cofralandes I: hoy en día, rapsodia chilena [*Cofralandes: Chilean Rhapsody*], dir. by Raúl Ruiz (2002)
Como me da la gana [*This is the Way I Like it*], dir. by Ignacio Agüero (1985)
Como me da la gana II [*This is the Way I Like it II*], dir. by Ignacio Agüero (2016)
Con el ojo en el visor (With the Eye Behind the Camera Lens), dir. by Sebastián Larraín (2004)
Conversaciones con el Cardenal Silva (Conversations with Cardinal Silva), dir. by Augusto Góngora, Ictus (1990)
Correcto... o el alma en los tiempos de guerra (Affirmative... or the Soul in Times of War), dir. by Orlando Lübbert (1993)
Crónica de un comité [*A Committee Chronicle*], dir. by José Luis Sepúlveda and Carolina Adriazola (2014)
Dear Nonna: A Film Letter, dir. by Tiziana Panizza (2004)

Det var några som hade kommit från Chile... [*They Were the Ones Who Came from Chile*], dir. by Claudio Sapiaín (1987)
Días de octubre (*Days of October*), dir. by Hernán Castro, Colectivo Cine Ojo (1989)
Dulce patria [*Sweet Country*], dir. by Andrés Racz (1986)
Ecos del desierto [*Echoes of the Desert*], dir. by Andrés Wood, Chilevisión / Wood Producciones (2013)
EEUU vs Allende, dir. by Diego Marín and José Alayón (2008)
Electrodomésticos: el frío misterio [*Electrodomésticos: The Cold Mystery*], dir. by Sergio Castro San Martín (2010)
El astuto mono Pinochet versus La Moneda de los cerdos [*Clever Monkey Pinochet versus La Moneda's Pigs*], dir. by Iván Osnovikoff and Bettina Perut (2004)
El caso Pinochet [*The Pinochet Case*], dir. by Patricio Guzmán (2001)
El color del camaleón [*The Color of the Chameleon*], dir. by Andrés Lübbert (2017)
El derecho de vivir [*Víctor Jara: The Right to Live in Peace*], dir. by Carmen Luz Parot (1999)
El diario de Agustín [*Agustin's Newspaper*], dir. by Ignacio Agüero (2008)
El eco de las canciones [*The Echo of Songs*], dir. by Antonia Rossi (2010)
El edificio de los chilenos [*The Chilean Building*], dir. by Macarena Aguiló and Susana Foxley (2010)
El hombre de la foto (*The Man in the Picture*), dir. by María José Martínez and Gonzalo Ramírez (2006)
El juez y el general [*The Judge and the General*], dir. by Elizabeth Farnsworth and Patricio Lanfranco (2008)
El lado oscuro de La Dama Blanca [*The Dark Side of the White Lady*], dir. by Patricio Henríquez (2006)
El memorial (*The Memorial*), dir. by Andrés Brignardello (2009)
El mocito [*The Young Butler*], dir. by Marcela Said and Jean de Certeau (2011)
El muro de los nombres (*The Wall of Names*), dir. by Germán Liñero (1999)
El pacto de Adriana [*Adriana's Pact*], dir. by Lissette Orozco (2017)
El país de mi padre (*My Father's Country*), dir. by Carmen Castillo (2004)
El soldado que no fue [*The Soldier That Wasn't*], dir. by Leopoldo Gutiérrez (2010)
El telón de azúcar [*The Sugar Curtain*], dir. by Camila Guzmán (2007)
El último combate de Salvador Allende [*The Last Stand of Salvador Allende*], dir. by Patricio Henríquez (1998)
El vals de los inútiles [*The Waltz*] (Edison Cajas, 2013)
En algún lugar del cielo [*Somewhere in Heaven*], dir. by Alejandra Carmona (2003)
En defensa propia [*In Self-Defence*], dir. by Claudia Barril (2009)
En nombre de Dios [*In the Name of God*], dir. by Patricio Guzmán (1986)
En resa till världens ände [*A Trip to the End of the World*], dir. by Simón Bergman (2011)
Éramos una vez (*Once We Were*), dir. by Leonardo de la Barra (1979)
Escucha Chile [*Listen, Chile*], dir. by Andrés Daie (2008)
Estadio Nacional [*National Stadium*], dir. by Carmen Luz Parot (2001)
Fernando ha vuelto [*Fernando is Back*], dir. by Silvio Caiozzi (1998)
¿Fernando ha vuelto a desaparecer? [*Is Fernando Missing Again?*], dir. by Silvio Caiozzi (2006)
Fragmentos de un diario inacabado / Otteita Keskenjääneestä Päiväkirjasta [*Fragments from an Unfinished Diary*], dir. by Angelina Vázquez (1983)
GAP: Amigos Personales, dir. by Claudia Serrano (2008)
Generation Exile, dir. by Rodrigo Dorfman (2010)
Gracias a la vida, o la pequeña historia de una mujer maltratada [*Thanks to Life, or the Little Story of a Mistreated Woman*], dir. by Angelina Vázquez (1980)

Héroes frágiles [*The Conspiracy*], dir. by Emilio Pacull (2006)
Huellas de sal [*Salt Traces*], dir. by Andrés Vargas, Grupo Proceso (1990)
I Love Pinochet, dir. by Marcela Said (2001)
I Wonder What You Will Remember of September, dir. by Cecilia Cornejo (2004)
Ich war, ich bin, ich werde sein [*I Was, I Am, and I Shall Be*], dir. by Walter Heynowski and Gerhard Scheumann (1974)
Il pleut sur Santiago [*Rain over Santiago*], dir. by Helvio Soto (1975)
Imágenes de una dictadura [*Images of a Dictatorship*], dir. by Patricio Henríquez (1999)
Imaginario inconcluso (*Unfinished Imagery*), dir. by Pablo Basulto, Colectivo Cámara en Mano (1990)
Je ne sais pas [*I Don't Know*] dir. by Marilú Mallet (1974)
La batalla de Chile I, II, and III [*The Battle of Chile*], dir. by Patricio Guzmán (1975–1979)
La batalla de la Plaza Italia (*The Battle of Plaza Italia*), dir. by Renato Villegas (2008)
La ciudad de los fotógrafos [*City of Photographers*], dir. by Sebastián Moreno (2006)
La conciencia de golpe, dir. by Manlio Helena-Urzúa (2009)
La cordillera de los sueños [*The Mountain Range of Dreams*], dir. by Patricio Guzmán (2019)
La cueca sola, dir. by Marilú Mallet (2003)
La femme au foyer (*The Housewife*), dir. by Valeria Sarmiento (1976)
La flaca Alejandra [*Skinny Alejandra*], dir. by Carmen Castillo and Guy Girard (1994)
La memoria herida (*Wounded Memory*), dir. by Francisco Casas and Yura Labarca (2004)
La muerte de Pinochet [*The Death of Pinochet*], dir. by Bettina Perut and Iván Osnovikoff (2011)
La nana [*The Maid*], dir. by Sebastián Silva (2009)
La quemadura [*The Burn*], dir. by René Ballesteros (2009)
La règle du jeu [*The Rules of the Game*], dir. by Jean Renoir (1939)
La realidad [*The Reality*], dir. by Andrés Lübbert (2009)
La sombra de Don Roberto [*Don Roberto's Shadow*], dir. by Juan Diego Spoerer and Håkan Engström (2007)
La venda (*The Blindfold*), dir. by Gloria Camiruaga (2000)
La verdadera historia de Johny (sic) *Good* (*The True Story of Johny Good*), dir. by Pablo Tupper and Patricia del Río, Grupo Proceso (1990)
Le Chili en transition [*Chile in Transition*], dir. by Gastón Ancelovici and Frank Diamand (1991)
Les murs de Santiago [*Chile: Ten Years of a Strong Man*], dir. by Fabienne Servan-Schreiber and Pierre Devert (1983)
Lettre d'un cinéaste ou le retour d'un amateur de bibliothèques [*Letter from a Filmmaker or the Return of a Library Lover*], dir. by Raúl Ruiz (1983)
Los perros [*The Dogs*], dir. by Marcela Said (2017)
Los 80 [*The 80s*], dir. by, Boris Quercia (Season 1–5) and Rodrigo Bazaes (Season 6), Canal 13 / Wood Producciones (2008–2014)
Los escolares se siguen amando [*Teenagers Keep on Loving*], dir. by Paco Toledo (2000)
Los niños de septiembre (*September Children*), dir. by Sergio Marras (1989)
Magic Magic, dir. by Sebastián Silva (2013)
Malditos, la historia de los Fiskales Ad-Hok (*Damned: The Story of the Fiskales Ad-Hok*), dir. by Pablo Insunza (2004)
Memoria desierta [*Deserted Memory*], dir. by Niles Atallah, Colectivo Diluvio (2006)
Mi hermano y yo [*My Brother and I*], dir. by Sergio Gándara (2002)
Mi vida con Carlos [*My Life with Carlos*], dir. by Germán Berger-Hertz (2010)
Min Mors Løfte [*My Mother's Promise*], dir. by Marianne Houghen-Moraga (2007)
Neruda en el corazón (*Neruda in the Heart*), dir. by Jaime Barros, Pedro Chaskel and Gastón Ancelovici (1993)

No, dir. by Pablo Larraín (2012)
No es hora de llorar [*This is not the Time to Cry*], dir. by Pedro Chaskel and Luis Alberto Sanz (1971)
No me amenaces [*Don't Threaten Me*], dir. by Andrés Racz (1990)
No me olvides [Don't Forget Me], dir. by Tatiana Gaviola, Ictus (1988)
No olvidar [*Not to Forget*], dir. by Ignacio Agüero (1982)
Nostalgia de la luz [*Nostalgia for the Light*], dir. by Patricio Guzmán (2010)
Noticias [*News*], dir. by Bettina Perut and Iván Osnovikoff (2009)
Nuit et brouillard [*Night and Fog*], dir. by Alain Resnais (1955)
Ojos rojos [*Red Eyes*], dir. by Ismael Larraín, Juan Ignacio Sabatini and Juan Pablo Sallato (2010)
Opus dei: una cruzada silenciosa [*Opus Day: A Silent Crusade*], dir. by Marcela Said and Jean de Certeau (2006)
Patio 29: historias del silencio [*Patio 29: Stories of Silence*], dir. by Esteban Larraín (1998)
Por sospecha de comunista [*Under Suspicion of Being Communist*], dir. by Cristóbal Cohen and Marcelo Hermosilla (2008)
Presencia lejana / Etällä ja läsnä: Kärsimyskertomus [*Far Away and Yet so Near*], dir. by Angelina Vázquez (1982)
Propaganda, dir. by Colectivo Mafi (2014)
Post mortem, dir. by Pablo Larraín (2010)
Raúl Silva Henríquez, El Cardenal (*The Cardinal*), dir. by Ricardo Larraín (1996)
Recado de Chile (*Message from Chile*), dir. by Guillermo Cahn, Carlos Flores del Pino, Alfonso Luco, Jaime Reyes, José Román, Raquel Salinas, José de la Vega, Fedora Robles, Pedro Chaskel and Nelson Villagra (1979)
Recuerdos del futuro: Raúl Pellegrín (*Memories of the Future: Raúl Pellegrín*), dir. by Colectivo Audiovisual Rodriguista, CARO (1994)
Reinalda del Carmen, mi mamá y yo [*Reinalda del Carmen, My Mother and Me*], dir. by Lorena Giachino (2007)
Remitente: una carta visual [*Postage: A Visual Letter*], dir. by Tiziana Panizza (2008)
Ruidos molestos (*Annoying Noises*), dir. by Viviana Sepúlveda (2007)
Salvador Allende, dir. by Gerardo Cáceres, Ictus (1992)
Salvador Allende, dir. by Patricio Guzmán (2004)
Septembre chilien (*Chilean September*), dir. by Bruno Muel, Théo Robichet, and Valérie Mayoux (1973)
Shoah, dir. by Claude Lanzmann (1985)
Si escuchas atentamente [*If You Listen Carefully*], dir. by Nicolás Guzmán, 2015
Somos +, dir. by Pedro Chaskel and Pablo Salas, Ictus (1985)
Soy testigo (*I Am a Witness*), dir. by Hermann Mondaca, Grupo Proceso (1990)
Testimonio 1 (*Testimony 1*), dir. by Hernán Fliman (1979)
Una vez más, mi país [*Once Again, My Country*], dir. by Claudio Sapiaín (1989).
Venían a buscarme [*They Were Coming to Get Me*], dir. by Álvaro de la Barra (2016)
Vereda tropical (*Tropical Pavement*), dir. by Pablo Lavín (1990)
Villa Grimaldi: Parque por la paz (*Villa Grimaldi: Park for Peace*), dir. by Juan Pablo Zurita (2002)
Volver a vernos [*Pinochet's Children*], dir. by Paula Rodríguez (2002)
Wo Ich Lebe / Aquí donde yo vivo [*Here Were I Live In*], dir. by Carlos Puccio (1994)

INDEX

Spanish-language films are found under their Spanish title, followed by their best-known English titles in square brackets. Translations in round brackets are the author's translations.

abject documentaries:
  abject, defined 165
  abjectivization, through close-ups 168–69
  El mocito [*The Young Butler*] (Said & de Certeau) 150, 153, 154, 163–67, 169–74, 180, 181
  La muerte de Pinochet [*The Death of Pinochet*] (Perut & Osnovikoff) 150, 154, 163–69, 173–74, 180
  overview 24, 150, 153–54
absolute solidarity 80, 93 n. 90
Abuelos [*Grandparents*] (Dávila) 73
Abu Ghraib 82–83
Academy Award nomination 150
Acta general de Chile [*General Statement on Chile*] (Littin) 101, 102–03
Actores secundarios (*Supporting Actors*) (Bustos & Leiva) 58 n. 116, 108–09, 151, 155–58, 160–61, 176 n. 56, 180
Adriazola, Carolina 181
aesthetics 15–16, 22–23, 111–13, 129, 137, 139–40
affect:
  defined 19, 30 n. 113
  see also cinema of affect; cinema of the affected
Afterimage (Hirsch) 16
Agrupación de Familiares de Detenidos Desaparecidos (Association of Relatives of the Detained and Disappeared, AFDD) 79
Agüero, Felipe 40, 69, 81, 85
Agüero, Ignacio:
  Como me da la gana [*This is the Way I Like it*] 1, 51
  Como me da la gana II [*This is the Way I Like it II*] 1
  El diario de Agustín [*Agustín's Newspaper*] 33, 51–52, 53, 61 n. 159, 61 n. 161
  on FIDOCS selections 45
  influence of 9
  No olvidar [*Not to Forget*] 1, 65–66
  as part of cultural resistance 48
Agüero-Meneses case 40, 69, 81, 85
Aguilar, Gonzalo 127, 139, 148 n. 37
Aguiló, Macarena:
  childhood memories 104, 112, 118–19, 130–31, 135–36, 138
  El edificio de los chilenos [*The Chilean Building*] 104, 110, 112, 114, 118–19, 126, 133, 135–36, 138, 153
  variety of media used by 111
Alayón, José 107, 153

Alegría, Fernando 116
Al final: la última carta [*In the End: The Last Letter*] (Panizza) 141, 144
Allende, Isabel 115
Allende, mi abuelo Allende [*Beyond my Grandfather Allende*] (Tambutti) 181
Allende, Salvador:
  commemoration of 41
  death of 66–67
  election of 3, 34, 78, 106, 144
  fall of 153
  government of 8, 55 n. 42, 97, 145
  as grandfather 181
  images of 66–67, 71
  last day of 67, 74
  monument of 40
alternative video movement (1980s) 71–72, 74
Amado, Ana 125, 131, 133
Ancelovici, Gastón:
  Chacabuco, memoria del silencio [*Chacabuco: Memories of Silence*] 70, 73, 81
  as Colectivo Cine-Ojo member 120 n. 9
  Le Chili en transition [*Chile in Transition*] 69, 88
  Neruda en el corazón (*Neruda in the Heart*) 71
Andermann, Jens 73, 113
Andes Mountains 72
Andrés de La Victoria (*Andrés from La Victoria*) (Di Girólamo & Ictus) 128
Angell, Alan 106
'Apoyo a la difusión de documentales nacionales ya producidos' (television) 60 n. 143
Apuntes para una historia del video en Chile (Liñero) 9, 35
Aravena, Claudia 107
Archaeology of Memory (Cruz) 70
archival material:
  body-landscape and 76–77
  in broader second generation documentaries 156–57
  children's subjectivity and 133–34
  in direct second generation documentaries 156
  in exilic director documentaries 106–07
  nostalgic uses of 128, 155
  overview 6
  soundtracks 74–75, 107, 139–40, 155
  unveiling memories through 69

volume of 54 n. 18
archive affect 159–61
Arendt, Hannah 169
Arriagada, Jorge 166, 172
The Art of Transition (Masiello) 126–27
Asociación de Documentalistas de Chile (Association of Chilean Documentarians, ADOC) 25 n. 17, 43, 46
Asociación de Productores de Cine y TV (Association of Film and TV Producers, APCTV) 49
Atacama Desert:
 description of 72–73
 as documentary setting 73
 see also Chacabuco concentration camp; *Huellas de sal*; *Nostalgia de la luz*; Pisagua concentration camp; Pisagua mass grave
Atallah, Niles 73
autobiographical documentaries 102–04, 111–13, 116–20, 126, 127, 129–37
Avelar, Idelber 10, 25 n. 7, 80
Aylwin, Patricio 3, 37, 38

Bachelet, Michelle 4, 41
Ballesteros, René:
 comparisons to 142, 146
 La quemadura [*The Burn*] 109, 126, 129, 137–38, 140, 142–43, 144–45
 on recalling the past not directly experienced 154
Banco del Estado (Chilean State Bank) 43, 57 n. 92
Barker, Jennifer 159–60
Baron, Jaimie 159
Barquero, Efraín 115
Barril, Claudia 128
Barrios, Jaime 71
Barros, César 107
Barthes, Roland 19, 135, 149 n. 44
Basulto, Pablo 70–71
Benedetti, Mario 96, 99, 120 n. 1
Benjamin, Walter 22–23, 32 n. 146, 114
Bennett, Jill 11, 146
Berger, Carlos 134, 148 n. 42
Berger-Hertz, Germán 11, 73, 104, 126, 134–35
Bergman, Simón 104, 126
Berríos, Violeta 73, 77
Bertrán, Eduardo 151, 155, 156, 162–63
Beugnet, Martine:
 on affective turn 12–13
 on body-landscape 76, 77
 on cinema of sensation 20, 137, 138–39, 142, 166
 on close-ups 168–69
Blaine, Patrick 76
bodies-as-landscapes 76–77
The Body in Pain: The Making and Unmaking of the World (Scarry) 80
Bonnefoy, Pascale 94 n. 126
Bossay, Claudia 9, 90 n. 18, 94 n. 124, 123 n. 61, 176 n. 56

Bossy, Michelle 103
Boym, Svetlana 18, 157
Bravo, Sergio 9
Brigada Lautaro 164, 170, 173
Brignardello, Andrés 84
broader second generation directors:
 abject bodies revealed by 154
 abject body revealed in 163–74
 kinship bonds in 153–54
 nostalgia and 154–63, 173
 overview 47–48, 130, 146–47, 150–54, 180
 see also Ballesteros, René; Panizza, Tiziana; Rossi, Antonia
Broderick, Mick 17
Bruno, Giuliana 113
Bruzzi, Stella 18, 99, 110, 129, 140
Buck-Morss, Susan 22–23, 32 n. 146
burden of representation 105–07, 139
Burns, Rob 12
Burton, Julianne 8
Bussi, Hortensia 115
Bustos, Pachi:
 Actores secundarios (*Supporting Actors*) 58 n. 116, 108–09, 151, 155–58, 160–61, 176 n. 56, 180
 on La Moneda bombing 108–09
 on narrative structure 155
Butler, Judith 23

Cabezas, Carlos 158, 162
Cabezas, Esteban 162
Cáceres, Gerardo 71
Cahiers du Cinéma 121 n. 32
Cahn, Guillermo 90 n. 14
Caiozzi, Silvio 67–69, 89, 91 n. 34 & 35
Cajas, Edison 181
Calle Santa Fe [*Santa Fe Street*] (Castillo) 110, 112, 116–18, 128, 153
Calles caminadas (*Walked Streets*) (Largo & Quense) 80
Camiruaga, Gloria 70, 85, 89
Canto a la vida [*Song to Life*] (Salinas) 70, 103, 110, 115–16, 140, 156
Canto Nuevo movement 156, 161, 176 n. 56
Cárcel de Alta Seguridad 175 n. 42
Carmona, Alejandra:
 childhood 112, 130, 138
 En algún lugar del cielo [*Somewhere in Heaven*] 104, 110, 114, 119, 126, 133–34
Carmona, Augusto 112
Cartas visuales [*Visual Letters*] trilogy (Panizza) 141
Caruth, Cathy 11, 12, 13
Casanova, Carlos 78
Casas, Francisco 73
Castillo, Carmen:
 Calle Santa Fe [*Santa Fe Street*] 110, 112, 116–18, 128, 153
 death of her partner 112

on domestic sphere 109
El país de mi padre (*My Father's Country*) 116–17
   as exilic director 48, 103
La flaca Alejandra [*Skinny Alejandra*] 45–46, 69, 70, 71, 82, 84–85, 89, 103, 114, 116–17, 127–28, 165, 172
   on *Les murs de Santiago* 116
Les murs de Santiago [*Chile: Ten Years of a Strong Man*], written by 58 n. 109, 116
   self-representation of 117–18
Castro, Hernán 80, 120 n. 9
Catálogo II Festival Internacional de Cine Documental en Santiago de Chile 58 n. 112
Catálogo Primer Festival 58 n. 112
Catastro virtual de la producción documental chilena (catalogue) 48, 59 n. 122
Caucoto, Nelson 170–71
Cementerio General 71, 90 n. 24, 139
Centro de Cine Experimental (Centre for Experimental Cinema) 33–34
Chacabuco, memoria del silencio [*Chacabuco: Memories of Silence*] (Ancelovici) 70, 73, 81
Chacabuco concentration camp 69–70, 72, 81, 86
chamber films 103, 111
Chanan, Michael 8, 42
Chaskel, Pedro:
   on Allende's government 34
   on FIDOCS selections 45
   influence of 9
   Neruda en el corazón (*Neruda in the Heart*) 71
   No es hora de llorar (*This is Not the Time to Cry*) 66
   Recado de Chile (*Message from Chile*) 90 n. 14
   Somos + 79–80, 160
Chicago Boys 163
Chi-Chi-Chi, le-le- le, Martín Vargas de Chile (Perut & Osnovikoff) 168
Chile, la herida abierta (*Chile: The Open Wound*) (Lübbert, O.) 67
Chile, la memoria obstinada [*Chile: Obstinate Memory*] (Guzmán, P.) 8, 11, 34, 44, 45, 86, 127–28
Chile, las imágenes prohibidas [*Chile, the Forbidden Images*] (television programme) 50, 60 n. 146, 154
Chile, los héroes están fatigados [*Chile, The Heroes are Tired*] (Enríquez-Ominami) 126, 131–33
Chile, no invoco tu nombre en vano (*Chile, I Don't Invoke Your Name in Vain*) (Colectivo Cine-Ojo) 98, 101–02
Chile actual: anatomía de un mito (Moulian) 36, 71
Chilean Cinema (Chanan) 8
Chilean documentaries, *see* post-dictatorship documentaries
ChileDoc 48, 49, 50, 53, 59 n. 124
Chile Films 35
Chion, Michel 75
Chomsky, Noam 107
CineChile 26 n. 17, 59 n. 123
CinemaChile 49

cinema de barricada 35, 65, 98
cinema of affect:
   abject bodies and 164–65, 166–67, 174
   affect, defined 19, 30 n. 113
   affective turn and 11, 110, 178–80
   defined 65, 154
   haptic memories and 19, 137–47
   overview 4–6, 17–23, 24
   tactile-like qualities of 12–13
   travelling memories and 111–17, 120
cinema of the affected:
   affect, defined 19, 30 n. 113
   affective turn and 11, 110, 178–80
   defined 64–65, 154
   overview 4–6, 12–17, 24, 47, 137
   urgency of 62–72
cinema of duty 12
cinema of sensation 20, 137, 138–39, 142, 166
Cineteca Nacional de Chile (National Film Archive) 1, 7, 121 n. 10, 178
Cineteca Nacional Online 7
Cineteca Universidad de Chile (Film Archive of the University of Chile) 7
Cineteca Virtual 7
The Clinic (newspaper), on TVN 51–52
close-up shots 6, 20, 76–77, 86–87, 134, 143, 145, 166–67, 168–69, 174
CNTV 50, 60 n. 143
Cofralandes (Ruiz) 74, 109
Cohen, Cristóbal 128
Cold War 33–34
Colectivo Audiovisual Rodriguista (CARO) 158, 175 n. 42
Colectivo Cámara en Mano 70–71
Colectivo Cine-Ojo 80, 98, 101–02, 120 n. 9
Colectivo Diluvio 73
Colectivo Mafi 181
collaborators, of Pinochet 5, 6, 82, 84, 137, 154, 164–65, 180
collective awakening 2, 14, 151–52, 157, 160–61
collective numbing 14, 22, 32 n. 146, 63, 64
Collins, Cath 36
Comené, María Elena 88
Comisión Ética contra la Tortura (Ethical Commission Against Torture) 40
Comisión Funa (Funa Commission) 40
Comisión Nacional de Verdad y Reconciliación (National Commission on Truth and Reconciliation, CNVR) 38
Comisión Nacional Sobre Prisión Política y Tortura (National Commission on Political Prison and Torture) 40, 56 n. 64, 64
Como me da la gana [*This is the Way I Like it*] (Agüero) 1, 51
Como me da la gana II [*This is the Way I Like it II*] (Agüero) 1

cómplices pasivos [passive accomplices] 42
concealed body, see abject documentaries
concentrationary imagination 85, 86, 95 n. 133
concentration camps 69–70, 72–73, 81, 85–86
Concertación de Partidos por la Democracia (Coalition of Parties for Democracy) 3, 4, 37, 78
Con el ojo en el visor (*With the Eye Behind the Camera Lens*) (Larraín, S.) 151, 155
conscripts (military) 6, 165–66
Consejo del Arte y la Industria Audiovisual (Council of the Arts and the Audiovisual Industry, CAIA) 48, 49
Consejo Nacional de la Cultura de las Artes (National Council for the Culture and the Arts, CNCA) 48
Consejo Nacional de Televisión (National Council for Television, CNTV) 50
contentious coexistence 164
Contreras, Manuel 94 n. 126, 164
Conversaciones con el Cardenal Silva (*Conversations with Cardinal Silva*) (Góngora & Ictus) 91 n. 41, 156
Cornejo, Cecilia 107, 126
Corporación de Fomento de la Producción (Chilean Economic Development Agency, CORFO) 49
Corporation of Repair and Reconciliation 25 n. 6
corpses, see human remains
Correcto...o el alma en los tiempos de guerra (*Affirmative... or the Soul in Times of War*) (Lübbert, O.) 46, 69, 83, 165
Corro, Pablo 66, 128, 138, 150, 166, 167, 168, 169
counter-nostalgia 99
Cozzi, Adolfo 87
Crónica de un comité [*A Committee Chronicle*] (Sepúlveda & Adriazola) 181
Cruz, Quique 70
Cuadra, Francisco Javier 161–62
Cuartel de la Brigada Lautaro 164, 170, 173
Cuartel Ollagüe 70, 84–85, 94 n. 121
Cuban revolution 33–34
Cuevas, Raúl 156–57
CULDOC 58 n. 114
culture of oblivion 36–37

Daie, Andrés 73
Dávila, Carla 73
Dávila, René 120 n. 9
Dear Nonna: A Film Letter (Panizza) 141
de Certeau, Jean:
    El mocito [*The Young Butler*] 6, 42, 109, 150, 153, 154, 163–67, 169–74, 180, 181
    Opus Dei: una cruzada silenciosa [*Opus Day: A Silent Crusade*] 165
de la Barra, Álvaro 181
de la Barra, Leonardo 112
de la Solidaridad, Vicaría 51, 95
de la Vega, José 90 n. 14
Deleuze, Gilles 12, 114

del Pino, Carlos Flores 90 n. 14
del Río, Patricia 67, 69, 71–72, 73, 74, 81, 89
de Luca, Tiago 170
Deren, Maya 103
desexilio narratives 11, 96–104, 110–20, 120 n. 1
detenidos desaparecidos (disappeared):
    documentaries addressing, in 1990 71–72
    kidnapping charges for 56 n. 54
    lack of resolution for 5, 44
    as maximal victims 64
    Pinochet's legacy of 3–4, 25 n. 6
    Recado de Chile (*Message from Chile*) (anonymous collective) 65–66
    symbolism of 75–76
    testimonies of relatives on 65, 67–68, 77–78
Det var några som hade kommit från Chile (*They Were the Ones Who Came from Chile*) (Sapiaín) 101
Devert, Pierre 58 n. 109, 116
Diamand, Frank 69, 88
Días de octubre (*Days of October*) (Castro & Colectivo Cine-Ojo) 80
diasporic cinema 12, 20, 101–03, 140
Díaz, Ágave 69
Díaz, Mario 120 n. 9
Díaz, Viviana 173
Didi-Huberman, Georges 80, 87
di Girólamo, Claudio 128
Dirección Nacional de Inteligencia (National Intelligence Agency, DINA) 84, 94 n. 119, 94 n. 121
disappeared, see detenidos desaparecidos
Doane, Mary Ann 169
documentaries, see post-dictatorship documentaries; *specific films*
Dokleipzig 49
domestic narratives:
    cinema of affect and 137–47
    by descendants of direct victims 131–37
    overview 125–31
Donoso, José 100
Dorfman, Ariel 107
Dorfman, Rodrigo 104, 126
Drake, Paul W. 34–35
Dulce patria [*Sweet Country*] (Racz) 103
Eaglestone, Robert 170
Eastman, Agustín Edwards 51
ECO 35
Ecos del desierto (*Echoes of the Desert*) (Wood) 149 n. 43
Edwards, Agustín 51–52, 61 n. 159
EEUU vs Allende (Marín & Alayón) 107, 153
80s: el soundtrack de una generación (*80s: The Soundtrack of a Generation*) (Bertrán) 151, 155, 156, 162–63
El astuto mono Pinochet contra La Moneda de los cerdos [*Clever Monkey Pinochet Versus La Moneda's Pigs*] (Perut & Osnovikoff) 74, 168
El botón de nácar [*The Pearl Button*] (Guzmán, P.) 72

El caso Pinochet [*The Pinochet Case*] (Guzmán, P.) 70, 73
El cine de Patricio Guzmán (Ruffinelli) 58 n. 112
El color del camaleón [*The Color of the Chameleon*] (Lübbert, A.) 181
El derecho de vivir [*Víctor Jara: The Right to Live in Peace*] (Parot) 70, 81–82
El diario de Agustín [*Agustin's Newspaper*] (Agüero) 33, 51–52, 53, 61 n. 159, 61 n. 161
El eco de las canciones [*The Echo of Songs*] (Rossi) 74–75, 104, 110, 119–20, 126, 136–38, 140–41, 143
Electrodomésticos 162–63
Electrodomésticos: el frío misterio [*Electrodomésticos: The Cold Mystery*] (San Martín) 151, 155, 157
El edificio de los chilenos [*The Chilean Building*] (Aguiló & Foxley) 104, 110, 112, 114, 118–19, 126, 133, 135–36, 138, 153
El Encapuchado [the Hooded Man] 87, 95 n. 137
11 de septiembre (Aravena) 107
11 September 1973:
    9/11 parallel 107–08
    collective numbing following 22
    commemoration 109, 139–40
    as coup against representation 2
    as cultural trauma 14
    as highly visual event 12
    symbolic circle of victims of 2
El hombre de la foto (*The Man in the Picture*) (Martínez & Ramírez) 81–82
El juez y el general [*The Judge and The General*] (Farnsworth & Lanfranco) 73
El lado oscuro de La Dama Blanca [*The Dark Side of the White Lady*] (Henríquez) 70, 87–88
El memorial (*The Memorial*) (Brignardello) 84
El Mercurio (newspaper) 51
El mocito [*The Young Butler*] (Said & de Certeau) 6, 42, 109, 150, 153, 154, 163–67, 169–74, 180, 181
El muro de los nombres (*The Wall of Names*) (Liñero) 70
El pacto de Adriana [*Adriana's Pact*] (Orozco) 6, 181
El país de mi padre (*My Father's Country*) (Castillo) 116–17
el pueblo [the popular subject] 126–29, 140
Elsaesser, Thomas 12–13
El soldado que no fue [*The Soldier That Wasn't*] (Gutiérrez) 73, 103–04, 165
El telón de azúcar [*The Sugar Curtain*] (Guzmán, C.) 104
Eltit, Diamela 41, 108
El Trolley 162
El último combate de Salvador Allende [*The Last Stand of Salvador Allende*] (Henríquez) 67
El vals de los inútiles [*The Waltz*] (Cajas) 181
emotion:
    affect and 19, 30 n. 113
    defined 19, 30 n. 113
    embodiment of 11, 15, 30 n. 113
    memory and 22, 179
    nostalgia and 113, 157–61

reenactments and 82–83
testimonies filled with 133, 134
enactment, reenactments vs. 81–82
En algún lugar del cielo [*Somewhere in Heaven*] (Carmona) 104, 110, 114, 119, 126, 133–34
En defensa propia [*In Self-defence*] (Barril) 128
Eng, David L. 18
Engström, Håkan 70, 73, 128, 165
En nombre de Dios [*In the Name of God*] (Guzmán, P.) 58 n. 101, 103, 160
En resa till världens ände [*A Trip to the End of the World*] (Bergman) 104, 126
Enríquez, Miguel 84, 112, 117, 131, 136
Enríquez-Ominami, Marco 126, 130–33
Éramos una vez (*Once We Were*) (de la Barra) 112
Erll, Astrid 21
Escucha Chile [*Listen, Chile*] (Daie) 73
España, Alvaro 161
Estadio Chile 70, 82
Estadio Nacional:
    commemorative public rituals at 79, 139
    images as proof of existence of 69–70, 106–07, 144
    prisoner statistics for 85–86, 94 n. 126
    survivor testimonies 81–82
Estadio Nacional [*National Stadium*] (Parot) 70, 85–87, 94 n. 124, 95 n. 137
exiled Chileans 4, 25 n. 6, 38, 104
exilic directors:
    about 121 n. 10
    context for 34, 35
    desexilio narratives 11, 96–104, 110–20, 120 n. 1
    female travelling trope and 110–20
    first-person narratives of 126
    memory struggles and 20–21
    Mouesca on 16
    overview 24, 96, 120, 180
    Pick on 8
    symbolic weight in 105–10

Fahrenheit 451 (Truffaut) 45
family and family ties:
    borrowing images of 141–42
    children of the revolution 131–37
    exile and destabilization of 99, 104
    extension and alternative conception of 153–54
    first-person narratives and 125–31
    haptic memories of 131–37, 138, 141
    overview 24
    repression and destabilization of 78–79, 99, 111–12, 118–19, 142–43, 146
Farnsworth, Elizabeth 73
Felman, Shoshana 11
female relatives of victims 1, 5, 64–65, 72, 77–80, 89, 158, 179
Fernando ha vuelto [*Fernando is Back*] (Caiozzi) 67–69, 89, 91 n. 35

¿Fernando ha vuelto a desaparecer? [*Is Fernando Missing Again?*] (Caiozzi) 69
Festival de Cine Recobrado de Valparaíso (Valparaiso Film Festival of Rediscovered Cinema) 26 n. 17
Festival Internacional de Cine de Valdivia (Valdivia International Film Festival, FICValdivia) 26 n. 17
Festival Internacional de Cine de Viña del Mar (Viña del Mar International Film Festival) 26 n. 17
Festival Internacional de Documentales de Santiago (Santiago International Documentary Film Festival, FIDOCS) 8, 25 n. 17, 44–46, 49, 52, 53, 57 n. 100, 58 n. 111, 58 n. 114
Festival Itinerante de Cine de Derechos Humanos 174 n. 5
Film Law (1967) 35
Film Law (2004) 48–49
film schools 33–34, 35
film's skin 4–5, 19–20, 31 n. 132, 64, 138, 142, 180
first-person narratives:
    as collective narrative 127–28, 129, 152
    in domestic narratives 127
    of exilic directors 99–100, 102–04, 110, 115–18, 119–20, 126
    of family and family ties 125–26, 131–37, 140–41, 142–43
    overview 5, 6, 9–10, 15–16, 17, 24
    post-2011 180–81
    term choice 129
    of torture 84–85
Fiskales Ad-Hok 161–62
flashback travelling 114
Fliman, Hernán 66
Flores, Carlos 9, 45, 58 n. 114
Fondo de Fomento Audiovisual (Audiovisual Promotion Fund, FFA) 48–49
Fondo Nacional de Desarrollo Cultural y las Artes (National Fund for the Development of Culture and the Arts, FONDART) 43
Formas de volver a casa (Zambra) 125
Foucault, Michel 100–01
Foxley, Susana 104, 110, 112, 114, 118–19, 126, 133, 135–36, 138, 153
Fragmentos de un diario inacabado/Otteita Keskenjääneestä Päiväkirjasta [*Fragments from an Unfinished Diary*] (Vázquez) 101–02, 115
Franco, Jean 78
Frazier, Lessie Jo 22, 76, 91 n. 50, 100–01
Frei, Eduardo 3, 39, 56 n. 60
Frente Patriótico Manuel Rodríguez (Manuel Rodríguez Patriotic Front, FPMR) 71, 158, 175 n. 42
Freud, Sigmund 13, 86
Fuenzalida, Valerio 50, 110
The Future of Nostalgia (Boym) 157

Gabriel, Teshome 9

Gaines, Jane M. 17
Galende, Federico 108
Gándara, Sergio 67
GAP: Amigos Personales (Serrano) 81–82
Garage Matucana 162
Garretón, Manuel Antonio 25 n. 7, 38, 63, 151
Gaviola, Tatiana 79–80
Generation Exile (Dorfman) 104, 126
Giachino, Lorena 129, 153
Girard, Guy 45–46, 69, 70, 71, 82, 84–85, 89, 103, 114, 116–17, 127–28, 165, 172
Goethe Institute 58 n. 111
Gómez-Barris, Macarena 79
Góngora, Augusto 91 n. 41, 151, 156, 174 n. 5
González, Juan-Pablo 155
González, Sebastián 181
Gracias a la vida, o la pequeña historia de una mujer maltratada [*Thanks to Life, or the Little Story of a Mistreated Woman*] (Vázquez) 98
gray zone 165–66, 173, 176 n. 71
Greene, Ricardo 58 n. 114
Grupo Proceso:
    about 91 n. 74
    grassroot movements and 35
    Huellas de sal [*Salt Traces*] 24, 43–44, 65, 71–76, 77, 79, 89, 179
    human rights trilogy 71–72
    La verdadera historia de Johny (sic) *Good* (*The True Story of Johny Good*) 67, 69, 71–72, 73, 74, 81, 89
    mission statement of 72
    Soy testigo (*I am a Witness*) 69, 71–72, 83, 89
Güell, Pedro 37, 39
Guerin, Francis 14
Guerrero, Manuel 90 n. 27
Gutiérrez, Leopoldo 73, 103–04, 165
Guzmán, Juan (judge) 56 n. 54
Guzmán, Camila 104
Guzmán, Nicolás 181
Guzmán, Patricio:
    Chile, la memoria obstinada [*Chile: Obstinate Memory*] 8, 11, 34, 44, 45, 86, 127–28
    daughter of 104
    on documentary concepts 58 n. 112
    on documentary distribution 52–53
    El botón de nácar [*The Pearl Button*] 72
    El caso Pinochet [*The Pinochet Case*] 70, 73
    En nombre de Dios [*In the Name of God*] 58 n. 101, 103, 160
    as exilic director 48
    FIDOCS and 44–46, 57 n. 100, 58 n. 114
    image in CinemaChile catalog 49
    influence of 8–9
    La batalla de Chile [*The Battle of Chile*] 8, 11, 34, 45, 58 n. 109, 74, 107
    La cordillera de los sueños [*The Cordillera of Dreams*] 72

Nostalgia de la luz [*Nostalgia for the Light*] 9, 24, 60 n. 148, 65, 72–74, 76–77, 79, 89, 109, 179
return from exile of 58 n. 101
Salvador Allende (2004) 49, 74, 77, 108, 128

H&S, *see* Heynowski, Walter; Scheumann, Gerhard
Hagener, Malte 12–13
Hallas, Roger 14
Händel, George Frideric 157
haptic images:
  affect and emotion in 19, 137–47
  Beugnet on 166
  defined 19–20
  of family ties and 131–37, 138, 141
  of human remains 179
  Marks on 19–21, 23, 111, 114, 158–59
  overview 76
  of shared traumatic experiences 115–16
  in videos 158–59
haptic turn 12, 30 n. 99
Hardt, Michael 19
Henríquez, Patricio:
  El lado oscuro de La Dama Blanca [*The Dark Side of the White Lady*] 70, 87–88
  El último combate de Salvador Allende [*The Last Stand of Salvador Allende*] 67
  as exilic director 48
  Imágenes de una dictadura [*Images of a Dictatorship*] 67, 87, 94 n. 131, 156–57
  on *Je ne sais pas* 66
  on photo origin 94 n. 131
  on torture reenactments 88
Henríquez, Raúl Silva 71, 91 n. 41
Hermosilla, Marcelo 128
Héroes frágiles [*The Conspiracy*] (Pacull) 103–04
Hertz, Carmen 134–35, 148–49 n. 43
Heynowski, Walter 46, 69–70, 86, 87
Hier, wo ich lebe/Aquí donde yo vivo (*Here Where I Live*) (Puccio) 46
Hiroshima mon amour (Resnais) 107
Hirsch, Joshua 15–17, 63–64
Hirsch, Marianne 21, 130, 138
Holocaust 10, 13, 16, 80, 104, 130, 135, 148 n. 32
homecomings, *see* exilic directors
Hougen-Moraga, Marianne 126
Huellas de sal [*Salt Traces*] (Vargas & Grupo Proceso) 24, 43–44, 65, 71–76, 77, 79, 89, 179
human remains:
  haptic images of 179
  images in documentaries 66–67, 179
  legacy of 179–80
  torture evidence on 66–67
human rights:
  advances for 138
  collective awakening and 152

men as main targets of 79
mourning process and 22
post-dictatorship context for 36–37
reparation policies for 36–39, 55 n. 42
revelation of bodies parallel with 179–80
Valech Report on 41
women's role in 1, 78–80
Hurtado, María de la luz 35
Huyssen, Andreas 15, 17–18

Ich war, ich bin, ich werde sein [*I Was, I Am, and I Shall Be*] (Heynowski & Scheumann) 69–70, 86, 87
Ictus:
  Andrés de La Victoria (*Andrés from La Victoria*) 128
  Conversaciones con el Cardenal Silva (*Conversations with Cardinal Silva*) 91 n. 41, 156
  grassroot movements and 35
  No me olvides [*Don't Forget Me*] 79–80
  Salvador Allende (1992) 71
  Somos + 79–80, 160
  video distribution by 54 n. 15
IDFA 49
I Love Pinochet (Said) 113, 165
Il pleut sur Santiago [*Rain over Santiago*] (Soto) 74
The Image and the Witness (Guerin & Hallas) 14
Imágenes de una dictadura [*Images of a Dictatorship*] (Henríquez) 67, 87, 94 n. 131, 156–57
Imagen latente [*Latent Image*] (Perelman) 102
Imaginario inconcluso (*Unfinished Imagery*) (Basulto & Colectivo Cámara en Mano) 70–71
Instituto Fílmico de la Universidad Católica (Film Institute of the Catholic University) 33–34
Instituto Nacional de Derechos Humanos (National Institute of Human Rights) 36
Insunza, Pablo 151, 155, 156, 157, 158, 161–62, 163
intercultural cinema 20–21, 31 n. 132
I Wonder What You Will Remember of September (Cornejo) 107, 126

Jaksić, Iván 34–35
Jarlan, André 128
Jelin, Elizabeth 37, 65, 78, 153
Je ne sais pas (*I Don't Know*) (Mallet) 66
Jocelyn-Holt, Alfredo 38, 156
Joignant, Alfredo 41
journeys, *see* travelling memories

Kaplan, E. Ann 11, 13, 15
Kazanjian, David 18
King, John 7, 97
Krassnoff, Miguel 84
Kristeva, Julia 165, 169
Kuhn, Annette 21, 129, 143

Labanyi, Jo 15, 19, 30 n. 113

Labarca, Yura 73
La batalla de Chile [*The Battle of Chile*] (Guzmán, P.) 8, 11, 34, 45, 58 n. 109, 74, 107
La batalla de la Plaza Italia [*The Battle of Plaza Italia*] (Villegas) 128–29
LaCapra, Dominick 81
La caravana de la muerte (The caravan of death) 38, 73, 80
La ciudad de los fotógrafos [*City of Photographers*] (Moreno) 109, 151, 153, 155, 158, 159
La conciencia de golpe (Helena-Urzúa) 123 n. 62
La cordillera de los sueños [*The Cordillera of Dreams*] (Guzmán, P.) 72
La cueca sola (Mallet) 70, 103–04, 113
La Dama Blanca (navy flagship) 70
La Esmeralda (navy flagship) 70, 87–88
La femme au foyer (*The Housewife*) (Sarmiento) 74
La flaca Alejandra [*Skinny Alejandra*] (Castillo & Girard) 45–46, 69, 70, 71, 82, 84–85, 89, 103, 114, 116–17, 127–28, 165, 172
Lagos, Ricardo 40, 131
La memoria herida (*Wounded Memory*) (Casas & Labarca) 73
La Moneda bombing:
commemorative public rituals for 139
context for 2, 3
footage of 12, 23, 34, 71, 163, 178
symbolic weight of 105–10
La muerte de Pinochet [*The Death of Pinochet*] (Perut & Osnovikoff) 109, 128, 150, 154, 163–69, 173–74, 180
Landsberg, Alison 21, 130, 140
Lanfranco, Patricio 73
Lanzmann, Claude 46, 81
La quemadura [*The Burn*] (Ballesteros) 109, 126, 129, 137–38, 140, 142–43, 144–45
La realidad [*The Reality*] (Lübbert, A.) 126
La règle du jeu [*The Rules of the Game*] (Renoir) 172
Largo, Eliana 80
Larraín, Esteban 48, 67–68, 89, 156
Larraín, Ismael 49
Larraín, Pablo 39, 74, 150–51, 154
Larraín, Ricardo 67, 91 n. 41
Larraín, Sebastián 151, 155
La sombra de Don Roberto [*Don Roberto's Shadow*] (Spoerer & Engström) 70, 73, 128, 165
Laub, Dori 11
La venda (*The Blindfold*) (Camiruaga) 70, 85, 89
La verdadera historia de Johny (sic) *Good* (*The True Story of Johny Good*) (Tupper, del Río, & Grupo Proceso) 67, 69, 71–72, 73, 74, 81, 89
Lavín, Pablo 48, 70–71
Lazzara, Michael 6, 42, 66, 165, 170
Le-Bert, Luis 176 n. 56
Lebow, Alisa 127, 129

Le Chili en transition [*Chile in Transition*] (Ancelovici & Diamand) 69, 88
Lechner, Norbert 37, 39
Leighton, Cristián 9
Leiva, Jorge 44, 155
Lesage, Julia 82–83
Les murs de Santiago [*Chile: Ten years of a Strong Man*] (Servan-Schreiber & Devert) 58 n. 109, 116
Letelier, Jorge 100
Lettre d'un cinéaste ou le retour d'un amateur de bibliothèques [*Letter from a Filmmaker or The Return of a Library Lover*] (Ruiz) 101, 102–03
Levi, Primo 165, 176 n. 71
Liñero, Germán:
Apuntes para una historia del video en Chile 9, 35
El muro de los nombres (*The Wall of Names*) 70
on independent film production 50
on redemocratization of Chile 35–36, 43, 70, 71, 72, 106
U-matic project 9, 54 n. 18
Lira, Elizabeth 40
literal second generation directors 47–48, 110, 118, 120, 126, 130
see also Aguiló, Macarena; Carmona, Alejandra
Littin, Miguel 101, 102–03, 105–06
Loach, Ken 107
Londres 38: 84–85, 172, 177 n. 107
long takes 65–66, 83–84, 133–34, 166, 170–71, 174
Lonquén case 1, 38, 66, 67
Los 80 (*The 80s*) (television programme) 50, 60 n. 146, 154
Los archivos del cardenal (*The Archives of the Cardinal*) (television programme) 51, 60 n. 147
Los escolares se siguen amando [*Teenagers Keep on Loving*] (Toledo) 74, 109, 139–40
Los niños de septiembre (*September Children*) (Marras) 74
Los perros [*The Dogs*] (Said) 177 n. 108
Los Prisioneros 162–63
Los zarpazos del Puma (*The Puma's Claws*) (Verdugo) 55 n. 49
Loveman, Brian 37–38, 40
Lübbert, Andrés 126, 181
Lübbert, Jorge 181
Lübbert, Orlando 46, 67, 69, 83, 165
Luco, Alfonso 90 n. 14

Magni, Cecilia 158
Malditos, la historia de los Fiskales Ad-Hok (*Damned: The Story of Fiskales Ad-Hok*) (Insunza) 151, 155, 156, 157, 158, 161–62, 163
Malik, Sarita 12
Mallet, Marilú:
as exilic director 9, 48
influence of 9, 110
Je ne sais pas (*I Don't Know*) 66
La cueca sola 70, 103–04, 113

Marín, Diego 107, 153
Marks, Laura U.:
    on cinema of affect 12–13
    on exilic productions 96, 101
    on haptic images 19–21, 23, 111, 114, 158–59
    on intercultural cinema 31 n. 132
    on sense memories 111
    on skin of film 4, 64, 142
    The Skin of the Film 4
Marras, Sergio 74
Martínez, Javier 152
Martínez, María José 81–82
Masiello, Francine 68, 126–27
mass demonstrations (1980s) 3, 34–35, 156
Massumi, Brian 19
Maureira, Elena 1
Mayol, Alberto 42
Mayolo, Carlos 105
Mayoux, Valérie 69, 86
McLuhan, Marshall 158
Mekas, Jonas 144
Mellado, Justo Pastor 106
Memoria desierta [*Deserted Memory*] (Atallah & Colectivo Diluvio) 73
memory struggles:
    everyday life details and 111–12
    FIDOCS and new season of memory 45–46
    layers of 91 n. 50
    legacy of 181
    'pacted transition' and 36
    postmemory 130, 146–47
    sense memories and 20–21
    trajectory of 88–89
    trauma's impact on 10–11, 15, 17–18
    travelling and 112–13
    unravelling impasse and 5, 18, 36–37, 65, 77, 138, 164–65, 179–80
    women and 77–79
Meneses, Emilio 40, 69, 81, 85
Meneses, Pedro (pseudonym) 65
Merino, Marcia 82, 84–85, 114
Mesa de Diálogo (Dialogue Table) 40, 56 n. 60
Mi hermano y yo [*My Brother and I*] (Gándara) 67
Mikkonen, Anita 102, 122 n. 38
Militarismo y tortura (*Militarism and Torture*) (Ruiz) 90 n. 19
military conscripts 6, 165–66
military coup, *see* 11 September 1973; Pinochet, Augusto
Ministry of Cultures 7
Min mors løfte [*My Mother's Promise*] (Hougen-Moraga) 126
MIR (Movimiento de Izquierda Revolucionaria) 84, 112, 117, 118–20, 130–32, 165
MiraDoc 49

Mi vida con Carlos [*My Life with Carlos*] (Berger-Hertz) 73, 104, 126, 134–35
Mondaca, Hermann 54 n. 18, 69, 71–72, 83, 89
Montealegre, Jorge 95 n. 132
Montiglio, Víctor 169
Morandé 80: 40
Moreiras, Alberto 14
Moreno, Sebastián 109, 151, 153, 155, 158, 159
Mouesca, Jacqueline 16, 43, 97, 98
Moulian, Tomás 4, 36, 71, 126
Movimiento de Izquierda Revolucionaria (Revolutionary Left Movement, MIR) 84, 112, 117, 118–20, 130–32, 165
Muel, Bruno 69, 86
Mulford, Marilyn 70
Müller, Jorge 49
Munjin, Vanja 181
Muñoz, Fernando 76
Museo de la Memoria y los Derechos Humanos (Museum of Memory and Human Rights) 4, 7, 36, 41, 52, 61 n. 159, 174 n. 5, 178
music scene (80s) 154, 155–56, 161–63, 175 n. 27, 176 n. 56

Naficy, Hamid 20–21, 96, 101, 113
Nancy, Jean-Luc 129
Navarro, Óscar 158
Neruda, Pablo 71
Neruda en el corazón (*Neruda in the Heart*) (Ancelovici, Barrios, Chaskel) 71
Nichols, Bill 18, 82–83, 140, 160, 166
9/11 attack (United States) 12, 107–08
1973 Revoluciones por minuto [*1973 Revolutions per Minute*] (Valenzuela) 74
No (Larraín, P.) 39, 150–51, 154
'No' campaign (1988) 3, 35–36, 37, 98, 151
No es hora de llorar (*This is Not the Time to Cry*) (Chaskel & Sanz) 66
Noguera, Héctor 115
No me amenaces [*Don't Threaten Me*] (Racz) 70
No me olvides [*Don't Forget Me*] (Gaviola & Ictus) 79–80
No olvidar [*Not to Forget*] (Agüero) 1, 65–66
Nora, Pierre 92 n. 52
nostalgia:
    Benedetti on 99
    Boym on 18
    collective awakening and 2
    defined 157
    for el pueblo 127–28
    emotion and 113, 157–61
    '*fiesta* sacrificial' and 156–63, 173
    overview 24, 150–54, 180
    politics of commemoration and 41
    Rebolledo on 99
    replaced by transito 113

Nostalgia de la luz [*Nostalgia for the Light*] (Guzmán, P.) 9, 24, 60 n. 148, 65, 72–74, 76–77, 79, 89, 109, 179
Noticias [*News*] (Perut & Osnovikoff) 166
Nuevo Cine Chileno 105
Nuevo Cine Latinoamericano (New Latin American Cinema, NLAC) 8
Nuit et brouillard [*Night and Fog*] (Resnais) 113

Oficina Nacional de Retorno (National Office for Return, ONR) 121 n. 21
Ojos Rojos [*Red Eyes*], (Larraín, Sabatini, & Sallato) 49
Olea, Raquel 151
Olivares, Fernando 68–69, 91 n. 35
Oñate, Rody 121 n. 21
Ondamedia 7
Opus Dei: una cruzada silenciosa [*Opus Day: A Silent Crusade*] (Said & de Certeau) 165
Oquendo-Villar, Carmen 75
Orozco, Lissette 6, 181
Osnovikoff, Iván:
  Chi-Chi-Chi, le-le- le, Martín Vargas de Chile 168
  on conventional historical discourses 154
  El astuto mono Pinochet contra La Moneda de los cerdos [*Clever Monkey Pinochet Versus La Moneda's Pigs*] 74, 168
  La muerte de Pinochet [*The Death of Pinochet*] 109, 128, 150, 154, 163–69, 173–74, 180
  Noticias [*News*] 166
  on political indeterminacy 167
Ospina, Luis 105
Oyarzún, Kemy 78–79

P+O 150
  see also Osnovikoff, Iván; Perut, Bettina
Pacull, Emilio 103–04
Page, Joanna 105
Palacios, José Miguel 115
Palma, Daniel 173
Panizza, Tiziana:
  Al final: la última carta [*In the End: The Last Letter*] 141, 144
  Ballesteros comparison to 142, 146
  Cartas visuales [*Visual Letters*] trilogy 141
  Dear Nonna: A Film Letter 141
  on director generations 47
  on memories 142, 154
  on recalling the past not directly experienced 154
  Remitente: una carta visual [*Postage: A Visual Letter*] 109, 126, 129, 137–38, 140–41, 144
  as second generation director 48
Paranaguá, Paulo Antonio 8
Parot, Carmen Luz:
  El derecho de vivir [*Víctor Jara: The Right to Live in Peace*] 70, 81–82

Estadio Nacional [*National Stadium*] 70, 85–87, 94 n. 124, 95 n. 137
Parra, Isabel 115, 116
Pascal, Andrés 136
Patio 29 (Graveyard 29) 39, 67–69, 89, 90 n. 24, 91 n. 35
Patio 29: historias del silencio [*Patio 29: Stories of Silence*] (Larraín, E.) 67–68, 89, 156
Payne, Leigh A. 164
Peirano, María Paz 45, 49
Pellegrín, Raúl 158
Pereira, Reinalda del Carmen 153
Perelman, Pablo 102
Pérez, Dago 158
Perut, Bettina:
  Chi-Chi-Chi, le-le- le, Martín Vargas de Chile 168
  El astuto mono Pinochet contra La Moneda de los cerdos [*Clever Monkey Pinochet Versus La Moneda's Pigs*] 74, 168
  La muerte de Pinochet [*The Death of Pinochet*] 109, 128, 150, 154, 163–69, 173–74, 180
  Noticias [*News*] 166
Philibert, Nicholas 46
Pick, Zuzana M. 8, 34, 53, 65, 74, 96, 97, 98–99, 103, 108
Piñera, Sebastián 4, 41–42
Pinochet, Augusto:
  assassination attempt on 158
  as commander in chief of the Army 3, 63
  death of 41, 141, 144
  defeat (1988) 34, 37
  demise of 41
  education system of 41
  iconic images of 71, 106–07, 143
  legacy of 1–2, 3–4, 36–37, 40–41, 84, 181–82
  London detention (1998) 3, 36, 37, 38, 39, 40, 56 n. 54, 78, 139, 152
  military coup 3, 14, 34. *see also* 11 September 1973
  'No' campaign (1988) 3, 35–36, 37, 98, 151
  on Patio 29 67
  post-dictatorship influence of 37–38, 39–40, 63
  redemocratization and 37–38
  as senator-for-life 3, 38
  supporters and collaborators of 5, 42, 109, 113–14, 137–38, 144, 154. *see also Correcto...o el alma en los tiempos de guerra; El mocito; I Love Pinochet; La flaca Alejandra; La muerte de Pinochet*
  tyranny of 81, 110, 112, 113–14. *see also* concentration camps; torture; *specific detention places and mass grave sites*
Pino-Ojeda, Walescka 84
Pinto, Iván 9, 108, 115, 181
Piper, Isabel 79
Pisagua concentration camp 69–70, 72–73, 81, 86
Pisagua mass grave 38–39, 55 n. 47, 55 n. 49, 66–67, 74

Plaza de Armas 128
Podalsky, Laura 11, 15
political transvestism 71
  see also transformismo
The Politics of Affect and Emotion in Contemporary Latin American Cinema (Podalsky) 11
porno-miseria (poverty-porn) 105
Por sospecha de comunista [*Under Suspicion of Being Communist*] (Cohen & Hermosilla) 128
post-dictatorship documentaries:
  access to 6–7, 25–26 n. 16–17
  background 8–11
  context for study of 3–4, 6, 10, 15–17, 23
  distribution issues 35, 44, 48–53, 54 n. 15, 60 n. 141, 60 n. 143
  economic crisis and 42–43, 97
  generational categories of directors 46–48, 58 n. 120
  identity crisis 42
  landscape and 72, 73, 95 n. 55
  overview 53
  politics of memory and 36–37
  post-2011 context 180–81
  pre-1990 context 33–36, 54 n. 18
  resources for 97
  strategies of 2
  trajectory of, as revelation of bodies 1–3, 10, 12, 19–20, 64, 178–80
  see also broader second generation directors; cinema of affect; cinema of the affected; exilic directors; literal second generation directors; 'silent' decade; *specific films*
postmemory 130, 146–47
Post mortem (Larraín, P.) 74
posttraumatic cinema 14, 16–17
Primavera con una esquina rota (Benedetti) 120 n. 1
Primer Festival Internacional de Cine Documental (First International Festival of Documentary Cinema) 57 n. 100
Project Home 118–19
Propaganda (Colectivo Mafi) 181
prosthetic quality of memory 130, 140–42, 147
Puccio, Carlos 46

Quense, Verónica 80
Quilapayún culture 105, 109
Quimantú books 142, 144, 145–46

Racz, Andrés 70, 103
Ramírez, Gonzalo 81–82
Rancière, Jacques 108, 111, 136
Rascaroli, Laura 15
Raúl Silva Henríquez, el Cardenal (*The Cardinal*) (Larraín, R.) 67, 91 n. 41
Rebolledo, Loreto 99
Recado de Chile (*Message from Chile*) (anonymous collective) 65–66, 90 n. 14, 98

Recuerdos del futuro: Raúl Pellegrín (*Memories of the Future: Raúl Pellegrín*) (CARO) 158, 175 n. 42
redemocratization of Chile:
  context for 4, 34–35
  fear and 63
  legacy of 39
  overview 4, 25 n. 7
  post-Pinochet's detention 39
  during the 'silent' decade 37–39
reenactments:
  for children's subjectivity 133–34
  defined 81
  of everyday life 136
  of exile 119
  flashback travelling and 114
  purpose of 81, 82–83
  torture evocation with 66, 80–89, 179
  of travelling shots 115–16
  unveiling memories through 69, 82
  for working through trauma 82–83
reflective nostalgia 157
Reinalda del Carmen, mi mamá y yo [*Reinalda del Carmen, My Mother and Me*] (Giachino) 129, 153
remains, *see* human remains
Remitente: una carta visual [*Postage: A Visual Letter*] (Panizza) 109, 126, 129, 137–38, 140–41, 144
Renoir, Jean 172
Renov, Michael 18–19, 127
reparation policies 36
reportaje de trinchera (cinema of barricada) 35, 65, 98
Resnais, Alain 107, 113
restorative nostalgia 157
Rettig, Raúl 38
Rettig Report 25 n. 6, 38, 40, 64, 81, 94 n. 119, 152
revelation of bodies, trajectory of 1–3, 10, 12, 19–20, 64, 178–80
Reyes, Jaime 90 n. 14, 120 n. 9
Rich, B. Ruby 110
Richard, Nelly 14, 15, 22, 64, 76, 117, 127, 154
Riegl, Alois 19
Robichet, Théo 69, 86
Robles, Fedora 90 n. 14
Rodríguez, Arnaldo 166, 172
Rodríguez, Paula 114, 151
Román, José 90 n. 14
Romo, Osvaldo 164
Rossi, Antonia:
  Ballesteros comparison to 142, 146
  El eco de las canciones [*The Echo of Songs*] 74–75, 104, 110, 119–20, 126, 136–38, 140–41, 143
  as second generation director 48
  use of animation and found footage 111–12
Ruffinelli, Jorge 58 n. 112
Ruidos molestos (*Annoying Noises*) (Sepúlveda) 151, 154, 156, 162, 163

Ruiz, Raúl:
    on Chilean cinema history 97, 100, 126
    on Chilean revolutionary process 106
    Cofralandes 74, 109
    as exilic director 48, 101, 121 n. 32
    on exilic production 105–06
    influence of 9, 97, 109
    Lettre d'un cinéaste ou le retour d'un amateur de bibliothèques [*Letter from a Filmmaker or The Return of a Library Lover*] 101, 102–03
    Militarismo y tortura (*Militarism and Torture*) 90 n. 19

Saavedra, Victoria 73, 77
Sabatini, Juan Ignacio 49
Said, Edward W. 101, 109, 114–15
Said, Marcela:
    on controversial subjects 165
    on *El mocito* 169–70, 173
    El mocito [*The Young Butler*] 6, 42, 109, 150, 153, 154, 163–67, 169–74, 180, 181
    I Love Pinochet 113, 165
    on landscapes in *El mocito* 171–72
    Los perros [*The Dogs*] 177 n. 108
    Opus Dei: una cruzada silenciosa [*Opus Day: A Silent Crusade*] 165
    on political indeterminacy 167
    on Salgado 177 n. 108
    as second generation director 48
Salas, Babi 54 n. 15
Salas, Pablo:
    on endangered gazes 160
    food redistribution footage by 158
    Pisagua mass grave images by 76
    Somos + 79–80, 160
    yellow car footage by 160
Salgado, Juan Morales 173, 177 n. 108
Salinas, Lucía:
    Canto a la vida [*Song to Life*] 70, 103, 110, 115–16, 140, 156
    on feeling of isolation 116
    as part of cultural resistance 48
Salinas, Raquel 90 n. 14
Sallato, Juan Pablo 49
Salt in the Sand (Frazier) 76, 91 n. 50
Salvador Allende (Cáceres & Ictus, 1992) 71
Salvador Allende (Guzmán, P., 2004) 49, 74, 77, 108, 128
San Martín, Sergio Castro 151, 155, 157
Santa Cruz, Guadalupe 72–73
Sanz, Luis Alberto 66
Sapiaín, Claudio 70, 101
Sarkar, Bhaskar 18
Sarlo, Beatriz 126, 130, 152–53
Sarmiento, Valeria 9, 74, 110
Scarry, Elaine 80, 83, 87
Scheumann, Gerhard 46, 69–70, 86, 87

Schumann, Peter 97
second generation directors, *see* broader second generation directors; literal second generation directors
Septembre chilien [*Chilean September*] (Muel, Mayoux, & Robichet) 69, 86
Sepúlveda, José Luis 181
Sepúlveda, Viviana 151, 154, 156, 162, 163
Serrano, Claudia 81–82
Servan-Schreiber, Fabienne 58 n. 109, 116
Servicio Médico Legal (Medical Legal Service, SMl) 66–67, 69
Shaviro, Steven 12–13
shell shock cinema 14
Shoah (Lanzmann) 81
Si escuchas atentamente [*If You Listen Carefully*] (Guzmán, N.) 181
Sight and Sound (journal):
    on *No* (Larraín) 151
    on state of Latin American cinema 105
'silent' decade (1990s):
    cinema of the affected and 62–72
    context for 42–46
    overview 37–39
    'The Pinochet Accident' and 39–42
    search in the Atacama Desert and 72–80
    torture and use of reenactment in 66, 80–89, 179
Silva, Sebastián 105, 106
16mm film 20, 87, 101, 111–12, 115–16, 139, 147
Skármeta, Antonio 97
skin of film 4–5, 19–20, 31 n. 132, 64, 138, 142, 180
The Skin of the Film (Marks) 4
Slit Throats case 90 n. 27
Sloterdijk, Peter 128
Smaill, Belinda 18
Sobchack, Vivian 12–13, 30 n. 99, 159, 172
Soja, Edward 113
Sommer, Doris 100
Somos + (Chaskel, Salas, & Ictus) 79–80, 160
Sontag, Susan 179
Sorensen, Kristin 50
Soto, Helvio 74
Soy testigo (*I am a Witness*) (Mondaca & Grupo Proceso) 69, 71–72, 83, 89
Spinoza, Baruch 19
Spoerer, Juan Diego 70, 73, 128, 165
Stark, Sergio Arellano 38, 80
Stern, Steve:
    on 80s nostalgia 156
    on Chile's cultural endpoint 152
    on commemoration of 11 September 108
    on death and disappearance statistics 25 n. 6
    on documentary distribution 54 n. 15
    on FIDOCS 45
    on Pinochet's dictatorship 38
    on Pisagua mass grave 38

on politics of commemoration 40–41
on popularity of *Los zarpazos del Puma* 55 n. 49
on Rettig Report scope 64
on symbolic circle of victims 5–6, 39–40
on unravelling impasse of memory 5, 18, 36–37, 65, 179
student protests (1980's) 34–35, 160–61
student protests (2011) 4, 41–42, 181
Sturken, Marita 21
Suleiman, Susan Rubin 148 n. 32
Super-8 footage 84, 101, 111–12, 115–16, 118, 134–35, 142, 147
symbolic circle of victims 2, 4, 5–6, 39–40, 152–53, 154–63, 164–66
synaesthesia 18, 30 n. 99, 32 n. 146, 101, 113, 138–39, 142

tactile qualities, *see* touch, in cinema of affect
Tambutti, Marcia 180–81
Teleanálisis 35
television:
  'Apoyo a la difusión de documentales nacionales ya producidos' 60 n. 143
  Chile, las imágenes prohibidas [*Chile, the Forbidden Images*] 50, 60 n. 146
  CNTV 50
  Los 80 (*The 80s*) 50, 60 n. 146
  Los archivos del cardenal (*The Archives of the Cardinal*) 51, 60 n. 147
  TVN 49–51, 60 n. 143, 61 n. 159
Televisión Nacional de Chile (National Television Channel, TVN) 49–51, 60 n. 143, 61 n. 159
testimonies:
  emotions and 133, 134
  expert accounts 155, 162
  of female relatives of victims 65, 67–68, 77–78
  as post-dictatorship documentary strategy 2
  of survivors 66, 81–82, 152–53
  trauma studies on 14
  witness accounts 155
Testimonio 1 (*Testimony 1*) (Fliman) 66
Theodorakis, Mikis 71
thirdspace chronotopes 113, 115, 118, 119
35mm film 20, 139
Tiempo Pasado (Sarlo) 126
Toledo, Paco 48, 74, 109, 139–40
topographical travelling 113
Torti, Juan Ángel 107, 123 n. 62, 178
torture:
  Abu Ghraib 82–83
  in early post-dictatorship documentaries 69
  excluded from CNVR investigations 38
  FIDOCS documentaries on 46
  first-person narratives of 84–85
  gendered dimensions of 85
  language of 80–81

Pinochet's legacy of 3–4, 25 n. 6
reenactments 66, 80–89, 179
Scarry on 83, 87
survivors recognized as victims 64
as taboo topic 40
testimonies of 66, 81–82, 152–53
tortured bodies 66–67, 81–89, 91 n. 34
unveiling memories of 69–70, 172–73
touch, in cinema of affect 12–13, 19–20, 23, 111–12, 115
transformismo (transformism) 36, 71
trauma cinema 14
Trauma Culture (Kaplan) 13
trauma studies framework:
  Hirsch on stages following traumatic event 63
  memory struggles and 13, 17–18
  overview 10–11
  of Pinochet's dictatorship 12
  political implications of 22
  for post-dictatorship documentary study 14–17
  problems with 179
  trauma, defined 12, 13
travelling memories 111–17, 120
travelling shots 6, 112–14, 132, 135–36, 137
Traverso, Antonio 10, 17
Trejo, Roberto 57 n. 92
Truffaut, François 45
Truth and Reconciliation Commission (Rettig Report) 25 n. 6, 38, 40, 64, 81, 94 n. 119, 152
Tupper, Pablo 67, 69, 71–72, 73, 74, 81, 89
TVN 49–51, 60 n. 143, 61 n. 159

U-matic footage 35, 54 n. 18, 74, 151
U-matic project 9, 54 n. 18
Una vez más, mi país [*Once Again, My Country*] (Sapiaín) 70
Unidad Popular (Popular Unity, UP) 3, 4, 5, 87, 127, 144
United States:
  approach to documentaries in 10
  9/11 attack 12, 107–08
  political intervention by 3, 97, 104, 153
  torture use by 82–83
Universidad de Chile 51
unravelling impasse 5, 18, 36–37, 65, 77, 138, 164–65, 179–80
unsettling accounts 164–65, 173
Uribe, Armando 4, 39
Urzúa, Macarena 161, 162

Valdés, Mauro 60 n. 148
Valdés, Pablo 168
Valech, Sergio 40
Valech Commission 40, 56 n. 64, 64
Valech Report 41, 69, 81, 110
Valenzuela, Fernando 74

Varda, Agnès 76
Vargas, Andrés:
  Huellas de sal [Salt Traces] 24, 43–44, 65, 71–76, 77, 79, 89, 179
  as part of cultural resistance 48
  poetic impulse of 72
Vázquez, Angelina:
  child of 104
  Fragmentos de un diario inacabado/Otteita Keskenjääneestä Päiväkirjasta [Fragments from an Unfinished Diary] 101–02, 115
  Gracias a la vida, o la pequeña historia de una mujer maltratada [Thanks to Life, or the Little Story of a Mistreated Woman] 98
  homecoming of 114
  influence of 9, 110
  Mikkonen collaboration 102, 122 n. 38
Velodrome 87
Venían a buscarme [They Were Coming to Get Me] (de la Barra) 181
Verdugo, Patricia 40, 55 n. 49, 56 n. 64, 81, 153
Vereda tropical (Tropical Pavement) (Lavín) 70–71
Vergara, Constanza 103
Vergara, Jorgelino 6, 42, 164–65, 166, 167, 169–73, 181
victimhood:
  defined 42, 165–66
  symbolic circle of 2, 4, 5–6, 39–40, 152–53, 154–63, 164–66
Victoriano, Felipe 85–86, 88
Vicuña, Miguel 4, 39

Vidal, Hernán 81
Viera-Gallo, María Teresa 159
Villagra, Nelson 90 n. 14
Villagrán, Fernando 51–52
Villa Grimaldi 84–85, 164
Villa Grimaldi: Parque por la Paz (Villa Grimaldi: Park for Peace) (Zurita) 70
Villegas, Renato 128–29
Villegas, René García 83
Viña del Mar 71
Visions du Réel 49
Volver a vernos [Pinochet's Children] (Rodríguez) 114, 151
Vuskovic, Sergio 88

Walker, Janet 15, 18, 81, 82
Wang, Ban 15
Water Music Suite 2 (Händel) 157
Waugh, Thomas 8
White, Hayden 15
Wilde, Alexander 14, 39, 55 n. 42, 58 n. 108, 152
Williams, Linda 15
Williams, Raymond 15
Wood, Andrés 149 n. 43
Woodward, Miguel 88
Woolf, Virginia 103

Zambra, Alejandro 125
Zúñiga, Francisco 91 n. 35
Zurita, Raúl 73